ROME, EMPIRE OF PLUNDER

Bringing together philologists, historians, and archaeologists, *Rome, Empire of Plunder* bridges disciplinary divides in pursuit of an inter-disciplinary understanding of Roman cultural appropriation – approached not as a set of distinct practices but as a hydra-headed phenomenon through which Rome made and remade itself, as a Republic and as an Empire, on Italian soil and abroad. The studies gathered in this volume range from the literary thefts of the first Latin comic poets to the grand-scale spoliation of Egyptian obelisks by a succession of emperors, and from Hispania to Pergamon to Qasr Ibrim. Applying a range of theoretical perspectives on cultural appropriation, contributors probe the violent interactions and chance contingencies that sent cargo of all sorts into circulation around the Roman Mediterranean, causing recurrent distortions in their individual and aggregate meanings. The result is an innovative and nuanced investigation of Roman cultural appropriation and imperial power.

MATTHEW P. LOAR is Assistant Professor in the Department of Classics and Religious Studies at the University of Nebraska–Lincoln. He is currently writing a book on the Cacus myth in Augustan Rome.

CAROLYN MACDONALD is Assistant Professor in the Department of Classics and Ancient History at the University of New Brunswick. She is currently writing a book on literary and visual responses to Rome's appropriation of Greek art.

DAN-EL PADILLA PERALTA is Assistant Professor in the Department of Classics at Princeton University. He is currently writing a monograph on the religious world of the Middle Republic.

ROME, EMPIRE OF PLUNDER

The Dynamics of Cultural Appropriation

EDITED BY

MATTHEW P. LOAR

University of Nebraska–Lincoln

CAROLYN MACDONALD

University of New Brunswick

DAN-EL PADILLA PERALTA

Princeton University

CAMBRIDGE
UNIVERSITY PRESS

CAMBRIDGE
UNIVERSITY PRESS

University Printing House, Cambridge CB2 8BS, United Kingdom

One Liberty Plaza, 20th Floor, New York, NY 10006, USA

477 Williamstown Road, Port Melbourne, VIC 3207, Australia

4843/24, 2nd Floor, Ansari Road, Daryaganj, Delhi – 110002, India

79 Anson Road, #06–04/06, Singapore 079906

Cambridge University Press is part of the University of Cambridge.

It furthers the University's mission by disseminating knowledge in the pursuit of
education, learning, and research at the highest international levels of excellence.

www.cambridge.org
Information on this title: www.cambridge.org/9781108418423
DOI: 10.1017/9781108290012

First published 2018

Printed in the United Kingdom by Clays, St Ives plc

A catalogue record for this publication is available from the British Library.

Library of Congress Cataloging-in-Publication Data
NAMES: Loar, Matthew, 1984- editor, author. | MacDonald, Carolyn, 1985- editor, author. |
Padilla Peralta, Dan-el, editor, author.
TITLE: Rome, empire of plunder : the dynamics of cultural appropriation /
edited by Matthew Loar, University of Nebraska, Lincoln, Carolyn MacDonald,
University of New Brunswick, Dan-el Padilla Peralta, Princeton University, New Jersey.
DESCRIPTION: Cambridge ; New York, NY : Cambridge University Press, 2017. |
Includes bibliographical references and index.
IDENTIFIERS: LCCN 2017017700 | ISBN 9781108418423 (hardback : alk. paper) |
ISBN 9781108406048 (pbk. : alk. paper)
SUBJECTS: LCSH: Civilization–Roman influences. | Rome–Civilization. |
Art thefts–Rome. | Cultural property–Rome.
CLASSIFICATION: LCC DG77 .R6729 2017 | DDC 937–dc23
LC record available at https://lccn.loc.gov/2017017700

ISBN 978-1-108-41842-3 Hardback

Contents

Figures

Contributors

THOMAS BIGGS is Assistant Professor of Classics at the University of Georgia.

MEGAN DANIELS is the former Redford Postdoctoral Fellow in Archaeology at the University of Puget Sound and the current IEMA Postdoctoral Fellow at SUNY-Buffalo.

BASIL DUFALLO is Associate Professor of Classical Studies at the University of Michigan.

CARRIE FULTON is Assistant Professor of Historical Studies and Classics at the University of Toronto.

AYELET HAIMSON LUSHKOV is Associate Professor of Classics at the University of Texas at Austin.

MATTHEW P. LOAR is Assistant Professor of Classics and Religious Studies at the University of Nebraska–Lincoln.

CAROLYN MACDONALD is Assistant Professor of Classics and Ancient History at the University of New Brunswick.

MICAH Y. MYERS is Assistant Professor of Classics at Kenyon College.

MARDEN FITZPATRICK NICHOLS is Assistant Professor of Classics at Georgetown University.

DAN-EL PADILLA PERALTA is Assistant Professor of Classics at Princeton University.

GRANT PARKER is Associate Professor of Classics at Stanford University.

STEFANO REBEGGIANI is Assistant Professor of Classics at the University of Southern California.

AMY RICHLIN is Professor of Classics at the University of California, Los Angeles.

JENNIFER TRIMBLE is Associate Professor of Classics at Stanford University.

Acknowledgments

The idea for this edited volume was hatched at "Cargo Culture: Literary and Material Appropriative Practices in Rome," a two-day conference held at Stanford University in March 2014. The conference was generously funded by Stanford's Department of Classics and by the Stanford Humanities Center; invaluable administrative and logistical support was provided by Valerie Kiszka, Lydia Hailu, and Lori Lynn Taniguchi. For initiating the proceedings *liquido auspicio*, we thank Alessandro Barchiesi; for gang-buster papers delivered at the conference but not included in this volume, we thank Joy Connolly, Nathaniel Jones, Isabel Köster, Scott McGill, Christopher Simon, William Stull, Chris van den Berg, and Ann Marie Yasin; and for responding to papers with verve and provocation, we thank Stephen Hinds, Grant Parker, and Jennifer Trimble. Alessandro Barchiesi, Denis Feeney, Stephen Hinds, and Walter Scheidel subsequently offered much-needed advice and encouragement as the volume began to take shape.

The editors would like to thank all the contributors for their enthusiasm for and support of this volume. We are also grateful to Princeton University's Kathleen Cruz for editing the manuscript and to the Princeton University Department of Classics Magie Fund for compensating her hard work. To Michael Sharp and Cambridge University Press for their interest in this project, and to the two anonymous referees who were so generous with their time and feedback, we give our warmest thanks.

Abbreviations

CIL	*Corpus Inscriptionum Latinarum*, Berlin 1863–.
Clauss-Slaby	Epigraphische Datenbank Clauss-Slaby, www.manfredclauss.de/gb/index.html.
D–S	Daremberg, C. and Saglio E. (1877–1919). *Dictionnaire des Antiquités Grecques et Romaines*, 5 vols., Paris: Hachette.
LTUR	Steinby, E. M. ed. (1993–2000). *Lexicon Topographicum Urbis Romae*, 6 vols., Roma: Quasar.
RE	Pauly–Wissowa, *Real-Encyclopädie des classischen Altertumwissenschaft*, Stuttgart 1894–München 1980.
RIC	Mattingly, H., & Sydenham, E. A. (1926). *The Roman Imperial Coinage*, Vol. II, *Vespasian to Hadrian*, London: Spink & Son, Ltd.
RIC²	Carradice, A. I. & Buttrey, T. V. (2007). *The Roman Imperial Coinage*, Vol. II Part. I. *From AD 69 to AD 96, Vespasian to Domitian*, second edition. London: Spink & Son, Ltd.
Tab. Vindol. II	Bowman, A. K., Thomas, J. D. & Adams, J. N. (1994). *The Vindolanda Writing–Tablets* (Tabulae Vindolandenses II), London: British Museum Press.
Tab. Vindol. III	Bowman, A. K. & Thomas, J. D. (2003). *The Vindolanda Writing–Tablets* (Tabulae Vindolandenses III), London: British Museum Press.
Tab. Vindol. IV	Bowman, A. K., Thomas, J. D. & Tomlin, R. S. O. (2010). "The Vindolanda Writing–Tablets (*Tabulae Vindolandenses IV, Part 1*)." *Britannia*, 41, 187–224.
TrRF	*Tragicorum Romanorum Fragmenta*. (2012–). 4 vols., Göttingen: Vandenhoeck & Ruprecht.

Introduction

Matthew P. Loar, Carolyn MacDonald, and Dan-el Padilla Peralta

How did the Romans become an imperial power? This was, understandably, a pressing question for Greek authors living in a world newly subject to Rome, and no less than three of them preserve variations on one Roman answer. On the eve of the First Punic War, a certain Roman Kaeso is reported to have boasted in the following manner to a Carthaginian senior official:[1]

… «ἡμεῖς» εἶπεν «οὕτως πεφύκαμεν (ἐρῶ δέ σοι ἔργα ἀναμφισβήβετα, ἵνα ἔχῃς ἀπαγγέλλειν τῆι πόλει) · τοῖς πολεμοῦσιν εἰς τὰ ἐκείνων ἔργα συγκαταβαίνομεν, κἂν τοῖς ἀλλοτρίοις ἐπιτηδεύμασι περίεσμεν τῶν ἐκ πολλοῦ αὐτὰ ἠσκηκότων. Τυρρηνοὶ γὰρ ἡμῖν ἐπολέμουν χαλκάσπιδες καὶ φαλαγγηδόν, οὐ κατὰ σπείρας μαχόμενοι · καὶ ἡμεῖς μεθοπλισθέντες καὶ τὸν ἐκείνων ὁπλισμὸν μεταλαβόντες παρεταττόμεθα αὐτοῖς, καὶ τοὺς ἐκ πλείστου ἐθάδας τῶν ἐν φάλαγγι ἀγώνων οὕτως ἀγωνιζόμενοι ἐνικῶμεν. οὐκ ἦν ὁ Σαυνιτικὸς ἡμῖν θυρεὸς πάτριος, οὐδ᾽ὕσσους εἴχομεν, ἀλλ᾽ἀσπίσιν ἐμαχόμεθα καὶ δόρασιν · ἀλλ᾽οὐδ᾽ἱππεύειν ἰσχύομεν, τὸ δὲ πᾶν ἢ τὸ πλεῖστον τῆς Ῥωμαικῆς δυνάμεως πεζὸν ἦν. ἀλλὰ Σαυνίταις καταστάντες εἰς πόλεμον, καὶ τοῖς ἐκείνων θυρεοῖς καὶ ὑσσοῖς ὁπλισθέντες ἱππεύειν τε αὐτοὺς ἀναγκάσαντες, ἀλλοτρίοις ὅπλοις καὶ ζηλώμασιν ἐδουλωσάμεθα τοὺς μέγα ἐφ᾽ἑαυτοῖς πεφρονηκότας. οὐδὲ πολιορκεῖν, ὦ Καρχηδόνιοι, ἐγινώσκομεν · ἀλλὰ παρὰ τῶν Ἑλλήνων μαθόντες, ἀνδρῶν τοῦ ἔργου πεπειραμένων, κἀκείνων τῶν ἐπιστημόνων καὶ πάντων ἀνθρώπων ἐν πολιορκίαι δεδυνήμεθα πλέον. μὴ δὴ Ῥωμαίους ἀναγκάσητε ἅπτεσθαι τῶν θαλαττίων · εἰ γὰρ ἡμῖν δεήσει ναυτικοῦ, πλείους μὲν καὶ ἀμείνους ὑμῶν ἐν ὀλίγωι χρόνωι κατασκευασόμεθα ναῦς, κρεῖττον δὲ ναυμαχήσομεν τῶν ἐκ πλείστου ναυτικῶν».

---

[1] This is the lengthiest version of Kaeso's speech, preserved in the Πλουτάρ<χου ἤ> Κεκιλίου Ἀποφθέγματα Ῥωμαϊκά ("Roman anecdotes of Plutarch or Caecilius"), which was discovered in a Vatican codex and published by H. von Arnim in 1892. Authorship and date are disputed: Beck's commentary and biographical essay at *BNJ* 839 posit an early first-century BCE date; Humm 2007 (followed with reservations by Woerther 2015: 139–43) attributes the work to the Augustan-era rhetorician and historian Caecilius of Kale Akte; Gabba 1991: 45–8 argues for post-Augustan composition. Another version of the speech is preserved in Diodorus (23.2) and its core argument is paralleled in Polybius (1.20.15).

... "We," he stated, "have thrived thus (and I'll tell you the most unambiguous things for you to take and announce to your city): we agree with our enemies to their terms, and we surpass in foreign customs those who have been practicing the same things for a long time. For the Etruscans had bronze shields and were in the phalanx when they fought us, and did not fight in maniples; and we, swapping our armor and taking up theirs, lined up in formation against them and striving in that fashion were victorious over men who had long been accustomed to fighting in the phalanx. The Samnite rectangular shield was not customary among us, nor did we make use of javelins; we fought with round shields and spears. Nor were we strong at cavalry-riding: all or nearly all of Roman military might was infantry in nature. But when facing off against the Samnites in war, we equipped ourselves with their shields and javelins and fought them on horseback, and with the help of foreign weapons and customs we enslaved those who were puffed up about themselves. We did not know how to wage siege warfare, Carthaginians; but after learning from the Greeks, men thoroughly knowledgeable about the practice, we have become superior to the experts and to all men in siegecraft. Do not force the Romans to take to the sea! For if we need a fleet, in a short time we will build more and better ships than yours, and we will prevail in sea-warfare over those who have been sailing for a long time."[2]

This speech is not solely an ideologically charged exaltation of the Romans as quick students: Emilio Gabba hits the nail right on the head in characterizing the passage as "a theory of *imitatio* applied to the history of a nation."[3] Revealingly, the competitive emulation through which (according to Kaeso) Rome made itself master over its adversaries is partly structured around objects and their appropriation: Roman spoliation of Etruscan armor and weapons allows them to imitate Etruscan tactics; likewise for Roman spoliation of Samnite armor and weapons. This discourse about Roman supremacy links the acquisition of new goods and social practices with knowledge of their proper deployment: the Romans (so the Greeks say the Romans say) master their empire by taking things over, appropriately. How was this understanding of imperial domination as mediated by successful appropriation reflected and refracted through Roman literature, art, and material culture – from the apex of the Republic to the apex of Empire?

---

[2] *Ineditum Vaticanum* § 3. All translations in this introduction are our own.
[3] Gabba 1991: 46. Polybius' representation of Romans as speedy learners: Walbank 1957–79: I.75. The innovations flagged in the *Ineditum Vaticanum* resulted in "one of the most significant military revolutions in European history": Potter 2014.

Taking up this question, this volume examines cultural appropriation by Rome and Romans, evident in literary practices ranging from plagiarism to quotation, and material practices ranging from spoliation to commercial import. As a critical term for the analysis of cultural products and practices, "appropriation" traces its origins to the American Appropriation artists of the 1970s (e.g., Jeff Koons, Sherrie Levine, and Richard Price) and to theoretical discussions of contemporary art from the 1980s and 1990s. The term has since been taken up (or taken over) by art historians working ever further afield from this charged moment in postmodern art-making and its specific interrogation of modern notions of authenticity, authorship, and originality. In transit, appropriation has become "a vertiginous concept," raising mutually entangled questions of "possession, ownership, making-one's-own ... [of] repetition, imitation, copying; [of] propriety, morality, ethics; [of] the dynamics of power, resistance, subversion."[4] Its definition and theoretical implications are best articulated in a 1996 essay by Robert Nelson, which already extends the term's applicability well beyond the contemporary art world: Nelson's paradigmatic example of appropriation in action is a statue group of four horses set above a cemetery gate in Texas, which he identifies as copies of the gilded bronze horses of San Marco in Venice, which had themselves been brought to Venice from Constantinople, and to Constantinople from Rome.

In his discussion of appropriation, Nelson draws particular attention to its "active, subjective, and motivated" nature. Situating himself within the French structuralist and post-structuralist traditions, Nelson introduces appropriation – in the context of the visual arts – specifically as an alternative to less precise and less agentive terms such as "borrowing" ("as if what is taken is ever repaid") and "influence" ("that elusive agency").[5] In casting aside this existing anodyne terminology, Nelson calls attention instead to the transformative, and in some ways violent, quality of the semiotic shift entailed by the act of appropriation. Indeed, appropriation does not happen incidentally, without conscious effort, but rather results from deliberate and purposeful actions on the part of identifiable actors or cultural forces. The net effect, however, is a distortion rather than a negation of what has been appropriated: the "prior semiotic assemblage" – an object, a motif – maintains its former connotations, albeit with a shift in meaning. Over time, then, varied and sometimes contradictory significations accrete, yielding a semiotic bricolage that always carries with it vestiges of its earlier lives. For this reason, plotting the life history of

---

[4] Mathur in Baselitz *et al.* 2012: 181; Kinney 2012: 1.   [5] Nelson 1996: 162.

appropriated texts and objects can represent in microcosm the study more broadly of cultural history, or indeed of culture itself.

Nelson was wary of this expansive potential: he cautions that, "taken too far, the act of appropriation becomes a theoretical Pac-Man about to gobble up all other theoretical terms and methods and thus to be rendered analytically useless."[6] In the twenty years since Nelson first published his essay, however, scholars working on everything from the postcolonial art of South Asia to the use of *spolia* in the Arch of Constantine have found in appropriation a rich analytical framework. Proponents now call not for limiting the concept, but for its continued expansion. Taking a "wide-angle view of appropriation's theoretical repercussions," art historian Saloni Mathur sees "the need to broaden the concept, to stretch it expansively across contemporary culture . . . and to enliven it with the enormous challenge of the most recent dynamics of global interaction."[7] This broad sense of appropriation's usefulness, as a way of getting at culture and at the interactions between cultures, undergirds the current volume – though of course our interests lie in Roman culture, and the dynamics of interaction across the ancient Mediterranean world.

By bringing an expansive concept of appropriation to bear on Roman literary and material practices, we hope to invigorate and intertwine two prominent strands in Classical scholarship. Scholars of Latin literature have long acknowledged the programmatic and cultural importance of Rome's competitive emulation of Greek literary models: this practice has been identified in the earliest moments of Roman literature, which indeed tropes itself as a "takeover" of a specific form of Hellenism.[8] In a similar vein, the proliferation of intertextual studies in Latin literature has drawn attention to the "dynamics of appropriation" at work when a Roman author quotes, cites, or otherwise alludes to another text, whether Latin or Greek.[9] Meanwhile, in the fields of Roman art and archaeology, there has been a surge of interest in plunder and the significance of its display in the city, along with a dramatic revision of how we understand Roman "copies" of Greek art.[10] These exciting conversations are taking place on

---

[6] Nelson 1996: 165.　　[7] Mathur in Baselitz *et al.* 2012: 182.

[8] Generally West & Woodman 1979; Hinds 1998; Hutchinson 2013, especially on the times and spaces where contacts between Greeks and Romans took place. On Roman literature's "takeover" of Hellenism, see Feeney 2005 and now Feeney 2016. For Roman takeover of Greek political/ philosophical ideas, see ch. 7 of Lane 2015.

[9] Hinds 1998 was trailblazing. For intertextuality's significance in classical studies, see Fowler 2000: 115–37; for a bibliography of major intertextual treatments of Latin poetry, see Coffee 2013.

[10] On plunder, see especially Miles 2008; Rutledge 2012. On the push against *Kopienkritik*, see Bergmann 1995; Perry 2005; Marvin 2008.

parallel but largely unengaged tracks, as disciplinary boundaries within Classics continue to obscure the interaction between literary and material modes of cultural appropriation. Only a small number of monographs have looked at both, and always with an eye to understanding one specific facet of what this volume will suggest is a multifaceted whole.[11] The need for interpretive frameworks capable of comprehending and evaluating literary and material appropriation as two sides of the same coin thus remains acute. Bringing together philologists, historians, and archaeologists, this volume bridges the disciplinary divides in pursuit of an interdisciplinary perspective on Roman appropriation – understood not as a set of distinct practices, but as a hydra-headed phenomenon through which Roman culture made and remade itself throughout antiquity.

To underline the interrelationship between the many heads of this hydra, our volume has adopted a shorthand name for the beast: *cargo*. As the excerpt from the *Ineditum Vaticanum* with which we began suggests, Romans were attentive to the significance of objects appropriated from others to their culture's historical trajectory. And yet, for the Kaeso of the excerpt, every successful appropriation of a class of weaponry was logical and inevitable; the model-cum-history of appropriation envisioned thus effaces the contingent and accidental in favor of the purposeful and deliberate. In counterpoint to the implicit triumphalism of the excerpt, our emphasis on cargo is in part motivated by a desire to recover precisely those contingencies that drove the incorporation of goods from all over the Mediterranean into Rome's many social worlds. This act of recovery entails a move from any narrative that would sanitize Roman domination and/or celebrate its value as self-evident and unproblematic. Rather, one of this volume's main objectives will be to probe the violent interactions through which cargoes are sent into circulation – and through which the individual and aggregate meanings of these cargoes experience distortion.

With this end in mind, this volume seeks both to highlight the significant points of contact between Roman literary and material appropriative practices and to formulate and apply interdisciplinary models for examining Roman appropriation. To that end, the theoretical perspectives adopted by our contributors take into consideration the broad sweep of recent scholarship on empire-building – Roman as well as modern. By way

---

[11] E.g., Marvin 2008, on Roman sculpture; Dufallo 2013, on Roman ecphrasis. Young 2015, esp. 52–88 on material and literary appropriation in Catullus' polymetrics, comes closest to our volume's intended cross-fertilization.

of contextualizing our volume's intended contributions, we turn next to
a summary of this research and its implications for our overarching
argument.

The motor of Roman appropriation was the imperial project that
shaped the trajectories of individuals and communities throughout the
Mediterranean world. In its exploration of this dynamic, *Empire of Plunder*
builds on the past several decades of prolific scholarship on the Roman
Empire's mechanisms for constructing and reaffirming local, regional, and
transregional identities. In a challenge to previous generations of scholarship that read provincial material culture as a marker of top-down Romanization (with sophisticated or unsophisticated locals on the receiving end),
Marcel Benabou and others have argued for resistance's role in the negotiation of imperial local cultures. In a pioneering 2001 article, Jane Webster
applied a model of creolization developed by specialists in early modern
and modern colonial cultures to the Roman provinces; Richard Hingley's
subsequent adaptation of theories of globalization for the study of the
Empire drew from another well of postcolonial research. C. R. Whittaker
and Greg Woolf have investigated how an "ethic of civilization" came to
be instantiated in the drive to restore discipline in the Roman East and in
the drive to create order in the West; Roman Roth and colleagues have
documented the tension between homogeneity and integration that con-
tinuously resurfaces in Roman texts and material cultures; and Andrew
Gardner has repurposed Anthony Giddens's concept of structuration to
elucidate how soldiers realized their identities through material culture in
Roman Britain.[12]

Although much attention has been (deservedly) paid to the articulation
of Roman power at the periphery, less often remarked is the extent to
which the productions of the periphery drive the internal redefinition of
Rome itself. In provincial settings as well as in Rome, the projection of
Roman power was not endorsed uncritically: anxieties over luxury and its
perceived social consequences gave birth to intellectual discourses and
"affective communities" concerned with critiquing empire.[13] Projection

---

[12] Resistance in North Africa: Benabou 1974; Mattingly 2003. Creolization: Webster 2001.
Globalization: Hingley 2005, now to be read with the essays in Pitts & Versluys 2015. The "ethic
of civilization": Woolf 1998. Homogeneity and integration: the essays in Roth & Keller 2007.
Structuration as a lens for Roman Britain: Gardner 2007. On cultural memory and imperial local
cultures, see now the essays in Galinsky & Lapatin 2016. For a modern take with examples drawn
from Cameroon, cf. Mbembe 1992.

[13] Roman critiques of luxury: Zanda 2011; cf. Gorman & Gorman 2014. The term and conceptual
rubric of "affective identities": Gandhi 2006.

generated more than contingent anxieties, however: our volume argues that the funneling of artifacts, bodies, and practices from periphery to center and center to periphery constituted Roman identity. In the exercise of empire, Rome *became* a culture of cargo.

Through its investigation of Rome's appropriative reach, this volume targets not only Romanists and students of the ancient world but also scholars working in other temporal and geographical settings; our expectation is that these different disciplinary communities will derive profit both from this volume's exposition of material and from the various theoretical frameworks employed to contextualize and tease out the material's significance. Postcolonial interventions such as Edward Said's *Culture and Imperialism* (1993) and Homi Bhabha's *The Location of Culture* (2004) are important to the story we seek to tell. In the spirit of Bhabha's call for understanding terms of cultural engagement as "produced performatively," our volume brings out the performativity of Romanness and the tactics and strategies deployed to stage it; indeed, as Dufallo's and Richlin's essays underline, it was on the stage itself that commodities of various kinds were converted into social values. Our volume's debts to postcolonial theory will also be apparent in the space we allocate not only to the elite but also to the sub-elite brokers of cultural traffic (slaves, merchants, soldiers) who roamed – or were dragged – across Mediterranean landscapes and boundaries.[14] The violence of these movements conditions the "geo-biography" of Roman literature (Myers on Gallus in Egypt)[15]; this same violence is, we argue, indispensable to understanding the range of significations that accrue to the spoliated and inscribed artifacts on display at Rome (Haimson Lushkov on annalistic spoliation, Biggs on re-spoliation).

In developing interdisciplinary models for examining Roman appropriation, this volume continues the trend in cultural studies of setting literary and material appropriative practices alongside each other.[16] The chapters that unravel the microhistories of displaced objects – Punic War monuments (Biggs), the Pergamene Gauls (Rebeggiani), and Egyptian obelisks (Parker) – bear on current discussions of appropriation within culturally mobile contexts, such as Stephen Greenblatt's edited volume *Cultural Mobility* (2009). Greenblatt's miniature history of appropriation opens

---

[14] Bhabha 2004: 3 on performativity, 17 and *passim* on "transnational histories of migrants, the colonized, or political refugees – these border and frontier conditions . . ."

[15] We borrow "geo-biography" from the afterword of Anderson 2006. For the diffusion of literary works in/alongside contemporary (globalized) commodity networks, see Moretti 2000, 2003; Parks 2015.

[16] As exemplified most recently by the essays in Huck & Bauernschmidt 2012.

with non-Roman appropriations of Rome in Late Antiquity; in a similar vein, recent years have seen a volume addressing appropriations of Rome from Late Antiquity to the modern age and another volume exploring appropriation as a widespread cultural phenomenon that likewise begins with Late Antique spoliations of Rome.[17] The range and disciplinary impact of these works bring into even clearer focus the need for a sustained exploration of appropriation in and by Republican and Imperial Rome.

One collection of chapters does come close to our own in interests and range: *Rome the Cosmopolis* (2003), edited by Catharine Edwards and Greg Woolf. Appropriation figures explicitly in some contributions (Edwards, "Incorporating the alien: the art of conquest"; Vout, "Embracing Egypt"), and implicitly in others (Beard, "The triumph of the absurd: Roman street theatre"; Elsner, "Inventing Christian Rome: the role of early Christian art"). In documenting the imbrication of city and empire – Rome as both *urbs* and *orbis* – the focus of *Rome the Cosmopolis* remains on the centripetal pull that the city of Rome exerts; its papers locate the act of appropriation in Rome itself. Our volume, however, decentralizes appropriation from the city of Rome, tracking the spread of cargo to Roman Italy (Richlin), Roman trade networks (Fulton), and other Roman provinces (Daniels, Myers, Parker). Our goal is to highlight the importance of appropriation as a foundational practice through which Rome (broadly conceived) made and remade itself, as a Republic and as an Empire, on Italian soil and abroad.

We come now to the arrangement of chapters. The volume is divided into three parts – "Interaction," "Distortion," and "Circulation" – each one containing three or four chapters and a short response penned by one of the editors. The groupings of chapters are thematic rather than chrono-logical, geographical, or generic: the goal in each part is to bring out a key facet of Roman appropriative practice and to explore its manifestations in different times and places, across different genres and media.

Under "Interaction," we trace how the Roman encounter with alterity was negotiated at sites of conquest and in the disposition of spoliated goods. These *spolia* – whether textual or material – acquired new (Roman-imposed) meanings as they were torn from their previous contexts of use and reception, reconstituted under the eye of the conqueror, and memorialized in Roman literature. The four chapters in this part therefore analyze how Latin literary works from different genres and historical periods comment on, enact, and even replicate material appropriations. Individually and as an ensemble, these contributions illustrate the

---

[17] The former: Prusac & Seim 2012. The latter: Brilliant & Kinney 2011.

sustained interaction and interrelation of literary and material appropriative practices. Basil Dufallo explains Plautus' *Menaechmi* as a dramatization of Roman material and cultural appropriation writ large (and the crises of identity attendant to these activities). Ayelet Haimson Lushkov reads Livy's source-citations about *spolia* in the aftermath of battle as if they too were war-won artifacts. Thomas Biggs unravels Augustan repurposings of Republican naval monuments and their (mis)readings in Augustan and post-Augustan literature. Stefano Rebeggiani traces the meanderings of Pergamene statues and Hellenistic poetry across the Mediterranean to Rome and the Vespasian Templum Pacis. In his response, Matthew P. Loar draws together the chapters' major themes, elaborating the potential usefulness of "microhistory" as a framework for writing Roman cultural history through the lens of appropriation.

In "Distortion," we engage explicitly with Robert Nelson's claim that "successful" appropriation is "a distortion, not a negation of the prior semiotic assemblage ... it maintains but shifts the former connotations to create the new sign."[18] The three chapters in this part examine the semiotic reconfigurations undergone by objects and motifs as they travel through the time and space of the Roman empire, with an eye to how prior meaning is preserved, transformed, or effaced – and to what end. In a close reading of Vitruvius' *De Architectura*, Marden Fitzpatrick Nichols shows that "preserving" the "original" meaning of appropriated architectural motifs was crucial to the process of repurposing them for Rome's world culture. Jennifer Trimble's contribution bears this out further by demonstrating that the Ara Pacis makes a very precise (but long unrecognized) citation of an Egyptian temple style, and the structure's full impact depends on viewers recognizing the citation and knowing the semantics of the original temples. Nichols and Trimble thus key us in to the delicate balance of meaning maintained and meaning changed in Roman appropriations and Roman discourses on appropriation. Grant Parker then tests the limits of this balance in the *longue durée*, tracing the manifold distortions of obelisks and obelizing objects in transit around the ancient Mediterranean and eventually across the modern Atlantic. Carolyn MacDonald's response concludes the section by reflecting on a crucial question that emerges from the three chapters: What does it mean to speak of Roman appropriation as "successful"?

In "Circulation," we examine how objects accumulated new meanings in and through travel. Different kinds of cargo (up to and including

---

[18] Nelson 1996: 119.

human) were variously susceptible to climatic, ecological, and/or administrative disruptions at each stage of transit. The four chapters in this part
challenge stemmatic understandings of the appropriative process, highlighting instead the importance of circulation and contingency. Amy
Richlin's contribution explores how Roman comedy bears traces of –
and witness to – the circulation of human cargo. With the help of *chaîne
opératoire* theory, Carrie Fulton studies the networks and middlemen
through which cargo was transported across the Roman Mediterranean.
Micah Myers brings to light how the Gallus papyrus from Qasr Ibrim was
implicated in and remains symbolic of multiple registers of textual and
human circulation. Taking up numismatic evidence, Megan Daniels
scrutinizes the circulation of Herculean iconographies in Iberia before
and after the Roman conquest. At section's end, Dan-el Padilla Peralta's
response assesses how each chapter advances our understanding of the
relationship between circulation and connectivity and sketches how one
might go about writing complementary histories of circulation's material
vectors.

We would be remiss in concluding this introduction if we did not
openly acknowledge two of this volume's limitations. The first is geographical. Responding to the interests and competencies of the editors, some of
the chapters circulate between Roman Italy and mainland Greece (Dufallo,
Richlin, Nichols); others voyage further afield to Egypt (Myers, Trimble,
Parker), Spain (Haimson Lushkov, Daniels), and Asia Minor (Rebeggiani).
Two chapters sail over the sea and the history of political and commercial
encounters on/underneath its surface (Biggs, Fulton). Whole regions of the
globalized Mediterranean have been skirted or sidelined: our chapters do
not engage extensively with the cultural and economic aftershocks of
Rome's encroachments upon the Near East; the shifts in identity para-
digms set in motion by the intensification of networks of trade and
plunder in Roman Britain and Gaul; the movements of troops, ships,
and cargo across the Balkan, Danubian, and Black Sea borderlands; or the
growing cultural and economic importance of North Africa's production
of commodities throughout our period.[19] However, in light of the salvoes
lately being fired at the "methodological nationalism" of traditional

---

[19] Generally on the need to look East in conceptualizing the Hellenistic and Roman worlds: Millar
1998; Purcell 2013. For the case of Roman Arabia, see Bowersock 1998. Britain: Mattingly 2007.
Gaul: Dietler 2010. Balkans and Danube: Bounegru 2006. Black Sea: Wheeler 2012. North Africa:
the essays in Milanese *et al.* 2010.

Roman provincial archaeology and historiography, the decision to limit geographic scope will (we hope) function as a heuristically productive constraint.[20]

The collection's second limitation is temporal. With the partial exception of Parker's chapter, our volume does not examine the *Nachleben* of Roman appropriation in the imperial and nation-state projects of modernity. Nonetheless, we are conscious of (and very much hope to convey in the scope and texture of our volume) the implication of our own subjectivities as editors and contributors in the cultural matrix of modern American empire: as Said famously insisted in his overview of nineteenth-century British imperial theory, there is no theorizing empire *from without empire*.[21] That "contemporary global sovereignty" continues to celebrate – and in many cases explicitly appropriate – the legacy of Roman plunder is evident in the academic and museological practices through which nation-states such as Britain, France, Germany, and the United States have claimed hegemony over the past; or in the epistemological technologies through which colonial and postcolonial spaces have been remapped as extensions of Roman *imperium* in twenty-first-century guise.[22] This volume thus makes no pretense of being the last word on Roman appropriation, far less appropriations of Rome. To the contrary, we are hopeful that the case studies and interpretive frameworks laid out here will spur and inform a great deal more research.

---

[20] For the phrase and critique, see Pitts & Versluys 2015, esp. 5–7.

[21] E.g., Said 1993: 154, commenting on the "commonplace of British imperial theory that the British empire was different from (and better than) the Roman Empire in that it was a rigorous system in which order and law prevailed. . ."

[22] The quoted phrase, and the notion of empire as "transtemporal": Willis 2007. The humanities as "epistemological technology" under the British Empire, with attention to the role of museums: Bradley 2010. Roman appropriation in the construction of Napoleonic France: Huet 1999. More generally on the toggle between ancient Rome as sign/signifier of cosmopolitanism on the one hand and Rome as brand for nationalistic projects on the other, see the other essays in Edwards 1999. On the United States as a second Roman Empire, compare Murphy 2007 and Smil 2010.

PART I

Interaction

CHAPTER I

The Comedy of Plunder
Art and Appropriation in Plautus' Menaechmi

Basil Dufallo

One way to assess the significance of the Romans' "culture of cargo," as described in the introduction to this volume, is to examine the history of their self-consciousness about it. In this chapter – appropriately enough for the volume's first chapter – I will argue that an acute self-consciousness about the crossover between literary and material appropriations at Rome is present already in the work of Plautus, the first Latin author whose works survive complete, and one whose Greek-style plays reflect a relatively early period in Rome's empire-building encounters with the Hellenic world. Further, I will maintain that the particular form of this self-consciousness in Plautine drama reveals something important about what happens when Roman society imagines "cargo" (re-)becoming "culture" through appropriation and vice versa, namely, that such imagining brings to the fore the class implications of this representational process itself.[1] It does so in Plautus' case by encouraging both comparison of the differing involvement of various classes in the activities surrounding cargo and those surrounding culture, and exploration of how such involvement by elite and non-elite, senator and merchant, slave and free relates to a collective identity as Roman. It thus reminds us of the difficulty of associating any aspect of Plautus' plays with the sole interests of a single class, and of the potential benefits as well as threats to all classes in the Plautine audience from the larger circulation of persons, goods, cultural products, and power

---

[1] My sincere thanks to the audience at the *Cargo Culture* conference, the editors, and the anonymous readers for the Press for their many helpful comments and suggestions.

For this purpose, I will understand "culture" in the last two of the overlapping senses of the word famously distinguished by Raymond Williams, i.e., culture as "the general body of the arts" and as "a whole way of life, material, intellectual and spiritual" (Williams 1983: *xvi*), but with some emphasis on the first sense, in light of my focus on drama and paintings. In this chapter "cargo" often signifies in its concrete sense as the "freight or lading of a ship, a ship-load" (*OED* 1a) but in some cases also as a "shorthand" term for objects of appropriation more broadly, as per the introduction to this volume. I acknowledge that no firm line exists between objects transported as cargo "in themselves" and as elements of "culture" – hence "(*re*-)becoming."

in the Mediterranean,[2] And, of course, when all this occurs in comedy it also provides abundant opportunity for laughter.

I will advance my case by focusing on Plautus' *Menaechmi*, and my initial point of entry into this brilliant and influential drama will be the passage containing a brief ecphrasis of art objects at *Men.* 143–9, a part of the play that I have discussed elsewhere with different emphases, and my earlier reading of which I will expand and develop.[3] Here Plautus employs ecphrasis to lend hilarious resonance to his characterization of the first Menaechmus twin, a Greek-named merchant's son from Syracuse, whose frivolous and effeminate identification with artistic images from Greek myth seems to foreground all that is most suspect about Greek culture from a Roman perspective. For all his absurdity, however, Menaechmus is nevertheless a figure with whom the Roman audience is encouraged to identify. He is the drama's comic hero, liberating himself from unpleasant personal entanglements with a wife and a prostitute and, together with his like-named brother, planning a joyful return home at the play's end. As a Syracusan, moreover, he hails from a city that not only lay within a Roman province but whose revolt against Roman power had also been crushed by the likely date of the play's first performance, and he currently resides in Epidamnus, another city that had, by this date, been the site of a decisive Roman victory.[4] Thus Menaechmus' doings have a special bearing on Rome's sense of its own implication in the Greek world.

---

[2] In this I build on a view advanced in particular by Amy Richlin, both in recently published work and in her contribution to the present volume. See, e.g., her discussions of the way different aspects of Roman comedy might have appealed to different social classes, including slaves (Richlin 2014, esp. 221; 2015), and her skepticism over the views of McCarthy (2000), Fontaine (2010), and Stewart (2012), insofar as they argue against the possibility of slaves as an audience targeted by Plautus (Richlin 2014: 180–1). See further her helpful remarks on the non-unitary quality of "elites" and other social groups in this period in Rome and the presence of slave volunteers in the Roman military (Richlin 2014: 209, 218), as well as on the implications of men's cross-dressing to play slave women onstage (Richlin 2015). Cf. Beacham 1991: 48; Sharrock 2009: 1, 23. For the mixed-status composition of Plautus' audience the *locus classicus* is *Poen.* 16–35. I differ from Richlin, however, in the extent to which I see any individual scene in Plautus as a discreet gesture of class resistance, easily assimilated, for example, to de Certeau's "tactics," the "ways of operating" in which persons excluded from power adapt and modify in "everyday life" the "strategies" of those in power for their own benefit and self-expression (de Certeau 1984: xix-xx; cf. Richlin 2014: 179). As I hope my reading of episodes from the *Menaechmi* will suggest, even individual Plautine scenes that cast ridicule on expressions of power by elites (and thus suggest the "tactical" operations described by de Certeau) may be so bound up with elite interests as to render problematic the very opposition between acts of resistance and acts of capitulation in this context (cf. my conclusions).

[3] See Dufallo 2013: 21–8.

[4] On the Roman attacks on Syracuse and Epidamnus, and the likely dating of the *Menaechmi*, see pp. 19–20.

This is true not least because, when he first emerges from his house near the play's opening, the first Menaechmus is effectively cross-dressed: underneath his male *pallium* ("cloak") he wears a women's *palla* (a loose "mantle"), which he has stolen from his overbearing wife as a form of payment to the prostitute, Erotium, whose nearby house is the goal of his foray from his own dwelling on this particular day. Menaechmus' transgressive choice of garment is not visible at first. After encountering his parasite Peniculus, however, he proudly compares himself, dressed in this fashion, with paintings of Ganymede and Adonis, images that would have been familiar to Plautus' audiences as a form of plunder from the Greek world through their display in triumphal processions of returning generals as well as in temples and the houses of the elite.[5] "Tell me," he says to Peniculus, "Have you ever seen, on a wall, a painted panel where an eagle snatches away Ganymede or where Venus snatches away Adonis?" "Often," Peniculus answers, "But what do those pictures have to do with me?" "Don't I utterly remind you of something?" Menaechmus presses, implicitly comparing himself with the two mythical pretty–boys and no doubt raising his *pallium* to make the *palla* visible.[6] "What's that fancy outfit you've got on?" asks Peniculus, but Menaechmus retorts, "Tell me I'm the most charming of men." Peniculus attempts to change the subject by demanding, "Where are we going to eat?" but eventually pays Menaechmus the compliments he requests, and at scene's end the pair have reached Erotium's house (*Men.* 143–81).

In this memorable episode, which the techniques of skilled actors must have greatly enhanced, it is as though Menaechmus becomes a walking painting, gleefully transporting himself to Erotium to purchase sexual favors by means of the plundered feminine garment that renders him pretty as a picture in the first place. This is a novel sort of cargo indeed, and one that both figures and interconnects at least three modes of appropriation, each with its own place among the activities of various Roman social classes: spoliation, the exchange of commercial goods, and the cultural borrowing that informed Plautus' own literary endeavors in a

---

[5] See n. 8. Although our sources emphasize the public display of captured paintings in this period, Polybius (9.10.13) notes that paintings that had been in private homes at Syracuse went to private owners in Rome. For discussion see Gruen 1992: 99, 103. Of course, such images could already have been familiar to the Romans from Hellenized Etruscan art (as Gratwick [1993: 152] points out in explaining the Etruscan provenance of the forms *Catameitum* and *Adoneum* [Pl. *Men.* 144]) even before the influx of war booty from Magna Graecia.

[6] On the handling of the *palla* as a stage property in the *Menaechmi*, see Ketterer 1986: 51–61; Marshall 2006: 105.

Greek comedic genre. The passage brings these three modes together through the figure of Menaechmus, whose loss, and subsequent reclaiming of his own identity (the "comedy of errors" that would make the play so appealing to Shakespeare), drives the engine of the drama. Thus our passage is integral to the larger exploration of identity in the *Menaechmi* as a whole, insofar as it emphasizes the ways in which Greece and Greekness – and beyond them the still more exotic Eastern identities represented by the specific cases of Ganymede and Adonis – pervade Roman identity at both a psychological and a material level. All this, I suggest, renders the *Menaechmi* an especially salient example of and commentary on Roman appropriation from the perspective on class and identity just outlined.

We see this especially, I maintain, by noting the way in which the play's ecphrasis is anticipated by the play's prologue and framed as well by the play's ongoing use of the *palla* to explore the links between aesthetic and commercial value, also in a highly comedic vein. For in the prologue we find an account of Menaechmus' status as a kind of commercial cargo himself and even as a kind of plunder, rendered such by the crowd-drawing power of Greek-style theatrical art. In the remainder of the play, the changing fate of the *palla* serves to keep the audience focused on material commerce, as well as on the play itself as a transaction between actors and audience. As the play opens, in other words, the associations between the appropriative practices to which I have referred first begin to take shape. The ecphrasis condenses and adds to these associations, and their further implications for my argument continue to emerge as the play unfolds. Thus approaching the *Menaechmi* from the vantage point afforded by this volume will, I hope, provide a fresh perspective on the ways in which this play situates itself within the structure of both Roman society and that of Rome's relations with the outside world.

Let us turn, then, to the *Menaechmi*'s prologue.[7] Like other Plautine openings, this one calls attention to the play as a Greek cultural borrowing (7–12). Yet, whereas other playwrights, we are told, set the action in an Attic Greek milieu so that the drama will "seem more Greek to you" (9, *vobis Graecum videatur magis*), this story will be told "with a

---

[7] Here I will be setting aside the question of whether the prologue (or parts of it) is actually by Plautus himself or reflects a somewhat later production. As Gratwick 1993: 30–4 discusses, the style looks genuine, but even someone writing these lines after the original performance date could have expected the same kind of interest in the social and cultural matters that I am ascribing to Plautus' original audience and emphasized these themes in the prologue as a way to highlight the play's relevance to such interests.

Sicilian accent rather than an Attic one" (11–12, *hoc argumentum ... non atticissat, verum sicilicissitat*), a reference to the Sicilian origins of its central characters. Suggestive remarks about the play's geographical setting continue as the Prologus describes how the Menaechmi twins came to be separated in childhood (17–36). Menaechmus' father, we learn, went on a sea voyage to Tarentum for commercial purposes and took one of the twins with him, while the other stayed in Syracuse. In Tarentum, a city known as a Greek theatrical center already by the late fourth century BCE, a dramatic festival was taking place, and among the crowds that had gathered to watch the productions (here described with the Latin term *ludei* [29]), the young Menaechmus wandered away from his father. A certain Epidamnian merchant was also at the festival, and he "snatched up" the boy and "carried him off" (33, *tollit avehitque*) to Epidamnus, the Greek city on the Adriatic where the *Menaechmi* is set. The father's loss of his son caused him such grief that he died at Tarentum a few days later. The Epidamnian made Menaechmus his heir and provided him with a wife sporting a large dowry, then died in turn: while heading to the country during a rain storm, he entered a rapid river and was washed away (60–6). Thus Menaechmus, although orphaned due to his father's distraction at a drama similar in kind to the one Plautus' audience is now witnessing, has been compensated for his misfortunes by becoming quite rich (67).

The first aspect of the prologue that I would like to bring out is its emphasis on places that we know to have been plundered of their Greek artworks by the Romans.[8] The event usually cited as opening the floodgates to this wave of spoliation is Marcellus' sack of Syracuse in 211 BCE. Given the interest that Erotium shows in Syracuse later in the *Menaechmi* (410–2), and the ironic reception of her bogus history of its rulers, the play most likely dates, as Gratwick argues, from after Rome's takeover, with the dramatic events set "within the living memory of most spectators."[9] Erotium names Hieron as the current ruler of Syracuse (411; the rule of Hieron II ended in 215 BCE), but she says this to the second Menaechmus twin, who has been away from Syracuse for over five years (234). His response – "You declare things, woman, that are scarcely false" (412, *haud falsa, mulier, praedicas*) – is clearly ironic, since she has included in her list the nonexistent ruler "Liparo" (411) as well as Phintia (410), who ruled at

---

[8] On the early history of Roman spoliation of Greek artworks and their display in Rome, see Pollitt 1986: 153–9; Gruen 1992: 84–130; Beard 2007: 143–6; Miles 2008; Dufallo 2013: 6–8.
[9] Gratwick 1993: 180.

Agrigentum.[10] The exchange potentially becomes even funnier for a Roman audience if Hieron can be thought to have died and Syracuse to have been captured by Marcellus during the time the second Menaechmus has been away looking for his brother, so that Menaechmus appears clueless about his city's momentous defeat by the Romans! Although ancient authors praise Marcellus for his restraint in victory, the conquest of Syracuse nevertheless produced an enormous quantity of loot, including art objects, and became something of a byword, as we see from Livy's description of the comparable spoils taken two years later by Fabius Maximus after his recapture of none other than Tarentum.[11] Fabius' conquest, Livy says, yielded vast quantities of silver and 3,080 pounds of gold, along with statues and paintings, the whole "almost" equaling what was taken from Syracuse (27.16.7).[12] (For Livy himself as an author capable of assimilating his use of earlier textual sources to Roman spoliation, see the following chapter by Ayelet Haimson Lushkov.) Thus the references in the *Menaechmi* to Syracuse and Tarentum, it is reasonable to assume, would have recalled impressive Roman victories and the lavish spectacles accompanying them.

But Syracuse and Tarentum were not simply rebellious Greek cities to be plundered and then abandoned: their presence as settings for the play's background action enfolds the drama within a geographical purview that was now Roman as well as Greek, and they thus imply a mixing and mingling of Greek and Roman identity in concrete terms. They share this trait with Epidamnus, the play's actual setting. The Romans had extended their power throughout the southern part of the Italian peninsula in the first half of the third century BCE, and after the conclusion of the First Punic War in 241 BCE, Sicily had become Rome's first province. In 229 BCE, moreover, a Roman force had invaded Epidamnus after an Illyrian attack, an intervention motivated at least in part by the worries of Italian merchants over disruptions of their sailing routes (cf. the mention of a pirate ship at *Men.* 344). And Rome sent forces to Epidamnus again in 205 in response to the aggressions of Philip V of Macedon. Thus the Epidamnian setting of the *Menaechmi* is far from arbitrary, but rather plays upon a Roman sense of increasing involvement in Hellas. In a moment, in fact, we will see Plautus playing upon the Latin resonance of the Greek name Epidamnus itself.

---

[10] Cf. Gratwick's astute remark that "things affirmed to be *haud falsa* in a bogus 'Epidamnus' (alias Plautopolis) are going to be *falsa* as far as the real Rome of the performance is concerned" (1993: 180).

[11] Tarentum had earlier succumbed to Roman power in 272 BCE.   [12] Cf. esp. Miles 2008: 61–9.

Within this world of Roman conquest and plunder, some much more mundane forms of appropriation are going on busily in the *Menaechmi*'s prologue. These involve the collection, transport, and sale of commercial goods. Yet, as one might expect from even the mundane aspects of Plautine drama, this, too, occurs in a comically suggestive fashion. In the passage cited, note especially Plautus' play with the language of cargo. The Menaechmi twins' father, we learn, loaded up a great ship with many goods. Then "the father put one of the twins on the ship and carried him off with him to Tarentum to market": *imponit geminum alterum in navim pater,* | *Tarentum avexit secum ad mercatum* (26–7). The language here is precisely that which is used not only of people but also of cargo when they are embarked and transported by ship. Both *impono* and *aveho* carry this double meaning.[13] Thus, whereas on the surface the *Menaechmi*'s Prologus can be heard simply to say that Menaechmus' father took the son with him to market, the image of loading cargo and son in quick succession jokingly suggests that even before the journey began the son was already being treated like an object of exchange, foreshadowing the way in which Menaechmus does in fact change hands, through theft, at the Tarentine *ludi*. The Epidamnian merchant, who also *avehit* (33, "carries off") Menaechmus, not only steals a son, but perpetrates a kind of material robbery, insofar as that son has already been assimilated to the commercial interests of his father.

Such connotations only deepen as the Prologus goes on to suggest, through comical punning on the name Epidamnus, that financial loss is the potential fate of any audience member who might have business dealings in that city (49–55). Saying that he must "return to Epidamnus" (49) as though he had traveled elsewhere in laying out the Sicilian and Tarentine parts of the background narrative, the Prologus suggests he can "set [the audience] right on this other account" (50) and proceeds to play on the Latin word *damnum* ("loss") that the Greek name Epidamnus would have conjured up to the Roman ear. "If any of you," he says, "should wish anything to be seen to in the direction of Epidamnus, let him boldly command and declare it" (51–2). Here the Roman audience can hear Epidamnus as a Greek/Roman amalgam joining *epi* and *damnum*, as well as both a place name and a comic adjective, so that the Prologus can

---

[13] See *OLD*, *impono* 4a; *aveho* 1. For the use of *aveho* in circumstances involving the kidnapping and actual sale of boys, see Pl. *Poen.* 73–4.

be understood to say "any Loss-ward thing."[14] This wordplay is confirmed by the paraprosdokian joke that he inserts next in insisting that any such transaction be on strictly cash-in-advance terms, for, he explains, those who do not pay up are wasting their efforts, whereas those who do pay up – are wasting their efforts still more (54–5).

Upon inspection, the class implications of the prologue's humor emerge as a richly ambiguous element of its potential appeal. If, on the one hand, business, commerce, and sea trade all point to danger and loss both here and elsewhere in Plautus' oeuvre, this is very much in keeping with the professed values of the senatorial elite who, through the *lex Claudia* of 218 BCE, forbid senators and their sons from owning large seagoing vessels capable of holding more than three hundred *amphorae* and thereby ostensibly barred them from the profits of overseas commerce. In general, as Matthew Leigh points out, the emphasis on the dangers and difficulties of sea trade in Plautus' work (notably in the *Mercator*) echoes elite prejudice against a form of profit directly threatening to the preeminence of Rome's old landed aristocracy.[15] The role of the senatorial class in organizing Rome's dramatic festivals and choosing the plays to be performed provides a ready motivation for such allusions. But on the other hand, the Prologus promotes the play itself, with all its emphasis on trade, as a successful form of appropriation – not merely of Greek culture but, as it were, of Greek territory. "This city [i.e., Rome] is Epidamnus as long as this play is being put on," he announces. "When another play is put on, it will become another town" (72–3). Through self-conscious reference to the dramatic illusion as well as to the conventions of comic prologues, the Prologus suggests that the entire audience is to enjoy, on its own turf, a city most likely occupied by Rome within recent memory.[16] Such reference to the military exploits of all the social groups represented in Rome's armies – and to the entire city of Rome – could potentially have defused any perceived criticism of the Roman trading class in particular, while

[14] See Gratwick 1993: 139. Cf., on the further pun on Epidamnus at *Men.* 263–4, Fontaine 2010: 28, 103 and, on Plautus' assumption of audience knowledge of Greek, Fontaine 2010: 163–4. Plautus' choice of Epidamnus as the city's name is rendered all the more significant by the fact that it was regularly known by its other name, Dyrrachium, by his day.

[15] See esp. Leigh 2004: 137–56. For more on the literary repercussions of the elite bias against profit from commerce, see Habinek 1998: 45–59. For further discussion of the *lex Claudia* see Fulton in this volume.

[16] For Rome as Epidamnus, cf. Anderson 1993: 138; on the adaptation of prologue conventions, Slater 1985: 152; on the theatrical importance of the Greek-and-Roman here, Moore 1998: 56–8; for the play with dramatic illusion throughout the Menaechmi's prologue, see esp. Sharrock 2009: 41–5. Gratwick 1993 transposes lines 72–6 to just after line 10 because the Prologus' insistence that he must "return" to Epidamnus (49) makes no sense without a previous reference to that city.

enhancing every spectator's sense of the play as a transaction for the benefit of the audience itself (cf. 3, *apporto vobis Plautum* ["I bring you Plautus"]).

In addition, Menaechmus, a resident of Roman Sicily, has been stolen from Tarentum by a merchant from Epidamnus, an outpost at the fringes of Roman power and trading interests on the Adriatic. His abduction suggests the fluidity of and, quite explicitly, the dangers posed by the circumstances of exchange even within an area of actual Roman dominion, and points to interactions of a kind (trade, theft) that would in reality have gone hand in hand with the expansion of Roman power. Yet the setting for Menaechmus' disappearance, a thronged dramatic festival in Tarentum, also confronts the audience with the connection between such risky exchange and the pleasure that the audience takes in the drama. Menaechmus' story is potentially more gripping for the whole Roman audience because of his association with the real, unpredictable circumstances of trade, the real fate of cargo, inanimate and animate, and the real familiarity with drama intrinsic to the Roman experience of empire. It is perhaps not irrelevant in this connection to recall that Latin versions of Greek drama itself were thought to have been introduced first at Rome by a Tarentine half-Greek, Livius Andronicus, supposedly brought to Rome enslaved after Tarentum's earlier defeat in 272 BCE.[17] And if the actors playing the parts of Menaechmus and Plautus' other characters were, as is very possible, Greek slaves themselves, this would only make the audience's profit from – and dependency on – the human cargo of the slave trade all the more obvious.[18]

Now let us turn back to Menaechmus' ecphrasis to see how its playful reference to paintings echoes, concentrates, and develops the themes of the prologue. The passage, as noted, recalls artworks taken from the Greek world and displayed by elites in processions as well as in religious and

[17] The long-lived Livius was apparently still active in 207 BCE, when we hear of his composition of an intercessory hymn to Juno, and so could even have been among the audience members at the *Menaechmi*'s first performance. For Livius' role in the Roman "translation project," see now the major discussion in Feeney 2016 (with 65–6 on the question of his free or slave status and 225–32 specifically on the hymn of 207 BCE).

[18] For slave actors see Amy Richlin's contribution to the present volume; play-texts themselves could also be thought of as cargo, as illustrated by the stories about Terence that she cites. For more on slave actors, cf. Christenson 2000: 141; Brown 2002: 235 on Pl. *As.* 2–3. As Richlin's chapter attests, the significance of Plautine drama's representation of slaves, who were members of the audience as well as actors, is currently a topic of considerable interest and debate. My argument engages with this question only to the extent that the idea of captive slave actors bears affinities to the notion of Menaechmus as a captive. I am additionally grateful to Amy Richlin for showing me her discussion of this aspect of the *Menaechmi* in her book manuscript on Plautus (Richlin forthcoming b). Cf. McCarthy 2000; Stewart 2012; Richlin 2014.

domestic settings. From a Roman perspective, Menaechmus' familiarity
with such images makes sense because, as the Prologus has pointed out, he
has become rich – a member of an elite, though himself the son of a
merchant – through his wife's dowry and his own inheritance. In fact,
when Messenio announces the auction of Menaechmus' belongings at the
end of the play, the list of his possessions suggests those of a well-to-do
Roman: "slaves, furniture, country estates, houses, everything" (1158, *servi,*
supellex, fundi, aedes, omnia). Within the drama's Greek-and-Roman fan-
tasy world, in other words, the first Menaechmus stands in for a Roman
elite in this ambiguous fashion. Peniculus, as a parasite seeking to attach
himself to wealthy members of society, could likewise be assumed to be
familiar with the type of art on display in opulent Roman houses.[19] Indeed,
part of the edgy humor of the scene possibly resides in an audience's
recognition of a Roman elite painting-owner in the libidinous, cross-
dressed Menaechmus. The fact that at least some portion of Menaechmus'
wealth is the result of overseas trade could have lent an added comical
resonance to his familiarity with such artworks, in light of biases reflected
in the *lex Claudia*. Menaechmus, the son of a merchant (or his adoptive
father, also a merchant), seems to have purchased the art that some Roman
elites would have considered it a point of pride to have acquired as spoils.[20]
In this connection, furthermore, the irony of a Syracusan Greek making
fun of the conventions of Roman triumphal processions (like the one in
which the art treasures of Syracuse had been displayed) would surely not
have been lost on at least some members of Plautus' audience.

Menaechmus' ecphrasis, however, not only plays to (and with) elite
interests in Greek painting, but also offers the whole Roman public the
pleasure of laughing at a comical Sicilian Greek identifying with these
fascinating artworks. Insofar as such paintings symbolize Rome's imperial
interests, another humorous aspect of Menaechmus' performance emerges
from its refusal to take entirely seriously objects that were nevertheless
recognized as significant Roman acquisitions, and from its transgressive
style of identification with these paintings. The very subject matter of the
artworks, furthermore, links them to essential elements of Rome's myths

---

[19] On the Roman associations of the parasite, a character with a rich Greek comedic background, see
Damon 1997; Tylawsky 2002. On the significance of Peniculus' Latin name, see Fontaine 2010:
102–10.

[20] The point is underscored for us by Julius Caesar's purchase, for the huge sum of eighty talents, of
paintings by the Greek artist Timomachus a century and a half later, a gesture whose significance lay
in part in its contrast with the conventional methods of obtaining such objects through spoliation.
Cf. Miles 2008: 236–7.

of origin, stories also borrowed from the Greek: Venus and the Trojan prince Ganymede. (As the Aeneas tale embedded in Naevius' roughly contemporary *Bellum Punicum* attests [frr. 4–23 Strzelecki], the Trojan legend had by this time become a feature of Roman self-mythologizing.) The fact, furthermore, that we are dealing with religious images perhaps also calls attention to the religious context of Roman drama, another important aspect of its status as both a possession and expression of Rome's entire citizenry. The pleasure that Menaechmus, a Greek resident of Roman Syracuse, takes in such stories therefore comically affirms their importance as narratives adapted to create a link between Greek and Roman culture, not only for the purposes of the elite, but also as a way of establishing the broader basis of Roman identity within the traditions of the Mediterranean. Menaechmus, an inhabitant at various times of two different cities seized by Rome, imagines himself as the prey of Venus, ancestress of the Roman line, and as the Trojan favorite of the supreme Olympian deity, whom Plautus' audience would regard as the Roman high god Jupiter (rather than the Greek Zeus).

Menaechmus' status as plunder himself – in a sense, cargo like the paintings with which he identifies – only strengthens his connection to the two mythical boys, both victims of divine plundering. It thereby adds to the potentially broad appeal of his ecphrasis, again in spite of its basis in images that served as markers of prestige for elites, as well as to the passage's resonance at both a material and a cultural level. Menaechmus has been snatched away by the merchant and brought to the "loss"-ridden city of Epidamnus, but through the image he ludicrously fantasizes himself transported to a better world, one in which he might enjoy the erotic attentions of Jupiter or Venus. Of course, he actually hopes to enjoy the attentions of a much less-exalted figure, Erotium. No doubt this, too, would have been part of the scene's comic potential: to see the conventions of prized Greek-style painting, the epitome of high cultural aspirations, reappropriated and brought low in this fashion.

As I have discussed more fully elsewhere, the way in which Menaechmus responds to the imagined art and the fluidity of identity embodied by these images in particular functions as a model for the audience's ideal response to the drama.[21] Menaechmus' wearing of the *palla*, his material embrace of stories from Greek myth, calls attention to both the pleasure and the risk in the audience's "trying on" of the Greek-and-Roman culture embodied by the play. The mock-heroic connotations of his name in Greek (literally,

---

[21] With the following paragraph, cf. Dufallo 2013: 26–8.

"Breakspear" or "Dauntless"[22]) point to his status as the play's hero, and so a figure worthy of the audience's identification in spite of his otherness. Ganymede and Adonis, however, are hardly obvious models for traditional Roman masculinity, since Ganymede is the love-object (*eromenos*) of Zeus, and Adonis is a young man loved by a more mature goddess.[23] The two boys, furthermore, are originally exotic foreigners even within the Greek tradition (being Phrygian and Near Eastern, respectively), and their liminality and effeminate sexiness are part of their allure.[24] Represented here, then, are Roman appropriations of Greek paintings depicting the erotic capture of unsettlingly non-Greek boys, a capture that is itself described in the language of Roman plunder (cf. *raperet*, 144).[25] This creates a kind of representational circularity in which a stable sense of ethnic or gender identity remains elusive, due specifically to the fact of appropriation within/as culture. And whereas the sympathetic audience member perhaps performs internally a transgressive identification with these ambiguously Hellenic others, Menaechmus performs this onstage, thus concentrating anxiety about such transgression in his own comical person. Plautus himself, finally, is not unlike Menaechmus in using aspects of Greek culture for his own purposes: in his case, the staging of a Roman play based on a Greek original (now unfortunately lost). From plunder to merchandise to cultural model – such is the varying fate of cargo.

Moving beyond the ecphrasis of the *Menaechmi* to the rest of the play, we see how the *palla*'s varying fate as an object of exchange underscores the comical elision of different modes of appropriation as markers of class and identity. Specifically, the treatment of the *palla* amplifies the play's simultaneous glorification and ridicule of plundered aesthetic objects as elite possessions while buying into elite suspicion of mercantile trade. Yet it also appeals to the broader audience's implication in such trade, imagines a prostitute as a possible beneficiary, and even points to embroidered goods as a sign of the foreign element within Romanness.

When Menaechmus first refers to the *palla* after exiting his house, he calls it *praeda* (134, "booty"). This makes him like a plundering Roman

---

[22] See Gratwick 1993: 138. I differ from his view of the name as "gratuitously" heroical, though I agree with him that the name could (simultaneously) have recalled that of the Syracusan mathematician Menaechmus (*fl. c.* 350 BCE) and his solution to the problem of the duplication of the cube, and so referred comically to the "twinning" of the play's protagonists.

[23] McCarthy 2000: 45–6.

[24] For confirmation of this aspect of Ganymede and Adonis in the Greco-Roman sculptural tradition, see Bartman 2002.

[25] My thanks to Matthew Loar for pointing this out to me.

general while anticipating the *palla*'s role in fashioning him, an object of theft, as similar to a plundered painting and to painted images of abducted boys. Similarly, when he first shows the *palla* to Erotium, he calls it *exuvias* (196, "spoils") and again situates it in within a mythological context by comparing it absurdly to the girdle of Hippolyta (200–1). By contrast, when the second Menaechmus, after arriving in Epidamnus in search of his brother, is seeking the favors of Erotium, who has mistaken him for his twin, she first makes him promise to take the *palla* "to an embroiderer" (426, *ad phrygionem*) to be spruced up. The word *phrygio*, repeated four times in the remainder of the play (469, 563, 617, 681) deserves special comment, since a remark by the Elder Pliny suggests that it refers to embroidery as a Phrygian invention (Plin. *Nat.* 8.196), and Plautus himself elsewhere associates Phrygia with Troy (*Bacch.* 953, a reference to the Phrygian Gate). Phrygian customs in Plautus' imagined Epidamnus thus continue to link the *palla* with Rome's Trojan origins as both a point of contact with the Greek mythical tradition and a locus of effeminate otherness.

Erotium's request returns the *palla* both to the status of merchandise and to that of an aesthetic object, however base the motives that appreciation of its physical appearance will serve. But when the second Menaechmus, about to enter Erotium's house, boasts to Messenio about soon gaining possession of the *palla*, he again refers to it as *praeda* (435, 441) in a comic echo of his brother's earlier description. After being confronted by Peniculus, however, with the charge of having worn the mantle earlier in the day, he rejects this as something a *cinaedus* (a Greek term for the passive partner in same-sex male intercourse) would do, transferring the mantle once again to an aesthetic realm of transgressive Greek self-adornment (511–5).

The possession of the *palla* by the second rather than the first Menaechmus leads to further associative overlap and confusion as the play continues.[26] After Peniculus lets it slip to Menaechmus' wife that her husband stole the *palla* from her and now (so he thinks) has taken it to the embroiderer, she demands it back from Menaechmus; when he denies having it, she bars him from their house until it is returned (559–664). When he subsequently tries to get it back from Erotium, who has given it unawares to his brother, she accuses him of theft (686) and bars him from her house, too (692–95). Then, in the following scene, when

---

[26] However much the *palla* as a stage property might have helped the audience distinguish between the twins. See Marshall 2006: 105.

Menaechmus' wife spots the second Menaechmus returning with the *palla*, his ignorance of what has just transpired between her and his brother prompts the accusations of insanity that lead, in turn, to the hilarious spectacle of his feigned madness (701–875). The first Menaechmus is still pondering the fate of the *palla* (907–8) when he is confronted by his wife's father and the doctor whom the latter has enlisted to examine his son-in-law. After escaping, with Messenio's help, from their clutches, he again tries unsuccessfully to recover the *palla* from Erotium (1049–50, 1060–1). Finally, in the play's last scene, the twins' recognition of each other clears up the matter of the *palla*, of which the second Menaechmus is still in possession (1137–45). Upon their decision to return home to Syracuse, the first Menaechmus decides to auction all of his belongings (1151–3), presumably with the *palla* among them.[27] Messenio invites the whole audience to be present at the auction, then requests its applause (1157–62).

The garment that began as a stolen, transgressive costume assimilating Menaechmus to plundered paintings of characters from myth ends up as material profit, perhaps to be sold to the audience in the near future. Its trajectory thus comically suggests the way in which the play functions as an object of exchange between the actors and the audience, a metaphor set in motion already in the prologue, as we have seen.[28] The *palla* helps frame the play's ecphrasis as a self-conscious staging of the links between different forms of appropriation, both cultural and material. Plautus thereby confronts his audience with both the richness and the disorder of a culture of cargo: not only the advantages it brings, but also the anxiety and vulnerability to which all such commerce is subject, and to which it opens its participants. Material exchange – cargo passing back and forth on ships along the often treacherous trade routes of the Mediterranean (cf. Carrie Fulton's chapter in this volume) – is woven into the very fabric of the *Menaechmi*, which, like Plautine drama in general, represents itself as a cultural import.

In calling attention, moreover, to the class implications of Roman cargo and the practices surrounding it, the *Menaechmi* reminds us of the difficulty of attributing any feature of Plautus' plays to a single class's interests. For all that Menaechmus' ecphrasis cleverly ridicules paintings as plunder, it nevertheless celebrates the military victories that have brought them to

---

[27] Cf. Ketterer 1986: 61. Alternatively, the first Menaechmus' pleasure in the fact that his brother has profited from getting the *palla* from Erotium (144–5) perhaps suggests that the second Menaechmus keeps it.

[28] For the *palla* as "possibly programmatic," see Sharrock 2009: 178 n. 40. Cf. Leach 1969: 42–3.

Rome, and thus points to the achievements of Rome's multi-class armies. Read with the play's prologue, it signals the role of resident Greeks – some of them slaves – in producing theatrical pleasure, even as it plays to the biases of the senatorial class who organized the Roman *ludi*. But such a broad appeal makes sense in historical terms. In the period of Plautus' career, when plundering by victorious Roman generals and their armies had begun to bring unprecedented riches and art treasures to Rome from the Greek world, Roman supremacy in the Mediterranean was nonetheless still far from a foregone conclusion, and civic cohesion was greatly to be desired. The Hannibalic War either coincides with or slightly predates the most likely date for the *Menaechmi*'s first production, and Macedon, under Philip V and then his son, Perseus, remained troublesome until after Plautus' death. To attend the *fabula palliata* ("comedy in Greek dress"), to identify with its characters, and to enjoy oneself fully in the way Plautus must have hoped that his audience would, was to be reminded of both security and risk, profit and loss, a sense of self and a dissolution of self, as they emerged from a broad spectrum of Roman interactions with the Greek world.

Laughing through such riskiness, however, may in the end reflect some of the most fundamental aspects of the comic impulse. And this in turn may help explain why a Roman audience might have been willing to stake its sense of itself as Roman – precious cargo indeed – on the success or failure of one ready to do business in Epidamnus.

CHAPTER 2

Citation, Spoliation, and Literary Appropriation in Livy's AUC

Ayelet Haimson Lushkov

That Roman texts often talk about cargo is an unsurprising observation in the context of an empire built on military conquest and trade. Indeed, as Basil Duffalo showed in the preceding chapter, cargo was something of a preoccupation not only for the upper classes, but also for the lower; and no wonder, since though it was the aristocracy that largely benefited, it was the lower classes that fought for the spoils of war, both physical and, as Amy Richlin demonstrates later in this volume, human. Cargo permeated all levels of Roman society, and it was not only there to be laughed at: cargo, especially the spoliated kind, was there to be used, admired, and reused. It was the subject of poems as well as inventory lists, the stuff of pageants as well as lowly transport ships.

My own contribution, however, takes cargo as an organizing metaphor. I argue that the act of reflecting on concepts fundamental to the idea of cargo – origin, transport, destination, plunder, and the market, to name only a few – can also suggest to a writer a closer connection between these processes of empire and his own activity within the literary tradition, as someone who translates or plunders sources, repurposes raw materials, and participates in a marketplace of ideas (though not necessarily a free market). This chapter, then, proceeds from the core idea that speaking about cargo in texts invites the reader to think about text as cargo.[1] More specifically, the chapter is interested in how this bidirectional analogy works to structure the historian Livy's accounts of war spoils in the aftermath of battle, which are often also accounts of Livy's own sources. I argue, therefore, that a parallelism exists in Livy between source text and war-won artifact, both areas fraught with concern over authority, ownership, and the question of how to render one's own something that properly belonged to someone else. Finally, I suggest that this relationship in turn

---

[1] This idea is particularly at home in the self-referential literary environment of Augustan and Imperial Latin literature, and especially with the notion of literary *silvae*, on which see n. 23.

tropes the writing of the *AUC* as an acquisitive procedure, parallel to conquering an empire and appropriating its goods. What Thomas Biggs in the following chapter sees as a process playing out across the whole city, I see as happening within the literary world of Livy's *AUC*, a world that is mimetic of the physical city, even if it is not perfectly congruent with it. Livy's spoils are literary ones, the remains of his predecessors and the information they contain; that he renders them into fragments is likewise a fitting parallel to Rome's imperial conquest. Rome became a museum of pillaged art, Livy of pillaged sources.

Undergirding this interest is the familiar (though hopefully now increasingly out of vogue) image of Livy as a bumbling armchair historian, putting together his vast history from scraps snatched from old scrolls, dutifully copying one source before repeating the same process with another.[2] Although this view is on the whole to be abandoned, the image of the cut-and-paste history nevertheless rewards closer inspection, albeit within a limited scope. For Livy's history relies on a heavy and extensive engagement with its predecessors for its architecture, lessons, and meaning, and especially for the construction of its author's persona and his place in the tradition he inherited. Livy's catalogues of historiographical predecessors are, therefore, in some fundamental ways self-referential, telling us more about Livy and his habits of thought than they do about the sources themselves.

For this reason, I import the architectural idea of *spolia* – originally war plunder removed from the body of a fallen enemy, and later coming to mean reused architectural elements like architraves, capitals, columns, tondos, and the like – as a way of thinking about both the aesthetics and the ideology behind Livy's deployment of his source citations.[3] More precisely, the chapter applies the metaphorical sense of *spolia* as recycled materials to Livy's discussions of war booty and his accompanying discussions of source citations, suggesting in effect that Livy's discussion of spoils encourages us to think of his source citations as *spolia*: literary booty recycled for a new purpose.[4]

---

[2] The practice, broadly speaking, is known as Nissen's Law: Nissen 1863; Pitcher 2009: 72–8. Livy earns his reputation especially well in the fraught episode of the Scipionic Trials (38.50–60), where Livy was thought finally to have washed his hands of Valerius Antias in favor of the more sober Claudius Quadrigarius; Luce 1977: 96–8.

[3] On architectural *spolia*: Krautheimer 1969; Deichmann 1975; Brenk 1987; Kinney 1997 and 2001; Elsner 2000; Hansen 2003; and the essays collected in Brilliant & Kinney 2011. Biggs in this volume explores the intricate dynamics, conducted in poetry as well as in stone, of Augustan "spoliating *spolia* from Republican victory monuments."

[4] The issue is especially well articulated in the early modern reception of the Classics, though it has broader applications, not least because Livy, too, is practicing a model of internal reception. For the

There are various advantages to such a paradigm, where *spolia* stand as a
marker for literary cargo, not least that it reminds us of the antagonism
inherent within a competitive literary tradition. In discussing architectural
spolia, Esch cautions against the over-free use of the comparison between
the use of *spolia* and literary citation, urging us to be "mindful that the use
of *spolia* destroys the old context, while the literary citation leaves the old
text intact."[5] This is certainly true, but it is also the case that new texts
made older texts redundant, so that citation was also a way to assert
authorial control over what remained of the literary past.[6] Conversely, as
Esch points out only a few pages earlier, "new uses preserve."[7] Quotation,
like spoliation, accounts for much of what remains from authors fallen
victim to the vicissitudes of the classical canon. But where the *spolia*
analogy is especially useful is in its evocation of qualities characteristic of
the ancient literary tradition and of the historiographical genre in particular: its monumentality, its mimetic function, the presence of the author
and identity politics more generally, and the overarching issue of morality
and moralizing. Both citation and *spolia*, moreover, deal in an aesthetic of
displacement and appropriation, assume a transportation of meaning and
presence from one place to another, and invite us to ask questions about
how such practices translate or impact our reading or viewing experiences.

The close convergence of English "spoils" and Latin *spolia* should
not efface the categorical difference between the two usages.[8] In this
chapter, I use *spolia* in the architectural sense, and "spoils" (*praeda, exuviae*)
as a catchall umbrella term for Livy's lists of plunder, a broad category of
objects, numbers, and persons, of which proper *spolia*, arms and armor

---

general issues: Swann 2001: esp. 149–93. Pugh 2010 and Chaudhuri 2014 both explore the unique
role of classical intertexts in their early modern contexts.

[5] Esch 2011: 26.

[6] For the ways reception determines how we read partially preserved texts: Hinds 1998: 63–74, with a
more expansive case study on Ennius in Elliot 2014: 75–197, as well as Biggs in this volume. Kinney
2001: 139–40, 147–50 discusses *spolia* in terms of a Bloomian "anxiety of influence" and argues that
some buildings assert a more emphatic ("stronger" in Bloom's terms) engagement with their
"sources."

[7] Esch 2011: 15. The letters of Theodoric attest that the idea was alive already in late antiquity: Brenk
1987: 107–8.

[8] The most famous English usage, "to the victor go the spoils," in fact originates from Sen. William
L. Marcy, in a New York congressional debate in 1832 (*Register of Debates in Congress,* vol. 8, col. 1325.
The actual quote is "They see nothing wrong in the rule, that to the victor belong the spoils of the
enemy"). In that context, the term "spoils" referred to the "spoils system," wherein the victor passed
political favors down to his supporters. Although this is clearly a metaphorical extension of the word's
basic semantic range, it does recall Roman concerns. Cato the Elder, for instance, averred that he
never distributed spoils among his friends (*ORF,* Cato 203), whereas soldiers regularly expected a
share in the profits the general made from the campaign (Gruen 1990: 138–9 shows the practice to
have been so prevalent that it appears even in Roman comedy).

stripped from an enemy body, were merely a subset.[9] Spoils of war had tremendous prominence in Republican culture: paraded in triumphs and displayed in private houses and public *atria*, the spoils of war demonstrated Rome's power and wealth, funded its public buildings, and provided financial incentive and relief to its population.[10] *Spolia* in its technical sense of materials recycled for new monuments, however, is a modern term given to an architectural practice that had its heyday from late antiquity onward, and whose most prominent exemplar is the Arch of Constantine, a monument showcasing a smorgasbord of older ornamentation brought out of storage or taken off older monuments in the service of the new.[11] Nevertheless, the linguistic convergence is telling: in both ancient origin and modern derivation, spoliation connotes a complex movement of physical cargo, flowing from one point of wealth and power to another, often as the result of war and always leaving behind some physical lacunae, if not outright destruction.

As a term of art, though not as a practice, the word *spolia* dates back to the sixteenth century, and to the antiquarian passions of Raphael and his circle and of Pope Julius II. The practice itself dates back securely to the age of Constantine, and indeed it was through observation of the monuments of that age, especially the Arch of Constantine in the Roman forum, that *spolia* obtained a technical descriptor.[12] The question remains, however, of their Augustan relevance: would Livy and his coterie have understood *spolia* to indicate ostentatious reuse, or would the term have remained for them strictly applicable to the arms taken off a fallen enemy? An exact answer is difficult to achieve, but it is nevertheless possible to see an Augustan interest in the modern, architectural sense of *spolia*, as well as in its relationship to physical spoils.[13]

A particularly good example of this comes from Vergil's *Aeneid*, an epic where spoliated arms play a crucial role both in the identity politics and the

---

[9] For what constituted spoils, at least from a triumphal point of view, see the catalogue in Östenberg 2009: 19–127.

[10] Spoils on public parade and private display: McDonnell 2006; Welch 2006; Östenberg 2009; Rutledge 2012: 117–38. As manubial construction: Orlin 2002: 117–38. As financial relief and incentive: Harris 1979: 54–104. Cf. the related question of the general's control over spoils and booty: Shatzman 1972 and *contra* Churchill 1999.

[11] The bibliography on the Arch is considerable. On the *spolia* and their interpretation, I have benefited especially from Kinney 1997 and Elsner 2000, both with extensive further references.

[12] Kinney 2001: 107–8. For the earlier ideology of spoliation: Brenk 1987.

[13] Cf. Marden Fitzpatrick Nichols's chapter in this volume on the Augustan author and architect Vitruvius. On the Augustan culture of display, see e.g., Hölscher 2006; Kellum 1990; Severy-Hoven 2007. For ancient idea of plunder and collecting: Miles 2008; Rutledge 2012. For the modern ideas: Rhodes 2007.

power plays that drive the plot. In 1982, Vincent Cleary surveyed the use of
spolia in the *Aeneid* and argued that the question of reuse is paramount in
the epic: wearing the armor of an opponent spells doom and destruction,
as Turnus learns at the close of the poem.[14] Indeed, most of the instances
of *spolia* in the *Aeneid* concern such exchanges, with arms worn in turn by
various heroes, used ritually or in display, or made into *tropaea*.[15] These
cases already show some sensitivity to the idea of scrambled reuse, not least
in the insistence that some of the essence of the rightful owner (or original
monument) inheres even as ownership of it changes.[16] One early instance
of *spolia*, however, stands out, precisely because here the *spolia* derive from
a world outside the scope of the *Aeneid*: the ecphrasis of the Temple of
Juno in Book 1, from which Cleary extracts the following passage:[17]

> ter circum Iliacos raptaverat Hectora muros
> exanimumque auro corpus vendebat Achilles.
> tum vero ingentem gemitum dat pectore ab imo,
> ut spolia, ut currus, utque ipsum corpus amici
> tendentemque manus Priamum conspexit inermis. (Verg. *Aen.* 1. 483–7)

> Achilles had dragged Hector three times around the walls of Troy, and was
> selling the dead body for gold. Then truly he [Aeneas] heaved a great sigh
> from the bottom of his heart, as he saw the spoils, the chariot, the very body
> of his friend, and Priam stretching out his unarmed hands.

Cleary is right that the precise meaning of *spolia* in the passage is not
entirely clear, and that it likely refers to Hector's armor, itself the spoils of
Patroclus, for whose death Achilles is here finally revenged.[18] This armorial
genealogy, however, alludes more broadly also to the literary filiation of the
Aeneid itself, since what Aeneas is seeing on the frieze of Juno's temple is
the cyclical epics narrating the fall of Troy, with the quoted passage in

---

[14] *Aen.* 12.941–4: *infelix umero cum apparuit alto | balteus et notis fulserunt cingula bullis | Pallantis
    pueri, victum quem vulnere Turnus | straverat atque umeris inimicum insigne gerebat* ("... when the
    unlucky belt appeared on his tall shoulder, and the girdles shone with the familiar studs of young
    Pallas, whom, defeated and wounded, Turnus slew, and now bore the hateful badge on his
    shoulders.") Cf. Cleary 1982: 24: "The second, and more important point, is that under no
    circumstances are these weapons, *spolia*, to be worn or used again by other than their original
    owner. Warriors who do wear or use again in battle the *spolia* of another inevitably meet death as a
    result of these actions."

[15] Cleary 1982: 24–5.

[16] Brilliant 2011: 169: "spoliation involves shifting 'presence' forward and is most effective when
    memory traces can be perceived or, at least, some awareness of the transgressive act of
    appropriation can be appreciated."

[17] On the scene and its ecphrastic context see further: Williams 1960; Thomas 1983; Clay 1988; Fowler 1991:
    32; Lowenstam 1993; Boyd 1995; Putnam 1998: 32–5; Beck 2007; and Duffalo 2013: 139, 142–7.

[18] Cleary 1982: 16.

particular capturing Books 22 and 24 of the *Iliad* (prepared for, perhaps, by *Iliades ... Iliacos* in 1.480 and 483).[19] The frieze as a whole is interested in weapons, chariots, and horses – epic equivalents to Livy's historical details – but it is the sight of Hector in particular, and indeed of the end of the *Iliad*, that moves Aeneas to sigh. This combination is a potent one for Vergil and for the *Aeneid*; it is the vision of Hector in *Aen.* 2.274–97 that galvanizes Aeneas to action. In taking up the charge, Aeneas is driven also into the plot of the *Aeneid*, an epic deliberately conceived as a continuation of, and literary inheritor to, the *Iliad* and *Odyssey*, as well as a textual vehicle for the transmission of actual Trojan remnants to Rome.[20] The act of seeing the *spolia*, ecphrastically embedded in a monument, thus mimics not only the reading of epic; it alludes also to its referential qualities: one epic becomes a monument contained within another epic, moving from oral performance to physical monument to narrative text. The scene on the frieze is a Homeric *spolium,* used by Vergil as fodder and inspiration, just as the *spolia* themselves become fodder for the epic plot.

Turning back to the *AUC*, we may note that the parallelism of citation and spoliation is not one that Livy makes explicit; this is hardly surprising in a historian who talks very little about his methods of discriminating between sources, or about how he conducted and wrote up his research. Nevertheless, it is clear that Livy's concept of his own work is bound up both in monumentality and in the building blocks from which the literary monument is comprised. The *AUC* opens, twice, with an explicit reference to other authors: once, at the beginning of the *Preface*, fretting over artistic competition (*Praef.* 1.1–3, with special reference to 1.3: *tanta scriptorum turba*), and again, at the beginning of the narrative proper, to establish a near consensus of the sources (1.1.1, *iam primum omnium satis constat*).[21] But the *AUC* is, above all things, a *monumentum* (*Praef.* 1.9, *omnis te exempli documenta in inlustri posita monumento intueri*), and one that grows along with the city whose historical progress it charts.[22]

---

[19] Barchiesi 1999: 334 observes that *orbem* (1.457) already puns on "cyclic" epic.

[20] Cf. *Aen.* 1.6 *inferretque deos Latio.* The Penates are themselves also a hyper-pious complement to the Palladium, and both are markers of Troy that are preserved and yet at the same time transformed through their association with the new nation of Rome. Note too that in other accounts (e.g., Varro *ap.* Serv. *ad Aen.* 2.166, Sil. *Pun.* 13.30–81) Diomedes gives the Palladium to Aeneas in Italy, thus almost un-spoiling (having already de-spoiled) Troy.

[21] Marincola 1997: 140–1 suggests that Livy's diffident pose is aimed to deflect attention from the issue of his qualifications as a historian. On *satis constat*: Miles 1995: 24–5.

[22] Kraus 1994: 270. On Livy's historical outlook and the gallery of *summi viri* in the Augustan forum: Luce 1990; on Livy and the dynamics of monumentality and destruction: Roller 2010.

Within this monument we find *exempla*, which Livy explicitly describes
as set within (*insita*) the textual monument, as well as a number of recycled
formal elements – *topoi*, annalistic notations, intra-texts, and the explicit
citation of sources, all of which expose, artfully and deliberately, the
procedures that give formal shape to the work. How much this is part of
a broader Augustan literary and visual culture is a topic for a separate
chapter, but I would like to suggest here that spoliation offers a useful
heuristic for thinking about a text that is overtly interested in the tension
between the new and the old, indeed in the ways in which the old might be
appropriated and made relevant to the here and now. Spoliated materials
or weaponry become both the subject of the text that reports their capture
as well as the materials with which the Romans will make war in Spain, for
example. They are, therefore, on some level a form of textual *silvae*, rough
timber from which the historian can craft his work, even as the spoliated
artifacts themselves find a new life somewhere in the Roman war
machine.[23] Citation, with its clear reference to another text, thus makes
for a rich parallel for both types of *spolia*. Having been transposed, they
create a chronologically dense moment in which one artifact produces
meaning by being visibly a foreign element in its immediate context.

Aesthetics and Appropriation

Source citations are ubiquitous in the *AUC* and engage with *spolia* and
spoliation in a variety of quite direct ways. One such way is mimicry,
which is important if only to establish from the outset that citation and
spolia are, or can often be, parallel constructions. Thus, Livy tells us about
the dedication of a shield allegedly belonging to the Carthaginian leader
Hasdrubal in the Capitol by one Lucius Marcius. The passage is a classic
instance of what I have elsewhere termed "variant citation," a citation type
wherein Livy lists a number of contrasting sources, often setting them
against some kind of common consensus.[24]

> ad triginta septem milia hostium caesa auctor est *Claudius, qui annales
> Acilianos ex Graeco in Latinum sermonem vertit*; captos ad mille octingentos
> triginta, praedam ingentem partam; in ea fuisse clipeum argenteum pondo
> centum triginta septem cum imagine Barcini Hasdrubalis. *Valerius Antias*

---

[23] Quint. *Inst. Orat.* 10.3.17 explains that *silva* is an unpolished literary text. The idea finds especial
vogue in Flavian Rome, where it features most prominently as the title of Statius' collection of
occasional poetry: Bright 1980: 20–42; Wray 2007. For earlier manifestations of the same idea, see
Kraus 2005 and Newlands 2011: 6–7.
[24] Haimson Lushkov 2013: 34–8, with further references.

una castra Magonis capta *tradit*, septem milia caesa hostium; altero proelio
eruptione pugnatum cum Hasdrubale, decem milia occisa, quattuor milia
trecenta triginta captos. *Piso* quinque milia hominum, cum Mago cedentes
nostros effuse sequeretur, caesa ex insidiis *scribit*. apud omnes magnum
nomen Marcii ducis est ... monumentumque victoriae eius de Poenis
usque ad incensum Capitolium fuisse in templo clipeum, Marcium appel-
latum, cum imagine Hasdrubalis. (Livy 25.39.12–17)

Claudius, who translated the annals of Acilius into Latin from the Greek,
puts the number of enemy dead at about 37,000, with some 1,830 taken
prisoner and massive amounts of plunder also won. The plunder, Claudius
claims, included a 137-pound silver shield bearing a portrait of Hasdrubal
Barca. In Valerius Antias' account, only one camp was taken, that of Mago,
and 7,000 of the enemy were killed; but there was, he says, a second
engagement, with Hasdrubal, who counterattacked from his own camp,
in which 10,000 were killed and 4,330 taken prisoner. Piso records that
5,000 were killed in an ambush, when Mago was in a disordered pursuit of
our retreating soldiers. In all the accounts Marcius, the commander, is well
celebrated. ... They also say that, to commemorate his victory over the
Carthaginians, a shield bearing the portrait of Hasdrubal and called "the
shield of Marcius" hung in the Capitol right down to the time when the
temple burned down.[25]

The topic at hand here is the number of camps taken, enemy soldiers
killed, and booty captured, of which Hasdrubal's shield is certainly the
pièce de résistance. The list is clearly arranged for rhetorical effect. The
names of the authors form a *tricolon diminuens*, from the elaborate
Claudius, qui annales Acilianos ex Graeco in Latinum sermonem vertit,
down through the unvarnished *Valerius Antias* to the almost austere
Piso, here referred to by cognomen only. The verbs assigned to each of
them meanwhile move from less to more assertive acts of composition:
thus we have *vertit* ("translated"), *tradit* ("reports"), *scribit* ("wrote").
More importantly, however, the sequence mimics, indeed spells out, a
progression from Greek to Latin that parallels the progression of the
spoils from the ends of empire to Rome, thus offering a textual version
of spoliation. This image is effectively capped by Livy's report of the
dedication of the shield, on which there is general agreement (*apud
omnes*), but whose capture is reported, at least according to Livy's
inventory, only by Claudius. This too, mimics spoliative procedure:
an individual's loot transformed into public property through the
parade and public display of those same objects. Complicating matters,

---

[25] Trans. adapted from Yardley, unless otherwise noted.

however, is the fact that the shield itself does not survive long enough
even for Livy to see it, since it was destroyed in the Capitoline fire of 81
BCE.[26] What remains, therefore, is only Livy's authority, relying necessarily on the sources. The passage, then, engages with multiple procedures and questions, chiefly the parallelism of citation and spoils, and the
broader question of authorial presence and credibility. Underlying all
this, however, is an alchemical process of transmutation, as physical
bodies – the shield, the camps, the combatants – become their own
textual representation.

As a showcase piece preserved for public display, the shield of Hasdrubal
represents a small but significant subgroup of *spolia*.[27] The majority of war
spoils, however, are more humble and functional, and include a varied
group of items, objects, and persons. Nonetheless, Livy's reports of these
other spoils resemble in form and structure the shield passage and its
variant sources.[28] Indeed, the very next Roman victory, the conquest of
New Carthage in Spain under the auspices of the young Scipio Africanus,
produced considerable spoils and extensive accompanying reports. The
victory itself was an important one, both for flagging Roman fortunes and
for Scipio, who was making his debut on the international scene; Livy
accordingly gives it pride of place at the end of Book 26, and dwells at
length on what the city yielded:

> captus et apparatus ingens belli; catapultae maximae formae centum viginti,
> minores ducentae octoginta una; ballistae maiores viginti tres, minores
> quinquaginta duae; scorpionum maiorum minorumque et armorum telor-
> umque ingens numerus; signa militaria septuaginta quattuor. et auri argenti
> relata ad imperatorem magna vis: paterae aureae fuerunt ducentae septua-
> ginta sex, librales ferme omnes pondo; argenti infecti signatique decem et
> octo milia et trecenta pondo, vasorum argenteorum magnus numerus;
> haec omnia C. Flaminio quaestori appensa adnumerataque sunt; tritici
> quadringenta milia modium, hordei ducenta septuaginta. naves onerariae
> sexaginta tres in portu expugnatae captaeque, quaedam cum suis oneribus,
> frumento, armis, aere praeterea ferroque et linteis et sparto et navali alia
> materia ad classem aedificandam, ut minimum omnium inter tantas opes
> belli captas Carthago ipsa fuerit. (Livy 26.47.5–10)

---

[26] Jaeger 1997: 126 argues that this effect is intended to juxtapose "vanished monuments" with the text
of the *AUC* itself.

[27] The shield is juxtaposed in the text with the more substantial spoils brought by Marcellus from
Syracuse, to which I will return later (Jaeger 1997: 124–31), and likewise intended for public display.
We might therefore read the eastward movement traced out by the citations as culminating with the
Syracusan spoils, as the two sets of spoils, one moving east and one west, converge in Rome.

[28] For humans as cargo, see the chapter by Amy Richlin in this volume.

The quantity of military equipment taken was enormous. There were 120 catapults of the largest dimensions, and 281 smaller ones; 23 large-scale and 52 smaller-scale ballistas; a huge number of the larger and smaller scorpions, and of weapons and projectiles; and 74 military standards. Large amounts of silver and gold were brought to the commander. There were 276 golden dishes, nearly all of them a pound in weight; there were 18,300 pounds of silver in bullion and coin, and a large number of silver vessels. All this was weighed and counted, and then put in the charge of the quaestor, Gaius Flaminius. There were 400,000 measures of wheat and 270,000 of barley. Sixty-three transport vessels were overpowered and captured in the harbor, some with their cargoes of grain and weapons, as well as bronze and iron, sail-linen, rope, and other materials for equipping a fleet. The upshot was that amidst all these riches taken as the spoils of war New Carthage represented the least significant prize of all.

Beyond establishing a Roman foothold in Carthaginian territory – a harbinger of greater things to come – the victory was so important because New Carthage held within its walls a veritable treasure trove: the better part of the Carthaginian war chest, their heavy artillery, and much of their political capital as well, in the form of a large group of Spanish hostages held against the good behavior and continued cooperation of their respective tribes. Indeed, Livy inventories the spoils with great care and greater detail. New Carthage thus yielded 74 military standards, 120 large catapults and 281 smaller ones, 63 transport vessels, 270,000 measures of barley, and exactly 276 golden dishes, to pick only a few of the eye-catching items from Livy's more considerable list.[29]

Despite this marvelous precision, however, the accounting does not quite add up. When it comes to the hostages, Livy reports, the sources can find no consensus. Indeed, he has found records of both 300 – an appealingly round and heroic number – and, on the other hand, the fabulously specific 3,742.[30] This first crack having appeared, others swiftly follow: there is no agreement, it turns out, on how many Carthaginian soldiers were captured, on who the generals were (surprisingly, on both Roman and Carthaginian sides, though Scipio, at least, is comfortingly above dispute), on how many ships or scorpions were taken, and finally, how much gold and silver was apprehended. The list of *spolia* unravels within one chapter of its report into fragmentary *aporia*.

[29] By comparison, Polybius (10.16.1–17.16) focuses more on the procedure of division and the probity of the Romans in not embezzling any of it, rather than on listing any particular items. It is worth noting, however, that Polybius acknowledges that the wealth of New Carthage, described in broad generalities in 8.1–5, was one of the main reasons for Scipio's desire to undertake the attack.

[30] On "typical numbers," especially in multiples of three: Fehling 1989: 221–2; Rubincam 2003.

tum obsides civitatium Hispaniae vocari iussit; quorum quantus numerus
fuerit piget scribere, quippe ubi *alibi* trecentos ferme, *alibi* tria milia
septingentos viginti quattuor fuisse inveniam. aeque et alia inter auctores
discrepant. praesidium Punicum *alius* decem, *alius* septem, *alius* haud plus
quam duum milium fuisse scribit. capta *alibi* decem milia capitum, *alibi*
supra quinque et viginti invenias. Scorpiones maiores minoresque ad sex-
aginta captos scripserim, si *auctorem Graecum sequar Silenum*; si *Valerium
Antiatem*, maior scorpionum sex milia, minorum tredecim milia; adeo
nullus mentiendi modus est. Ne de ducibus quidem convenit. *plerique*
Laelium praefuisse classi, *sunt qui* M. Iulium Silanum dicant; Arinen
praefuisse Punico praesidio deditumque Romanis *Antias Valerius*, Mago-
nem *alii scriptores tradunt*. non de numero navium captarum, non de
pondere auri atque argenti et redacta pecunia convenit; si aliquis adsentiri
necesse est, media simillima veri sunt. (Livy 26.49.1–6)

Scipio then had the hostages from the Spanish communities summoned to
him. The number of these I am reluctant to put on the record, as I find it
set at about 300 in one source and at 3,742 in another. There is as much
discrepancy between the historians on other items, too. One records that
the Punic garrison was 10,000 strong, another that it was 7,000, and yet
another that it was not more than 2,000. In one source I find the number of
prisoners taken as 10,000, in another more than 25,000. If I follow the
Greek author Silenus, I should put at about 60 the number of larger and
smaller scorpions that were captured; if I follow Valerius Antias, then there
were 6,000 larger scorpions and 13,000 smaller ones – so unbridled are the
fabrications of historians! There is no agreement even about the command-
ers. Most claim that Laelius commanded the fleet, though some say it was
Marcus Junius Silanus. Valerius Antias informs us that it was Arines who
commanded the Punic garrison, and surrendered to the Romans; other
writers say that it was Mago. No agreement is found on the number of ships
captured, and none on the weight of gold and silver taken, or the amount of
money realized from it. If one must agree with some of these sources,
figures halfway between the extremes seem closest to the truth.

As with the Marcius passage, the aesthetics of form and structure help
build the tension between the two lists: if Livy's first list of New Carthaginian spoils derives its punch from the precise enumeration of detail and
the parade of spoils before the reader's eyes, his second replaces the *spolia*
themselves – now proven problematic and suspicious – with the report on
the *spolia*, that is, with Livy's own sources. Where the first list has *variatio*
in the size, kind, and number of items, the second one has its *variatio* in
the names and reports of the various sources, and in fact it tropes the very
idea of *variatio* in demonstrating the great variations that exists in the
sources. But where these two passages are most striking is in how they
marry *spolia* and source citation in the process of constructing and

deconstructing Livy's text. In fact, the two lists exemplify the process of reading history: as we read, and as we move from one list to the other, the physical spoils become textualized spoils, and they are transmuted accordingly from objects to fragments, bits of writing to replace bits of clay and metal.[31]

Of course, the move from physical to textual is a freighted one, and it suggests a correspondingly agonistic relationship between Livy and his source texts. To this we may add also a pronounced tension between text as a commemorative medium and the materiality of physical remains.[32] These issues are programmatic for Livy, and they converge in particular on the mediating presence of the author himself, who, as researcher and writer, is the one to perform the alchemical procedure required to capture the stuff of history.[33] The act of citation conflates these two aspects of the author; it advertises his diligent work, and allows him to nod toward or elaborate on earlier accounts of the same event. With reports of *spolia* and booty, however, the most pressing question is that of reliability or credulity, and here the authorial purpose usually takes on a more agonistic dimension – correcting, improving on, or acceding to another's authority.

Indeed, what is immediately apparent in the move between one list and another is the presence of source citation in the latter, and its absence in the former. The two passages in effect offer two corresponding catalogues, one of the actual spoils, and another of the points of contention and disagreement among sources. Livy refers several times to anonymous sources as well as explicitly naming Silenus and Valerius Antias, all the while conducting an elaborate balancing act (note the repetition of *alibi . . . alibi*), looking at one source and then another in an effort to illustrate the intricacies of the transmission. The effect is immediate; where the first list sounds authoritative and reassuring in its multiplicity of detail, the second bears out the maxim that some things really are too good to be

---

[31] On the movement from text to object, see my discussion on the *Aeneid*, pp. 33–5.

[32] For the relationship among lists, objects, and historiographical narrative, see now Kirk 2014, who sees Herodotus' catalogues of objects as "enumerative display[s] in words"; for the idea of Livy's text as monument parallel to empire: Kraus 1994: 86, and 1998; for the tension between monument and *fabula* and its attendant issues, especially truthfulness and reliability: Miles 1995: 8–74. Brilliant 2011: 176 suggests that "spoliation . . . seems to assert claims for truth in representation, at least in the art of representation itself, alienated from claims of authenticity dependent on concepts of the primacy of an originating source."

[33] Cf. Kraus 2011: 408, "This is a genre that aims . . . not only to rival but to (re)present past experience in language, to create a verbal image of lived events."

true. Importantly, however, the two lists also offer two views of authorship
and authority: Livy's voice is the stronger in the first list, from which he is
entirely absent, simply because there is nothing to disrupt the smooth
listing by the invisible narrator. When Livy's personal voice intrudes into
the second list, his presence increases, while the credibility of the material
diminishes, as it is tied more and more to external authorial voices.

In the *AUC*, and in the annals of scholarly work on it, there is perhaps
no more famous external authority than Augustus himself. The infamous
Cossus digression in Book 4 is therefore perhaps the clearest example of
Livy's staging of his own authority; despite his own research and better
judgment, the historian cedes to the authority of Augustus and includes a
version of events in which Cossus is consul rather than tribune.[34] Here, the
process we saw in the New Carthage example is reversed – the parsing out
of conflicting sources is replaced by the single authority of Cossus, which is
to say, of Augustus:

> sed, ut ego arbitror, vana versare in omnes opiniones licet, cum auctor
> pugnae, recentibus spoliis in sacra sede positis, Iovem prope ipsum, cui vota
> erant, Romulumque intuens, haud spernendos falsi tituli testes, se
> A. Cornelium Cossum consulem scripserit. (Livy 4. 20.11)

> But, to my mind, it is pointless to deal with every opinion, when the author
> of the battle, as he lay down his newly won spoils in their sacred place,
> practically gazing at Jupiter himself, to whom he vowed them, and at
> Romulus – witnesses to a false inscription who cannot be easily dismissed –
> wrote that he was A. Cornelius Cossus, consul.

The overlap between textual and physical evidence is clear here, bol-
stered by the language of testimony and the sacred. While Livy lingers
over the physical aspects of the dedication – the *spolia*, the ritual statues
of the gods – Cossus assumes the attributes not only of the dedicator
but also of the author. He is *auctor pugnae*, a phrase with strong
authorial connotations; his act of dedication, technically epigraphic, is
encapsulated in the verb *scripserit*, a regular verb for marking source
citations.[35] The passage further resembles one of Livy's more standard
instances of variant citations. The initial contrast between *omnes opi-
niones* and *auctor pugnae*, however much Livy attempts to skew it in
favor of Cossus, repeats the standard historiographical procedure of
singling out a variant from a broader consensus.[36] Further, Jupiter

---

[34] On the Cossus digression: Syme 1959; Flower 2000; Sailor 2006.
[35] E.g., Livy 8.19.14, 25.39.15, 34.10.2. For *scribere* in an epigraphic sense: *OLD* s.v. *scribo* 2.
[36] E.g., Livy 32.6.5: *Valerius Antias ... tradit ... Ceteri Graeci Latinique auctores ... tradunt.*

and Romulus share the description *haud spernendos falsi tituli testes* with no less an authority than Polybius himself (Livy 30.45.5–6, *haud spernendus auctor*), likewise an author whose presence, at least before the fourth decade, is external and invisible.[37] Thus, in both form and content, the passage elides citational practice and the dedication of the *spolia*. For all that it carefully distances Livy's authority from the information he is reporting, it nevertheless implicates *spolia* deeply within the *AUC*'s citational dynamics.

Surprisingly, perhaps, Augustus has good company. In Book 45, Livy describes the spoils brought to the treasury after the triumph of Lucius Anicius over the Illyrians in 167 BCE:

> sestertium ducentiens ex ea praeda redactum esse auctor est Antias, praeter aurum argentumque, quod in aerarium sit latum; quod quia unde redigi potuerit non apparebat, auctorem pro re posui. (Livy 45.43.8)

> According to Antias, 20,000,000 sesterces were realized from the booty, beyond the gold and silver that was deposited in the treasury. But since it was not clear from where this sum could be realized, I have put down the source rather than just the information itself.[38]

Valerius Antias was famous for his exaggerated numbers – Livy rolls his eyes at precisely the same thing in the New Carthage passage – and this certainly makes sense of Livy's reluctance to endorse his account.[39] What is of greater interest for present purposes, however, is the phrase *auctorem pro re posui*, in which Livy performs much the same substitution we have already seen: an external authority is allowed to enter the text in order to neutralize a problematic source, allowing Livy to disavow responsibility for an absurd figure or claim. Our visualization of Cossus' corselet or Anicius' spoils is thus displaced and any vividness dulled; we see now the process of research rather than the smooth surface of the finished text. In fact, I would suggest, this too is a variation on the broader theme. The textual account displaces the description of the spoliated object, be it precious metal or aged linen, by adverting clearly and explicitly to Livy's own spoliated source.

---

[37] On the complex relationship of Livy and Polybius, see now Levene 2010: 126–63, and 2011.

[38] Trans. Chaplin.

[39] On Antias' numbers: Laroche 1977. On Livy's negotiation of citations from Antias: Haimson Lushkov 2010: 98–119, with 101–2 on this passage. As a general rule, Livy's references to Antias' numbers divide about evenly between acceptance (signaled by reportage without comment) and outright criticism.

Morality

One of the great spoliative moments in Roman history was surely the arrival in Rome of the spoils of Syracuse after Marcellus' capture of the city:

> dum haec in Hispania geruntur, Marcellus captis Syracusis, cum cetera in Sicilia tanta fide atque integritate *composuisset* ut non modo suam gloriam sed etiam maiestatem populi Romani *augeret*, ornamenta urbis, signa tabulasque quibus abundabant Syracusae, Romam devexit, hostium quidem illa spolia et parta belli iure; ceterum inde primum initium mirandi Graecarum artium opera licentiaeque hinc sacra profanaque omnia volgo spoliandi factum est, quae postremo in Romanos deos, templum id ipsum primum quod a Marcello eximie ornatum est, vertit. (Livy 25.40.2–3)

> Such were the events in Spain. Marcellus, meanwhile, had been so scrupulous and honest in all his dealings in Sicily following the capture of Syracuse, as to increase not only his own reputation but the majesty of the Roman people as well. The artwork of the city, however, the sculptures and paintings with which Syracuse was richly endowed, he shipped off to Rome. True, they were enemy spoils, won under the rules of warfare, but this was what first started the appreciation for Greek works of art, and the license we now see in the widespread looting of all manner of things sacred and profane. This eventually recoiled on the Roman gods, and did so first of all on the very temple that was superbly furnished by Marcellus.

This is clearly a moment of some moral significance, reminiscent of (though not verbally alluding to) Sallust's passage on *fortuna*, and pregnant with foreboding.[40] Indeed, unlike the *spolia* lists we have seen already, there are no "real" numbers of the sort Livy presents for Marcius' victory in Spain, or Scipio's in New Carthage, where the armies and enemy dead are enumerated, and the various authors laid out and discussed. Further, there are no reports about conflicting sources of any kind. In fact, the Syracusan spoils are the culmination of a narrative marked by the absence of source citation, with the result that Marcellus' spoils are never displaced by any

---

[40] Sall. *BC* 10.1: *sed ubi labore atque iustitia res publica crevit, reges magni bello domiti, nationes ferae et populi ingentes vi subacti, Carthago aemula imperi Romani ab stirpe interiit, cuncta maria terraeque patebant, saevire fortuna ac miscere omnia coepit.* ("but when the state has grown large by hard work and good faith, when great kings were vanquished in war, and fierce nations and vast peoples were subjected by force, and when Carthage, the rival to Roman dominion, perished root and stock, and all the seas and lands lay open, then Fortune began to rage and mix everything up.") On the connections between Livy and Sallust, especially in the third decade: Feldherr 2010; on the various points identified by Roman writers as the beginning of moral decline: Lintott 1972.

textual artifact, but rather become absorbed in the Roman cityscape, and, more crucially, in the Roman psyche.[41]

There is nevertheless payment to be exacted, and just as Livy reports that the "love of despoiling" eventually results in the destruction of the temple – ironically and appropriately dedicated to *Virtus et Honos* – in which Marcellus houses his spoils, so too Marcellus himself is the one to suffer the textual indignity of fragmentation. Of all the great Romans in Livy's text, Marcellus is perhaps the spoliator *par excellence*: not only the winner of the *spolia opima*, but also the one to introduce to Rome the love of spoliation characteristic of empire.[42] Indeed, the language used of Marcellus assimilates him to an author figure: he puts in order (*composuisset*) the affairs of Sicily and augments (*augeret*) the glory and majesty of Rome, in which two acts he parallels Livy the historian, if not also foreshadowing Augustus the emperor. Marcellus' death, the last of the great Roman losses before the conclusion of the Second Punic War, is an exemplary case of the vulnerability of the historical narrative to its conflicting sources. The events are clouded by mystery, and Livy declines to confirm anything beyond stating that many versions existed; Coelius alone knew of three, at least one, though not the one he affirms to be true, from an eyewitness.[43] Marcellus the spoliator thus ends up nothing so much as a collection of literary *spolia*, animated and reconstituted by Livy's authorial hand.

In a work conceived as a physical monument, physical artifacts naturally have a heightened potential for significance, and I would like to conclude by revisiting my initial suggestion that spoliation in this text functions as a metaphor for various processes of appropriation and imperialism, both physical and textual. Livy's citations are certainly embedded within a

---

[41] They feature, for instance, when Manlius Torquatus imagines the dead king Hiero coming back to life to see his city's spoils transferred to Rome in 26.32.4. Nevertheless, Livy makes sure (cf. *templum ... vertit*) that the Syracusan spoils are in a state of imminent destruction from the moment they arrive. Jaeger 1997: 124–31 argues that Livy aims to reconstruct verbally monuments that are no longer extant, a procedure similar to what I am proposing for *spolia* and citation here.

[42] On Marcellus' career of plunder: Miles 2008: 61–9.

[43] Livy 27.27.12–4: *multos circa unam rem ambitus fecerim si quae de Marcelli morte variant auctores, omnia exsequi velim. ut omittam alios, Coelius triplicem gestae rei †ordinem edit, unam traditam fama, alteram scriptam in laudatione filii, qui rei gestae interfuerit, tertiam quam ipse pro inquisita ac sibi comperta affert. ceterum ita fama variat ut tamen plerique loci speculandi causa castris egressum, omnes insidiis circumventum tradant.* ("I would be covering the same ground again and again if I were to follow all the variants authors give on the death of Marcellus. I have therefore omitted a few. Coelius gives three accounts of the same event: one is the traditional story; another that was written in the eulogy given by his son, who was a participant in the events; and a third, which he hands down as researched and established by himself. But however much the story varies, still many say he left camp to reconnoiter, and everyone says he was ambushed.")

broader culture of display, as trophies of conquest and as relics of a literary past now subsumed within a newer work, but they also do more specific work in thinking about the location of authority within and outside the text, and the processes of importation that link the *realia* of history with the artifice of the textual construct. The *AUC* is fascinated by the parallelism of form and content, and so it is hardly surprising that the story of Rome's acquisition of an empire and its goods should be paralleled by the story of Livy's mastery of a literary empire, with its own remnants of what came before. This metaphor has some further implications, in line with what I have argued elsewhere concerning Livy's authorial demeanor: it lets us see Livy as himself a spoliator, an aggressive and domineering author, whose mild-mannered coyness hides a genuine desire to encompass everything within the *AUC*, creating a *monumentum* of both history and historiography.[44] If in this he resembles Augustus, that is no bad thing; like the emperor, Livy appropriated Rome's literary past for his own project. His sources, broken down, processed, and newly displayed, were preserved within the new edifice. A good thing, too; new uses preserve.

---

[44] Haimson Lushkov 2010 and 2013. These articles, as well as the present one, are all part of an ongoing project on the dynamics of source citation in the *AUC*. I thank the organizers of the *Cargo Culture* conference for the opportunity to explore another facet of the topic, and the conference attendees for their useful comments; as ever, I am grateful to Pramit Chaudhuri for his comments.

CHAPTER 3

A Second First Punic War
Re-Spoliation of Republican Naval Monuments in the Urban and Poetic Landscapes of Augustan Rome

Thomas Biggs

quantam statuam statuet Populus Romanus
quantam columnam quae res tuas gestas loquatur?[1]

How great a statue will the Roman people set up,
How great a column, to speak of your deeds?

In the telling fragment quoted here, the poet Ennius evokes the connection between words, deeds, and monumental commemoration. The ability of monuments to "speak" the *res gestae* they recollect and the people who performed them points to the semiotic qualities that permeated the Roman built environment – qualities that can be seen in referential or even intertextual terms.[2] What statues and columns signify, however, depends in large part on when and to whom they "speak." Just as texts in reception give rise to numerous readings, the same problems and possibilities are inherent in the consumption of monuments: some crumble; some are reused as *spolia* for new polyphonous structures; and some, when viewed diachronically, take on new meanings, though they have not changed their original form. The latter two processes, centered on both active and passive "misreadings," share significant ground with the practices of literary appropriation.[3] And in an attempt to better understand such cross-media interaction, the present study turns to the naval *spolia* of the First Punic War and their material and literary reuse in Roman culture. By examining the reappropriation of objects that themselves had already been reappropriated (*spolia*), I suggest that we can better understand not only the palimpsestic afterlife of the First Punic War as evoked by spoliate monuments, but also the very semiotic functions that underpin such instances of reappropriating the Republican past. In particular, we will see how

---

[1] Skutsch 1985, *Op. Incert.* iv.   [2] Cf., e.g., Hölscher 2004 and Roller 2013.
[3] See Haimson Lushkov in this volume for *spolia*, spoliation, and the parallel practices of Livy's literary engagement with his historiographical predecessors. Cf. Kinney 2001. "Misreading" as I employ it can be understood as an act of resemanticizing.

memories of the First Punic War and its Carthaginian *spolia* were used and reused by poems and monuments to construct conflicting narratives of victory in Triumviral and Augustan Rome.

Spoliation, of course, is not an act specific to any period of Roman history. Nonetheless, scholars have largely adopted the term to designate the architectural reuse of Roman materials in late antique and medieval structures.[4] In fact, many see architectural spoliation as a process that first takes shape under Constantine.[5] This view of *spolia*, however related, is not what is at stake in the present study. In a Roman context, *spolia* were, at their root, the spoils of war; they were cargo, the booty taken from a defeated foe and put on display for public observation and the production of glory that was at once individual and collective.[6] Romans of later eras even held in their memory a clear view that such monumental reuse dated to the foundations of Rome itself.[7] But the process of reusing *spolia* that had already been on display at Rome for the construction of subsequent Roman monuments has largely been discussed without a critical vocabulary or approach.[8] Modern notions of Roman *spolia* have focused so singularly on art objects (especially those imported from Greece) and on later periods of engagement with a discontinuous "Classical" past that Roman self-spoliation has received little attention as a distinct appropriative act.[9]

With such complexities in full view, locating a fruitful entrée into the topic of re-spoliation seems a daunting task. Yet as Ennius indirectly suggests, zeroing in on particular *statuae* and *columnae* and the memories they communicate may offer a solid foundation. Indeed, within Basil Dufallo's contribution to this volume we have already seen how productive approaching interpretation through a spoliate object can be; as he

---

[4] For a brief history of the term, see esp. Kinney 2006 and 2011; Esch 1969 is still important. Brilliant 2011: 168 discusses *spolia* in terms of appropriation: "*Spolia*, which constitute a subset of the broader category of appropriation, involve the physical incorporation of artworks, or fragments thereof, into new artistic contexts; the term includes, as well, the replications of other originals or reproductive images of them, inserted for their iconographic and visual effect into later or 'foreign' works of art."

[5] Brenk 1987: 103–7; Elsner 2000; Kinney 2006.

[6] Haimson Lushkov in this volume discusses Livy's source citations as *spolia* that serve as literary booty recycled for a new purpose.

[7] For Romulus and the *spolia opima*, see Livy 1.10; cf. Flower 2000.

[8] I refer here to Rome up to the third century CE. The formal process of architectural reuse is sporadically discussed in terms of self-spoliation but not in relation to objects and structures that were already considered *spolia* or spoliate. Cf. Kinney 2006: 234.

[9] In architectural conceptions of *spolia*, the engagement with a Classical world that is clearly severed from the present time is essential. Of course, the notion of a "Classical" past is itself a fluid conception. See esp. the contributions of Citroni, Hölscher, and Elsner in Porter 2006. Kinney 1997 pushes on the standard boundaries of the definition.

demonstrates, Menaechmus' *palla* and the subtextual resonance of Rome's plundering of Syracuse and Tarentum activate issues like aesthetic and commercial value, and class and identity at Rome. Accordingly, the core of this chapter is made up of a series of engagements with the memory of the First Punic War as evoked by *spolia*: in this case, the rams of warships – *rostra* – and their display on *columnae* and *templa*.

I begin with the monuments of C. Duilius (cos. 260 BCE), especially his rostral column and Temple of Janus in the Forum Holitorium.[10] The next section expands the scope to provide a brief snapshot of the wide array of naval commemorations in Triumviral and Augustan Rome.[11] The third section turns to recent archaeological discoveries to further develop our image of the rostral *spolia* that would have adorned Duilius' column and, through comparison, Octavian's later column for the Battle of Naulochus. The act of "conceptual" spoliation at stake in this section is akin to Richard Brilliant's *spolia in re* (virtual spoliation) as opposed to *spolia in se* (physical spoliation), a distinction that will resurface throughout the present study.[12] In conclusion, the final section intensifies the focus on text and connects the various arguments of this chapter. An interpretation of the opening of Vergil's third *Georgic* shows how a history of "misreading" arose from the poetic blurring of time and space surrounding a monument based on Octavian's column for Naulochus at a time when (and in a poetic context where) all things pointed to Actium. Ancient and modern readings of the rostral columns depicted on the *templum* in *Georgics* 3 exemplify how particular facets of literary reception can be seen as a practice akin to physical reappropriation: once perceived through a Vergilian lens, the *spolia* of Naulochus became the virtually re-spoliated *rostra* from Actium.

Monumenta Duilii

Beginning in the 30s BCE the city of Rome increasingly presented to a viewer not only the monuments of the First Punic War that had stood the test of time, but also art, architecture, and inscriptions newly restored and

---

[10] Duilius' building program and its Augustan afterlife have recently been studied in terms of textual and material referentiality in Roller 2013.

[11] In this chapter, Triumviral refers to the Second Triumvirate unless otherwise noted; that is, the period of time from 43 BCE until Lepidus' fall from power in 36 BCE.

[12] Brilliant 1982. The ideological shifts attendant upon reuse and redisplay of objects at Rome, especially those of foreign manufacture, receive a complementary analysis in Rebeggiani's chapter in this volume, wherein Greek art objects (the Pergamene Gauls) and their imprint upon Roman literary texts tell multiple stories concerning civil and foreign war.

some even newly erected.[13] The battles of the First Punic War (264–241 BCE) were among the most significant sources of naval *spolia* and maritime symbolism before the wars of Octavian gave rise to new forms of naval commemoration.[14] And within this particular class of monuments from the First Punic War, one stands out for its mid-Republican importance and afterlife. Set up in the Forum Romanum to commemorate Rome's first naval triumph at the Battle of Mylae (260 BCE), the rostral column of Gaius Duilius was the first structure of its kind at Rome.[15] Duilius' column of captured Carthaginian rams was later restored and adapted by Octavian, but the specifics of the changes he made remain largely unknown.[16] What is clear is that the column was juxtaposed with Octavian's new rostral column for the Battle of Naulochus (36 BCE), a battle fought on the same waters as Mylae – the nail in the coffin for Sextus Pompey's *Bellum Siculum*.[17]

Statuae of each victorious general stood atop these rostral *columnae*, the figures elevated high above the city and the people of the Forum Romanum.[18] In his narrative of the war against Sextus, the historian Appian summarizes Octavian's honors after Naulochus (*BC* 5.130):

> Of the honors voted to him, he accepted an ovation and annual solemnities on the days of his victories, and a golden image to be erected in the Forum, with the garb he wore when he entered the city, to stand on a column surrounded by the beaks of captured ships. There the image was placed bearing the inscription: "Peace, long disturbed, he reestablished on land and sea."[19]

---

[13] For Rome as a museum, see esp. Rutledge 2012; Edwards 1996 *passim*. Cf. Barchiesi 2005b for limitations to seeing Rome in museological terms. For elite collective memory in the Roman Republic cf., e.g., Walter 2004; Hölkeskamp 2006.

[14] Though the speaker's platform near the Comitium became the "Rostra" after 338 BCE when C. Maenius affixed rams taken from the Antiate fleet to the tribunal, the naval aspects of the structure are rarely viewed as its primary symbolic feature. For a quick taste of the vast dedications made during the First Punic War, consider the fifteen listed for the period in Ziolkowski 1992 (the list is not exhaustive) and the details provided for only a few of the First Punic War dedications in Pietilä-Castrén 1987: 28–48. There were, of course, other naval monuments between the First Punic War and the Triumviral and Augustan periods (those of Pompey stand out) but a majority of attested examples come from these eras: see Dart & Vervaet 2011.

[15] On Duilius, see, e.g., Bleckmann 2002: 113–31; Kondratieff 2004; Beck 2005: 217–29; Roller 2009 and 2013. C. Maenius also erected a column known to later authors as the *Columna Maenia*; its nature is unclear. See Pliny *HN* 7.212 and 34.20.

[16] This statement excludes the altered inscription from the base of Duilius' column, for which see n. 23 below.

[17] I revisit this geographic "coincidence" below. On Sextus, cf. Welch 2012; Powell & Welch 2002.

[18] Cf. *RIC* 1(2) 271 for a numismatic rendering of what is likely Octavian's column; Roller 2013. Our current conception of Duilius' column derives from brief literary sources, the extant inscription from the base, and extrapolation from possible numismatic depictions of Octavian's later rostral monument.

[19] Trans. White 1913 (modified).

Looking at the monumental landscape of the Forum Romanum in the wake of this new installation allows us to encounter the present and the First Punic War past face to face at the center of Rome: through the rostral columns we witness the enactment of a key historical dialogue between these moments in time. The column for the consular hero's victory over Carthage, indeed the symbolic nature of the Forum Romanum itself, is given new meaning when viewed in relation to Octavian's civil war monument as it pierces the landscape of Republican commemoration with a discourse at once strange and familiar. And it is the *rostra* themselves that provide these monuments with *spolia* capable of closing and, so too, increasing the distance between the comparison's Republican "source" and Triumviral "target." Through this monumental comparison, Octavian's victory over Sextus can be seen – at least superficially – as a victory over a foreign enemy and one worthy of its great Republican predecessor at Mylae. Yet the dynamics of the comparison are not so clear-cut: all *rostra* are not created equal. After all, Sextus was no foreign king or marginal bandit. Rather, in 43 BCE he was officially appointed *Praefectus Classis et Orae Maritimae* by the Senate;[20] it is texts such as *Res Gestae* 25 that give us Sextus the *praedo,* the *pirata,* fully transformed into a personification of stereotypes often applied to Carthaginians (*Punica fides* indeed).[21] In the third section this reductive analogy between Sextus and a Carthaginian general will ultimately find itself undermined.

Though the evidence surveyed so far suggests that Octavian cultivated a self-elevating connection with Duilius in the mid-30s BCE and that this particular connection survived here and there without recourse to Actium, it is to a post-Actium Rome that we now turn in more detail. A new monumental Duilius appeared in Rome nearly thirty years after the commemoration of Naulochus had tied him so publicly to Octavian and the defeat of Sextus Pompey. This time he stood among the so-called *summi viri* of Augustus' Forum, a great figure of the Republic adapted to serve as an *exemplum* for a new era.[22] Although the Republican consul was a key model for representing the defeat of Sextus during the civil wars of

---

[20] A title commonly featured on Sextus' coinage along with symbols of naval power such as rams and the god Neptune. Cf., e.g., Crawford 1974: 511/4a.

[21] See Rebeggiani in this volume for the ways in which art and text coalesce to allow for the ideological transformation of civil conflict into a narrative of foreign war. See Lange 2013 and 2009: 79–90 for bibliography on the nature of such wars as "civil" or "foreign." For a negative image of Sextus, see Vell. 2.73.

[22] Geiger 2009: 144–5; see discussion and bibliography in Roller 2013: 123–4. Cf. also Itgenshorst 2004.

the Second Triumvirate, naval commemoration after Actium and during the emergence of the Principate unavoidably changed his significance.

His statue in the Forum Augustum was accompanied by an *elogium*, a brief text marked by allusions to the inscription on Duilius' column in the Forum Romanum.[23] Moreover, this Republican inscription was also likely reinscribed and reappropriated under Augustus in a striking instance of *metagraphe* that served to realign the commemorative teleology of the monuments.[24] The tone and language of each are quite similar, the result of the Augustan author's decision to activate the formal elements of monumental discourse in the archaizing "original." In each, the role of the *primus* is stressed[25] and the naval triumph referred to specifically: aspects of aristocratic self-presentation that may not be markedly surprising, but still serve to connect the inscriptions. Even more striking, however, is the Augustan *elogium*'s focus on the monuments and temples that Duilius erected,[26] a referential system into which Augustus actively inserted himself through his vast campaign of adaptive reuse and historic preservation (see the following example). As in the column contrast in the Forum Romanum, it is the reappropriation of the First Punic War that endows such self-depiction with meaning; and the *elogium* intervenes and comments on these appropriative acts in a strikingly self-conscious fashion, reframing the process and the product. Through textual representation, the inscriptions strove to guarantee that Duilius' building projects would be forever bound to the *princeps*.

Although the catalogue of First Punic War monuments restored and, so too, re-spoliated by Octavian-Augustus is extensive, analysis of a rather telling example drawn from the post-Actium period will have to suffice for our present goals. Janus, god of past and present, forward and backward, was a divinity with immense public significance during the First Punic War – an

---

[23] For the *elogium*, see *CIL* 6.40952 [31611 = I² p. 193 no. XI = *ILS* 55] = *Inscrlt.* XIII.3 13; Geiger 2009: 144; Sehlmeyer 1999: 117–19; Roller 2013: 123 n. 12. For the inscription from the rostral column of Duilius, see *CIL* I² 25 = *ILS* 65 = *ILLRP* 319 = *Inscrlt.* 3.13.69. Cf. Sehlmeyer 1999: 117–19; Bleckmann 2002: 113–39, esp 119–21; Kondratieff 2004: 7–14; Roller 2009 and 2013: 122.

[24] See Roller 2013: 122 n. 11 for dating; also, e.g., Gordon 1983: 124–7. Consider the Augustan *Fasti* and the suggestion that Augustus' second triumph was likely recorded *navalis ex Actio*, enacting its own revisionary view of the past. Dart & Vervaet 2011: 280: ". . . it would have been an original way both to revive and conclude a glorious republican tradition, established some 230 years ago on behalf of C. Duilius, and to herald in a golden new age of peace and prosperity."

[25] Being *primus* is a consistent feature of elite self-presentation, though paradoxically at odds with Roman views of tradition. See Biggs 2017 on Carthage and Rome.

[26] It is possible that the original did so as well, but the supplements in the inscription are too contentious to support much on their own, even if Roller 2013 gets some traction out of accepting them.

often-overlooked aspect of this god's history. Not only did Duilius dedicate a Temple of Janus in the Forum Holitorium (260 BCE),[27] but the god also appeared on the obverse of similarly dated issues of *aes grave* coupled with a reverse depicting the ram of a warship.[28] For a mid-Republican viewer of this coin's iconography, the god's connection to the great war at sea was solidified in a specific way that extended far beyond his war gates in the Forum Romanum. In fact, Janus and his connection to the maritime culture of the First Punic War remained of interest far into the empire: as Plutarch reports at *Quaestiones Romanae* 41, this early coinage continued to fascinate ("Why did their ancient coinage have stamped on one side a double-faced image of Janus, on the other the stern or the prow of a ship?").[29]

Moreover, for Duilius' Temple of Janus, landscape demands as much attention as structure: the Forum Holitorium was an urban space highly associated with the First Punic War through multiple temple dedications[30] and through its potential prewar connection with the Carthaginian population of Rome.[31] As we have already noted, Augustus began the restoration of this Forum's Temple of Janus and was widely compared with the victor at Mylae in various other media. Pointed restoration and the parallel textual presentation of the act (epigraphic and literary) reframed the Forum Holitorium, like the Forum Romanum, for an Augustan "now": structures and monuments were reappropriated, but so too were the spaces in which they stood. Duilius and Rome of the First Punic War became virtual *spolia* for a conceptual, totalizing monument to the idea of an Augustan Rome and, in turn, played a significant role in creating that cultural construct.

In fact, if one steps forward in time and considers the way that Tacitus describes the completion of the Temple of Janus' restoration under Tiberius, it becomes clear that the symbolic bond between Duilius and Augustus crafted at this precise point in time had solidified in both collective and literary memory (*Ann.* 2.49):

> Isdem temporibus deum aedis vetustate aut igni abolitas coeptasque ab Augusto dedicavit ... et Iano templum, quod apud forum holitorium

---

[27] 17 August 260 BCE is the date given for its dedication in the Fasti Vallenses and Allifani. See Pietilä-Castrén 1987: 33; Ziolkowski 1992: 61.

[28] See, e.g., Crawford 1974: no. 322/2; Mattingly 1929. Janus was not the only god to appear in this configuration.

[29] *Moralia* 274 E 4–6.

[30] Duilius – Janus in 260 BCE; A. Atilius Caiatinus – Spes in 258 or 257 BCE. For the Temple of Janus, see Pietilä-Castrén 1987: 32–3; Ziolkowski 1992: 61–2, with Levene 1994. For the Temple of Spes, see Pietilä-Castrén 1987: 41–3; Ziolkowski 1992: 152–4.

[31] Palmer 1997: 53–73, 115–20.

C. Duilius struxerat, qui primus rem Romanam prospere mari gessit triumphumque navalem de Poenis meruit.

During the same period he dedicated shrines of the gods which, destroyed by age or fire, had been projects of Augustus' . . . and the temple of Janus which had been set up in the Forum Holitorium by C. Duilius, who was the first to pursue the Roman cause successfully at sea and win a naval triumph over the Poeni.[32]

The Temple of Janus in this Tacitean *Res–*almost*–Gestae Augusti* prompts the historian to relate not only that Duilius built it, but also that he was Rome's first successful commander at sea and first naval *triumphator.* Though discussion of a temple's founder is itself not all that significant, it is the expansion Duilius receives in an otherwise restrained catalogue that signals his marked status. Tacitus confirms that even in Flavian Rome the temple would still firmly evoke the First Punic War and Duilius' role in Roman cultural history. But it is surely the expansive and public connection Augustus' monumental program constructed between himself and Duilius (and that connection's literary and cultural afterlife) that informs Tacitus' perspective and prompts his narrative expansion on the Republican consul's own *res gestae* (*rem . . . gessit*). Tacitus engages with the Republican past through its Augustan reception and reappropriation: the evocation of one is the activation of the other's resonance. The memory of the First Punic War becomes the virtually re-spoliated material for the interpretation of this reframed monument to Janus and Rome's first victory at sea. For this Flavian reader, the First Punic War no longer belonged to Duilius alone.

The Bigger Picture

In the late first century BCE, symbols and iconography of Roman naval victory were found in settings as diverse as the wall paintings of domestic dining rooms and the Actian rams adorning various structures in the Forum Romanum.[33] It is well known that Agrippa set up dolphins on the *spina* of the Circus Maximus following Naulochus and that Augustus later installed an Egyptian obelisk at the same location.[34] As Andrew Feldherr remarks, the dolphins "celebrate the defeat of Sextus Pompey at

---

[32] Trans. Woodman. The full passage contains several other structures omitted for space.
[33] See Kellum 2010 for Actium in the pictorial programs of houses.
[34] Nelis-Clément & Nelis 2011: 5; Dio. 49.43.1–2. Dolphins also appear on the shield of Aeneas at *Aen.* 8.673. The circus was damaged by a fire in 31 BCE (Dio 50.10.3), an event that likely prompted some of this modification.

the naval battle of Naulochus, and the obelisk, like its partners elsewhere in Rome, recalled Augustus' conquest of Egypt at the battle of Actium."[35] Agrippa later built a Basilica of Neptune (c. 25 BCE), a structure that clearly served as a memorial of his naval victories.[36] The city of Rome was progressively dotted with more and more markers of naval victory that, over time, became tokens of Augustan supremacy. The urban landscape also presented lingering memorials of those now defeated, who had also co-opted Rome's systems of monumental communication, who had also refashioned the First Punic War – its heroes, symbols, and *spolia* – to commemorate the present. For example, one thinks of Cn. Domitius Ahenobarbus and the Temple of Neptune he restored or revowed in the late 40s BCE, a structure originally erected by a Republican naval victor from his family.[37]

It may not be surprising, then, that in such a climate new structures seemingly unconnected with the First Punic War or the naval achievements of Augustus were also imprinted with the significance of the maritime. For example, the "platform" of the Temple of Caesar, dedicated in 29 BCE but already vowed in 42 BCE, was affixed with *rostra* from the recent battle of Actium.[38] This temple was sited across the Forum to the southeast of the Rostra, and, in turn, created a dialogue between these structures. Consider Paul Zanker's interpretation: "[t]hus the prows from the Battle of Actium were unmistakably linked with those from a much earlier victory over the Antiates in 338 B.C. and consciously set up a comparison between a victory in civil war and a historic naval victory of the old Republic."[39] The temporal and spatial dynamic created by this rostral referentiality transformed Rome's past naval victories and the divine Julius himself into the public expression of Augustus' naval prowess and subsequent position of power: a near instance of *spolia in re* (virtual re-spoliation). This "positive" act of transhistorical allusion is in line with the reading of the columns offered in the first section: as Robert Nelson puts it, "[w]hen successful, [appropriation] maintains but shifts the former

---

[35] Feldherr 1995: 248. See Parker in this volume for the impact of Egyptian obelisks throughout Roman history. For a solid reevaluation of Augustus' obelisks, cf. Swetnam-Burland 2015: 15, 97–103.

[36] Ziolkowski 1992: 118–9. The Basilica (stoa) is mentioned by Dio at 53.27, 66.24 and *SHA* 19. Cf. Zanker 1988: 143: "The fresco cycle of the Voyage of Argo in one of the long colonnades and the name Basilica Neptuni probably contain an allusion to his service as admiral, for which Augustus had already bestowed on him a *corona rostrata* adorned with ships' prows (cf. fig. 168a) after the Battle of Naulochoi." Cf. Lucas 1904; Shipley 1933.

[37] Cf. Plin. *HN* 36.26.1–6; Ziolkowski 1992: 117–19; Welch 2012: 194–5.

[38] Frontin. *Aq.* 129.1; Coarelli 1985: 308–24; Ulrich 1994, *passim*; *LTUR* III: 116–19.

[39] Zanker 1988: 81. Cf. Rebeggiani 2013: 57.

connotations to create the new sign and accomplishes all this covertly, making the process appear ordinary or natural."[40]

Nonetheless, the spatial contrast between the Augustan Rostra and the rostra at the Temple of Caesar was by no means monologic. Although it seems clear that these structures now surrounded the Forum and its Republican past with a rather dynastic frame,[41] reference to the Republic through the use of the (Augustan) Rostra – still evocative of that earlier stage for Republican oratory and aristocratic display – seems a potential counterweight to increasingly imperial gestures. Accordingly, we are led to ask how "Republican" could these rostral structures seem in such changing times?[42] Could they have lessened the shock of the growing Julian monopolization of public commemorative space? Consider Brilliant's view that "[s]poliation reintroduces the past and the 'other' into the present."[43] If this is how *spolia* function, can Zanker's image of "a comparison between a victory in civil war and a historic naval victory of the old Republic" withstand the ambiguity of language and the space between symbols?

It Came from the Deep

The communicative potential of *spolia* is never straightforward. *Spolia* are foreign objects taken from the defeated and resemanticized through the dialogue enacted between their new cultural contexts and their original, inimical intentions.[44] *Spolia* are also "[e]lements 'that can't be replicated' ... [they] announce their origin in a different context from the one into which they have been (re)built."[45] To take such factors fully into account for the present argument, we must first ask what can be said about the naval *spolia* of the First Punic War, especially the rams that would have adorned the column of Duilius. Surprisingly, with only a little speculation we can say quite a lot about these *rostra* thanks to the ongoing excavation of the site of the Battle of the Egadi Islands (10 March 241 BCE).[46] While *spolia* "are survivors of violence, about which they might be mute ... or eloquent," the cache of Carthaginian and Roman rams from the last major battle of the First Punic War speaks both verbally and symbolically, like the statue and column of the Ennian fragment with which this study began.[47]

---

[40] Nelson 2003: 163–4.   [41] Cf. Sumi 2009: esp. 19–20.
[42] When does the idea of "The Republic" as a past tense truly arise? For explorations of this notion, see Gowing 2005 and Farrell & Nelis 2013.
[43] Brilliant 2011: 168.   [44] Cf. Davies 2011: 384; Nelson 2003.   [45] Kinney 2011: 3.
[46] See Tusa & Royal 2012.   [47] Kinney 2011: 4.

The single Carthaginian ram brought up from the seabed so far contains an inscribed Punic prayer for Roman defeat.[48] Known as the Egadi 3 ram, part of its inscription has received several provisional translations:[49] Giovanni Garbini translates a segment of the inscription, "We pray to Baal that this ram will go into the enemy ship and make a big hole;" Philip Schmitz offers "Tanit, for in it are its *officers*. Blow, gales of Reshep! and build the surge/overflowing/wave und[er (?) ...]."[50] The current readings, though different, indicate that the sea, storm, curselike prayer, and the influence of the gods pervade the Carthaginian view of battle – perspectives also found on the Roman side in dedications such as Scipio's Temple of the Tempestates and the maritime iconography of the war's monuments.[51] In fact, the Roman and Carthaginian rams both have fins in the shape of a trident, a symbol that clearly suggests a shared focus on the god of the sea.[52] For the present argument, however, it is the mere existence of the Punic inscription, its clearly hostile intent, and the comparative value it may provide that are of interest.

If, as it seems, the rams of the Carthaginian ships taken by Duilius at Mylae contained similar inscriptions, his rostral column in the Forum would have displayed a tower of visibly Carthaginian rams also marked by the Punic language.[53] Set in the center of Rome, these enemy rams and their prayers for Roman loss might have seemed conquered and neutralized (through a spoliate *evocatio* of a sort),[54] but, all the same, their inimical force might have remained for each viewer to experience. The *spolia* would have allowed for such varied interpretations whether the viewer was capable of reading the inscribed prayers (Punic may not have been widely

---

[48] It is significant that the inscription was made through the wax layer of the ram's mold before casting, a factor indicating it was not an afterthought. The method also implies, but cannot prove, that inscribing rams was regular Carthaginian practice. Tusa & Royal 2012: 18.

[49] Tusa & Royal 2012: 43. For the Punic text of the inscription, see the corrected page on the *JRA* website.

[50] Tusa & Royal 2012: 43. Schmitz informs me *per litteras* that the final version of his translation will differ greatly from that printed in *JRA* 2012. Cf. Prag 2015: 86 for a more recent translation of the Punic text.

[51] For more on this see Biggs 2017. See Pietilä-Castrén 1987: 28–48; Palmer 1997: 54–6. On the inscription, Tusa & Royal 2012.

[52] Tusa & Royal 2012: 42: "Although less is known of the iconography associated with Punic sea deities, it seems the trident was familiar at Carthage by the 3rd c. B.C."

[53] Several of the excavated helmets from the site are also inscribed in what could be Punic. See Tusa & Royal 2012: 27.

[54] Cf. Davies 2011: 381: "The obelisks worked metonymically: just as they were subordinated to the power of the Roman people, so was Egypt. For them to function in their new context, their Egyptian origin was paramount, and so was an understanding that through capture they were rendered Roman. This transformation in identity is played out in the superposition of *Aegypta* over *Populi Romani* [in the inscription from the *Horologium Augusti*]."

known, but was likely recognizable),[55] or solely reacted to rams that might have taken Roman life. Accordingly, the key aspect (the *spolia*) of this new type of Roman monument resists full appropriation, allowing it to highlight the foreignness of the conflict – a foreignness necessary to the objects' very ability to adopt new semiotic resonance in their present cultural context.[56] The rams of Duilius' column must have created a palpable tension that rendered the *spolia* intelligible at Rome (no longer a Punic weapon, but a symbol of Carthaginian defeat), while simultaneously indicating a victory over those who did not *Latine dicere*. But what of the reframed context introduced by Octavian and his own rostral column? Our earlier readings of the comparison highlighted Octavian's alignment of his own civil war against Sextus with the reductive Rome/Carthage antithesis often put forward in black and white narratives of Republican victory. There is, however, much more at stake.

First, the influence of Actium's subsequent centrality has led many to forget Naulochus and read Octavian's rostral column as an Actian monument; hence one likely to bear rams from Antony and Cleopatra's eastern fleets, rams marked by a plethora of non-Roman visual and linguistic codes. As we will soon see, such opinions are still quite pervasive. Nonetheless, Octavian's only well-attested rostral column commemorated the victory over Sextus Pompey at Naulochus.[57] At the time of that battle

[55] Consider the implications of interpreting the "Punic" monologues in Plautus' *Poenulus*. Indeed, the hieroglyphics of Egyptian obelisks present a similar situation: cf. Nelis-Clément & Nelis 2014: 130 on the obscure but still communicative nature of hieroglyphics at Rome. Concerning knowledge of hieroglyphics and Egyptian aesthetics at Rome, see Swetnam-Burland 2015: 11, 41, 45–6, 48–9, 90–3, and *passim*; Parker in this volume. The issue of the visibility of the Punic inscriptions themselves is pressing, especially when they had been weathered by time. Yet even in their original state, they may have sat quite high upon the column. Answers are impossible, but if inscribing rams was a regular practice, as it seems, the expectation that inscriptions were there could circumvent their invisibility from the ground.

[56] For the Roman absorption of foreign elements and the enduring preservation of their disparate origins, especially as construed textually to reflect on facets of sociocultural practice in Augustan Rome, see Nichols's discussion of Vitruvius in this volume.

[57] Pollini 2012: 74 argues against identifying the rostral column depicted on Octavian's coinage (e.g., *RIC* 1[2] 271) as that of Naulochus (Zanker 1988, Gurval 1995, Sehlmeyer 1999, and Hallett 2005 all identify it as the Naulochus column). Pollini contends that Octavian's garb does not match Appian's depiction (quoted on p. 50), and uses this apparent discrepancy as evidence for an Actian rostral column. He aligns this view with Servius ad *Georgics* 3.29 – a passage that also implies the existence of Actian columns. He does not consider (as we will in the fourth section) that Servius, too, depends on Vergilian virtual re-spoliation – the transformation of the Naulochus column into an Actian monument in reception. Beyond Servius' problematic remarks, an Actian rostral column is otherwise unattested. The expectation of numismatic imagery to perfectly reflect either the monument's "true" form or a literary representation of it is also faulty (Pollini 2012: 74: "That is clearly not how he appears on the column on the coin!"). Consider, for example, the temporal distance between Claudius' Triumphal Arch (not completed until 51–52 CE) and its

(36 BCE), Sextus' Sicilian fleet still contained a core of the former Pompeian navy, buttressed by levies from, among other places, Italy, Sicily, Spain, and Sardinia: the concept of a runaway fleet of bandits and slaves is most certainly a skewed perspective, even if it is based on some truths concerning Sextus' manpower.[58] Questions inevitably remain, then, concerning the appearance of the spoliate rams affixed to Octavian's column. Would they have struck viewers as markedly Roman, Italian, or Greek in style? Might they even have borne Latin inscriptions? Unfortunately, any answers to these questions are even more speculative than those concerning the column of Duilius: we do not have contemporary evidence like the Egadi rams nor do we know the full makeup of Sextus' fleet, especially regarding mitigating factors such as the reuse of enemy ships and rams.[59] Moreover, as Sebastiano Tusa and Jeffrey Royal warn,

> [t]he material associated with the Battle of the Egadi Islands is pertinent to warships and their operation in the 3rd c. B.C. only. . . . Comparisons can be made to remains from different eras, such as the Athlit ram or Augustus' Victory Monument at Nicopolis, but the results will be limited to general diachronic changes.[60]

For all that, we can still hazard a few suggestions. Concerning the possibility that Latin inscriptions were present on the rams of Sextus' fleet, the First Punic War evidence provides a precedent. The Roman rams from the Egadi Islands contain Latin inscriptions that document Quaestorial oversight,[61] while also displaying what can be described as Roman decorative features that would have resonated in the late third century BCE.[62] If any ships in Sextus' fleet were contracted through *probatio* they might have followed suit, but unfortunately this knowledge sits outside our ken. Though the Republican information may not be very useful for visualizing the rams of later eras, it does allow us to better conceive of the rams at the

---

depiction on his coinage (already in 46–50 CE), just one factor that could produce a numismatic image that differs in form from the structure it portrays. Cf. Hurley 2001: 137.

[58] Welch 2012: 21, 37–43; Pitassi 2009: 184–91.

[59] Concerning potential reuse in the Battle of the Egadi Islands, see Tusa & Royal 2012: 45.

[60] Tusa & Royal 2012: 35.

[61] Cf. Prag 2014: 728; Coarelli 2014; Cébeillac-Gervasoni 2014. See also Gnoli 2011 and 2012a.

[62] These include the trident and winged victories holding laurel crowns and palm fronds. See Tusa & Royal 2012: 42–3. In their discussion, indebted to Hallett, Hölscher, and Crawford, they note that "the Victory Motif on the two rams is similar to that on Roman didrachms minted between 265 and 241 B.C. (Crawford, *RRC* no. 22/1)." Also rightly introduced in their discussion is the fact that the Temple of Victoria on the Palatine had been dedicated in 294 BCE and would have played a symbolic role in the first great war to follow. Concerning Actium, a prow in the British Museum found near Actium and generally considered to have come from a small ship that took part in that battle is conceivably Roman in aesthetics as well (GR 1872.12.14.1).

other end of this monumental comparison – those of Duilius. The question that remains, then, is as follows: when a more concrete image of Duilius' rostral *spolia* is brought to bear on this column contrast, what might the rostral referentiality enacted by Octavian's monument have actually conveyed to its viewers?

Surely the spatial and allusive contrast was meant to imbue Octavian's naval success with the elevating symbolic force of victory over Carthage, a city with a long history of interactions with Rome, but whose people were, all the same, collectively construed as Rome's first great overseas enemy and antagonist in its greatest naval war:

> By appropriating the monuments and iconography of a famous victory over a feared external enemy, Octavian also parades his recent victory, won over Roman citizens, as a "normal" victory over foreigners – or, at the least, he occludes the distinction between civil and external war.[63]

This explanation goes some of the way in conveying why Octavian would have elected to restore and virtually re-spoliate Duilius' column in the first place.[64] Indeed, we already engaged with particular aspects of this historical comparison in the first section. But it is now time for some corrective considerations. Aspects of the *spolia*'s past associations will and, in fact, must resurface when re-spoliated (*in se* or *in re*) – a facet of their communicative power that new frames and contexts can only attempt to control.[65] At first glance, the columns in the immediate wake of Naulochus seem to represent a perfect realization of Zanker's "comparison between a victory in civil war and a historic naval victory of the old Republic."[66] Nevertheless, a viewer set within the spatial axis of these two monuments would have found them similar in aesthetic and architectural form, but dangerously distinct in the semiotic potential of their *spolia*.

---

[63] Roller 2013: 122 n. 10.

[64] Whether this act involved restoring the original Carthaginian rams, recasting them, or replacing them with new rams from recent victories is unknown, but all options provide immense interpretive fodder. Moreover, the sacral aspect of the victory monument lends some weight to arguments in favor of the retention of the original Carthaginian rams (or rams thought by most to be such).

[65] Brilliant 2011: 169: "[f]or *spolia* to succeed as evidence of the swing between two sites, the original source cannot be fully obscured if the newly combined elements are to have meaningful saliency in the present."

[66] Or even Roller's more nuanced formulation concerning Duilius and Augustus: ". . . the new Augustan monuments . . . work together to provide a frame for the two old (but restored) monuments and draw them into a new, teleological story. Duilius' victory is decisively confirmed as a great achievement, but is at the same time positioned as a precursor . . . to Octavian's allegedly similar yet greater victory" (2013: 124). The two monuments he refers to are the rostral column and the Temple of Janus.

Instead of allowing Octavian's column to re-spoliate its predecessor and align the symbolic potential of the Mylae monument with the needs of contemporary legitimation (achieved here by co-opting Republican non-civil victory), the clear narrative of Roman victory over an external threat seen in Duilius' column – a narrative told through its aesthetics, form, and *spolia* – may very well have resisted conforming to the newly desired teleology. The act of reappropriating the Republic, of reusing the Roman past, was unavoidably a Pandora's box for those attempting to restrict its potential meanings. A hypothetical Roman viewer of both columns and their *spolia* could have been forced to contrast Carthaginian and Roman visual cues and iconography – to contrast Punic and Latin inscriptions. And even if we concede, as we must, that the origin of Sextus' rams is truly beyond our knowledge, we can still rest assured that they were not Carthaginian. Whatever the Naulochus column's goals, any attempt to view the *spolia* of Octavian's monument as something other than civil – to see them as the virtual spoils of a replayed First Punic War – might have been in vain.[67] Whether *in re* or *in se*, re-spoliating the symbols of a monument to foreign victory and reframing them in a civil war context, like a quotation from an earlier text, seems to activate more than its author may have anticipated. Though the *spolia* from each column share many features, what distinguishes them is potentially damning.

Poetic Re-Spoliation

The Battle of Naulochus largely failed to hold the attention of later authors and seems to have ceded its place in Roman collective memory to the mythologized victory at Actium.[68] Indeed, at *Res Gestae* 25 Augustus moves from Naulochus to Actium in the very same breath;[69] in the *princeps'* teleology, the first battle was just a stepping-stone to greater things.

---

[67] Lange 2009 and 2013, as well as others such as Beard 2007: 303, have seen Actium as a victory openly celebrated as a civil war (with, of course, foreign elements as well). Be that as it may, a tendency to construe contemporary conflict in terms of Republican victory over foreign enemies is beyond doubt, thus creating a civil–foreign tension regardless of how much one may want to accept that victory in civil conflict was not as much of an evil as modern scholarship has held.

[68] For this general idea of a "mythologized" Actium, cf. Gurval 1995 *passim* with Pelling 1997; Labate & Rosati 2013.

[69] *Mare pacavi a praedonibus. Eo bello servorum, qui fugerant a dominis suis et arma contra rem publicam ceperant, triginta fere millia capta dominis ad supplicium sumendum tradidi. Iuravit in mea ver[ba] tota Italia sponte sua et me be[lli], quo vici ad Actium, ducem depoposcit.* Interpretations of the war against Sextus as a Sicilian slave war are discussed with bibliography in Lange 2009: esp. 33–8, 79–90 and 2013: 81–2. This view of the war is often related to its civil aspects and the *ovatio* that Naulochus received instead of a triumph.

Accordingly, in an attempt to draw together all of the arguments made in the first three sections of this chapter, the final pages turn to a similar process, tracking how a Roman poem (*Georgics* 3) and its ancient and modern readers (e.g., Servius, Thomas, Erren, Meban) engage in an interpretive maneuver that itself virtually re-spoliates the *rostra* of the earlier naval victory at Naulochus to symbolize that later success at Actium.

The opening lines of Vergil's third *Georgic* contain one of the work's most studied passages, in which the poet builds a monument of words for a victorious post-Actium Augustus (*G.* 3.16–18):[70]

> in medio mihi Caesar erit templumque tenebit:
> illi victor ego et Tyrio conspectus in ostro
> centum quadriiugos agitabo ad flumina currus.

> In the middle will be Caesar, and he will possess the temple.
> For him, I, as victor, conspicuous in Tyrian purple will drive a
> hundred four-horse chariots along the river.

The poetic *ego* in Tyrian purple is a complex image when the semantics of Carthaginian war are activated,[71] but it is the temple itself that interests us at present. This Mantuan *templum*, beyond its role within the poem, is often read as "a metaphorical construct standing for a future poetic project of epic proportions."[72] The instinct to read the *Aeneid* back into this passage emerges immediately, with *in medio* providing an oft-noted retroactive connection with the shield ecphrasis of *Aeneid* 8. The shield, of course, contains a famous poetic depiction of the Battle of Actium – a scene filled with language that can intertextually alter any later reader's ability to interpret *Georgics* 3 without thinking of *Actia rostra* and *Actia bella* (8.675–88):[73]

> in medio classis aeratas, Actia bella,
> cernere erat, totumque instructo Marte videres
> feruere Leucaten auroque effulgere fluctus.
> hinc Augustus agens Italos in proelia Caesar
> cum patribus populoque, penatibus et magnis dis,
> stans celsa in puppi, geminas cui tempora flammas
> laeta vomunt patriumque aperitur vertice sidus.

---

[70] Text of Vergil throughout is Mynors 1969.   [71] Cf. *Aen.* 4.260–4.

[72] Thomas 2004: 130. Cf. also Hardie 2002 and Meban 2008. Armstrong 2009: 86 refers to it as a "temple epic."

[73] In fact, the imagery of the circus and temple dedication in *Georgics* 3 has led some rightly to see it "as replete with allusion to the contemporary political scene of the years immediately after Actium." Nelis 2008: 514.

parte alia ventis et dis Agrippa secundis
arduus agmen agens, cui, belli insigne superbum,
tempora navali fulgent rostrata corona.
hinc ope barbarica variisque Antonius armis,
victor ab Aurorae populis et litore rubro,
Aegyptum virisque Orientis et ultima secum
Bactra vehit, sequiturque (nefas) Aegyptia coniunx.

In the middle one could discern bronze ships, Actian war, and you could see all Leucate seethe in Martial preparation and the waves glitter with gold. On one side Augustus Caesar stands on the lofty stern accompanied by the senate and people, by the Penates and the great gods, as he leads the Italians into battle. His happy brow emits twin flames and his father's star is visible on his head. In another section Agrippa leads the battle line from on high, winds and gods in his favor, and proud in his honor of war, his brows gleam with the rostrate naval crown. On the other side Antony, with barbarian wealth and strange weapons, the victor over the peoples of the east and the Indian shores, brings Egypt with him, and the forces of the Orient, and remote Bactria; and his Egyptian consort (shameful to say) follows him.

Viewed through these lines of the *Aeneid*, *Georgics* 3 certainly appears a poem fully focused on depicting, and, so too, creating an Actian Roman world. And in many ways, this perspective is exactly right. The *Georgics* do present us with a clear instance of poetry after Actium.[74] Nonetheless, the Actian perspective, inevitable as it may now seem, has obscured a few aspects of the poem and its reception. For example, in these lines of *Aeneid* 8, Naulochus is present in a way that complicates any conception of the poem's *rostra* as fully Actian. Some of the passage's key naval imagery is introduced through Agrippa's naval crown (*tempora navali fulgent rostrata corona*), and although Agrippa is depicted in the midst of battle at Actium, we must recall that this naval crown was awarded for Naulochus.[75] The gleaming rams of his *corona rostrata* once signified victory over Sextus Pompey, but Vergil's placement of the crown so close to words like *Actia bella*, *barbarica*, *Aegyptum*, and *Aegypta*, virtually re-spoliates the rams of Agrippa's crown for Actium. This is the same complex process of re-spoliation at work in *Georgics* 3, to which we now return.

[74] See Nappa 2005.
[75] Liv. *Per.* 129; Vell. Pat. 2.81.3; Plin. *HN* 7.115; 16.7; Dio 49.14.3. Servius describes the origin of the crown in his note on 8.684, as do Eden 1975 and Gransden 1976. Neither modern commentator considers the potential effects of focusing on the crown from an earlier naval victory in the midst of Actium.

After setting out the riverside landscape of the temple, the poet describes its doors and the scenes they contain (*G.* 3.26–9):

> in foribus pugnam ex auro solidoque elephanto
> Gangaridum faciam victorisque arma Quirini,
> atque hic undantem bello magnumque fluentem
> Nilum ac navali surgentis aere columnas.

> On the doors I will fashion a battle from gold and solid ivory, the arms of the peoples of the Ganges and of victorious Quirinus, and here I will fashion the Nile swelling and overflowing with war and columns rising up [adorned] with the bronze rams of ships.

The flowing Nile evokes the war against Antony and Cleopatra, while the use of a topographic reference to Egypt locates the landscape of the phrase far from Rome. At first glance, the movement to Egypt seems capable of effacing any difference between a civil and a foreign war – one potential result of comparison that we have already encountered. Nonetheless, the phrase *navali surgentis aere columnas* bridges the boundary between (the monumental landscape of) home and away.[76] Servius in his *Commentary* on the *Georgics* makes the key connection between art and text:

> And columns rising up with prows of bronze: He means the columns which were set up in honor of Augustus and Agrippa, decorated with the prows of warships. Augustus, the victor over all of Egypt, which Caesar had conquered in part, captured many prows in a naval battle. When these had been gathered together, he made four columns, which later were situated on the Capitolium by Domitian; these we see today, whence he says "columns rising up with prows of bronze." Duilius set up columns decorated with prows, after the Phoenicians [Carthaginians] were conquered in a naval battle, one of which we see on the rostra, the other in front of the circus on the side by the doors.[77]

Confused about the number of columns erected in either historical context,[78] Servius certainly sees line 29 as a reference to Octavian's rostral

---

[76] See Hardie 1987: 164.

[77] Servius *ad Georg.* 3.29 (trans. J. W. Crawford: http://dlib.etc.ucla.edu/projects/Forum/resources/ primarysources/Servius_ad_Georg.3.29): *columnas dicit, quae in honore Augusti et Agrippae rostratae constitutae sunt. Augustus victor totius Aegypti, quam Caesar pro parte superaverat, multa de navali certamine sustulit rostra, quibus conflatis quattuor effecit columnas, quae postea a Domitiano in Capitolio sunt locatae, quas hodieque conspicimus: unde ait "navali surgentes aere columnas". nam rostratas Duilius posuit, victis Poenis navali certamine, e quibus unam in rostris, alteram ante circum videmus a parte ianuarum.*

[78] No other source indicates that Duilius erected more than one rostral column. So, too, no other source indicates a rostral column for Actium. See Pollini 2012: 74 (and n. 57 herein) for the opposing view that Octavian's column is one of the alternate Actian columns only mentioned by Servius and,

column and an evocation of Duilius' monument.[79] His leap from one to the other highlights the connection prompted by their (once) juxtaposed position in the Forum and in the subsequent literary tradition. As the vast naval semiotics of the city pointed out in this chapter suggest, the built environment of Rome's monuments encouraged such leaps.[80] Yet Servius' reading also reflects the overpowering impact of Actium in the cultural myth of the Augustan age. Later views of the victory over Egypt (and Antony) have obscured the full allusive texture of the phrase. In a very Actian poem, Servius could only see these particular *rostra* as Actian: should we follow his lead?

Concerning these very *rostra* David Meban has suggested that "[l]ines 29–30 . . . likely refer to Octavian's victory at Actium and the rostra seized during the battle," while Richard Thomas has noted that "[i]f, as is likely, V[ergil] intends a reference to the *rostra* taken at Actium. . . and incorporated into the Temple of Divus Julius (29 B.C.), as distinct from the Augustan *rostra* (*rostra vetera*), then the line gives further evidence of the late date of the poem."[81] With even more confidence and without the "likely" found in both Meban and Thomas, Manfred Erren states that the temple doors will not just illustrate Octavian's battles and victories, but will also specifically depict the Battle of Actium.[82] There is good reason for scholars to read the symbolism of the *rostra* in such a way. In fact, we must concede from the outset that the poem's temple is a fictional structure; it can contain *rostra* from any battle it likes. Nonetheless, if one desires to undo readerly re-spoliation and to locate the full range of structures that could have informed the visualization of these *navali surgentis aere columnas*, some rather significant complications remain.

As we have already noted, five years before Actium, Augustus defeated Sextus Pompey off the coast of Sicily in the battle of Naulochus. This was the battle commemorated by Octavian's rostral column – the primary monument evoked by the temple doors in *Georgics* 3. Though Actium gave

---

further, that the column depicted on the coins of Octavian could not be the same as that described by Appian for Naulochus.

[79] Silius Italicus also felt the connection and engages with it in his allusive depiction of Duilius' column at *Punica* 6.663–6: *Aequoreum iuxta decus et* **navale** *trophaeum| rostra gerens* **nivea** *surgebat mole* **columna**;| *exuvias Marti donumque Duilius, alto| ante omnis mersa Poenorum classe, dicebat*. Cf. *G.* 3.29: *Nilum ac* **navali** *surgentis aere* **columnas**.

[80] For example, consider how Pliny at *HN* 16.7.1–16.8.8 moves seamlessly from one set of *rostra* to another.

[81] Meban 2008: 170. Thomas 1988 *ad loc.* Cf. also Mynors 1990 *ad loc*; Pollini 2012: 74.

[82] Erren 2003: 573: "Die Türflügel des Tempels sollen auf Bildsteifen von Schlachten und Siegen Caesars erzählen, und zwar stellt der eine die Schlacht von Actium dar."

rise to numerous rostral monuments, from the temples of the Forum Romanum to the Victory Monument at Nicopolis, as we have seen, there is no solid evidence for an Actian rostral column. So, one asks, whereas *navali surgentis aere* could potentially been seen as Actian at first,[83] why do Vergil's *columnae* not temper this view?

In order to trace out the symbolic connections, we must begin with the links between Republican past and Augustan present. First, it is most significant to recall that Naulochus, *not* Actium, essentially took place at the same location as Duilius' *spolia*-producing victory at Mylae; the spatial correspondence is what really makes the comparison exceptional in its communicative potential. Consider David West's comments on the Horatian depiction of the First Punic War as *Siculum mare| Poeno purpureum sanguine (Odes* 2.12.2–3): "no Roman could read of the Sicilian sea purpled with blood without thinking of the battles fought in Sicilian waters by Octavian and Agrippa against Sextus Pompeius."[84] For this reader, the evocation of the First Punic War was an evocation of Octavian's victory at sea (and vice versa).[85] We here see the full realization of the compressed semiotic field of commemoration that Octavian's column contrast worked to produce. In the mid-30s BCE the Battle of Mylae could seem a ready-made *exemplum* for Naulochus: Actium begged for such a choice *exemplum*, and in many ways it is Vergil who most clearly delivers it.

Octavian's column alluded to that of Duilius, temporally moving and transforming the latter into a symbol for contemporary victory in a civil war, virtually re-spoliating its material form and potential meanings for a Triumviral context.[86] The *elogium* for Duilius in the statuary galleries of the Forum Augustum alluded to the rewritten inscription from the Republican consul's column, updating the First Punic War once again for the Roman world after Actium. Vergil's textual strategy enacts a similar, but, as it turns out, more complete resemanticization: physical *spolia*, by nature, retain a connection to their differing, original contexts, but in *Georgics* 3 the history of this column has largely been erased.[87] We here encounter a "full" (if not fictional and self-subverting) reappropriation of the First Punic War, Naulochus, and all earlier ties between them. Yet we must not flatten the potential ambiguities. Those who recall Lucan's geographical syllepsis of Pharsalus and Philippi into a single "Emathian,"[88]

---

[83] Whether those on the Temple of Caesar, the Augustan Rostra, the Temple of Castor, or any other structure, is up in the air until line end.

[84] West 1998: 81.   [85] See Nisbet & Hubbard 1978 *ad loc.*

[86] Not without the potential for subversion.

[87] As we saw earlier with Agrippa's *corona rostrata* in *Aeneid* 8.   [88] Reed 2011: 25.

what John Henderson calls "the 'always already' cyclicity of *Pharsalus-Philippi*,"[89] will know how slippery such conflations can be. Actium was not Naulochus, neither battle was Mylae.

Though it is nearly certain that the physical columns Servius saw evoked by the imagery of *Georgics* 3 were not originally monuments erected for Actium, at least one of them became Actian for Roman viewers and readers. The semantic transition from Naulochus to Actium that happens when conceptualizing the *same* monument occurs via reinterpretation, a virtual re-spoliation encouraged by Vergil's coupling of the Naulochus monument depicted on the *templum* of *Georgics* 3 with images of Egypt. Just as Augustus punctured the urban fabric of Rome with Egyptian obelisks,[90] each deictic needle a *spolium* that pointed to foreign victory, and each capable of transporting the viewer across the Mediterranean, Vergil subtly transports the rostral column and its civil *spolia* to Egypt. A new hybrid monument is created as the rams of the civil *Bellum Siculum* become symbols for *Aegypto capta*; the latter, of course, the outcome of a war easily seen as civil if one chooses not to privilege the Egyptian side of things. And this potential lack of a clear-cut foreign foe is where comparison with Republican victory over Carthage in the First Punic War comes into play – a historic victory over the city founded by that proto-Cleopatra, Dido. Such comparisons, however, only become active in reception: it depends on the reader whether the transposition serves to reduce the civil resonance or reintroduce it into what was already skewed as foreign by other media.

This process of poetic re-spoliation – of virtual re-spoliation – would have been possible with any of the naval monuments in the city, be they Antiate, Carthaginian, or Pompeian: in *Aeneid* 8, Agrippa's naval crown no longer symbolizes Naulochus as it gleams on Actian waters. Semantic translocation is always possible and, indeed, possibly the goal of such pointed interventions in the culture of spoliate cargo at Rome.[91] Servius

---

[89] Henderson 2010 [1987]: 488.

[90] See Parker in this volume; Davies 2011; Swetnam-Burland 2015.

[91] For a strong example of how far such post-Actium reappropriation reaches, we can recall in passing the very real possibility that the Temple of Apollo on the Palatine, the hallmark of Actian symbolism, was originally dedicated for Naulochus. Miller 2009: 191–2: "Roman generals had long memorialized their military achievements with temples or other structures. ... After defeating Pompey's son in 36, Octavian followed this tradition by vowing a temple to Apollo. Velleius clearly situates the promise in the context of the recent victory (2.81.3 *victor...promisit*). Concluding the hard-fought campaign against Sextus Pompey at Naulochus certainly merited such commemoration." Cf. also Dio 49.15.5. For a different interpretation, see Gurval 1995: 118–27. The same has even been suggested for Octavian's arch next to the Temple of Caesar. As Zanker remarks (1988: 81), it was voted "for his victory at Actium (or was it for the earlier Battle of Naulochoi?)."

and many modern commentators thus make an anticipated move in virtually re-spoliating the Naulochus column and in resemanticizing its *rostra*. Readerly reconstruction of the monument for the next great naval conflict, although activated by Vergil's ecphrastic imagery of Egyptian war, is nonetheless incorrect. But "incorrect" is not quite right either: to say so would miss the point of intrusive reappropriation, of poetic re-spoliation. The column *was* an Actian monument and its naval *spolia* surely came from Cleopatra's fleet – just not at first.

CHAPTER 4

Buried Treasures, Hidden Verses
(Re)Appropriating the Gauls of Pergamon in Flavian Rome

Stefano Rebeggiani

In the *Naturalis Historia*, Pliny mentions a famous speech by Agrippa in which Augustus' collaborator remarks on the need to display in public the Greek works of art that have become the possession of Roman aristocrats.[1] In praising Agrippa's oration, Pliny notes that public display is preferable to the current tendency in Rome, in which such works of art are held in exile (*exilia*) in the aristocrats' houses. This chapter examines the end of one of these exiles, which coincided with the first public appearance of one of the most famous Greek statuary complexes appropriated by Rome: the Galatae from Pergamon, initially kept in the Domus Aurea of Nero, but displayed publicly in Rome in 75 CE. Their public exhibition, which has received little scholarly attention, is part of a complex cultural process that involves ideology, literature, and the arts.

The story of the Pergamene statues provides an excellent case study for reflecting on the dynamics of appropriation. This chapter will show that the appropriation, reuse, and transformation of Greek materials at the level of texts and monuments share important features, and that there is a high degree of mutual interaction and interdependence between literary and material appropriations. By interaction and interdependence I do not mean the simple fact that the presence of certain artifacts may prompt writers to interact with texts of analogous subjects (although this, too, is a phenomenon often overlooked). I am rather concerned with the factors shaping ancient and modern receptions of the appropriated materials in their new contexts. Specifically, a long history of appropriations of certain Greek cultural narratives (Celtomachy), texts, and artifacts sets the scene for a specific reading of the Greek pieces of art in their new Roman context. This chapter will accordingly move toward a more inclusive view of appropriative practices in Roman society, one that is less mindful of

---

[1] Pliny *HN* 35.26. Cf. Zanker 1988: 141.

boundaries between disciplines, and one that assumes some degree of correspondence in the semantics of both literature and figurative arts. More to the point, because of their interconnected nature, Roman appropriative practices are best studied through an interdisciplinary approach; they should be examined as part of complex cultural narratives that capitalize on a variety of experiences (visual and textual, e.g.), and so evidence from different fields (literary, artistic) should be taken into account. In this chapter, I (almost always) imply intentionality on the part of the practitioners involved in these appropriations, but I also argue that intentionality is irrelevant; earlier acts of appropriation become part of the way viewers experience and make sense of the newly appropriated materials. They necessarily affected ancient readings of the artifacts no less than they shape modern scholarly interpretations today.

It is useful first to provide some background information about the Pergamene Gauls. At the beginning of the third century BCE, Greece suffered one of the most frightening attacks of its history. Celtic tribes invaded the Greek peninsula and went so far as to attack the sanctuary of Apollo at Delphi.[2] According to a widespread story, the god himself defended his shrine by causing an earthquake and a snowstorm that prevented the Gauls from sacking his temple.[3] The incident became legendary – a turning point in Greek history and a symbol of Greece's ability to defend freedom against barbarians – and was soon regarded as a parallel to the Persian wars. Greek cities and kingdoms sought to join in the Delphic triumph. The Aetolians, for instance, claiming to have helped the god defend his shrine, dedicated shields in the temple of Apollo at Delphi – shields that were similar to those dedicated after the Persian wars.[4] Hellenistic kings, too, claimed for themselves the role of defendants of Hellenization against the barbarians.[5] Antigonus Gonatas boasted about his victory over the Gauls at Lysimacheia, which made him master of Macedonia. Conversely, in his wars with Gonatas, Pyrrhus defeated a force of Gallic mercenaries in 274 BCE, which he considered the most glorious aspect of his success.[6] In his *Hymn to Delos*, Callimachus makes the most of a minor victory achieved by

---

[2] On the Gallic assault on Delphi (279 BCE) and its sources, in both literature and archaeology, see Nachtergael 1977: 15–174.
[3] Paus. 1.4.4; 10.19–23; Diod. 22.3–5, 22.9; Just. 24.4–8.   [4] Paus. 10.19.4.
[5] Nachtergael 1977: esp. 176 on Celtomachy in the Hellenistic period.
[6] Plut. *Pyrr.* 26. 9. Cf. Momigliano 1975: 60–2; Nachtergael 1977: 168 n. 192, 177–81 on Antigonus Gonatas; 181–4 on Pyrrhus.

Ptolemy II against Gauls to link his sovereign's success to the Delphic triumph of Apollo (Call. *Hymn* 4.171–6):[7]

καί νύ ποτε ξυνός τις ἐλεύσεται ἄμμιν ἄεθλος
ὕστερον, ὁππόταν οἱ μὲν ἐφ' Ἑλλήνεσσι μάχαιραν
βαρβαρικὴν καὶ Κελτὸν ἀναστήσαντες Ἄρηα
ὀψίγονοι Τιτῆνες ἀφ' ἑσπέρου ἐσχατόωντος
ῥώσωνται νιφάδεσσιν ἐοικότες ἢ ἰσάριθμοι
τείρεσιν, ἡνίκα πλεῖστα κατ' ἠέρα βουκολέονται.

Yea and one day hereafter there shall come upon us a common struggle, when the Titans of a later day shall rouse up against the Hellenes barbarian sword and Celtic war, and from the furthest West rush on like snowflakes and in number as the stars when they flock most thickly in the sky.[8]

Callimachus uses Gigantomachy as a mythical framework for the Gallic assault on Delphi. The metaphor places the fight on the cosmic level: the Celts are equated to the impious underworld creatures who sought to overthrow the cosmos; Mount Parnassus defended by Apollo parallels Olympus, defended by the gods.

Celtic victory was, however, nowhere as central to the ideology of the ruling class as in Pergamon. Here, the Attalid dynasty closely linked its power to successes against the Celts. Attalus I, the initiator of the dynasty, began his reign with a brilliant success over the Gauls in the valley of the river Caicus, through which he freed the kingdom of Pergamon from the tribute imposed by the Gauls (he took the name of Soter thereafter). The Caicus victory was celebrated through a number of monuments. In the precinct of the temple of Athena Nikephoros on the acropolis of Pergamon a tall inscribed circular base was raised, supporting a statuary group portraying the defeated Gauls (Tolistoagii is the name of the Celtic tribe defeated by Attalus I). The original bronze statues are lost, but a number of Roman copies, mainly from the first century CE, have been identified.[9] These include the famous Dying Gaul, now in the Capitoline Museum, as well as the Ludovisi Gaul. A second monument was later dedicated on the Athenian acropolis. This monument, described by Pausanias, associated the victory over the Gauls with three famous paradigmatic battles: Gigantomachy, Amazonomachy, and the battle of Marathon.[10] Gigantomachy was also the subject of one of the friezes of

---

[7] See Stephens 2015: 206–8; Nachtergael 1977: 184–90.   [8] Trans. A. W. Mair.
[9] Wenning 1978: 1–36.
[10] Paus. 1.25.2. The monument aligned Celtic victory with the success against the Persians. Besides the representation of Marathon, the iconography recalled a monument deeply connected to the Persian

the Great Altar of Zeus, perhaps the most famous monument of Hellenistic art, erected by Attalus' successor Eumenes II. The historical occasion behind the dedication of this latter monument is highly debated, and it is not clear that there was a direct connection with the celebration of a Gallic victory.[11] What matters for us is that later viewers experienced Gigantomachy and Celtomachy as part of the same celebratory complex. Readers of Callimachus' *Hymns* would have found it natural to connect the historical and mythical events commemorated by the monuments, and it is possible that the allegory was articulated in other, now lost, Hellenistic celebratory poetry. After all, Celtic victory and the defeat of the Giants were associated on the Acropolis monument.

The success of Celtomachic imagery centering on the Delphi episode was soon exported to the Italian peninsula. The Romans had suffered a terrifying Gallic invasion about a century earlier than the Celts' incursion against Delphi. In 390 BCE the Senones, a Gallic tribe, defeated the Romans at the river Allia and then proceeded to sack and burn down the city, with the sole exception of the Capitol, which miraculously survived (according to the prevalent version of the legend) thanks to the heroism of its defendants and divine help.[12] The influence of the Delphi episode on Roman versions of Celtomachy is evident in a number of places. The name of the Gallic chieftain is shared by both legends (both in Rome and in Delphi Gallic hordes are led by one Brennus). Moreover, scholars find it likely that the story of the Capitol's survival, probably a later addition to the legend, received its decisive momentum under the influence of the Delphic episode, where the citadel was believed to have survived.[13] Roman generals follow in the footsteps of Hellenistic rulers in seeking to align their Gallic victories with the Delphic triumph. Thus, cauldrons are offered to Apollo at Delphi after the victory of Clastidium, and the story of the Gallic attack on Delphi is modified to accommodate the needs of Marius' Cimbric triumph.[14]

---

victory, the Athenian Parthenon (Gigantomachy and Amazonomachy featured on the metopes). On the Athens dedications, see Palma 1981 and Stewart 2004. Earlier discussions: Hansen 1971: 290 n. 147; Allen 1983: 31 n. 8; Hardie 1986: 133; Hannestad 1993.

[11] See Stewart 2000.

[12] On the sources, see Williams 2001: 142–50; Ogilvie 1965: 719. The fullest account is Livy 5.33–50. Extensive narratives also in Dion. Hal. *Ant. Rom.* 13.6 ff.; Plut. *Cam.* 15–30; Diod. 14.113–7. Cf. also Pol. 1.6.2–4; 2.18.1–4; 2.22.4–5; App. *Gall.* frr. 1.1, 2–9; *Ital.* fr. 8.2; Dio fr. 25, with Zon. 7.23; Florus 1.7.13–9; Eutr. 1.20; *De vir. ill.* 23.

[13] Ogilvie 1965: 719; Williams 2001: 165–7.

[14] On Clastidium: Plut. *Marc.* 8; Williams 2001: 165. On the Cimbric wars, see the strange version by Appian (*Ill.* 4) according to which the Cimbri and Illyrians attacked Delphi.

Romans find in this legend an important tool in shaping their relation-ship with Greeks and the other peoples of Italy: that they have been fighting against barbarians proves to the Greek world that they are not barbarians; they can also go so far as to claim for themselves the role of the defendants of Greece, casting their (Greek) enemies into the role of barbarians.[15] The Greek narrative transforms Roman accounts, but it is also transformed by them, receiving different emphasis in its new Roman contexts. In Rome Celtomachy is not simply seen as a fight of civilization and monstrosity, tyranny and freedom. Because of the symbolic value attributed to the Capitoline as a pledge of Rome's eternity, Celtomachy begins to be closely associated with Roman con-cerns about the city's survival and its identity.

The influence of the Pergamene monuments on Augustan culture has been documented by recent studies.[16] The Gallic attack against Delphi was represented on the doors of the temple of Palatine Apollo built by Augustus after his victories in the 30s BCE.[17] The metaphorical/allegorical meaning of the relief is heavily discussed, as is almost everything that pertains to the iconography of the Palatine complex. The temple was inaugurated on the occasion of Octavian's triple triumph (for the war against Illyrians, the battle of Actium, and the conquest of Alexandria). A simple, first level reading would consist of relating the imagery to Augustus' triumphs against barbarians. There is some evidence that during the time of Octavian the Illyrians had been, somewhat forcefully, linked to the Celts who attacked Delphi.[18] And Egyptians easily could be cast in the role of uncivilized barbarians. Yet very few viewers would have failed to extend the imagery to the triumph over Antony. One such attentive viewer, Virgil, clearly did not fail to do so.

Philip Hardie has drawn attention to the pervasiveness of the imagery associated with the Pergamene monuments in the works of Virgil.[19] In his ecphrasis of Aeneas' shield Virgil combines Celtomachy and Gigantoma-chy. The narrative of the battle of Actium is shot through with images of Gigantomachy, but the shield of Aeneas also displays the attack of the

---

[15] See Williams 2001: 162–4.
[16] Hardie 1986: 120–43. Marszal 2000: 218–19 lists a few adaptations of Celtomachy in the late Republic and Augustan period.
[17] Prop. 2.31.9–14.
[18] The evidence comes from Appian (*Ill.* 4), whose surprising theory that the Illyrians had played a role in the Gallic assault on Delphi is likely to be influenced by Augustan sources, perhaps even Augustus' own *Memoirs*, on which Appian based his account (Appian *Ill.* 42–3).
[19] Hardie 1986: 120–43.

Gauls on the Capitoline in 390 BCE.[20] There is a strong sense of symmetry and interconnection between the two pictures.[21] Hardie suggests that Virgil's depiction of the Gauls on Aeneas' shield – note especially the reference to their white complexion at 8.660 (*lactea colla*) – may evoke the parallel episode of the attack on Delphi as it was represented on the ivory doors of the Capitoline temple. While exploiting the imagery linked to Greek Celtomachies, Virgil is also aware of the specific connection the story had developed at Rome; the narrative of the shield of Aeneas aligns the Gallic sack of 390 BCE with the defeat of Antony at Actium.[22] That same defeat is celebrated by Octavian in the Palatine temple, on whose doors was depicted Apollo defeating the Gauls at Delphi. Thus, Antony is cast in the role of the impious barbarian who dares to assault the gods (and who is defeated by them), as in the Delphic narrative, but he also features as the Gaul who threatens to bring Rome to its final destruction, as in the legend of the Gallic sack.[23] If the Republican appropriation of Hellenistic Celtomachy had turned the story into a twin of Roman legends about the city's survival, then the Augustan appropriation takes it a step further. The story is part of Roman strategies to barbarize the enemy, as during the Republic, but this time the enemy is a Roman, not a Macedonian. Celtomachy is harnessed to consolidate the image of Antony the barbarian, thus turning civil war into a fight between civilization and chaos, freedom and tyranny. Augustan adaptations of Celtomachy contribute to configure the war as a foreign assault.

With this background information about the Pergamene Gauls in place, we can now turn to their appropriation by the Flavian entourage. After being removed from their original context and transferred to Rome, the statues from Attalus' monument on the Pergamon acropolis became part of Nero's collection in the Domus Aurea.[24] It was only the death of Nero, and the ensuing civil war of 69 CE, that created the conditions for a

---

[20] The Gallic attack on the shield of Aeneas: *Aen.* 8.659–62. The battle of Actium: *Aen.* 8.671–713. Gigantomachy and the battle of Actium: Hardie 1986: 97–110. The same combination (Gigantomachy) is employed also in the duel between Turnus and Aeneas, with Turnus cast in the role of both a Giant and a Gaul. See Hardie 1986: 118–19, 149–54.

[21] See Harrison 1997: 75.　　[22] Hardie 1986: 120–5.

[23] The destruction of Rome by the Gauls in 390 BCE was followed by a proposal to move the city to Veii, an event which, in Camillus' view in Livy, would have erased Rome's identity. Cf. Livy 5.51–4; Harrison 1997: 72–3. A design of making Alexandria the center of the Roman state was attributed to Antony (cf. Cassius Dio 50.4.1), and Augustan authors speak of Cleopatra's desire of destroying Rome (see, e.g., Horace *Od.* 1.37.6–8; Harrison 1997: 75).

[24] Pliny's passage (*HN* 34.84; quoted here) contrasts Vespasian's public dedication with Nero's previous use of the statues; this seems to suggest that there was no public access to the Pergamene Gauls in Nero's palace.

completely different exploitation of the Pergamene group. Vespasian placed the Pergamene statues within some of the monuments he erected in Rome after his victory of 69 CE, including the Templum Pacis. The evidence comes from a passage in Pliny (*HN* 34.84):

> Plures artifices fecere Attali et Eumenis adversus Gallos proelia, Isigonus, Pyromachus, Stratonicus, Antigonus, qui volumina condidit de sua arte . . . Atque ex omnibus, quae rettuli, clarissima quaeque in urbe iam sunt dicata a Vespasiano principe in templo Pacis aliisque eius operibus, violentia Neronis in urbem convecta et in sellariis domus aureae disposita.

> Several artists have represented the battles of Attalus and Eumenes against the Gauls, Isigonus, Pyromachus, Stratonicus, and Antigonus, who wrote books about his art. . . . And among the list of works I have referred to all the most celebrated have now been dedicated by the emperor Vespasian in the Temple of Peace and his other public buildings; they had been looted by Nero, who conveyed them all to Rome and arranged them in the sitting-rooms of his Golden Mansion.[25]

We do not know which other buildings hosted the statues, and we do not know exactly which of the many Attalid Gauls were displayed, but we know enough about one of the complexes in which the statues where displayed, the Templum Pacis.[26] This innovative complex, dedicated in 75 CE after Vespasian's triumph over Judaea, consisted of a large square portico encircling a temple to the goddess Peace.[27] The portico was adorned with a collection of Greek masterpieces, to which the Pergamene Gauls were added.[28] What is the point of this operation? How did viewers react to the presence of the Pergamene statues within the collection of the Templum Pacis? The question of how to read collections of Greek art in

---

[25] Trans. Rackham.

[26] It is impossible to say which of the many statues attributed to the Attalid monuments came to Rome, and from which monuments they came (the Athenian monument, or the Pergamene bases). If the text of Pliny should be corrected to read Epigonos instead of Isigonos, as many scholars believe (e.g., Michaelis 1893: 119–34; Künzl 1971: 6–7, 33–9; Wenning 1978: 1–5; Schober 1938: 137 and 1951: 67–8, with summaries in Marszal 2000: 194, 224 n. 7 and 197, 226 nn. 26–7, respectively), we can at least trace one of these statues. Elsewhere Pliny refers to a statue that has been unanimously identified with the Dying Gaul in the Capitoline Museum as a masterpiece by Epigonos (*HN* 34.88); the name of Epigonos has been found in one of the inscriptions on the statuary bases in the precinct of the Athena temple. The Dying Gaul thus comes from the bases in the Athena precinct, and since Pliny writes that the "most famous" of the works of Epigonos found its way to the Flavian collection, it is very likely that the Dying Gaul was among them. For a convenient summary and review of the scholarly debate about the Attalid statues, their attribution and location, see Marszal 2000.

[27] On the Templum Pacis see the relevant articles in Coarelli 2009: 158–201 and *LTUR* IV: 67–70 (F. Coarelli).

[28] On the collection, see Bravi 2012: 167–81, esp. 175–8 on the Pergamene Gauls.

Rome is a hotly debated topic, one that is central to investigations of Roman appropriative practices. Were these collections like modern museums, where works of art are selected especially in light of their artistic value? Or was there an ideological design governing the selection of pieces and their subject, a design connected to the specific function of the building? Different answers have been offered by different scholars, and different things will be true in the different contexts. As for the Templum Pacis, a few elements seem to suggest the presence of an "ideological" design. Other pieces in the Templum Pacis collection can be aligned with the ideological function of the building, namely the celebration of the Flavian dynasty. For instance, a massive statue of the Nile reminded the viewers of the beginnings of Vespasian's ascent to power, when in Alexandria a number of miracles, including an overflow of the Nile, announced that he had been chosen by the gods as the new emperor. Likewise, a famous painting of Alexander's victory at Issos provided an obvious parallel for the Emperor's triumph over Easterners.[29]

So, what about the Pergamene Gauls? Were they meant to evoke Vespasian's triumph in Judaea? Or perhaps the campaign by Mucianus and Domitian against the Batavian rebel Julius Civilis? The first option is ruled out by the clear ethnic characterization of the Galatae as Celts.[30] A direct reference to Julius Civilis cannot be excluded, but seems, on the balance, less probable.[31] The presence of a certain narrative centering on Celtomachy, propagated by the regime, was bound to press a different interpretation on those statues.

To make full sense of Vespasian's appropriation of the Pergamene Gauls we need to reconstruct a complex ideological narrative, which surrounded the events of 69 CE, the year of the four emperors. Here I build on the notion that the celebratory monuments erected by Vespasian, including the Templum Pacis, while nominally celebrating Vespasian's victory over Judaea, also adumbrated his more important triumph, the victory over Vitellius, through which he had restored peace to the world.[32] Vitellius was governor of Germany. Many of his soldiers were ethnically Germans and

---

[29] Bravi 2012: 170–5.

[30] In addition, as we have seen earlier, Roman appropriations of Celtomachies are associated with conflicts that can be configured as foreign invasions against Rome, which is hardly true for the Judaean campaign of Vespasian.

[31] The statues referring to Julius Civilis: Bravi 2012: 177–8. Civilis was not defeated in battle; the revolt was settled through an agreement, and no triumph was celebrated over him. Domitian and Mucianus did not even make it to the operation field (cf. Levick 1999b: 107–12).

[32] We know that the troops who defeated Vitellius participated in the triumph of 71 CE. Important evidence is the coinage. Vespasian celebrated his triumph on coins with legends such as *Libertas*

he was joined by a number of Gallic tribes. His troops behaved, indeed, like barbarians during their descent into Italy, and one of Vitellius' generals, Caecina, went so far as to appear in public dressed as a Gaul (wearing *brachae* – a traditional Gallic garment).[33] In addition, Vitellius was believed to have ignored the prohibition against performing civic duties on the day of the Allia defeat.[34] This escalation of bad portents climaxed in an episode which was seen by many as a repetition of the Gallic invasion of 390 BCE. Brennus' incursion had culminated in an attack against the Capitoline, and exactly the same occurred with Vitellius' invasion of Italy. After a fight with Vespasian's brother Sabinus and his men, Vitellius' soldiers attacked and burned the Capitol, bringing to completion what Brennus had failed to achieve in 390.[35] The parallel with the Gallic sack of 390 BCE is noted by Tacitus, who stresses that, more than anything else, this event made people believe that the end of Rome's *imperium* had arrived, for even when the city had fallen to the Gauls the Capitoline had survived intact.[36]

This presentation of Vitellius' descent into Italy as a new barbaric invasion is also reflected in contemporary poetry. The victory of 69 CE was celebrated by panegyric epic. One such poem was composed by the elder Papinius, Statius' father.[37] Statius himself briefly recalls the episode that provided the subject matter for his father's poem (Stat. *Silv.* 5.3.195–8):

> Talia dum celebras, subitam civilis Erinys
> Tarpeio de monte facem Phlegraeaque movit
> proelia. sacrilegis lucent Capitolia taedis,
> et Senonum furias Latiae sumpsere cohortes.

> Such was your occupation when the Fury of civil war sud-
> denly raised her torch from the Tarpeian mount and stirred
> battles as of Phlegra. The Capitol was alight with sacrilegious
> brands, and Latian cohorts borrowed Senonian rage.[38]

Statius' passage depicts the attack by Vitellius' soldiers as a Gallic invasion, which he associates with the Gallic incursion of 390 BCE.[39] More than this,

---

Restituta or *Adsertor Libertatis*: see Levick 1999b: 71 and 229 n. 18; *RIC* 49 no. 290; *RIC* 65 no. 411; 70 no. 45 5f. (70 and 71). He clearly boasted that he had freed Rome from slavery of the Vitellians.

[33] Tac. *Hist.* 2.20.   [34] Tac. *Hist.* 2.91.   [35] Tac. *Ann.* 3.63–74; Suet. *Dom.* 1.2; *Vit.* 15.3.

[36] Tac. *Hist.* 3.72.

[37] The elder Papinius' poem is mentioned at *Silv.* 5.3.199–202. Another poem on the subject was composed by Domitian, the future Emperor. This poem is praised by Martial as an equal of Virgil's *Aeneid*, in one of his epigrams – probably not the most sincere of his collection: Mart. 5.5.7–8. On Domitian's poem see Penwill 2000; Coleman 1986: 3089–90; Nauta 2002: 327 n. 2.

[38] Trans. Shackleton Bailey.

[39] On this passage and the elder Papinius' poem, see Gibson 2006: 343–4.

his coupling of Celtomachy and Gigantomachy is influenced by the tradition that ultimately goes back to Callimachus and the Pergamene monuments. Statius describes the Vitellians as engaging in Gigantomachic battles (*Phlegraea proelia*) and as borrowing the fury of the Senones, just as Callimachus describes the Galatae as "latter-day" Titans who raise the sword of the Celts against Greece. Statius' diction is also reminiscent of a well-known Roman rewriting of the Callimachus passage, that by Propertius in 3.13.[40] It is possible that a sustained engagement with Gigantomachy and Celtomachy featured in the elder Papinius' epic on the 69 CE civil war, which was roughly coeval with the opening of the statuary collection of the Templum Pacis.

The impact of Roman appropriations of Celtomachy is even more remarkable in Statius' major epic poem, the *Thebaid*. In the course of his epic, Statius plays on the idea of Thebes as an image of Rome. In the tenth book, these suggestions acquire a more specific poignancy, for Statius' narrative of the siege of Thebes interacts considerably with mythologized accounts of the 69 CE civil war. There is no space here for a detailed study of Statius' interactions with narratives of the Flavian victory, but a few points will suffice.[41] To begin with, the Argives' assault on Thebes is presented through a sustained engagement with the same two myths that feature in Statius' description of the 69 CE war in the *Silvae*, namely, Gigantomachy and the Gallic sack. As for the former, Gigantomachic imagery constantly surfaces in Statius' description of the attack on Thebes in Book 10. The main agent of the Argive attack, Capaneus, is compared several times to a Giant. It is sufficient to quote the first grand simile which marks the start of Capaneus' *aristeia* (*Theb.* 10.848–52):

> alterno captiva in moenia gressu
> surgit ovans: quales mediis in nubibus aether
> vidit Aloidas, cum cresceret impia tellus
> despectura deos nec adhuc inmane veniret
> Pelion et trepidum iam tangeret Ossa Tonantem

> Step upon step he rises exultant against the captive walls. So the ether saw the Aloidae amid the clouds when the impious earth was growing as though to look down upon the gods; vast Pelion was not yet come, and already Ossa touched the frightened Thunderer.[42]

More surprisingly, Statius' war is shot through with allusions to Celtomachy, a kind of imagery that is at odds with the mythical setting of his

---

[40] Prop. 3.13.51–4.   [41] See Rebeggiani, forthcoming.   [42] Trans. Shackleton Bailey.

narrative. This appears clearly in the scene that opens Statius' account of the siege of Thebes. It is worth examining it in some detail. In Book 10, the Argive heroes lay siege to Thebes. The city gates are closed with all haste, but Echion, a Theban hero, is slower than the others. Some Argives thus manage to slip in before he shuts the gate. Finding themselves trapped within the walls, they are soon overwhelmed by their opponents. Among these is a hero named Amyntor, whose death is described in some detail (*Theb.* 10.513–18):

> par operis iactura lucro, quippe hoste retento
> exclusere suos; cadit intra moenia Graius
> Ormenus, et pronas tendentis Amyntoris ulnas
> fundentisque preces penitus cervice remissa
> verba solo vultusque cadunt, colloque decorus
> torquis in hostiles cecidit per vulnus harenas.

> The labour balanced gain and loss, for keeping the enemy within they shut their comrades out. Grecian Ormenus falls inside the walls. As Amyntor stretched forth his upturned arms and poured out entreaties, his neck is cut right off, words and countenance fall to the ground, his handsome necklace dropped from his throat through the wound onto the hostile sands.[43]

At first sight, there is nothing remarkable in this scene. The passage is modeled on a similar incident from the *Aeneid*.[44] There is, however, a strange detail in Statius' picture. Amyntor, a Spartan, is wearing a *torquis* (l.518).[45] This kind of collar was known to the ancients for being an ethnic attribute of barbarians, and especially of Celts.[46] Archeological evidence shows that citizens from Gaul advertised their ethnic origin by portraying themselves wearing *torquis*-style collars, and a *torquis* is commonly the hallmark of defeated Gauls in public and private reliefs.[47] That this unnecessary detail is not just an attempt to make the picture more exotic is confirmed by the presence of an allusion to the Propertius passage which I have mentioned previously (Prop. 3.13.51–4). The use of Celtomachic imagery here, disguised under the surface of Statius' mythical narrative, is part of Statius' strategy of alluding to Roman history, and especially to the

---

[43] Trans. Shackleton Bailey.   [44] *Aen.* 9.722–7.

[45] Or *torques*, as the spelling varies: see *OLD* p. 1951 s.v. *torques*.

[46] When the term is used properly – that is, to describe a male garment – it usually refers to barbarians or Celts (or to people who have acquired it as a spoil from them). Cf., e.g., Luc. 11.409 Marx; Quad. *Hist.* 10b Peter; Hor. *Od.* 3.6.12; Prop. 4.10.44; Curt. *Hist. Alex.* 3.3.13; Val. Fl. 2.112 and D–S 5.375–8, *RE* 6A. 1800 ff. For the *torquis* as a Gallic spoil, see Liv. 24.42.8. *Torques* were conferred to Roman soldiers as military awards (cf., e.g., *CIL* 1.709.4.5; *OLD* p. 1951 s.v. *torques*); this use stems from the fact that this object was associated with victories over Celtic enemies.

[47] See D–S 5.375–8 and following text on the Dying Gaul.

most recent civil conflict of 69 CE. By assigning Gallic features to his
Argive hero Statius is able to evoke Roman narratives of barbaric threats
against the city of Rome, from the time of Brennus to that of Vitellius.
After all, Statius' portrait of this dying "Gaul," with visible *torquis* on his
neck, is virtually a textual materialization of the Dying Gaul of Pergamon
(the latter likewise wears a *torquis*) which the *Thebaid*'s readers could
admire in the Templum Pacis or some other monument erected by
Vespasian.[48]

This ideological use of Greek and Roman Celtomachic imagery to frame
Vitellius' invasion is likely to go back to Flavian sources (Pliny the Elder,
from whose *Histories* both Tacitus and Suetonius depend, is a major
suspect). A reconstruction of this narrative casts a new light on Vespasian's
appropriation of the Pergamene Gauls. The inclusion of the Pergamene
statues in the collection of the Templum Pacis conveyed a clear message:
Vespasian advocated for himself the role of Attalus. He had defeated the
sacrilegious barbarians (the Vitellians) who attacked the seat of Jupiter (the
Capitoline), just like Attalus defeated the Gauls who attacked Apollo's
temple in Delphi. The effect of the strategy was grand. The statues
impressed for their aesthetic power and worldwide fame, but they also
immensely increased Vespasian's prestige by aligning him with a glorious
Greek tradition of battles for freedom. He appeared as the last representative in a tradition that went back to Greece's wars against Persians and
Gauls. He also relied on the tendency in both Republican and Augustan
receptions of Greek Celtomachies to align the Gallic sack of Rome with
the Delphic invasion of the Gauls. The Gallic invasion had nearly marked
the destruction of Rome, yet the city had survived and rose stronger from
its ashes. Thus, Vespasian could advertise his *Roma Resurgens* on his
coinage and style himself as a new Camillus, the man who rescued the
city from the Gallic threat and inaugurated a new phase of Rome's
history.[49]

The use of the Pergamene Gauls also forged a connection between the
Templum Pacis and the temple of Palatine Apollo. Both temples had been

---

[48] This tactic of connecting the mythical narrative to the historical context through a well-calculated
use of names and identities of otherwise irrelevant characters should not surprise readers of Statius,
who are familiar with similar strategies employed by Statius' foremost model, Virgil. See, e.g., Reed
1998.

[49] Cf. for instance *RIC*[2] I, 109, p. 67: reverse with the personification of Roma, kneeling, raised by
Vespasian, with the legend ROMA RESURGE(N)S. Images of prosperity and the return of
Fortune: *RIC*[2] I, 1, p. 59; 33–4 and 36, p. 61; 62, p. 64. References to the Romulus legend and
the foundation of Rome: *RIC*[2] 960–2, p. 128 she-wolf with the twins (struck under the name of
Domitian).

erected after the new emperor's success in civil war; both also commemorated victories against foreigners. Octavian's temple featured the Gauls on
its doors, whereas Vespasian could impress his spectators even more by
displaying the original statues from Pergamon. Vespasian's use of Celtomachy clearly recuperated an element which had been typical of Augustan
receptions of Pergamene imagery, namely using this paradigm to make the
enemy into a barbarian, thus reframing civil war as a foreign conflict. It
was part of a strategy of turning Vitellius into a barbarian, so as to allow
celebration of that victory without evoking the scandal of civil war. I am
inclined to think that Vespasian and his entourage would have been
sensitive to the potential inherent in the display of these statues, and that
their public display, coinciding, it is reasonable to think, with the opening
of the Templum Pacis was designed as an emphatic gesture. However, my
main contention is that, regardless of the original intention behind the
display of the Pergamene Gauls, the long story of reception of Celtomachies in Roman culture, which we have outlined, would have informed the
reading of these pieces of art in their new context. The viewer's own
experience of earlier, ideologically charged appropriations of Celtomachy,
both literary and monumental, was bound to affect the most recent
reactions to these figures in their new space.

This chapter has examined the appropriation of the Pergamene monuments in Flavian culture. It began by highlighting the historical importance of the Pergamene statues and the events with which they were
associated, namely Hellenistic triumphs over Gauls. It then sketched a
history of their reception in Rome, both in Republican culture and during
the Augustan period. In Roman culture the story tends to be regarded as
an equivalent of the Gallic sack of Rome of 390 BCE; hence it becomes a
battle for the survival of Rome. During the Augustan period, Celtomachy
becomes associated with strategies of barbarizing the enemy in the context
of civil war. These shifts in meaning are documented by the different
contexts, both literary and monumental, in which Celtomachy appears. All
these earlier appropriations contribute to shape viewers' responses to
Vespasian's appropriation of Pergamene monuments, which are best
understood in the context of the Flavian strategy of recontextualizing the
civil conflict with Vitellius, as well as forging a connection with other
genetic moments in Roman history, such as Augustus' Principate and
Camillus' second foundation of Rome.

CHAPTER 5

Interactions: Microhistory as Cultural History

Matthew P. Loar

As stated at the outset, one of this volume's primary objectives is to identify some of the significant points of contact between Roman literary and material appropriative practices. The preceding four chapters have done just that, offering a series of examples in which literature is simultaneously the nexus for various modes of Roman appropriation – plunder, spoliation, and reuse – and a proxy for the very activities that it narrates. Literature, in other words, alternately names, reifies, and becomes cargo; it is both an integral ancillary to the physical relocation of appropriated objects and an appropriated object in its own right. In what follows, I will recapitulate the highlights from each of the four chapters, drawing out their major themes and identifying those places where the chapters can further our understanding of the relationship between literary and material appropriative practices. I will conclude with some thoughts on the directions these chapters might encourage us to pursue in future work.

Basil Dufallo opens the section by attempting to raise class consciousness, explicating the identity politics at work in Plautus' *Menaechmi*. Dufallo shows how the play, both by its subject matter and performance context, already reflects an acute self-awareness about the overlap between Roman literary and material appropriative practices. Key to this argument are the abundant knowing nods underlying the play: it is a *fabula palliata* in which the comedy hinges on the exchange of a *palla*, a story about loss that is set in the city of loss (Epidamnus), and a tale of transaction that is itself a kind of transaction – a dialogue between actors and audience. Even the first lines of the play's prologue hint at this self-awareness, as the speaker teasingly tells the assembled crowd, "I bring you Plautus – with my tongue, not my hand!" (*apporto vobis Plautum, lingua non manu*, Pr. 3). The joke is a groaner, something of a paraprosdokian, and yet it works precisely because, as Amy Richlin argues later in her contribution to this volume, it is entirely possible that the person of Plautus, and not simply his

82

words, could be paraded onstage.[1] Indeed, in relating the comedy's backs-tory only a few lines later, the narrator reveals that the transport of human cargo – the [commodified] Menaechmus twin who, as a child, had been loaded onto a merchant ship by his father (*imponit geminum alterum in navim pater*, Pr. 26) – actually is the subject of the play. Whether by *lingua* or *manus*, for the comedy's purposes the display of cargo is the same. From the very start, then, the play presents itself as a literary performance that simultaneously narrates and tropes material appropriation; it represents, in other words, both text-about-cargo and text-as-cargo.

All of this gains greater significance from the play's historical context. Written in the aftermath of major Roman victories during the Second Punic War, it offers something of a commentary on the mass influx of foreign wealth and *spolia* into Rome and other Roman cities that those victories precipitated and hastened. By drawing out the historical condi-tions influencing the play's composition, and by relating these conditions to the identity politics already at work, Dufallo ultimately reads the play as a performance intended to visualize and dramatize Romans' (and non-Romans') efforts to navigate their own sense of identity in a heterogenous Mediterranean world that was more and more bearing the marks of Roman intervention.[2]

Most significantly for this volume's aims, Dufallo untangles this wider web of cultural interactions by tracking the movement of a single displaced object throughout the play: the *palla*, a non-Roman garment whose use and exchange both facilitates and models the dynamics of material appro-priation. The *palla* is the disguise by which the first Menaechmus presents himself as cargo, it is described as itself a kind of cargo, and then at the end it becomes cargo – an object to be sold for material profit. This strikes me as one of the real contributions of Dufallo's piece, namely that something as small and quotidian as an item of clothing can come to embody and instantiate the larger mechanisms of Roman cultural appropriation. Duf-fallo's own concise summary bears repeating: "from plunder to merchan-dise to cultural model: such is the varying fate of cargo" (p. 26).

---

[1] Indeed, *apporto* can refer either to the movement of goods (*TLL* 2.0.304.22–53) or the delivery of words (*TLL* 2.0.304.54–70) or people (*TLL* 2.0.304.71–4). One could also think of the homology between text and author that prevailed in ancient Greek and Roman literature, as in, e.g., Plat. *Phaedr.* 228d–e, where Socrates implores Phaedrus not to pretend to "remember" Lysias' speech when he has Lysias with him – a reference to the text that Phaedrus carries beneath his cloak.

[2] On local communities negotiating the influence of Roman expansion on their own sense of identity, see the essays in Galinsky & Lapatin 2016, esp. by Noreña, Elsner, Kamash, and Jiménez.

The transmutation of cargo from plunder into model likewise lies at the center of Ayelet Haimson Lushkov's discussion of Livy's spoliated citations in the *AUC*. Picking up from Dufallo's reading of Plautus' *Menaechmi* as both a text-about-cargo and a text-as-cargo, Haimson Lushkov identifies a similar phenomenon in Livy: the historian effectively treats other authors' literary accounts of *spolia* in the aftermath of battle as if they too were *spolia*. Source texts about Roman plunder are thus assimilated to the actual plunder they enumerate. Haimson Lushkov extrapolates from this a parallelism between the processes of empire and Livy's place within the historiographic tradition. In other words, Livy's brief citations speak to broader historical trends, providing a model for understanding the larger dynamics of Roman appropriation: "Rome became a museum of pillaged art, Livy of pillaged sources" (p. 31).

The same semantic realignment that accompanies the act of material appropriation is therefore also at work in Livy's appropriation of other historical works. Livy is not, however, adopting other historians' work *tout court*; instead, he fragments and decontextualizes his sources – an activity not at all unlike the movement of physical *spolia* from one location to another. By removing his sources from their respective works, Livy makes subject to debate texts that once presumably carried the weight of authority and historical accuracy in their original literary contexts. In effect, he constructs for his pillaged sources not only new frameworks of interpretation, but also new networks of transmission, tying their circulation to his own: where Livy goes, so go his citations. The aftershocks of Livy's approach are felt even today, as many ancient historians' works are known chiefly through the relics preserved in Livy's history. Haimson Lushkov's chapter ultimately underscores the close relationship between fragmentation and preservation, an idea that gets taken up more fully at the end of the volume by Micah Myers in his discussion of the Gallus papyrus.

With the third chapter in this opening part, Thomas Biggs transitions from spoliated citations to another type of Augustan appropriation-cum-reuse: Octavian's imitation of C. Duilius' rostral column in commemorating his own naval victory – though not over Antony at Actium, as became the consensus among the ancients, but rather over Sextus Pompey at Naulochus. Biggs is quick to point out that this architectural borrowing is only one piece in a larger effort by Octavian to recast himself, if not as a second Duilius, then at least as an inheritor of the Punic War tradition. Octavian also renovated Duilius' Temple of Janus in the Forum Holitorium, and he included Duilius among the gallery of *summi viri* encircling the Forum Augustum.[3] By reclaiming the memory of Duilius, Biggs proposes, Octavian attempted to rebrand his civil war victories as conquests over foreign foes.

It is a testament to the power of literature and the literary tradition that Biggs must "correct" the ancients and remind us that Octavian's rostral column celebrated his victory over Sextus Pompey at Naulochus and not over Antony at Actium. After all, as Biggs shows, later literary receptions of Octavian's naval victory and rostral column – including the *Res Gestae* itself – tend to elide the distinction between the two battles, giving Actium pride of place. The misreading of the column's significance in literature points up the primacy of text in dictating the terms of an object's reception: whereas physical *spolia* can still signify their original context (what Biggs, borrowing from Richard Brilliant's terminology, labels *spolia in se*), textual "appropriations" (labeled conversely as *spolia in re*) can fully efface that context, assimilating one monument into the dominant discourse tied up in others.[4] Indeed, what Biggs' piece makes absolutely clear is that literature creates (oftentimes *ex post facto*) the conceptual framework necessary for making sense of cargo in its new context. Critically, this is not to say that literature always makes sense of cargo in "historically correct" ways; sometimes literature misreads cargo, falsifying its semantic pedigree. Thus Octavian's naval monument comes to commemorate his victory over Actium, not Naulochus. Ideology – in this case, the prominence of the Augustus-as-vanquisher-of-Antony narrative – trumps reality.

At the same time, the fact that the literary reception of Octavian's monumental repurposing subordinates Naulochus to Actium raises a second issue about the historical development of appropriation in the Roman world. The rotating patterns of Republican office-holding meant that Duilius' naval monument, constructed to commemorate his victory at Mylae during his consulship in 260 BCE, was – and could only be seen as – a one-off dedication.[5] Subsequent years would witness subsequent consuls guiding subsequent victories, and so Octavian's later adoption of Duilius' monument as a model could only ever link Octavian to a single, specific historical moment: Duilius' naval triumph. Octavian's new monument, however, was not bound by such semiotic fixity. Thanks in large part to Augustus' decades-long reign, the original meaning of monuments could evolve, adapting to suit historical exigencies. Literature, then, may

---

[3] See Gros 1976 on Augustus' temple restorations. On Augustus' efforts to position himself within the Republican triumphal tradition through the gallery of *summi viri*, see Itgenshorst 2004; cf. Loar 2017.
[4] Brilliant 1982.   [5] I must thank Dan-el Padilla Peralta for calling my attention to this.

simply be complicit in the long process of writing and rewriting monumental significations – a reflection, and not a dictator of larger cultural narratives.

The centrality of literature to understanding material appropriation – and the fluid meanings attached to such appropriations during the Imperial period – likewise defines Stefano Rebeggiani's contribution to the volume, which draws attention to the migrations of the Pergamene Galatae over the span of a few centuries. As with Biggs' chapter, however, the new significations of the Galatae remain inaccessible without considering complementary literary evidence. As such, Rebeggiani's chapter does much more than simply track the movement of statues. It traces the migration of Celtomachic tropes from Callimachus' *Hymn to Delos* to Vergil's *Aeneid* to Statius' *Thebaid*,[6] from the decoration on the Athenian Acropolis to the Roman Palatine to the Templum Pacis, from historical accounts of the assault on Delphi to those of the assaults on Rome – not only by the Gauls, but also by the legions of Vitellius. Additionally, the chapter illuminates the movement of the Pergamene Galatae from Attalus' monument on the Pergamon acropolis to Nero's Domus Aurea, and eventually to Vespasian's Templum Pacis.

In this neat bit of detective work, Rebeggiani carefully details how the wayward path of the Galatae from Pergamon to Rome mirrors and accompanies the movement across the Mediterranean of Celtomachy (and Gigantomachy) as a literary and visual leitmotif. And it is only by recognizing how deeply imbricated these material and literary appropriations are that Rebeggiani is able to draw out the statues' significance in their new context, namely within their display in the Templum Pacis: as a commemoration of Vespasian's victory over Vitellius in 69 CE. More to the point, even if Vespasian did not explicitly intend this connection, Rebeggiani argues, the long history of Roman cultural appropriation that preceded the arrival of the Galatae – specifically the incorporation of Celtomachy into Roman literary and visual culture – creates the conditions for such an interpretation. The assimilation of Greek cultural narratives (Celtomachy and Gigantomachy), Greek texts (Callimachus' *Hymn to Delos*), and Greek artifacts (the Pergamene Galatae) into Roman literary and visual culture thus nicely crystallizes the overarching theme of the volume's first section: the changing symbolism of the Galatae does not

---

[6] See Stephens 2003: 114–21 on a reading of Callimachus' *Hymn to Delos* within the context of the Ptolemaic court – an important point since both the *Aeneid* and the *Thebaid* can be construed as Roman court poetry.

make sense without the literary and historical armature that originally attended their arrival in Rome. Concomitant or prior literary appropriations are just as, if not more, important than their material counterparts.

To conclude, there are three larger points that I want to make about these four chapters. First, each chapter accomplishes its aims by tracing the "microhistories" of appropriated texts or objects: Duffalo's contested *palla*, Haimson Lushkov's literary *spolia* (historical fragments that I would call, tongue–in–cheek, "microhistories"), Biggs's rostral column, and Rebeggiani's Pergamene Galatae (and accompanying narratives of Celtomachy). And in all four cases, the cargo at the heart of the investigation has a way of synecdochically representing – or at least touching on – the larger processes of empire and expansion. This is one of the defining features of microhistory, according to Jill Lepore: "however singular [an object's life history] may be, the value of examining it lies not in its uniqueness, but in its exemplariness, in how that [object's] life serves as an allegory for broader issues affecting the culture as a whole."[7] Thinking through microhistory, then, entails turning our focus away from the riches of plunder to culture itself.[8]

By writing these microhistories, all four chapters raise in some form or fashion questions of naturalization and assimilation: what are the mechanisms for incorporating cargo into Roman culture, and does this cargo ever cease to show remnants of its pre-appropriated existence? These questions loom largest in the following section of the volume, particularly in the chapters by Marden Fitzpatrick Nichols and Grant Parker, but some tentative answers already emerge from this first section. On the one hand, the cargo that Duffalo and Haimson Lushkov consider are never actually stripped of their original meaning; there is no attempt to fully assimilate the appropriated items into a new symbolic system, and so they still signify their manifest alterity. The *palla* remains marked as a non-Roman garment used by a non-Roman individual to imitate similarly non-Roman

---

[7] Lepore 2001: 133. Lepore is writing about the similarities and dissimilarities between biography and microhistory. The original quote begins, "however singular a person's life may be," with the final clause opening, "in how that person's life ..." This is what Lepore calls "proposition 1" in her distinctions between biography and microhistory. "Proposition 2" likewise points to microhistory's value for understanding larger cultural trends: "microhistorians, tracing their elusive subjects through slender records, tend to address themselves to solving small mysteries, in the process of which a microhistorian *may* recapitulate the subject's entire life story, though that is not his primary purpose. *The life story, like the mystery, is merely the means to an end – and that end is always explaining the culture*" (133, emphasis mine).

[8] On the importance of this distinction to discussions of "cultural mobility," see Greenblatt 2009: esp. 7–11.

paintings, and this is one reason why it serves so effectively as an index of identity in flux. Livy's spoliated citations, though inserted into a new context, nonetheless often retain the names of their original authors, ensuring that they never become fully Livy's. The point, in fact, is for the citations to maintain their original authorial associations so that Livy can either assert his own historiographic superiority (in cases where he finds other accounts beyond belief), or at least avoid intervention (in cases where the facts are so in doubt that Livy would prefer to stay out of it: *adeo nullus mentiendi modus est*, 26.49.4). Meaning, in other words, can and should still be contested, which is why Livy takes such care to chronicle the competing accounts and, in some cases, name the authors of those accounts (*auctorem pro re posui*, 45.43.8).

Biggs and Rebeggiani, on the other hand, describe the opposite phenomenon: imperial figures (Octavian and Vespasian) take previously appropriated non-Roman objects that have already been integrated into Roman culture – Duilius' column of captured Carthaginian rams and the Pergamene Galatae – and reappropriate them for new purposes. As such, both chapters treat objects that had already acquired new meaning in their adopted Roman context, and so the reappropriations of these objects cement their naturalization within Roman culture. Nevertheless, in both cases the objects have been naturalized in unnatural ways, which is to say that the objects have been endowed with significations at odds with their original appropriation. Roman authors assimilated Octavian's imitation of Duilius' column into an ideological discourse inconsistent with its original intended meaning. Likewise, Vespasian's repurposing of the Pergamene Galatae relied on an anachronistic historical parallel already evident in the Augustan period: the Roman borrowing of the third-century BCE Gallic attack on Delphi as a way of understanding the fourth-century BCE Gallic attack on Rome. In other words, Vespasian can only use the Galatae as a marker of his victory over Vitellius' barbarism because the Galatae already had acquired strong Roman significations.

Lurking beneath the surface of the last three chapters is a third theme that warrants brief consideration: time. Rebeggiani's chapter in particular should encourage us to think laterally to the broader Roman impulse for historical synchronization. As Denis Feeney has shown, Roman authors gradually developed a tendency to chart Rome's past and present onto "Panhellenic grids of time."[9] Such synchronizations not only enabled Rome to put notable events from its own history in line with the Greek past, but it also

---

[9] Feeney 2007: 4, with analysis of this synchronization in chapters 1 and 2.

gave Romans a way of dating that was reminiscent of the Hellenistic habit of counting down from significant points in time, thereby circumventing the rigidity (and banality) of consular dating. As Greek history merges with Roman history, as Greek historical frameworks become Roman historical frameworks, Rome reorients and re-centers Mediterranean history around itself.

On the topic of time, it should come as no surprise that all four chapters treat in some way material relating to the third and second centuries BCE. Nor should it be surprising that, with the exception of Rebeggiani's contribution, the chapters all pinpoint, implicitly or explicitly, the first two Punic Wars as turning points in the development of Rome's appropriative impulse. After all, this is the period singled out by ancient Roman authors themselves as the watershed moment in Rome's engagement with, and importation of the corrupting influence of Greek culture.[10] This is also the moment at which a Latin literary tradition finally begins to emerge, which might make us wonder whether the [material] appropriative impulse is synchronous with the emergence of Latin literature.[11] Such coincidence certainly explains the interrelationship of literary and material appropriative practices, and especially the indispensability of literary narratives to making sense of material appropriation.

This final point brings us back to the remit of the volume's first section, namely to identify some of the significant points of contact between Roman literary and material appropriative practices. This set of chapters shows that literary and material appropriative practices do not simply interact, but rather are interdependent, with each critical to understanding the other. Whether through the performance of Plautine comedy, the citation of historical sources, the imitation of Republican monuments, or the movement of Pergamene statues, Roman appropriation proves itself to be a multimodal and multimedia operation.

---

[10] E.g., Hor. *Ep.* 2.1.156–57 (*Graecia capta ferum victorem cepit*), though Nenci 1978 argues that these lines may refer instead to Mummius' sack of Corinth in 146 BCE.
[11] On this question, see Feeney 2016.

PART II

Distortion

CHAPTER 6

Plunder, Knowledge, and Authorship in *Vitruvius'* De Architectura

Marden Fitzpatrick Nichols

The preface to the first book of Vitruvius' *De architectura* identifies Augustus' building program as the impetus for the treatise.[1] The author dedicates his work to the emperor *ut eas adtendens et ante facta et futura qualia sint opera per te posses nota habere* ("so that laying out both how these works were made before and how they will be [made] in the future, you might be able to inform yourself," 1.praef.3). The contents that follow, however, fall short of expectations: absent are many architectural features we now consider most distinctively Roman during the period of *De architectura's* composition (ca. 20s BCE).[2] Instead of describing native Roman conventions, Vitruvius catalogues monuments and forms around the Mediterranean. He interweaves technical descriptions with symbolic, and often fantastical, narratives set in the East. This chapter argues that Vitruvius' recurrent and varied engagement with Greek culture neither conflicts with, nor detracts from, the author's presentation of a Roman world. In fact, such recourse to Greek *exempla* is essential to his literary project.

I propose that *De architectura's* claim to relevance within its own time and architectural milieu relies on a definition of Romanness as self-consciously composite, distinguished not only by its absorption of foreign

---

[1] *De arch.* 1.praef.3: *haec tibi scribere coepi; quod animadverti multa te aedificavisse et nunc aedificare* ("I began to write these things for you; because I observed that you have built, and are now building, many things"). Unless otherwise noted, all Latin quotations are from Vitruvius' *De architectura*. I follow the Budé editions. Translations are my own. For insightful comments and good conversation, I am grateful to Catherine Keesling, Charles McNelis, Mika Natif, Carey Seal, Alexander Sens, Michelle C. Wang, and Katherine Wasdin, as well as to the editors and anonymous readers of this volume. This material is explored at greater length in my forthcoming book, *Roman Author and Audience in Vitruvius'* De architectura (Cambridge University Press).

[2] On the date and authorship of the treatise, see Baldwin 1990. Vitruvius mentions major Roman innovations such as the amphitheater fleetingly (1.7.1) and has little interest in the possibilities of vaults and domes. Cf. Wallace-Hadrill 2008: 144.

elements, but also by enduring preservation of their disparate origins.[3] Vitruvius' expansive approach to the topic of architecture reflects his participation in the late Republican intellectual and literary project – shared among Varro, Cicero, Lucretius, and others – of reconceiving Greek knowledge in Roman terms.[4] Andrew Wallace-Hadrill has shown how in setting up dichotomies between "Greek" and "Roman" practice, Vitruvius builds Roman identity through and against the Greek.[5] I will argue here that the Greek world functions not only as a distant other, but also as a part of the recently expanded, heterogeneous whole of the Roman Empire. After all, *De architectura*'s first sentence pins the treatise's *kairos* to the end, in some sense, of a non-Roman world: *Cum divina tua mens et numen, Imperator Caesar, imperio potiretur orbis terrarum* ("When your mind and divine spirit, Imperator Caesar [i.e., Augustus], were taking hold of an empire of the entire world"), Vitruvius did not dare (*non audebam*) to present *De architectura* to its dedicatee (1.praef.1).[6] In this variation on the trope of hesitation to approach a ruler-reader, the moment for circulating a *corpus* of architecture composed of elements from across the known world is precisely the moment when Rome and the world occupy the same space.[7]

Vitruvius refers not only to the buildings, topography, and inventions of faraway lands, but also to the spoils of war and privileges of empire through which Rome fed its appetite for the treasures of the Eastern Mediterranean. Scholarship on the Roman recontextualization of such *aliena* in houses, temples, and public spaces has argued that their presence evoked varying reactions: statues, paintings, and other precious materials

---

[3] See now Feeney 2016 on the uniqueness of Rome's appropriative relationship to Greek literature and culture. Cf. also the complementary model of Roman religion in Feeney 1998.

[4] *Architectura*, by Vitruvius' definition, extends beyond construction to encompass sources of water (Book 8), the heavens (Book 9), and machines of war (Book 10). On *De architectura*'s intellectual context, see Rawson 1985; Romano 1987; Schrijvers 1989; Gros 1997; Wallace-Hadrill 2008: 144–210; Courrént 2011; Cuomo 2011. Vitruvius names Lucretius, Varro, and Cicero as Roman literary models (9.praef.17).

[5] Wallace-Hadrill 2008. In my use of the term "Greek," I follow Vitruvius' own application of the descriptor *Graecus*. In *De architectura*, this label characterizes not only the language from which the author translates technical terms, but also the peoples in various parts of the Greek-speaking world (e.g., Corinth or Ephesus). We should be wary of imposing our own scholarly interest in cultural differences across the Mediterranean on an author who derives meaning from the concept of a homogeneous "Greek" culture.

[6] This anticipates Augustus' *Res Gestae*, in which "the empire was a world, almost a new world which had been discovered, explored, and mastered" (Nicolet 1991: 24). Given Vitruvius' claim to have had a military role in this conquest (1.praef.2), we may also assume that the cessation of war was an appropriate moment for him as well.

[7] See, e.g., Hor. *Epist.* 2.1.1–4; *Epist.* 1.13.1–5. See König 2009; Nichols 2009: 111–13. On Vitruvius' use of the word *corpus*, e.g., at 1.1.12, see McEwen 2003; Oksanish [forthcoming].

displayed as a "hegemonic visual discourse throughout the city" could also provide "embarrassing demonstrations of Roman artistic inferiority."[8] Vitruvius makes an important contribution to our understanding of Rome's aesthetic eclecticism in the first century BCE by configuring a world in which transplanted objects are not merely by-products of empire or triumphal showpieces. Rather, they represent attempts to preserve the *memoria* of the Greek East and to promote Rome as heir to the achievements of the Mediterranean world. The result, to borrow a phrase from Grant Parker, is a "colonization of time."[9]

Vitruvius' approach to conquest and plunder relates productively to his attitude toward literary models, elaborated most extensively in the preface to Book 7.[10] This preface, often read as a denunciation of plagiarism, touts the author's memorialization – and repurposing – of Greek textual sources. Through a thinly veiled analogy, Vitruvius compares his authorial accomplishment to the intellectual feat of the Hellenistic librarian Aristophanes of Byzantium, who is able to recognize any *volumen* by its recited excerpt. In so doing, Vitruvius advocates that Rome import the model of the library of Alexandria and its associated literary activities.[11] Knowledge of the canon is as important to Vitruvius as his creation of a novel and perfect work; *De architectura* is unabashedly derivative. Harsh words against literary *furtum*, however, argue for the importance of preserving and acknowledging the identities of past creators. Roman culture, for Vitruvius, is continuous with and retentive of the Greek past.

This chapter explores three figures whom Vitruvius identifies as key actors within Rome's culture of appropriation: the architect, the author, and the general. I trace similarities across the approaches to plunder and knowledge that Vitruvius outlines for each. The architect, master of military machinery, constructs and destructs engines of war; steeped in *historia*, he also creates monuments that configure Roman identity through reference to a larger Mediterranean past and ensures, through acts of explication, that these references are preserved. The author both imports a Greek canon, which becomes the font of Roman textual production, and retains the memory of authors within this canon through the act of inscribing their names within new compositions. The general, having

---

[8] For quotations, see Rutledge 2012: 29; Edwards 2003: 54. See also Gruen 1992; Edwards 2003; Welch 2006; Miles 2008; Rutledge 2012, *inter alia*.

[9] See Grant Parker's chapter in this volume. See also Jennifer Trimble's chapter on the Ara Pacis as a construction of Rome as heir to Egypt.

[10] On the intersection of these issues in late antiquity, cf. Hansen 2003.   [11] Tomlinson 1989: 71.

conquered and plundered, transforms the city of Rome into a repository of transplanted knowledge by erecting monuments that highlight the brilliance and strangeness of Greek achievements.

In his approach to texts as well as objects, then, Vitruvius suggests that Romanness is a dynamic concept, which involves both a continual pulling in of divergent materials from across the empire and the persistent recognition of the origins of these materials. As Robert Nelson reminds us, however, acts of appropriation are subject to entropy.[12] If transferred passages and objects lose their otherness, Roman culture loses its self-definition as variegated and appropriative. Vitruvius' authorial personae and his text perform crucial roles in protecting a completed empire against cultural stagnation.

The Architect

Architectura, for Vitruvius, encompasses not only public and private building projects, but also the manufacture of war machines. In the opening paragraphs of the treatise, he claims to have been responsible for the construction and repair of military engines and artillery under Julius Caesar (1.praef.2).[13] This conspicuous reference to his own contribution to imperial expansion underscores the close relationship between the project of empire and Vitruvius' literary program. Moreover, in Book 10, dedicated to armaments, he relates the parable of Diognetus, an *architectus* at Rhodes with a similar remit (10.16.3–8). The people of Rhodes, easily impressed by a charlatan named Callias and his flashy presentation of grand designs, transfer Diognetus' salary to Callias (10.16.3). The foolish Rhodians later regret such disloyalty, however, when it becomes apparent that the contraption that Callias has built to destroy the approaching siege engine (*helepolis*) of Demetrius Poliorcetes is ineffective.[14] In a series of events unattested in other accounts of Demetrius' siege of Rhodes, only Diognetus can save the city from destruction.[15] Diognetus agrees to help the Rhodians, on the condition

[12] Nelson 2003.

[13] On Vitruvius' career as a *scriba armamentarius*, see Purcell 1983: 156; Baldwin 1990: 431–3; Masterson 2004: 390–2; Nichols 2009; Cuomo 2011.

[14] The context for this anecdote must be Demetrius Poliorcetes' siege of Rhodes in 304 BCE, described in Diod. Sic. 20.82ff; Plut. *Demetr.* 21–2. Cf. Callebat & Fleury 1986 *ad loc*; Roby 2016: 107–8. Neither Diognetus nor Callias is attested elsewhere.

[15] In *De architectura*, architects are not the only intellectuals who offer rulers invaluable insights. On Vitruvius' characterization of Archimedes' discovery of the *furtum* of precious materials from Hieron's crown (9.praef.9–12) as a "challenge to aristocratic values," see Jaeger 2008: 18–31.

that the engine of war he captures be given to him. Diognetus stops the siege engine in its tracks by diverting an enormous amount of water, mud, and refuse out of the city; the machine is caught in the mire.

In the first book, Vitruvius likens the mastery of theory and practice to the wearing of armor (1.1.2): *At qui utrumque perdidicerunt, uti omnibus armis ornati, citius cum auctoritate quod fuit propositum sunt adsecuti* ("But those who have mastered both [manual skill as well as literature and theory], like men equipped in full armor, have achieved their goal more quickly, and with authority").[16] In the tenth book, he shows that intellectual prowess generates its own kind of *manubiae*: after Diognetus defeats the *helepolis*, the people heap *honores* and *ornamenta* upon him; he assumes the persona of a general.[17] Diognetus returns the *helepolis* to the people, setting it up in public space with an inscription: DIOGNETUS E MANUBIIS ID POPULO DEDIT MUNUS ("Diognetus gave this gift to the people from the general's share of the plunder," 10.16.8).[18] Such dependence on the unequivocally Roman concepts of *munus* and *manubiae* confirms that this inscription is no translation from the Greek.[19] By couching the consequences of Greek victory in Roman terms, Vitruvius produces a Greek precedent for his portrayal of the high-status, powerful architect, who not only behaves like a general, but also is supplicated like a patron (10.16.7).[20] The ending Vitruvius provides differs greatly from Pliny the Elder's: Pliny claims that Demetrius left his war machinery behind, which the Rhodians then sold, using the profits toward their Colossus (Plin. *HN* 34.41). Demetrius supposedly received the name of Poliorcetes ("the Besieger") because his inventiveness exceeded that of a master builder (Diod. Sic. 20.92). Vitruvius confronts and upends that tradition. In his retelling, the architect not only is general-like in his mastery of strategy, but also receives the credit and honors that are a general's due.

Vitruvius elaborates on the role of the architect in creating and interpreting war monuments midway through his description of the architect's

---

[16] The only other occasion where Vitruvius refers to *arma* is 6.1.10, in which Northern peoples *ad armorum vehementiam paratiores sunt* ("are more prepared for the fervency of battle").

[17] Vitruvius likewise dedicates his ninth preface to demonstrating that writers like himself are just as deserving of *honores* as athletes, see Fögen 2009: 126.

[18] Grant Parker's chapter in this volume discusses the epigraphic dedication of obelisks as *munera*.

[19] Vitruvius self-aggrandizes in a similar manner when he refers to his treatise as a *munus omnibus gentibus non ingratum* ("gift thankfully received by all peoples") (6.praef.7). Definitions of *manubiae* and *praeda* are a vexed issue, cf. Orlin 2002: 117–22. Gellius, for example, considers them a unity (Gell. *NA* 13.25).

[20] Cf. Gros 1983.

education (1.1). *Architecti* must be familiar with *historiae* in order to provide the *rationes* for architectural *ornamenta* (1.1.5):[21]

> Historias autem plures novisse oportet quod multa ornamenta saepe in operibus architecti designant de quibus argumentis rationem cur fecerint quaerentibus reddere debent.

> [The architect] must acquaint himself with a great amount of history, for architects often design many ornamental features within their works, of which they must be able to give a reasoned account, to those who ask why they made them.

Architects, in other words, read *historiae* not only to enrich the composition of their *commentarii*, but also to serve as vessels and conduits of knowledge in a world beyond the text.[22] The built environment is replete with encoded architectural messages, legible only to the educated architect. Vitruvius proves his point using the example of sculptures of conquered people in postures of submission (1.1.5):

> Quemadmodum si quis statuas marmoreas muliebres stolatas, quae caryatides dicuntur, pro columnis in opere statuerit et insuper mutulos et coronas conlocaverit, percontantibus ita reddet rationem.

> For example, if anyone erects marble statues of robed women, which are called caryatids, instead of columns on his buildings, and places mutules and crowning members above them, this is how he will explain them to inquirers.

The Peloponnesian city of Carya, Vitruvius explains, sided with Persia against Greece.[23] The victorious *Graeci* took revenge on Carya. Not content merely to slaughter the Caryan men and enslave their women (*uti non una triumpho ducerentur* ["so that they might not be led in only one triumph"]), the betrayed Greeks immortalized their degradation of the Caryan women in stone, as an *aeterno servitutis exemplo* ("eternal reminder of slavery," 1.1.5).

By Vitruvius' day, monuments incorporating this type of imagery, including Pompey's theater complex, with its personifications of the fourteen nations he had conquered, had become visible reminders of

---

[21] On Vitruvius' conception of *historia*, see Romano 2011; Oksanish 2016. *Ratio* is the second most common noun (after *pars*) in *De architectura*; its frequency (331 instances) speaks to the importance of ordering and reason to Vitruvius' literary project.

[22] See also Fleury 1990: 94–5; McEwen 2003: 17–31; Romano 2011; Oksanish 2016; Oksanish [forthcoming] on Vitruvius' engagement with the genre of *commentarii*.

[23] Elisa Romano links Vitruvius' etiological and etymological impulses with Varro's. Cf. Romano 2011: 190–3. See also Wallace-Hadrill 2008: 150–1.

Roman conquest within the cityscape.[24] As Catharine Edwards explains, "these powerful alien bodies were frozen in perpetual submission as a permanent reminder of Roman superiority."[25] According to Servius, Augustus also created a portico referred to as *Ad Nationes*, which included personifications of the conquered (Serv. *A.* 8.721).[26] Although this structure and its figures of the *gentes* have not survived, the tradition of such imagery is well-attested in later Roman sculpture, particularly reliefs.[27] Burkhardt Wesenberg offers the tantalizing suggestion that Vitruvius includes this story as a nod to Augustus' construction of his Forum, with its rows of caryatids replicating those of the Erechtheion in Athens, and that Vitruvius situates the narrative in Periclean Athens in order to strengthen the connections Augustus was making between that golden age and his own.[28] Kristina Milnor, while rejecting this specific reference, likewise underscores mention of the *stola* in Vitruvius' description of these figures as *statuas marmoreas muliebres stolatas*, arguing that this diction helps create an iconographic link to Rome.[29]

Such analyses of Vitruvius' caryatids within a Roman frame, though valid and important, can obscure the significance of the author's choice to present yet another triumphal narrative in which Greeks, not Romans, are the conquerors. The architect, Vitruvius suggests, not only draws upon an ornamental lexicon steeped in convention, but also ensures that older meanings are maintained, even as their political relevance dims. Furthermore, lest we see the Golden Age of Greece too neatly as a model for Rome, the caryatids, in Vitruvius' formulation, memorialize a dark, if fictitious, chapter in Greek imperialism: the duplicity of one Greek city-state against another – and its subsequent subjugation. To many a passerby observing Greek columnar maidens in buildings projects at Rome, such images likely symbolized the Roman annexation of the Greek world. Vitruvius, who may well have known little about the origins of the form, retrojects this contemporary valence when he depicts victorious Greeks leading their captives in a Roman triumph. All the while, however, his

---

[24] Suet. *Ner.* 46; Plin. *HN* 36.41. See Kuttner 1995a: 69–93.   [25] Edwards 2003: 66–7.
[26] Cf. also Plin. *HN* 36.39. Coarelli suggests that the statue groups mentioned in association with Pompey's theater complex and Augustus' porticus are one and the same. Cf. Coarelli at *LTUR* IV: 138–9.
[27] Cf. Toynbee 1934: 8; Zanker 1970: 512; Smith 1988: 70; Edwards 2003: 65–8.
[28] Wesenberg 1984. Cf. also McEwen 2003: 30. Bibliography on Vitruvius' caryatids is extensive, and I will not attempt to reproduce it here.
[29] Only Roman women wore the *stola*. Cf. Milnor 2005: 112–15. Vitruvius also refers to these garments in his description of the development of the Ionic column, in which he likens fluting to *rugae stolarum* ("the folds of *stolae*," 4.1.7).

overarching aim is to restore a native Greek significance to the caryatid. For Vitruvius, the Roman architect is a master of cultural appropriation, who creates a Rome in which the Greek past is preserved, not effaced.[30]

Vitruvius' version of events cannot easily be reconciled with what we know of fifth-century Greece.[31] Similar complaints, of course, are often lodged against Vitruvius' portrayal of Roman architecture, the nominal focus of the treatise. Just as Vitruvius' stated aim of describing Roman architecture seems to chafe against the content of *De architectura*, so too his proclaimed interest in *historia* appears at odds with the historical inaccuracies apparent in each Greek anecdote discussed in this chapter. Admittedly, it may seem perverse for a Roman author to restore Greek significance to an architectural form by repeating, or even inventing, a Romanized fiction about its Greek origins. However, Vitruvius' purpose is not to retell history, but rather to develop a vivid rhetorical argument about proper behavior using carefully crafted parables.

Vitruvius couples his tale of the caryatid with another that enriches the intended lesson. The Spartans, having overcome the Persians at Plataea, *acto cum gloria triumpho spoliorum et praedae, porticum persicam ex manubiis* ("celebrated a glorious triumph with the spoils and the booty, and erected the Persian Stoa from the general's share of the plunder," 1.1.6). Here again the image is of *captivorum simulacra barbarico vestis ornatu . . . sustinentia tectum* ("likenesses of their prisoners, dressed in rich, barbaric clothes, holding up the roof," 1.1.6). This monument punishes the Spartans' enemies for their haughty pride; it warns future enemies of the Spartans' power; and it encourages contemporary and future Spartans to remain proud and ready to defend their homeland (1.1.6). A perhaps unintended consequence, however, is the lesson it provides to future architects: *Itaque ex eo multi statuas persicas sustinentes epistylia et ornamenta*

---

[30] Jennifer Trimble suggests, in her chapter in this volume, that both the Roman senate and the *princeps* belonged to a learned subset, whose education and experiences rendered them conversant in the languages of both Egyptian and Greek architectural forms. Such knowledge, actual or feigned, would be a meaningful element of status. In light of Trimble's argument, Vitruvius' continual assertion of his own exigency as translator of architectural bricolage may be read as an impertinent stance toward his Augustan addressee and elite readers.

[31] Coincidence with historical fact culminates in a possible allusion to an underlying current of Peloponnesian medism. See Huxley 1967; Romano 2011. The early fifth-century Persian invasions, which are an important element in Vitruvius' narrative, never extended to the Peloponnese. The Laconian city of Carya was still flourishing in the fourth century BCE. There is no evidence that the ancient Greeks referred to these statues as caryatids. In Greek contexts, most notably the Erechtheion on the Athenian acropolis, caryatids do not necessarily carry connotations of subjugation. Cf. Ridgway 1999: 145–50 on the varying meanings of caryatids throughout Greek and Roman history.

eorum conlocaverunt ("and so from that time many builders placed in their works statues of Persians holding up architraves and their attendant ornaments," 1.1.6).[32] This trend changes a site-specific gesture of domination into an architectural trope, as is indicated by Vitruvius' suggestion that *ex eo argumento varietates egregias auxerunt operibus*, ("this theme enabled them [other architects] to increase notably the variety of their creations," 1.1.6). Vitruvius thereby reminds his reader of the diffusion of Greek architectural motifs, even as he argues for the importance of maintaining discrete narratives of origin.

The Author

In *De architectura*'s seventh and longest preface, Vitruvius reflects upon his appropriation of (primarily[33]) Greek literary sources. As elsewhere in the treatise, the author outlines the contours of his position through vehement disavowal of behaviors he avoids – in this case, literary theft (*furtum*) (7.praef.3):

> qui eorum scripta furantes pro suis praedicant sunt vituperandi, quique non propriis cogitationibus scriptorum nituntur, sed invidis moribus aliena violantes gloriantur, non modo sunt reprehendendi, sed etiam, quia impio more vixerunt, poena condemnandi.

> They ought to be scolded, those who as they steal the works [of earlier authors] proclaim them to be their own, those who are not supported by their own engagement with authors, but with an envious character pride themselves as they violate the property of others; not only should they be censured but even, since they lived in a wicked way, they should be sentenced to punishment.

By referring to these writers as *furantes*, Vitruvius equates a type of literary borrowing not only with petty thievery,[34] but even with the looting of a province. Cicero, prosecuting the provincial governor Verres for his seizure of precious objects from Sicilian houses and sacred sites, uses the word *furtum* to emphasize the illegality and vulgarity of Verres' crimes.[35]

---

[32] Compare Ovid's image of Persia born of Danae (*Danaeia Persis*), amidst figures of countries in an imagined triumph of Gaius, Augustus' grandson (*Ars* 1.225).

[33] See Vitruvius' expression of disappointment that, unlike the *Graeci*, Roman architects, such as Cossutius and Gaius Mucius, did not leave behind written accounts (7.praef.17–18). In this preface, he cites three Latin authors amidst dozens of Greeks: Fuficius, Terentius Varro, and P. Septimius.

[34] Vitruvius also uses *furtum* to denote the theft of metal from a crown that set in motion Archimedes' fabled bathtub discovery (9.praef.10–12).

[35] Frazel 2005. See also Frazel 2009.

For Cicero, the pillaging of foreign lands, an activity sanctioned by gods and men in wartime, violates the laws of peace (*Verr.* 2.4.123). Vitruvius' diction in 7.praef.3 (*aliena, violantes, gloriantur*) also evokes foreign conquest and plunder in order to depict these literary brigands as unlawfully ransacking a Greek East that is now at peace with, and even contained within, the Roman world. *Aliena*, here denoting a stolen text, recurs across *De architectura* in contexts conveying foreignness, or simply otherness, including the preface to Book 6, where the unknown shores upon which the wise man will feel at home are described as *alieni loci* (6.praef.2). Vitruvius' assertion in 7.praef.3 that wicked people *gloriantur* calls to mind his descriptions of the Greek triumphs over the Caryans and Persians (*gloria* [x2], 1.1.6; *gloriose*, 1.1.5), as well as the first sentence of the treatise, in which *triumpho victoriaque tua cives gloriarentur* ("the citizens prided themselves in [Augustus'] triumph and victory," 1.praef.1). Recourse to the language of righteous conquest in the context of punishment-triggering activities associated with *invidi mores* configures plagiarism as a violation of the rules of engagement between conqueror and conquered.

Vitruvius elaborates his concept of literary *furtum* in two parables, in which he criticizes poets who engage incorrectly with literary models (explicitly Homeric in one case, more broadly poetic in the other). In the first, Ptolemy sponsors a competition of poets in the library of Pergamum (7.praef.4–7).[36] Aristophanes of Byzantium identifies the poems that please his fellow judges most as having been lifted from library scrolls.[37] Only one poet has recited his own verses. When Aristophanes produces proof to this effect, Ptolemy reluctantly agrees that the unpopular poet is the victor. Vitruvius narrates neither the punishments nor the prize; instead, he praises Aristophanes and mentions his resultant promotion to librarian. By making Aristophanes the hero of the episode, as well as a foil to his own authorial persona, Vitruvius advances his argument for a correlation between well-earned professional success and a thorough knowledge of Greek source material (1.1.5–6).

Based on their analyses of Aristophanes' unmasking of the poetasters, scholars of plagiarism have styled Vitruvius "the earliest surviving Latin

---

[36] See Kuttner 1995b: 163–4 for analysis of the significance of the Pergamene location.

[37] Aristophanes of Byzantium was both the first Alexandrian scholar to establish contacts with Pergamum (he was subsequently imprisoned to prevent him from emigrating there) and the first critic to write a book on plagiarism. See Fraser 1970: 119. Scholars agree that Varro was probably Vitruvius' source for this tale. Like the caryatid tale, it contains some historical inaccuracies. Fraser 1970: 18; Roscalla 2006: 71; Romano 2011; McGill 2012: 36.

author ... to apply the category [of plagiarism] to a scholarly text."[38] For Scott McGill, the passage hinges on issues of creativity: "the problem is actually that the authors inertly follow their models rather than engage with them creatively to advance the study of the topic as Vitruvius does."[39] Though classical authors did not practice direct citation, the poets disparaged by Vitruvius "still should have been open to having their debts discovered."[40] Pamela Long, meanwhile, suggests that since texts were not considered marketplace commodities in the ancient world, Vitruvius must here be decrying the theft of such immortal fame as attended authorship.[41]

According to my reading, however, criticism of plagiarism chiefly offers support for Vitruvius' demonstration of his esteem for the literary canon: in other words, his ability to rehearse a litany of earlier authors and his eagerness to acknowledge and engage with them. The majority of the preface is devoted to just such an activity (7.praef.11–17). Vitruvius' contention is not just that a failure to innovate would be uncreative, or that a slight to an earlier author's reputation would be unjust. Rather, Vitruvius defines his enterprise as a Roman author by his appropriative relationship to Greek literature. For Vitruvius, indebtedness to and critical engagement with predecessors are prerequisites to securing his place within the tradition.

To advance his declaration of authorial blamelessness, Vitruvius adapts the literary commonplace of drawing water from a spring (7.praef.10).[42] He claims that he engages with the works of his literary predecessors *uti fontibus haurientes aquam et ad propria proposita traducentes* ("like those who draw water from springs and siphon it for their own purposes," 7.praef.10). His recourse to the imagery of the font offers a variant on the tradition; Vitruvius does not contrast muddy or unclean waters with pure ones (e.g., Callim. *Hymn* 2.105–13; Hor. *Sat.* 1.10.50–1; Ov. *Pont. Tr.* 4.2.15–20). Nor does he follow the Alexandrian convention by drinking from Hippocrene on Mount Helicon (e.g., Callim. *Aet.* 112.5–9 Pf.; Pers. *Preface* 1–3). Water is not inspiration to be imbibed, but a commodity to be repurposed. Unlike Manilius (2.53–9), who employs very similar

---

[38] McGill 2012: 40. Cf. Fraser 1970: 16; Long 2001; McGill 2012: 33–73.   [39] McGill 2012: 40.
[40] McGill 2012: 41.   [41] Long 1991: 856.
[42] Cf. Brink 1972: 553–6; Jones 2005: 51–69 on aquatic imagery and literary inspiration. Book 8, dedicated to sources of water, reflects engagement with Hippocrates. The different characteristics of peoples result from the waters of their native lands. In the eighth preface, Vitruvius uses another metaphor for the literary tradition; he follows in the footsteps of earlier authors (*quorum secutus ingressus*, 8.3.27). See now König 2016 on Book 8 and its centrality to Vitruvius' literary project.

imagery in defense of his originality, Vitruvius does not flinch at the idea of "channeling" early authors.[43]

It is logical, then, that Vitruvius associates failed authorship with want (*inopia*). In the second parable of the seventh preface, Zoilus the Home-romastix makes a career of disparaging Homer.[44] Eventually, however, this revenue stream runs dry: *Zoilus autem, cum diutius in regno fuisset, inopia pressus misit ad regem postulans ut aliquid sibi tribueretur* ("Zoilus on the other hand, when he had lived for a long time in the kingdom, pressed by want sent word to the king demanding that something might be paid to him in tribute," 7.praef.8). Vitruvius' statement that his ability to write *De architectura* is predicated on his freedom from fear of want (*inopiae timor*) conditions our reception of this anecdote (1.praef.3). In both cases, the type of *inopia* invoked is ostensibly financial. Ptolemy's response nevertheless advances Vitruvius' conception of literature as the font of literature (7.praef.9):

> Rex vero respondisse dicitur Homerum, qui ante annos mille decessisset, aevo perpetuo multa milia hominum pascere, item debere qui meliore ingenio se profiteretur non modo unum sed etiam plures alere posse.

> The king is said to have replied that Homer, who had died a thousand years before, through an unbroken eternity nourished many thousands of men, and therefore someone who professed that he had greater talent ought to be able to feed not one but many others as well.

According to this model, an author provides unceasing sustenance (*pascere, alere*) to his thousands of successors. Here again the tradition is a renewable resource, though the metaphor has shifted from the font to the field (or, perhaps, nursemaid). The Zoilus anecdote thus enriches Vitruvius' characterization of the relationship authors should have to the literary canon. Zoilus, like the plagiarizing poets, feeds on the tradition like a parasite. Vitruvius introduces these negative *exempla* in order to disavow their method of consuming and either effacing or denigrating their predecessors. After he then names and extols a stream of authorial forefathers, his lesson on the proper relationship that Roman writers should have to Greek tradition is complete.

---

[43] On Manilius and this imagery, see Volk 2010, especially 190–1 on the legal rubric of *aquae ductus* and water rights; on the need to reemphasize the conceptual significance of water for the movements of Roman cargo see Padilla Peralta in this volume.

[44] Fraser 1970: 119 considers the Zoilus anecdote "a fragment of a Pergamene literary history or similar work."

The General

Vitruvius, by and large, avoids direct references to the politics, architectural projects, and events of his own time. Most individuals in the treatise have Greek names and historical origins east of Italy. Yet the general Mummius and the aediles Varro and Murena also appear – each in reference to an importation of Greek material into the city of Rome. These very brief accounts, when considered within their narrative context, offer a perspective on Rome's absorption of Greek objects that coheres well with the anecdotes and parables that I have discussed thus far. Once in the hands of Roman *auctores,* in neither instance do repurposed goods lose their Greekness. Rather, their incongruous fit within both building and cityscape allows them to serve as markers of geographical and cultural distance.

Across Roman literature, the figure of Lucius Mummius and his sack of Corinth (146 BCE) serve as a lightning rod for debate about Eastern expansion and the ownership and display of spoils.[45] Vitruvius refers to this victory in the context of a disquisition on theaters in Book 5, the volume dedicated to public buildings. Vitruvius claims that Mummius seized bronze vessels (*echea*) designed to enhance theatrical acoustics from the theater at Corinth and that their dedication in the Temple of Luna was the first time when vessels of this type entered Rome (5.5.8).[46] He admits that there is no example within the city of *echea* used acoustically (5.5.8):

> Sin autem quaeritur in quo theatro ea sint facta, Romae non possumus ostendere, sed in Italiae regione et in pluribus Graecorum civitatibus.

> But if you ask in what theater this is done, we cannot show any at Rome, but we must turn to the region of Italy, and to many Greek cities.

Nevertheless, on account of the general's importation of these objects, Vitruvius identifies Mummius as their Roman *auctor* (5.5.8):[47]

> Etiamque auctorem habemus Lucium Mummium, qui, diruto theatro Corinthiorum, ea aenea Romam deportavit et de manubiis ad aedem Lunae dedicavit.

---

[45] Cf. Yarrow 2006b.

[46] Vitruvius explains that when theaters are built of solid materials (*solidae res*) that cannot resound, bronze vessels (*echea*) can enhance their acoustics (5.5.7). According to legend, Servius Tullius commissioned the Temple of Luna. Cf. Richardson 1992: 238.

[47] *Auctor* appears four other times in *De architectura*, indicating nonhuman origins (3.1.8) as well as literary authors. On *auctoritas* in *De architectura*, cf. Gros 1989; Callebat 2003.

We have as our author Lucius Mummius who, when the Corinthians' theater was destroyed, transported these bronze vessels to Rome and dedicated them, from the general's share of the plunder, at the temple of Luna.

Vitruvius' classification of a general dedicating *manubiae* as an *auctor* reinforces his portrayal of Roman authorship; a Roman *auctor* imports and recontextualizes Greek knowledge.[48]

Allusions to the scale and quality of his plunder pervade extant literary references to Mummius (Cic. *Verr.* 2.1.55; Vell. Pat. 1.13.3–5; Plin. *HN* 33.149, 37.12; Eutr. 4.14). Yet here emphasis lands on the objects' geographic and architectural contexts and the *auctor* responsible for their transplantation, rather than on their quantity and cost. The *echea* in the Temple of Luna appear amidst a description of how vessels are used in theatrical acoustics *in Italiae regione et in pluribus Graecorum civitatibus* (5.5.8), even though they cannot perform the same function in a temple context. The paradox is significant. *De architectura* presents these materials as vessels of knowledge, to be interpreted, ordered, reconfigured, and recontextualized at Rome.

The same literary strategy manifests itself in a passage on the aediles Varro and Murena. Vitruvius mentions the (now obscure)[49] "Varro and Murena" in Book 2, which is dedicated to the materials used in architectural construction. Varro and Murena distinguish themselves during their time in office by importing Spartan paintings to Rome for display in the Comitium (2.8.9):[50]

---

[48] Compare Mary Jaeger's suggestion that the *auctor* often sits at a remove from a monument, as the author and guarantor of its representation, but that "that representation can convey a memory quite different from the one preserved by the original." Jaeger 2002: 49. See Liv. 4.20 with Haimson Lushkov in this volume for varying uses of *auctor* in discussion of the *spolia opima* and the restoration of the Temple of Jupiter Feretrius. See also Heinze 1925; Béranger 1953: 114–31; Galinsky 1996: 10–41; Sailor 2006.

[49] Though the date of their aedileship cannot be established with certainty, there is reason to identify Vitruvius' aediles as C. Visellius Varro and C. Licinius Murena (59 BCE). Cf. Plin. *HN* 35.173; Cic. *Brut.* 264. For Broughton 1952: 189, they are the curule aediles of 59 BCE, C. Licinius Murena and C. Visellius Varro (Cicero's mother's nephew). (See also Croisille 1985: 275 and Callebat & Gros 1999: 127, who argue that the aedileship of Varro and Murena occurred in 68 BCE.) McDermott 1941: 258 and Croisille 1985: 275 also suggest that Vitruvius may have intended A. Terentius Varro Murena, who was consul in 23 BCE. Sauron 1994: 283, however, convincingly rejects this, partially on the grounds that both Pliny and Vitruvius clearly join the two names with *et*. In any case, Varro and Murena's appropriation of the Spartan paintings occurred long after Sparta became part of the Roman Empire in the second century BCE.

[50] The triumphal display of art and other spoils in the Comitium is well attested (Suet. *Iul.* 10; Liv. 2.10; Cic. *Verr.* 2.1.49). Cf. Miles 2008: 177. Cicero describes how C. Claudius borrowed, and subsequently returned, a statue of Cupid from Messana in order to adorn the Forum while he was an aedile (Cic. *Verr.* 2.4.6). Such loans were not always returned; in the case of the excised paintings, it seems unlikely that they would be reintegrated into the Spartan walls. Cf. Rawson 1985: 194.

Item Lacedaemone e quibusdam parietibus etiam picturae excisae intersectis lateribus inclusae sunt in ligneis formis et in comitium ad ornatum aedilitatis Varronis et Murenae fuerunt adlatae.

Likewise in Sparta, pictures of inlaid brick, cut out of certain walls, in fact were enclosed in wooden frames and were brought to the Comitium to adorn the aedileship of Varro and Murena.

This anecdote appears amidst descriptions of brick-walled palaces at Tralles, Sardis, and Halicarnassus, as a further example of the use of bricks (2.8.9–10). Such an anomalous Roman entry within the list might appear to indicate the presence of the author's personal experience (firsthand knowledge).[51] Vitruvius, however, has not diverged from his usual argument structure; directly before this cluster of palaces, we read of Athenian city walls, a temple at Patrae, and a wall at Arezzo (2.8.9). Vitruvius thus nests this marker of Rome's territorial expansion within his illustration of a Greek architectural practice. Relocated, neither the *echea* nor the *picturae* retain their original function; while the bronzes do not amplify sound, the paintings no longer decorate brick walls. Furthermore, both examples commemorate (in Vitruvius' account as well as in their Roman dedication) the destruction – or at least debasement – of their original (Greek) architectural contexts. Vitruvius reminds his reader that, when an architect provides the *ratio*, Greek plunder becomes Roman knowledge.

This story recurs in Pliny the Elder's disquisition on brickwork. Many details in Pliny's recounting of the episode echo Vitruvius', yet Pliny specifies that these paintings were chosen *propter excellentiam* ("because of their preeminence") and comments that *cum opus per se mirum esset, tralatum tamen magis mirabantur* ("although the work had been admired for its own sake, nevertheless they [the panels] were admired more for their transportation," *HN* 35.173). This jubilant gloss underscores Vitruvius' comparative subtlety. Whereas Vitruvius reveals only where the paintings came from and where and by whom they were displayed, Pliny remarks upon their quality and the wonder of their transportation. Pliny's more confident posture reflects a later author for whom Rome's appropriation of "foreign *mirabilia*" has become intrinsically connected with a triumphalist narrative of empire.[52]

---

[51] Callebat & Gros 1999: 127.

[52] Cf. Carey 2003: 90. On Vitruvius' resistance to such astonishment, see Courrént 2004. On Pliny's use of Vitruvius as a source, see Barresi 1989; Schuler 1999: 15–24 and 328–9; Fane-Saunders 2016. See Grant Parker's chapter in this volume on the significance of transportation within the Roman dynamics of appropriation.

Both of these Vitruvian examples, *echea* and *picturae excisae*, fall neatly into the categories of legitimate removal and transfer of patrimony advocated by Cicero: generals collecting booty and aediles decorating the city with the gifts of foreign subjects act on behalf of the state, to serve a common good (*Verr.* 2.4.126; cf. also *De or.* 3.92). Vitruvius' explanation of the moral justification and purpose of these behaviors is far more oblique; he introduces the importation of foreign objects as a way of integrating Rome within a larger Mediterranean context and calling attention to Rome's synthesis of the Greek world within its urban fabric.

Conclusion

By amassing examples from across the known world and collecting them into one *corpus*, Vitruvius illustrates the abundance of Greek sources now available for the Romans, to use for their own purposes (*ad propria proposita*). His shape-shifting authorial persona assumes the features of an architect, author, and general. Reflecting on each of these varied roles, Vitruvius draws together a coherent approach to incorporating, and acknowledging, the Greek past. Making his case through faraway parables as well as direct instructions, Vitruvius draws attention to the Greek knowledge embedded within Roman architecture and literature. Most persuasively, he inserts allusions to Corinthian and Spartan objects, relocated to Rome, within technical descriptions of Greek architectural practices. Roman *auctores* create a contemporary culture utterly reliant on the past, with full citations as well as revisions. Without the *rationes* Vitruvius – or one of his educated architects – supplies, the promise of a Roman world culture remains unfulfilled.

CHAPTER 7

Appropriating Egypt for the Ara Pacis Augustae*

Jennifer Trimble

Introduction: Appropriation and the Ara Pacis

The Ara Pacis Augustae is famously the product of a modern appropriation (Figure 7.1). Fragments were known already in the sixteenth century, and there was serious interest in the nineteenth, but the decisive intervention came under Mussolini in 1937–1938, when Giuseppe Moretti's team excavated the majority of the altar in a spectacular feat of engineering that included freezing the groundwater at the site.[1] The subsequent reconstruction presented a monument that was compellingly whole. Within a new pavilion designed by Vittorio Ballio Morpurgo, it could be visited and walked around, its program and sculpture studied in detail. This splendid presence was coupled with a striking absence. The monument had been removed from its original location in the Campus Martius and reconstructed as the fourth side of the Piazzale Augusto Imperatore; the other three sides were new buildings framing Augustus' Mausoleum.[2] The *Res Gestae* of Augustus was reproduced on the external wall of the Ara Pacis pavilion facing the Mausoleum, whereas on the Piazzale's modern buildings, modern inscriptions and imagery evoked ancient Roman themes. Excavated and reconstructed in this way to mark Augustus' bimillennial anniversary, and inaugurated in 1938 on the ancient emperor's birthday of 23 September, the Ara Pacis Augustae linked the Fascist political program

---

* I am grateful to the editors of this volume for their stimulating questions about appropriation. For comments on earlier drafts, I thank Alessandro Barchiesi, Melissa Bailey, Jaś Elsner, Walter Scheidel, Bernard Frischer, and Carolyn MacDonald. The initial stimulus for this chapter was a talk on the White Chapel at Karnak, delivered by John Baines at the University of Michigan in the late 1990s; for a Romanist, the building's architectural similarity to the Ara Pacis Augustae was striking and demanded further investigation. A first version of this chapter was written several years ago but remained unpublished; major gains since then in the scholarship on Aegyptiaca in Rome and on the northern Campus Martius make the topic worth revisiting, and the chapter has been revised accordingly.

[1] Moretti 1948.   [2] Kostof 1978: 270–325; see also Cooley 2009: 51–5.

Figure 7.1.   The Ara Pacis Augustae in Rome. Constructed 13–9 BCE, reconstructed
in 1938

to the Imperial past through direct analogy and through the process of
reclamation and reframing.[3]

Mussolini's Ara Pacis strikingly illustrates two key points in Robert
Nelson's classic discussion of appropriation. It is not a neutral or passive
process, but involves active selections for new purposes.[4] More importantly, a "distortion" is inherent in any appropriation, and this shift
involves neither unbroken continuity nor a complete semiotic break.[5]
The Ara Pacis retained much of its original structure and visual impact in
its reconstructed form in Mussolini's Rome. Still, its new physical setting
and changed political and cultural contexts gave it a very different
reception and impact there. Analyzing appropriation, then, means not
only looking at the movement of artistic objects and ideas, but also
asking why certain forms or motifs were taken up for a new purpose,

[3] The new pavilion designed for the Ara Pacis by Richard Meier and opened in 2006 adds more layers
to the altar's modern receptions: Strazzulla 2009.
[4] Nelson 1996: 118. Recarving in antiquity and post-antique restorations represent additional
appropriations; see La Rocca *et al.* 1983 and Conlin 1997. For a critical discussion of appropriation
in modern and ancient art history, Kinney 2012.
[5] Nelson 1996: 119.

how and why they were "distorted" in that transformation, and what resonance and significance they had in their new settings. This poses new questions and challenges. What aspects of meaning are retained in an appropriation and what shapes their distortion? Who sees and responds as desired by whoever performed this active selection and reframing, and how can we know?

These issues come vividly to the fore in considering the cultural and artistic appropriations that produced the Ara Pacis Augustae in the first place. Augustan Rome is a particularly rich locus for study because of the extraordinary self-consciousness of the period's visual and textual appropriations. Marden Fitzpatrick Nichols's chapter earlier in this section explores Vitruvius' citations of Greek writers as an imperialistic form of intellectual heritage. Grant Parker's following chapter discusses the way obelisks brought to Rome were made to represent the nature of the empire and its ruler – with ongoing reappropriations and new distortions of meaning evolving all the way into the modern period. My own chapter focuses on the symbolic role of pharaonic Egypt in Augustan Rome. Specifically, I argue that peripteral jubilee chapels from New Kingdom Egypt were appropriated as architectural models for the Ara Pacis. More broadly, reconstructing this process highlights pharaonic Egypt's importance in Augustan state expressions of dominion over time as well as space, and illuminates the innovative and experimental nature of the Augustan monumental project.

The chapter is divided into three sections. The first establishes some necessary context for Augustan appropriations from ancient Egypt. The second examines peripteral chapels in Egypt as architectural precedents for the Ara Pacis. The third section returns to Rome to ask how and why pharaonic precedents were meaningful on the Ara Pacis. I interpret them as part of a freighted ideological communication between the Senate and the *princeps*. More broadly, paying attention to Egypt illuminates Augustan appropriations for a new cultural synthesis that expressed the aspirations of Roman power and Augustus' rule.

This synthesis has previously been recognized for the Italic and Greek allusions on the Ara Pacis, but not for the Egyptian. Why not? One reason may be disciplinary: since the late nineteenth century, Classics and Classical Archaeology have specialized in Greece and Rome whereas Egypt has been studied in a separate discipline. Egyptian precedents for Roman monuments can therefore seem impossibly remote, whereas Greek connections seem familiar and accessible. And in fact, scholars

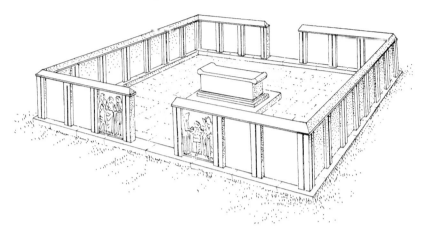

Figure 7.2.   Reconstruction drawing of the Altar of the Twelve Gods in the Athenian
Agora, 522/521 BCE

from the 1950s onward have found architectural precedents for the Ara
Pacis in Classical and Hellenistic Greek altars, including the Altar of the
Twelve Gods in the Athenian Agora (Figure 7.2), the altar court at
Samothrace (Figure 7.3), and a monumental altar in the sanctuary of
Poseidon and Amphitrite on Tenos in the Cyclades.[6]

Another reason may be historical. After World War II, scholarship
turned strongly away from the fascist appropriations of Imperial Rome;
indeed, Augustan visual culture did not return to the scholarly main-
stream until the 1980s.[7] For the Ara Pacis, the postwar period saw a more
guarded focus on native Italian sources and on developments in the
capital alone. Later twentieth-century Italian and German scholars found
meaningful precedents for the altar within Italy and Roman religion,
citing Etruscan funerary architecture, the U-shaped altars at Lavinium,
the archaic Roman *templum minus*, and the Temple of Janus Geminus in
the Roman Forum.[8] However, a wave of recent work on Egypt and

---

[6] Altar of the Twelve Gods: Thompson 1952; see also Toynbee 1953. Samothrace: Lehmann and
Spittle 1964. Tenos: Etienne & Braun 1986. Additional parallels are discussed in Tuchelt 1975:
130–6.

[7] Landmark events were an exhibition in Berlin, *Der Kaiser Augustus und die verlorene Republik* (Hofter
1988), and the influential publication in German and English of Paul Zanker's *Augustus und die
Macht der Bilder* (Zanker 1987).

[8] Simon 1967; Borbein 1975; La Rocca *et al.* 1983: 13; Torelli in *LTUR* IV: 70–4; Tortorici in *LTUR* III:
92–3 with further references.

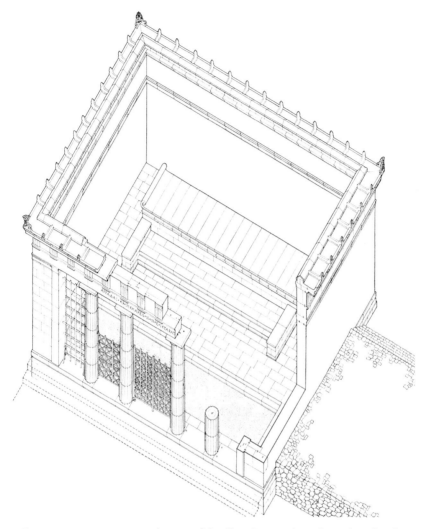

Figure 7.3.   Reconstruction drawing of the Altar Court at Samothrace, later fourth century BCE

Egyptian culture in Rome has begun to restore our sense of the imperialistic breadth and scope of Augustan monumental appropriations.[9]

---

[9] Important works include Versluys 2002, Bricault *et al.* 2007, Swetnam-Burland 2015. The term "Aegyptiaca" has come into use to avoid anachronistic distinctions between Egyptian vs. Egyptianizing objects or artworks, arguably not relevant within an ancient context (Swetnam-Burland 2007). In this chapter, I employ the term "Egyptianizing" to refer to things in Rome that were Egyptian, looked Egyptian, or appealed to Egypt in some way.

In adding Egypt to the cultural sources for the Ara Pacis, I am benefitting from and continuing this important reevaluation.

Ancient Egypt and Augustan Rome

Any cultural appropriation is contingent; it is shaped by its broader context, dependent on that context for its significance, and meaningful only in relation to it. This context is a full partner in the process, in that appropriation (in Robert Nelson's sense) does not happen or have meaning without it. Before discussing the Ara Pacis in particular, therefore, this section establishes what was at stake in Augustan state appropriations from Egypt more generally. First, Egypt was enormously important for Rome in the charged politics of the end of the Republic. Second, the extensive Augustan building program in Egypt demonstrates that the *princeps* and his representatives in Egypt were highly knowledgeable about the religious landscape of Egypt. Third, Augustan state Egyptianizing in Rome drew on a specific strand of thinking in the Hellenistic Mediterranean: pharaonic Egypt as a symbol of deep time, sacrality, and rule over the *oikoumene*.

Ancient Egypt and Rome were far more deeply intertwined than modern disciplinary boundaries indicate.[10] During the last two centuries BCE, the weakening Ptolemaic kingdom was caught up in elaborate diplomatic, economic, and military connections with an increasingly powerful Rome. The final stages of this history need no repeating: Cleopatra VII's attempts to exploit civil strife at Rome to create dynastic alliances in the interests of Ptolemaic Egypt; Mark Antony's choice of Egypt as a power base; Octavian's defeat of Cleopatra and Mark Antony at Actium in 31 BCE and his emergence as sole ruler of Rome and the Mediterranean world. Interactions between Rome and Egypt went beyond the military and political, however. The conquest of Egypt was part of Alexander the Great's enduring mythology and political importance, in Rome as elsewhere in the Hellenistic world. Alexandria, as a major capital of the Hellenistic world, drew writers and artists from all over, with profound cultural effects on Rome. The worship of Isis and her consort Serapis spread around the Hellenistic Mediterranean, including in Italy. In Roman art and visual culture, Egyptian decorative motifs became widely

---

[10] Hölbl 2000, 2004, 2006. A short but useful overview is Van't Dack 1983. The long-standing view of Roman Egypt's administrative and cultural isolation from the rest of the Empire after Augustus was challenged in Bowman & Rathbone 1992.

known and popular.[11] Augustus commemorated his conquest of Egypt in coinage and celebrated a triple triumph at Rome in 29 BCE for his victories in Illyricum and Egypt as well as at Actium. He also banned the worship of Isis; however, this did not indicate a blanket anti-Egyptian position but is better understood within the long tradition of state attempts at Rome to control and limit unruly religious gatherings.[12] Roman attitudes toward Egypt were multifaceted, and Roman engagement with Egyptian culture took many forms. Within this complex picture, I will focus on Augustan state Egyptianizing, that is, appropriations from Egypt undertaken by the *princeps* or other members of the Augustan state.

To understand this state Egyptianizing, we must also recognize that the Augustan regime was deeply invested in the traditional religious landscape of Egypt. As part of consolidating Roman control over Egypt, Augustus became a major building patron of temple complexes all along the Nile.[13] This was a different political and cultural context from Greek Alexandria, where in 30 BCE Augustus ostentatiously refused to pay his respects to the dead Ptolemies after visiting the grave of Alexander the Great (Cass. Dio 51.16). South of Alexandria, the Roman treatment of the Ptolemaic legacy was very different. Augustan interventions there followed a long-established pattern by which new rulers of Egypt stressed continuity of rule and religion.[14] Augustan additions to or completions of earlier temples include Dendera, Kom Ombo, Elephantine, Khonsou, Biggeh, Dabod, Kalabsha, Dakka, 'Ain Birbijeh, probably Maharraqa, and perhaps 'Ain Amur. Religious structures were built on Philae and at Qertassi, and high Roman officials built temples at Philae and Dendur. New temples in the traditional Egyptian style were built at El-Qal'a, Shanhour, Taffeh, and probably Deir El-Shelouit. Especially in Nubia, Augustus' patronage of temples of Isis is strongly marked. With his religious building program

---

[11] On Isis worship, Takács 1995. On Alexandria, see, e.g., Hunter 2006 and Stephens 2010. On "Egyptomania" in early Imperial painting and mosaics, Roullet 1972, de Vos 1980, Versluys 2002, Bricault *et al.* 2007, Swetnam-Burland 2015. For Egypt in love elegy, see, e.g., Koenen 1976 and Bowditch 2011.

[12] Takács discusses the marked difference between the measures taken against the cult of Isis and the popularity of Egyptianizing art (Takács 1995: 75–80; see also 56–70).

[13] Hölbl 2000, 2004, 2006; Arnold 1999: 248–73; Herklotz 2007: 137–206. Herklotz points out that much of the Augustan building program concentrated on strategic areas of Egypt.

[14] Ptolemaic temple building outside Alexandria followed 13th Dynasty precedents very closely, and Augustan interventions in turn emphasized continuity with the Ptolemaic. The following list of interventions is distilled from Arnold 1999: 230–48. More broadly on the Roman imperial engagement with Egyptian temple complexes, Hölbl 2000, 2004, 2006. For a detailed example of how this accretive continuity worked, from the 18th Dynasty through the Ptolemaic and Roman periods, see Laroche-Traunecker 1998.

along the Nile, Augustus inserted himself into a centuries-old Egyptian tradition of accretive layering as a way to legitimize the current ruler.

This extensive building program attests to a detailed Augustan knowledge of the religious landscape of Egypt. It is not known who was responsible for deciding exactly where and what to build; certainly, these projects must have involved a great number of Egyptian temple priests, architects, craftsmen, and laborers. However, given the enormous expense and political importance represented, these interventions must also have involved the *princeps* himself, if only through proxy agents who could be trusted to make expensive and delicate decisions. Evidently, Egypt's ancient religious past was both visible and important to these Augustan builders, and they were able to draw nuanced differences between ancient and more recent constructions in the Egyptian religious landscape. In Egypt, the Augustan building program demonstrated a knowledgeable continuity with tradition; in Rome, however, Augustan Egyptianizing involved a deliberate and classicizing selection of ancient Egyptian rather than more recent Ptolemaic models.

This classicizing attitude drew on a specific strand of Hellenistic thought. *Ancient* Egypt had a symbolic significance in the Mediterranean that was quite distinct from attitudes toward recent history. Pharaonic Egypt was seen as a repository of deep history, religious solemnity, and civilized knowledge, and as a touchstone for the sanction of world rule.[15] Roman imperialist thought appropriated this existing eastern Mediterranean view of Egypt. Conquering Egypt meant dominion over time as well as space, and possession of the powerful symbolism that the Mediterranean world invested in pharaonic Egypt. Book 17 of Strabo's *Geography* exemplifies this Roman appropriation of Hellenistic ideas about ancient Egypt; it is dedicated to Egypt, Ethiopia, and Libya, where Strabo traveled in the mid-20s BCE with the prefect C. Aelius Gallus and his entourage.[16] Strabo positions the Roman conquest within a much longer historical context and as an improvement on Ptolemaic rule (17.1.11–13). He also demonstrates just how much detailed information about Egypt was available to the Roman political elite. Drawing on Greek historical and scientific writings,

---

[15] Ferrari 1999 shows how the Hellenistic conception of deep Egyptian time and space could be expressed in a single image, the second- or early first-century BCE Nile Mosaic from Praeneste. From the perspective of the mosaic's viewer, both space and time recede from the here and now of Ptolemaic Alexandria through the traditional temples along the Nile all the way to Ethiopia and the sources of the Nile, depicted as fantastic and primitive. See also Meyboom 1995. Coarelli 1990 relates the mosaic to the *pompe* of Ptolemy Philadelphos.

[16] On Strabo's role within Hellenistic geography, Clarke 1999a.

Strabo discusses Egyptian geography, customs, religion, administrative boundaries, ancient monuments, and scientific knowledge.[17] Moving south from Alexandria, his group visits many of the great pharaonic sites, from the ancient royal center of Memphis, to Thebes (Luxor), to ruined Heliopolis—the source of two obelisks that Augustus would move to Rome some years later. En route, Strabo explains the nilometers at Elephantine and Philae (17.1.48–9), as well as traditional Egyptian temple architecture (17.1.28). He even describes the content of hieroglyphic inscriptions on obelisks (17.1.46), information presumably obtained from the temple priests.[18] He thus presents the ancient religious landscape of Egypt as both known in detail to the Roman political elite and important to know about. Through his synthesis of Hellenistic ideas about ancient Egypt, Rome emerges as the culmination of rule in the Mediterranean.

These themes are brought together in the best-known example of Augustan state Egyptianizing: the import of two obelisks from Heliopolis to Rome in 10/9 BCE.[19] They have been frequently discussed; Grant Parker's chapter in this volume, Chapter 8, treats them from the original perspective of appropriation in the long-term. They matter here as an example of a knowledgeable and synthetic Augustan state appropriation from pharaonic Egypt. There, obelisks were installed in pairs at the entrances to temples, but in Rome, Augustus installed one on the central barrier in the Circus Maximus and the other in the northern Campus Martius, near the contemporaneous Ara Pacis (Figure 7.4). Molly Swetnam-Burland has recently explored the obelisks' simultaneous continuity and distortion of meaning in their new contexts.[20] Rome's political elite knew that Egyptian obelisks were monarchic symbols and religious dedications to the sun.[21] The text inscribed onto the new bases of

---

[17] Strabo engages with earlier Greek writers and their descriptions of Egypt, sometimes repeating previous contributions, sometimes refuting or claiming to improve on existing ideas. Named references in Book 17 include Eratosthenes, Plato, Poseidonius, Callisthenes, Aristotle, Thrasyalces, Pindar, Homer, Artemidoros, and Callimachus.

[18] The text's social sympathies lie firmly with the temple priests: among all Egyptians in the past they were dedicated to philosophy and astronomy, and were close to the king (17.1.3).

[19] Most recently, La Rocca 2014; Swetnam-Burland 2010 and 2015: 65–104. Augustus had previously brought obelisks from Heliopolis to Alexandria (Herklotz 2007: 221–3).

[20] Swetnam-Burland 2010 and 2015: 65–104. See also D'Onofrio 1992: 369–421 and Arnold 2003: 165.

[21] Plin. *HN* 36.64–74. On obelisks as monarchic, often jubilee monuments, see Herklotz 2007: 220. In removing two obelisks from Heliopolis, Augustus was following much older monarchic practices (cf. Pliny, *HN* 36.14; Arnold 2003: 150). On the dedication of Augustus' obelisks to the sun, La Rocca 2014: 140–57.

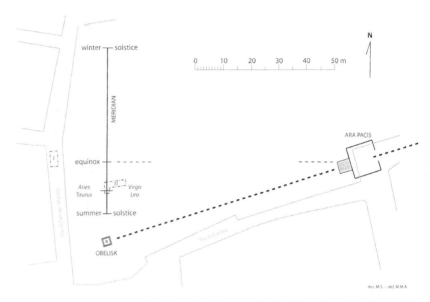

Figure 7.4.   Map showing the relationship between the obelisk and meridian line at left
and the Ara Pacis at right in the northern Campus Martius

Augustus' two imports highlights these ancient functions while reframing
them in terms of Roman conquest (*CIL* 6.701–2 = *ILS* 91):

> Imp(erator) Caesar Divi f(ilius)
> Augustus,
> pontifex maximus,
> imp(erator) $\overline{\text{XII}}$, co(n)s(ul) $\overline{\text{XI}}$, trib(unicia) pot(estate) $\overline{\text{XIV}}$,
> Aegypto in potestatem
> populi romani redacta,
> Soli donum dedit.

> The emperor Caesar Augustus, son of the Deified [Caesar], as pontifex
> maximus, imperator for the twelfth time, consul for the eleventh
> time and with tribunician power for the fourteenth time, with Egypt
> brought under the dominion of the Roman people, gave this as a gift to
> the Sun.

As renewed dedications to the sun god, made in relation to the extraordinary powers of the *princeps*, Augustus' obelisks expressed the symbolic
importance of ancient Egypt for representing Roman rule over space and
time within a sacral framework.

Augustus' obelisks also represent a double appropriation, most easily seen in the northern Campus Martius. Both came from Heliopolis, a center in Egypt for the worship of the sun god and for knowledge about the calendar and the measurement of the year (Strabo 17.1.29). The Campus Martius obelisk was reinstalled as the *gnomon* of a monumental meridian instrument; every day at noon, it cast its shadow against a measured north–south line laid out on the ground (Figures 7.4, 7.5).[22] That line was labeled with zodiac and seasonal inscriptions in Greek. The exact date at which the meridian line was built is disputed, but it is increasingly considered an original part of the obelisk's reinstallation in Rome.[23] This spectacular instrument was thus not only a direct appropriation from Egypt, a physical object brought from far away and valued for its sacral and monarchic connotations. Its new installation *also* represented the appropriation and synthesis of Egyptian and Greek scientific knowledge concerning the measurement of time. As such, this monument was directly related to Augustus' calendar reforms.[24] The obelisk in its new installation was simultaneously a religious and monarchic object from ancient Egypt, a Greek scientific apparatus concerned with the control of time, and a triumphal appropriation of all of these to celebrate Rome's conquests and Augustus' power over time as well as space.

To summarize: Augustan state Egyptianizing was both highly knowledgeable and ideologically charged. Detailed information as well as symbolic ideas about ancient Egypt were known and important to the Augustan state and were sometimes actively sought out for their ability to communicate messages about Roman rule and Augustus' power. Augustan state Egyptianizing was classicizing, favoring models from the distant Egyptian past over Ptolemaic or contemporaneous developments. This was also a double form of appropriation, not only taking specific ideas and objects from ancient Egypt, but also demonstrating a sophisticated cultural layering that combined Egyptian, Greek, Hellenistic, and Roman strands in the service of Rome and its ruler. All these themes will reappear

---

[22] Recent scholarship has thoroughly refuted Edmund Buchner's reconstruction of the Horologium Augusti as a massive sundial measuring the hours of the day. The papers and bibliography in Haselberger 2014 offer a valuable entry point into the controversies. Key works among many include Buchner 1982, Schütz 1990, Heslin 2007, Albèri Auber 2011–2012, Frischer & Fillwalk 2014.

[23] The supposed Flavian date of the excavated portion of the meridian line rests on shaky ground; more convincing is the Augustan date proposed by Albèri Auber 2011–2012: 467–70. See the useful discussion in Haselberger 2014: 181–4.

[24] On Augustan appropriations of time and the calendar reforms: Wallace-Hadrill 1987; Feeney 2007. On obelisks and time, Parker 2007.

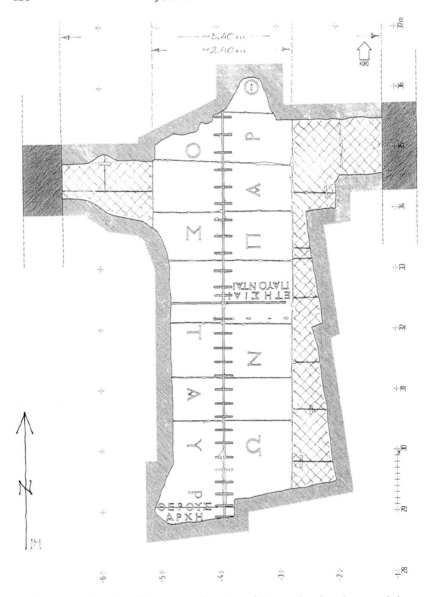

Figure 7.5.   Drawing of the excavated portion of the meridian line that extended northward from the base of the Egyptian obelisk in the northern Campus Martius

on the Ara Pacis. First, however, I turn to Egypt and a group of pharaonic chapels that are strikingly similar to the Ara Pacis in their architectural design.

New Kingdom Peripteral Chapels and the Ara Pacis Augustae

The Hellenic and Italic precedents mentioned in this chapter's introduction (e.g., Figures 7.2, 7.3) clarify many aspects of the Ara Pacis. Still, none of them quite accounts for the architectural design of the altar as a small, freestanding stone building with a nearly square plan, two central entrances opposite one another, and external walls enclosing an ambulatory around a sacred central structure (Figure 7.6). In this second section, I explore an Egyptian architectural precedent for the Ara Pacis Augustae: New Kingdom peripteral chapels. Built at temple sites along the Nile, they share formal, functional, and spatial characteristics with the Augustan altar.

A peripteral chapel from Elephantine illustrates the architectural parallels (Figure 7.7). On the occasion of his first jubilee, Amenhotep III (18th Dynasty, first half of the fourteenth-century BCE) dedicated this peripteral chapel to Khnum at the southern end of the island near the eastern shore.[25] It was a freestanding, rectangular building on a low platform. Shallow steps on either side led up to two axial doorways and a barque repository at the center. Low parapet walls connected the piers along the longer north and south sides, but the east and west façades were tripartite, with a wide central doorway flanked on either side by window-like openings above parapet walls below. Other New Kingdom peripteral chapels share these architectural features: a chapel of Thutmose III (18th Dynasty, 1479–1425 BCE) at Karnak (Figure 7.8), a second chapel on Elephantine, one built by Amenhotep III at Kuban, and a poorly preserved 18th Dynasty chapel at Amada.[26] An important predecessor for these structures was the Middle Kingdom White Chapel at Karnak, built by Senwosret I (12th Dynasty, 1971–1926 BCE) for Amun-Ra (Figure 7.9).[27] All these Egyptian chapels

---

[25] This chapel was documented by the Napoleonic expedition but was completely destroyed some years before 1838 (*Description* 1809: vol. I, ch. 3, pp. 4–11; vol. V, pls. 34–8; Borchardt 1938: 95–8, fig. 28, pl. 21).

[26] Karnak: Borchardt 1938: 90–3, fig. 27, pl. 19. The second chapel on Elephantine stood somewhere north of the first; it was dedicated by the 19th Dynasty pharaoh Ramesses II (*Description* 1809: vol. I, ch. 3, pp. 11–12; vol. V, pl. 38.2–4; Borchardt 1938: 100–1, pl. 21, lower left). Kuban: Borchardt 1938: 98–9, pl. 22 top. Amada: perhaps built by Amenhotep IV (Akhenaten) or his father and dedicated to Harmachis (Borchardt 1938: 99–100, pl. 22).

[27] The White Chapel was destroyed and buried in the foundations of Amenhotep III's pylon in the Temple of Amun, and so was not visible during the Augustan period, but it was an important model

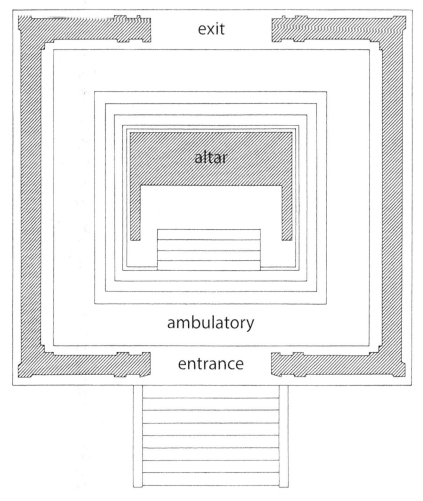

Figure 7.6.   Plan of the Ara Pacis Augustae

are truly peripteral whereas the Ara Pacis is only illusionistically so, being punctuated by pilasters at the four corners of the solid external walls. However, in both Egypt and in Rome, these external walls were all divided into upper and lower registers, with a screen wall below and open air above – actual in Egypt, depicted in Rome.

for several New Kingdom chapels that did survive into the Roman period. Borchardt 1938: 56–7, fig. 19; Lacau & Chevrier 1956; Kees 1958; Simpson 1991.

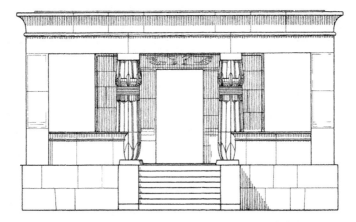

Vorderansicht der südlichen Kapelle

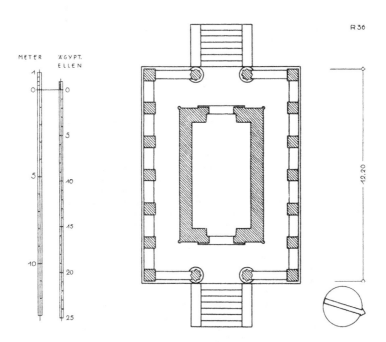

Grundriß der südlichen Kapelle

Figure 7.7. Elevation drawing and plan of the chapel of Amenhotep III at Elephantine

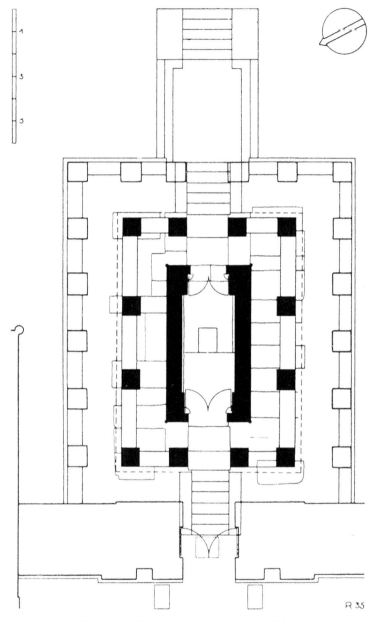

Figure 7.8.   Plan of the jubilee chapel of Thutmose III west of the holy lake in Karnak.
The dark fill marks the first phase of the structure.

Figure 7.9. The "White Chapel" at Karnak, built for the jubilee celebrations of Senwosret I, buried in the foundations of the pylon of Amenhotep III, reconstructed in 1938

There are functional and spatial parallels as well. Like the Ara Pacis, the Egyptian chapels were designed for processional movement through the building, with an internal ambulatory around a central focal point for religious ritual. For example, in the first phase of the jubilee chapel of Thutmose III at Karnak, a barque socle stood at center, arranged lengthwise to facilitate ritual movement through the space (Figure 7.8). This and similar chapels functioned as a stopping place during processions of the sacred barque, a long, narrow boat transporting the god's image and carried by priests in procession. The barque ritual is specific to Egyptian religion and quite different from the animal sacrifices that took place at the central altar within the Ara Pacis. There are strong parallels, however, in ritual movement. In the Egyptian chapels, the procession entered through one door and set down the barque on the central repository in a ritual pause before continuing out through the opposite door. At the Ara Pacis, the ritual procession entered through the western door and paused to make the sacrifice at the central altar before leaving the building through the eastern door.[28]

In Egypt as in Rome, buildings and movement were carefully situated within a larger ritual landscape. The chapel at Amada was axially placed in relation both to the main temple and to the Nile. Amenhotep III's chapel at Kuban functioned as a processional station within a temple complex situated on the road to the Nubian gold mines. The best surviving evidence for careful placement is Thutmose III's chapel at Karnak (Figure 7.8), built just west of the Sacred Lake and against the external wall between the seventh and eighth pylons. It stood on axis with a pair of obelisks at the entrance of the seventh pylon, foreshadowing the pairing of the obelisk and the Ara Pacis in the northern Campus Martius in Rome.

A final parallel is that these Egyptian chapels celebrated the ruler and his reign. Several can be linked to the Heb-Sed, a jubilee celebration that took place after thirty years of the pharaoh's rule and then again every few years after. Amenhotep III's chapel at Elephantine celebrated his first jubilee; so did Senwosret I's White Chapel at Karnak. Thutmose III's chapel at Karnak had two phases; the second phase was built to celebrate his second jubilee, suggesting that the chapel was initially built for his first. In the final section of this chapter, I will suggest that the Ara Pacis likewise celebrates a jubilee of Augustus.

Strikingly, the designers of the Ara Pacis Augustae seem to have bypassed later, more contemporaneous versions of these peripteral chapels. From the Kushite through the Hellenistic and Roman periods, peripteral chapels continued to be built, but these "kiosks" are *less* close to the Ara Pacis in form and design than the New Kingdom examples.[29] The kiosks, too, are also small, stone, freestanding, peripteral buildings with a sacred function. By contrast, however, they stand at ground level, with no steps up to the entrances, as at Qertassi (Figure 7.10), Philae, and Dendera.[30]

---

[28] Elsner 1991. On the Ara Pacis, the sculptural program depicts and facilitates this direction of movement.

[29] Dieter Arnold analyzes change and continuity between the older chapels and these newer kiosk forms (Arnold 1999: 284). See also Weber 1910.

[30] Qertassi, about 40 km south of Philae, was part of Isis' annual Nubian circuit. On the kiosk there: Borchardt 1938: 17, pl. 9; Arnold 1999: 237–40, figs. 197–8; Hölbl 2004: 101–2 and fig. 136. The giant kiosk at Philae (15 by 20 m in plan, 15.45 m in height) has often been considered Trajanic, but an Augustan date has also been proposed (Haeny 1985); Borchardt 1938: 13–14, pls. 5 and 6; Hölbl 2004: 86–7; Arnold 1999: 235–6, figs. 193–4. Dendera: Borchardt 1938: 14–7 and pls. 7 and 8; Arnold 1999: 215 and figs. 165 and 166; Chassinat and Daumas 1978: 1–70. Additional kiosks are known at Philae (Hölbl 2004: 86–7 and fig. 124; Arnold 1999: 119–22, figs. 74–8); Dionysias (Borchardt 1938: 17–18, pl. 9; Arnold 1999: 254); Tebtunis (Borchardt 1938: 18; Arnold 1999: 155 and 254); Tanis, and the El-Kharga oasis (Arnold 1999: 107 and 113–15).

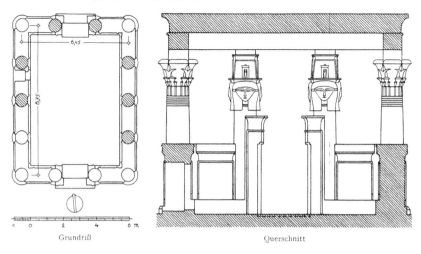

Grundriß   Querschnitt

Figure 7.10.   Plan and elevation drawing of the Augustan kiosk at Qertassi

Instead of having two axial entrances, they often have additional doorways in the long sides, and the roof chapel at Dendera has two doors placed diagonally to one another in the north and east façades. The older chapels and the Roman altar had a flat roofline or no roof; the later kiosks were topped with a low, vaulted, wooden roof.[31] The late period kiosks do show a tripartite structure of the entrance façade as well as a division between solid parapet walls below and an open register above. However, they are surrounded by plant or Hathor columns, not the piers seen on most earlier chapels. And the kiosks' parapet walls are not low and flush with the vertical plane of the façade but tall, with extruding cavetto moldings that interrupt the solid lines of the exterior in a new emphasis on ornament and a lightened visual effect.[32]

There are changes in function as well. The late period kiosks continued to be built in locations suggesting that they provided shaded stops or way stations for a deity's image along a processional route.[33] However, unlike the earlier chapels, these kiosks did not celebrate the pharaoh's jubilee.[34] The Ptolemaic or Augustan kiosk at Dendera, which stood on the

[31] Compare the Hellenistic kiosk depicted on the Praeneste mosaic. The kiosk at Qertassi, with its 7-meter-long, flat, sandstone roofing slabs, is an exception (Figure 7.10).
[32] On these later screen walls, Arnold 1999: 302–3.   [33] Borchardt 1938: 19–20; Arnold 1999: 284–5.
[34] Nectanebo's fourth-century BCE kiosk on Philae and the Augustan kiosk at Qertassi were almost certainly barque stations on ritual processions for Isis. So, probably, was the huge, unfinished, Roman-period kiosk on Philae.

southwest corner of the roof of the temple of Hathor, shows no trace of an internal structure.[35] Rather, a light well in the center of the floor illuminated the room below. Inscriptions and two nearby staircases show that this kiosk was part of the processional movement of the New Year celebration, during which the cult image was brought up into the sunlight from the *wabet*, or "pure hall," directly underneath. All in all, these late period kiosks – including the ones built under Augustus' rule – are less comparable to the Ara Pacis than are the New Kingdom chapels.

To sum up, my argument is that New Kingdom peripteral chapels in Egypt were appropriated as architectural and functional models for the design of the Ara Pacis Augustae in Rome. As seen earlier, this was certainly possible at the level of knowledge and transmission. Many of these chapels were still standing and visible during the Augustan period – indeed, some survived above ground another two millennia to be recorded in modern times. And, far beyond architectural survival and simple visibility, the temple complexes in which they stood continued to be ritual centers and the focus of an extensive Augustan building program. It is not clear if it mattered to the Augustan designers that these chapels dated to ancient Egypt in general, to the New Kingdom more particularly, or to a specific pharaoh's reign. However, it does seem to have mattered that these were sacred buildings from Egypt's deep past. A second key point thus emerges: like the appropriation of the two obelisks brought to Rome in 10/9 BCE, the appropriation of Egyptian jubilee chapels for Rome was a deliberately classicizing gesture, bypassing more recent religious architecture to appropriate instead from the pharaonic past.

The Ara Pacis as an Egyptianizing Monument

Appropriation, in Nelson's terms, is an active selection carried out for particular reasons; it takes over – and distorts – cultural objects or ideas that are in this way made valuable for the new context. It is not enough, then, to identify Egyptian parallels for the Ara Pacis, or even to show that knowledge of them in Rome was certainly possible. A full analysis must also show that these pharaonic precedents had meaning and value as appropriated for the Ara Pacis Augustae. Like the adjacent obelisk

---

[35] The temple proper was begun in the New Kingdom, enlarged by Nectanebo I, replaced by Ptolemy XII starting in 54 BCE, continued under Cleopatra VII, and finally dedicated by Augustus in 20 BCE. Borchardt 1938: 14–17 and pls. 7 and 8; Arnold 1999: 215 and figs. 165 and 166; Chassinat & Daumas 1978: 1–70.

described earlier, the Ara Pacis exemplifies a double appropriation, and this section is accordingly divided into two parts. I first consider the pharaonic precedents alone, then evaluate them as just one appropriation within the monument's layered synthesis of Italic, Greek, Hellenistic, and Ptolemaic cultural elements.

The Egyptian chapels discussed earlier are here considered as precedents for key *architectural* features of the Ara Pacis; its sculptural styles and iconography drew on other cultural sources. The similarities between pharaonic jubilee chapels and the Roman altar, coupled with the symbolic importance of Egypt in Augustan Rome, suggest that this was a deliberate appropriation. I interpret it in relation to the Ara Pacis' commission by the Senate. The *Res Gestae* of Augustus describes the occasion (12.2):[36]

> cu]m ex H[isp]ania Gal[liaque, rebu]s in iis provincis prosp[e]re [gest]i[s], R[omam redi], Ti(berio) Nerone P(ublio) Qui[nctilio c]o(n)s(ulibus), aram [Pacis A]u[g]ust[ae senatus pro] redi[t]u meo consa[c]randam [censuit] ad campum [Martium, in qua m]agistratus et sac[er]dotes [vi]rgines[que] V [est]a[les ann]iver[sarium sacrific]ium facer[e iussit].

> When I returned to Rome from Spain and Gaul, having settled affairs successfully in these provinces, in the consulship of Tiberius Nero and Publius Quinctilius, the senate decreed that an altar of Augustan Peace should be consecrated in thanks for my return on the field of Mars, and ordered magistrates and priests and Vestal Virgins to perform an annual sacrifice there.

This account, finalized a generation after these events, stresses the *princeps'* effectiveness as ruler, the honorific nature of the monumental gift, and the ritual aspects of the altar's dedication.[37] It does not mention the political dynamics of 13–9 BCE or the altar's appearance, cultural allusions or spatial connections. However, given that the Senate commissioned this altar, its pharaonic allusions can be interpreted primarily as political communication between the senators and the *princeps*.

It was one thing for Augustus to create Egyptianizing monuments at Rome, as in the import of two obelisks from Heliopolis. It was another thing entirely for the Senate to do so. Egypt had been formally ceded to Augustus' control as part of the constitutional settlement of 27 BCE (Cass. Dio 51.19.6, 53.12.7). To reduce the danger of an Egypt-based political threat, Augustus installed as governor an equestrian, not a senatorial,

---

[36] Text and translation are from Cooley 2009: 70. On the different sources of this composite text, Cooley 2009 with additional bibliography.

[37] On the late Augustan date of the *Res Gestae*, Cooley 2009: 42–3.

prefect of Alexandria and Egypt (Cass. Dio 53.13.2).[38] Egypt as an actual place was therefore a difficult subject in Roman governance, while Egypt as a symbolic idea remained powerful. The Ara Pacis displays a carefully considered celebration of Augustus' reign, with an even more careful evocation of Egypt – a classicizing pharaonic appeal, bypassing more recent Ptolemaic models.[39] This parallels the Greek classicism of certain parts of the altar's sculptural decoration but with very different political connotations. The Senate avoided the fraught recent politics of Egypt and instead appropriated its powerful ancient symbolism to celebrate Augustus: religious solemnity, the conquest of time as well as space, and the importance of Egypt as a touchstone of rule over the *oikoumene*. From this perspective it is no surprise that a monument created to honor *res bene gestae* in Spain and Gaul drew on Egyptian and Greek precedents; they gave the altar the necessary imperial scope.

An additional possibility is worth considering. Middle and New Kingdom peripteral chapels celebrated the ruler's thirty-year jubilee; was this idea appropriated for Rome as well? For at least some people at the elite levels of Roman politics, the celebration of a thirty-year jubilee may have been a valuable connotation.[40] The Ara Pacis was commissioned by the Senate in 13 BCE. Thirty years before, in the year 43, Augustus (then Octavian) held the consulship for the first time. It is possible that, with this monument, the Senate paid the *princeps* the compliment of a thirty-year regnal jubilee celebration, suggesting that Augustus' legitimate rule dated back to his first consulship – never mind the intervening civil wars and proscriptions, Actium in 31, or the political settlement of 27.[41]

These pharaonic precedents take on additional significance in relation to the nearby obelisk in the northern Campus Martius. On both

---

[38] Roman senators and high-ranking equestrians were no longer permitted to visit Egypt without Augustus' permission (Tac. *Ann.* 2.59). The Senate, apparently anxious to reassure the *princeps* that it did not pose a threat, had passed a *senatusconsultum* that made the date of Octavian's triumphal entry into Alexandria a holiday.

[39] On classicism in Roman art, Elsner 2006, Hölscher 1987/2004 and 2006.

[40] Perhaps not coincidentally, the meridian obelisk, erected in the same year the Ara Pacis was completed and in rectilinear alignment with it, was originally commissioned by Psammetichus II (26th Dynasty, 595–589 BCE) to celebrate his thirty-year jubilee (D'Onofrio 1992: 369–421; Swetnam-Burland 2010). The hieroglyphic inscription is transcribed and translated in Budge 1926: 219–24.

[41] The *Res Gestae*'s account of the Ara Pacis makes no reference to this, but it was probably finalized decades after the altar's dedication; what had seemed valuable to emphasize in the years around 10 BCE was no longer right for a very changed situation. The *Res Gestae* emphasizes the web of ritual connections between Augustus and Rome's political and religious bodies rather than his own monarchical power.

monuments, ancient Egypt was recruited to play an architectural and structural role. The obelisk was made the gnomon of a monumental meridian instrument, while pharaonic jubilee chapels were treated as architectural models for the Ara Pacis. Neither monument was complete with only its Egyptian aspects; both also drew on other cultural sources, as in the Latin inscription on the obelisk's new base and the Greek labels along the meridian line on the ground, or the mix of Roman iconography and Hellenizing styles animating the sculptural decoration of the Ara Pacis. The altar and the obelisk were finished in the same year and stood almost ninety meters apart in an apparently open area (Figure 7.4).[42] They were aligned with each other and also with the preexisting Augustan monuments in the zone. The obelisk was famously not aligned with the north–south meridian line that it served as a gnomon, but was instead positioned so as to be nearly parallel to the east and west walls of the Ara Pacis and to face Augustus' Mausoleum to the north, linking these three monuments.[43] Their alignment recalls the alignment of the seventh pylon obelisks and the jubilee chapel of Thutmose III at Karnak, discussed earlier. More broadly, Egyptian temple and mortuary complexes connected different kinds of religious buildings through careful alignments across large spaces. That practice, too, may have been a source for the spectacular Augustan monuments in the northern Campus Martius.

The Ara Pacis was a senatorial commission but also part of a larger monarchic complex; in this balance lies further significance. Though the obelisk and the altar were highly coordinated, there are important differences in the dynamics of appropriation. The obelisk was an actual object brought from Egypt, while the Ara Pacis drew architecturally on an Egyptian building form, among other models. Obelisk and altar also drew on the symbolic force of ancient Egypt in different ways. Augustus' obelisk ostentatiously celebrated the *princeps'* conquest of Egypt and his control over the measurement of time. The Ara Pacis expressed a more restrained view of his power; with its allegorical and ritual imagery, it situated his rule firmly in the context of proper Roman religious observation. In this way,

---

[42] The date of the re-erection of the obelisk is provided by the Latin inscription on the base. We do not know exactly when the meridian line was first installed, but it seems most plausible to date these to the same time (see n. 30). On the revised measurement of the distance between obelisk and Ara Pacis as 89 rather than 87 meters, Frischer & Fillwalk 2014: 79.

[43] Carlos Noreña has further observed that a line projected westward from the Ara Pacis through the obelisk will bisect, at its halfway point, the north–south line between Agrippa's Pantheon and Augustus' Mausoleum (Noreña 2013: 56). For this reason and others, he proposes to locate the *ustrinum* of Augustus at this halfway point.

we see the Senate intervening in the high-stakes politics of Augustan monuments. The Egyptianizing Ara Pacis was a pendant to the nearby obelisk but also a counterpoint, a careful foil that drew on the same symbolism of ancient Egypt to mitigate the obelisk's more strongly monarchic force.

Who in Augustan Rome could have recognized an architectural reference to Egyptian jubilee chapels? The same question, of course, arises for Augustus' obelisks, the first such objects from Egypt to arrive in Rome.[44] It is possible that Egyptian allusions were more recognizable in Augustan Rome than they are now. People may have learned about Egypt from their army service, commercial or administrative work there, visual displays paraded during Augustus' triumph, or everyday conversations in Rome about the spectacular new monuments being built in the northern Campus Martius. Still, the primary audience for these Egyptianizing monuments does not seem to have been the Roman public. Pharaonic precedents on the Ara Pacis would have been meaningful above all to the *princeps* and the Senate at Rome, and to knowledgeable spectators from around the Mediterranean who were in a position to understand the ways in which Rome was expressing its power in relation to Mediterranean history. For other spectators without this level of knowledge and without the same investment in monumental gamesmanship at Rome, these connotations would have been less visible and probably irrelevant; for them, the monument worked in other ways and at other levels.

The Ara Pacis' appropriations from pharaonic Egypt are about more than specific references treated in isolation; they are equally important for the way they interact with Greek, Italic, and Ptolemaic sources in a layered synthesis. Like the meridian obelisk, the Ara Pacis can be seen to perform a double appropriation involving both direct quotations from Egypt and a sophisticated cultural layering from multiple times and places, all in the service of Augustan Rome.[45] This cultural synthesis was carefully structured. The altar's architectural design, iconography, style, and decorative organization all differed with respect to cultural appropriation.[46] As already

---

[44] As Grant Parker reminds us elsewhere in this volume, repeated appropriations have given obelisks a spectacular and familiar public role at Rome and in other western capitals that pharaonic jubilee chapels never had; obelisks look immediately and obviously Egyptian to modern eyes in a way that the Ara Pacis does not.

[45] Tonio Hölscher has shown that Augustan art drew on different periods and styles of Greek art for semantic purposes; particular styles of Greek art were consistently associated with particular Roman themes and values (Hölscher 2004). Egyptianizing art at Rome responds to a similar approach.

[46] Compare the Augustan-period tomb of C. Cestius Epulo at Rome, which also draws directly on pharaonic architectural models. It is shaped like an Egyptian (more accurately, Nubian) pyramid

seen, pharaonic chapels were adapted for the altar's architectural form. This by no means excludes the Archaic Italian or classical and Hellenistic Greek architectural precedents identified by previous scholars; notable in all these sources is their classicizing reach into the Italian and Mediterranean past. The altar's iconography and style, by contrast, drew primarily on Greek and Italian artistic traditions. At this level, Egyptianizing elements appeared as a decorative margin only, as in the border of palmettes and lotus buds on the interior of the temenos walls.[47]

The decorative organization of the exterior temenos walls – how the visual field was organized and what kind of imagery was placed where – was handled in yet another way. Two Ptolemaic visual practices may have been among its sources. Women and children famously appear in Roman state relief for the first time on the Ara Pacis, but visual models for this dynastic practice were well established in Ptolemaic Egypt.[48] Equally fundamental is the juxtaposition of figural relief sculpture in the upper register with vegetal ornament below. David Castriota has explored the sacred symbolism of this vegetal ornament in relation to Hellenistic Greek precedents;[49] I would suggest that those Hellenistic precedents included Egypt. Ptolemaic and Roman temple art in Egypt frequently combined a figural relief above with a sacred vegetal zone of papyrus or lily below.[50] In other words, the designers of this new Augustan monument drew on monarchic and cultural precedents from around the Mediterranean; the pharaonic allusions were but one cultural strand within a carefully constructed synthesis of Egyptian, Italic, and Greek sources, drawn from the distant past as well as from more recent developments. The resulting Ara Pacis was a layered and allusive synthesis of conquered cultures.

but includes no Egyptian motifs or imagery inside. The pyramid form seems to have brought Egyptian sacrality to the tomb and to have created a prestigious and up-to-date public display (see Versluys 2002: 367–8).

[47] Elsewhere in Augustan art, too, and by contrast to architectural citations, Egyptianizing iconography and style were employed in marginal zones and as framing elements rather than in the central spaces. Consider, for example, the position of the Egyptianizing elements in the wall paintings of the Augustan villa at Boscotrecase (von Blanckenhagen & Alexander 1990: pls. 2–5, 8–9, 28, 34–5, 38, and 41).

[48] For example, on the outer rear wall of the Temple of Hathor at Dendera, Cleopatra VII presents Caesarion (Ptolemy XV Caesar), her son by Julius Caesar, to the gods. These Cleopatran reliefs were left unharmed during the Augustan completion of the temple, either because of their connection to Julius Caesar or because of the priority placed on religious and political continuity in these temple complexes.

[49] Castriota 1995.

[50] Finnestad 1997. For example, papyrus dados provide a sacred connection to the Nile for the figural imagery above on the reliefs of the Ptolemaic pronaos at Kom Ombo (Arnold 1999: fig. 264) and on the façade reliefs of the Augustan temple house at Dendur (Arnold 1999: fig. 205).

Questions about audience arise again. Who in Rome could fully see and understand allusions to the classicizing Greek style of the processional reliefs or the archaic Roman *templum minus*, or the sophisticated ways in which different times and places were interwoven on the altar? Presumably not many, but a universally understood message was not the goal. The Ara Pacis' designers, like those of the obelisk-meridian, worked in a high-stakes political climate of visual experimentation, and they had available to them the full knowledge resources of the empire.[51] All of these were appropriated and reconfigured to represent Roman rule and the power of the *princeps*.

Conclusion

In this chapter, I have argued that pharaonic jubilee chapels were among the architectural models for the Ara Pacis Augustae. Exploring this specific line of appropriation has more broadly highlighted the symbolic importance of pharaonic Egypt in Augustan cultural politics, as well as the complexity and sophistication of Augustan cultural appropriations. Specific ideas were appropriated from Egypt, but so were classical and Hellenistic intellectual traditions about Egypt. This double appropriation echoes Marden Fitzpatrick Nichols's exploration, in Chapter 6, of the self-conscious Roman takeover of existing ideas and forms of authority. It also echoes Grant Parker's emphasis on the colonization of time. In their sophisticated layering of Egyptian, Greek, and Roman styles and ideas, Augustan monuments appropriated time as well as space to position Rome as the geographic and chronological culmination of Mediterranean rule.

We can develop aspects of Robert Nelson's model of appropriation with Augustan appropriations in mind. Nelson stresses the active, motivated nature of this process; as seen earlier, in the Ara Pacis and other Augustan state monuments, appropriation was actively and self-consciously imperialistic. It was also classicizing, in the sense of creating the value of the past by means of its much later treatment.[52] The past (be it pharaonic Egyptian, classical Greek, archaic Italian) played an essential role, but there was no stable "original" meaning that was then taken up and distorted for new purposes; this was not a binary model or linear sequence in which an untouched and unchanging original was reused later in a different way. Rather, the Augustan nature and significance of the past was created through this active, retrospective selection. Two distortions operated

---

[51] On knowledge and empire, Murphy 2004; König & Whitmarsh 2007.
[52] Jaś Elsner has articulated the way in which this simultaneity works: Elsner 2006.

simultaneously: one was the meaning projected back onto the past, and the other was the distortion inherent in the actual appropriation, reshaping that projected meaning for the new context. The retrospective meaning attributed to the past itself evolved over time and in different Hellenistic, and then Roman, contexts, and this malleability facilitated new kinds of appropriation that could nonetheless claim recognizability and continuity.

A final question is why there was no further Egyptianizing of this particular kind after the construction of the Ara Pacis. Egypt continued to be a rich source of imagery and symbolism in Imperial Rome after Augustus; obelisks had a long afterlife in Imperial Rome, as did more syncretic Egyptianizing ideas and motifs.[53] However, no other surviving buildings at Rome seem to allude to pharaonic jubilee chapels – or, apparently, to the Ara Pacis itself.[54] It is possible that such references exist in later Roman buildings but have not yet been recognized. Alternatively, this may not have been a successful appropriation; in Nelson's terms, perhaps these pharaonic references did not experience distortion, in which some original meaning was retained even as they were reconfigured, but rather a negation, a complete semiotic loss.[55] I would suggest, however, that Nelson's discussion of contingency offers a better way forward. Appropriations depend heavily on context for their motives and significance; they will lose or change meaning as that context changes.[56] An immediate implication is that appropriations – even spectacular monumental ones – are by definition temporary and situational.

Just so, the transient value of pharaonic jubilee chapels in Rome was due to the specific political and cultural situation in the middle years of Augustus' reign. Within that period's monumental politics, especially in relation to the obelisk-meridian and the larger landscape of the Campus

---

[53] An important recent study is Swetnam-Burland 2015.

[54] We do not know what some contemporary or subsequent altars looked like, so this is by no means certain. The Ara Fortuna Redux, dedicated by the Senate on Augustus' return in 19 BCE and erected outside the Porta Capena, took a far more basic and traditional form than the Ara Pacis (*LTUR* II: 275 and fig. 103). We do not know the architectural shape of the Julio-Claudian Ara Pietatis (*LTUR* IV: 87–9). A monument excavated in 1886–7 in the Campus Martius was reconstructed by Lanciani as having three screen walls concentrically arranged around a central altar and punctuated by doorways on a central axis, but this reconstruction has since been rejected (*LTUR* II: 19; compare *LTUR* IV: 273–4).

[55] I thank Carolyn MacDonald for this intriguing idea.

[56] "Appropriation ... breaks down over time, either fading away or mutating into a new myth" (Nelson 1996: 119). Elsewhere in this volume, Grant Parker and Marden Fitzpatrick Nichols show how the force of an appropriation could be kept alive either by subsequent appropriations (e.g., of further obelisks from Egypt) or by being explicit (as Vitruvius is in deliberately naming his Greek predecessors and sources). The Ara Pacis, however, neither makes its pharaonic models explicit nor has successors that draw on the same models.

Martius, this reference to pharaonic Egypt worked very well as communication between the Senate and the *princeps*. That context, however, changed with time. In the decades after Augustus' death, with the consolidation of dynastic rule and the increasingly autocratic position of the emperor, obelisks were apparently deemed more useful than jubilee chapels for celebrating the Roman emperor. More broadly, after Augustus, there was less need to represent Rome as the culminating power in relation to Hellenistic ideas about space and time; that had been accomplished.

In short, Egyptian allusions on the Ara Pacis may have suffered the fate of many appropriations, which is to fade from significance as the immediate context changes. This does not mean that the pharaonic models were not successful at the time. Similarly, no subsequent monuments employed Greek and Hellenistic stylistic and iconographic precedents in quite the same way as the Ara Pacis, nor, for that matter, is there evidence at Rome of a second monumental meridian. Later emperors always could, and indeed had to, engage with the legacy of Augustus as founder of the Principate, but different aspects of Augustan visual culture were appropriated for future uses. For example, Hadrian's Mausoleum visibly echoed Augustus' but surely did not embody the complex cultural appropriations activating the earlier one. In these ways, then, focusing on the Egyptianizing aspects of the Ara Pacis highlights not only the symbolic importance of Egypt in Rome and the synthetic complexities of Augustan cultural appropriations, but also the experimental aspects of political art and cultural expression throughout the Augustan era.

CHAPTER 8

Monolithic Appropriation? The Lateran Obelisk Compared

Grant Parker

> Patris opus munusque [ ] tibi, Roma, dicavit
> Augustus [Constan]tius orbe recepto,
> et quod nulla tulit tellus nec viderat aetas
> condidit ut claris exa[equ]et dona triumfis.
>
> (1–4)

> When Constantius Augustus had recovered the world, he
> dedicated the ... work and gift of his father to you, Rome,
> and established what no land brought forth and no epoch
> had seen, so that he makes his gift match his triumphs.[1]

So begins an inscription on the base upon which the emperor Constantius
had an obelisk of red granite erected in the Circus Maximus (*CIL* 6.1163).
The text, now lost, is known from a sixteenth-century transcription. The
obelisk itself was moved in 1588 to Piazza San Giovanni in Laterano, where
it was placed on a new base with a new inscription. The fourth-century
inscription will be our starting point, for it puts the focus on a retrievable
moment in late antique history, providing tantalizing information about
the life story of an artifact and, beyond that, framing a discussion about the
dynamics of appropriation in the Roman world. Indeed, in such a context
the obelisk offers a test case by which to tease out not only the possibilities
but also the limitations of appropriation as a concept.

Those very possibilities will constitute the core of this chapter, which
moves beyond the Lateran obelisk to compare other monoliths transported
across the Mediterranean. The first section focuses on the Lateran obelisk,
after which the second section takes a broader view of obelisks and their
narratives. The third section outlines various senses in which obelisks are

---

[1] The translation is adapted from Courtney 1995: 57, inscription no. 31, with critical edition and
commentary. The standard scholarly edition is *CIL* 6.1163, which is taken up into other important
collections of inscriptions: *ILS* 736 = *CLE* 279. It was first published by Mercati (1589: 291–2), who
was instrumental in its excavation and repair.

entangled with narratives of appropriation, whereas the fourth section briefly diverts to a limit case in the form of Diocletian's stele in Alexandria: a monolith, in many ways comparable to obelisks, that defies the predominant south-to-north momentum. A brief conclusion revisits the usefulness of appropriation as a concept.

In the bigger picture of this volume it should be said that appropriation is here taken as not a given but a productive problem. Without doubt, uncritical and overly broad use of the concept attenuates its significance. No less troubling is the concomitant risk of reifying cultural boundaries. Is it possible to imagine culture without appropriation? Any such thought would bring us uncomfortably close to Herder's notion of cultures as discrete entities. Yet it seems axiomatic that the dynamics of exchange feature prominently in contemporary understandings of culture. Appropriation thus risks becoming an awkward surrogate for culture itself. That said, the concept indeed has use if it directs us towards the ways in which objects and meanings are taken over, displaced, replaced, creatively adapted for new purposes. It seems most useful as a means of articulating the transition between the physical and the symbolic, the ideological and the metaphorical. Appropriation might help us to think not just of Rome's deployment of exotic cultural productions but also of its engagement with Roman and other pasts – what we might call its colonization of time. Beyond their spatial movement, obelisks have huge transhistorical resonance, encapsulating a heady mix of Egyptian, Roman and other pasts.

If this is, *prima facie*, a story about appropriation, it is also one about distortion. Just as the opening lines of the poem highlight the unprecedented nature of Constantius' gift, creating an unspoken paradox with the prevalence and antiquity of Rome's preexisting obelisks, so the current chapter requires tightrope walking. If we wish to evaluate the dynamics with which obelisks were integrated into Roman settings, we must balance the longevity of the objects with the novelty and variety of their new settings, all too readily glossed as "contexts." Here we can try to attend to the ways in which new contexts come into being, and how the surviving monoliths carry meaning within them.

An Obelisk

The biography of the obelisk now at the Piazza di San Giovanni Laterano in Rome begins with the pharaoh Thutmose III (1479–1425 BCE), who had it hewn from Aswan red granite. It was finally raised at Karnak by his grandson, Thutmose IV (1400–1390 BCE), and remained there for over seventeen centuries until the emperor Constantine had it brought to Alexandria with a view to transportation northward. It was not until the rule of his son and successor, Constantius II, that the obelisk was moved to Rome, shortly before his visit there in 357 CE. It was placed on the *spina* of the Circus Maximus, which already accommodated one obelisk.[2] There it stood until its collapse at some undisclosed time, probably in the early Middle Ages. In 1587 Pope Sixtus V had it excavated and repaired by his architect Domenico Fontana, and the next year it was erected at the Piazza San Giovanni in Laterano.[3] This bare bones account provides our starting point for further reflection. Such data emerge from the object itself, from its description by Ammianus Marcellinus, and not least from two inscriptions: one in Middle Egyptian on its flanks and the lost Latin on what used to be its base.

With its recurrent theme of precedent, the Latin inscription conveys a strong sense of time depth. Dynastic continuity is emphasized from the beginning (*patris opus munusque*, 1), indicating Constantius' *pietas* towards Constantine. At the same time, the scale of the obelisk confers an exceptional quality on Constantius' act of moving it (*nulla tulit tellus.* . ., 3, with strong alliteration). In fact, at 32.18 meters this is today the tallest obelisk standing at Rome, even after some four meters were lost in its sixteenth-century reconstitution.[4] This accident of survival seems to substantiate the emperor's proud claim. The inscription continues as follows:

> hoc decus ornatum genitor cognominis urbis
> esse volens caesa Thebis de rupe revellit,
> sed gravior divum tangebat cura vehendi
> quod nullo ingenio nisuque manuque moveri
> Caucaseam molem discurrens fama monebat.
>
> (5–9)

> His father [Constantine], wishing this monument to adorn the city named after him, hewed it from the rock at Thebes, but the greater worry of transport troubled the sanctified emperor, in that far-spread rumor warned that the mass of Caucasian proportions could not be moved by any ingenuity or physical effort.

Constantius' act of bringing the obelisk to Rome emerges as homage to the empire's original capital and to his father. Whereas Constantine had intended the obelisk for Constantinople, the new Rome on the Bosporus,

---

[2] In 10 BCE Augustus had two obelisks brought to the city of Rome, to the Campus Martius and the Circus Maximus. The latter was moved to the Piazza del Popolo at the instruction of Pope Sixtus V. Habachi 2000: 73–5.

[3] Fontana left his own detailed account of engineering aspects: Fontana 1590.

[4] Habachi 2000: 67.

Constantius redirected it to Italy.[5] The fact that transportation was a
"greater worry" (*gravior. . .cura vehendi*, 7), with emphatically placed comparative adjective, shows that the process of transportation eclipses even
the obelisk itself in significance. Put differently, and as the rest of
the inscription indicates, the process (of moving) subsumes the product
(obelisk), thus making the mover (Constantius) paramount.

> At dominus mundi Constantius omnia fretus
> cedere virtuti terris incedere iussit
> haut partem exiguam montis pontoque tumenti
> credidit et placido [flu]ctu
> litus ad Hesperiam [   ] mirante carinam.
>
>   (10–14)

> But Constantius, lord of the world, confident that everything
> yields to excellence, gave orders that the sizeable slice of
> mountain should proceed over the land and entrusted it to
> the swelling sea, and (had it carried) to the shores of Italy
> while the calm waves wondered at the . . . boat.

That the logistical feat predominates is a very Roman imperial inflection
of the epigraphic habit. Here we see a variant on inscriptions honoring
extraordinary building projects throughout the empire; engineering signifies the conquest of nature and brings credit to the emperor with whom
the building project is proximately associated.[6] In reality the voyage from
Alexandria to Ostia or Pozzuoli (14 days) is longer than that from
Alexandria to Constantinople (5);[7] that difference may be hinted at here,
so that Constantius' achievement surpasses even Constantine's original
ambition.

> interea Romam ta[et]ro vastante tyranno
> Augusti iacuit donum studiumque locandi
> non fastu spreti, sed quod non crederet ullus
> tantae molis opus superas consurgere in auras.
> nunc veluti rursus ruf[is] avulsa metallis
> emicuit pulsatque polos.
>
>   (15–20)

---

[5] Well may we wonder about the reason for this change of plan, especially given the contradictory
statements from the historian Ammianus Marcellinus (*Res gestae* 16.10.17; 17.4.12), discussed later.

[6] DeLaine 2002.

[7] According to ORBIS, the geospatial network model of the Roman world, a voyage from Alexandria
to Constantinople could take as few as 12.3 days (in January) and as many as 15.7 days (in July),
whereas Alexandria to Ostia would take between 16 days (April) and 20.4 days (July). See http://
orbis.stanford.edu.

> In the meantime while the foul usurper was devastating Rome
> the gift of Augustus and zeal to put it in situ were abandoned,
> not because it was rejected in contempt, but because nobody
> believed that such a massive work could be raised into the air.
> But now, as if again hewn from the red quarry, it has leaped
> up and knocks at heaven's door.

Enter Magnentius, a soldier-turned-count who seized power in the western provinces in the years 350–353 by gaining the support of the army.[8] Eventually the rising was crushed, and Magnentius himself committed suicide in 353. Just as Horace in the Cleopatra ode avoids naming the defeated Egyptian queen ("no ordinary woman," *non humilis mulier*, *Odes* 1.37.32), so Magnentius is identified in the inscription by means of a charged periphrasis.

Nobody believed that the obelisk could be re-erected (*non crederet ullus*, 17); in fact, widespread rumor (*discurrens fama*, 9) had predicted that the planned move would fail to materialize. In this light the successful move and re-erection are a double improbability. The emphasis on the ambiguities of *fama* contributes to a sense of uncertain outcomes,[9] amplifying the emperor's achievement by reflecting on the dangers successfully negotiated.

The poem compares the re-erection at Rome with the original quarrying in Upper Egypt, at the red granite quarries around Aswan ("as if," *veluti*, 19). The later moment explicitly reprises the earlier ("again," *rursus*, 19). If we take these temporal markers together, the longest possible span frames the life history of the object, from its first quarrying to the culminating point of its installation, at Constantius' behest, at Rome on the Tiber. This long-term life history is delicately balanced against the intentions of the two emperors (*volens*, 6, and *iussit*, 11), amid popular misgivings about the likelihood of realization, and the implied potential interference on the part of the usurper.

In the immediate sense, the "gift of [the] Augustus," i.e., Constantius, refers to the obelisk itself, but it may also draw a connection with the obelizing activity of the first Augustus, who had obelisks brought to the Campus Martius and the Circus Maximus. The monoliths did much to give a new character to those locations and make them highly visible public spaces.[10] And yet the inscription presents Constantius' obelisk as an innovation, trumpeting that it defies nature's constraints: a skyscraper that "knocks at heaven's door" (*pulsat. . .polos*, 20).

---

[8] Matthews 1989: 33. The beginning of Ammianus' surviving text (book 14.1) opens with the punishment of Magnentius' supporters.
[9] Hardie 2012: esp. 3, "duplicities of *fama*."   [10] Zanker 1988: 145–6.

haec gloria dudum

auctori servata suo c[um c]aede tyranni
redditur, atque aditu Ro[mae vi]rtute reperto
victor ovans urbiq[ue   ]e tropaeum
principis et munus condi[t   ]que triumfis.

(20–4)

This glory, long kept in store for its author, is now duly awarded to
him along with the death of the usurper, and the celebrating
victor, having found the path to Rome through his courage and
favoring the city, has established his trophy and an emperor's gift
and consecrates it by his triumph.

Gloria in the usurper's death spurs a triumphal moment. In this the obelisk
participates as a trophy (*tropaeum*, 21).[11] It would have been unthinkable to
celebrate a triumph over a domestic opponent in the early or high Empire.
Yet there were instances of smaller *tropaea* dedicated at temples to mark
failed conspiracies.[12] Octavian's victory over Egypt in 31 BCE was at the
same time a victory over Mark Antony, yet some twenty years later
Augustus chose two obelisks to monumentalize his success. An *exotic*,
Egyptian object therefore seems to have been chosen to signify victory in
civil war. Constantius' triumph over Magnentius comes at the end of the
inscription as the immediate point of memorialization and at the same
time constitutes a strong point of closure. The word *triumfis* may be taken
as a poetic plural, specifically denoting victory over Magnentius;[13] yet at
the same time it suggests that future triumphs can be expected.

The evidence for Constantine's intentions is contradictory. The inscription says he wanted to bring the obelisk to his eponymous city, i.e.,
Constantinople (line 5); yet Ammianus seems to imply that he always
had Rome in mind.[14] On its own terms, the historical question has little
impact here, but it points to the idea, seen in both the inscription and in
Ammianus, that the life of an object itself sometimes defies the intentions
of monument-makers.

---

[11] A loanword from the Greek, this could be used of either small or large objects. Lewis & Short,
A Latin Dictionary, s.v. trop(h)aeum.

[12] Caligula thus dedicated three daggers after a failed conspiracy in 39 CE (Suet. *Cal.* 24.3; Dio Cassius
59.22.7); and Vitellius in Cologne dedicated the dagger with which Otho took his life (Suet. *Vit.*
10.3). See further Rutledge 2012: 135.

[13] Courtney 1995: 251.

[14] Each view has modern supporters. For Rome as the intended destination, following Ammianus, see
Fowden 1987; for Constantinople, in keeping with the inscription, Nicholson & Nicholson 1989.
See now Kelly 2008: 225–30.

What does Ammianus say about the Lateran obelisk? As it happens, this is the one obelisk he describes in detail. He tells us that the obelisk was erected in the Circus Maximus as a deliberate means for ¡Constantius to memorialize his visit to Rome, which took place on 28 April 357 CE (16.10). After this initial reference he includes a lengthy excursus on obelisks, including a translation of the inscription of the flanks into Greek (17.4). This translation he ascribes to a certain Hermapion, about whom nothing else is known. The retention of the Greek in quoting Hermapion's translation reflects a tradition of Egyptology going back to Herodotus; it is also in keeping with Ammianus' use of Greek when rendering oracles.[15]

In the *Res gestae*, Constantius' appearance in Rome is dramatic – the late antique ceremony of *adventus* or ceremonial arrival seen at its most elaborate[16] – but it is also a tense moment in the balance of ¡power between emperor, senate, and people, between old Rome and the empire. Constantius is especially overawed (*obstupuit*) when he comes to the rostra, mindful of its role over the course of history (16.10.13).[17] ¡Amazed at the monumentalized city, his response is to contribute in kind:

> Multis igitur cum stupore visis horrendo imperator in fama querebatur ut invalida vel maligna, quod augens omnia semper in maius erga haec explicanda quae Romae sunt obsolescit: deliberansque diu quid ageret, urbis addere statuit ornamentis, ut in maximo circo erigeret obeliscum, cuius originem formamque loco conpetenti monstrabo. (16.10.17)

> So then, when the emperor had viewed many objects with awe and amazement, he complained of Fame as either incapable or spiteful, because while always exaggerating everything, in describing what there is in Rome, she becomes shabby. And after long deliberation on what he should do there, he determined to add to the adornments of the city by erecting in the Circus Maximus an obelisk, the provenance and figure of which I shall describe in the proper place.

The obelisk is thus intended as an intervention in collective memory and a way of counteracting the unreliability of fame. Later in the work, Ammianus' general account of the hieroglyphs on the obelisk flanks again emphasizes intentionality:

> Volucrum enim ferarumque, etiam alieni mundi, genera multa sculpentes ad aevi quoque sequentis aetates ut impetratorum vulgatius perveniret memoria, promissa vel soluta regum vota monstrabant. (17.4.9)

---

[15] Hartog 2001: 41–78; Matthews 1989: 462. For a modern translation of the inscription on the flanks: Ciampini 2004: 56–87.

[16] MacCormack 1981.   [17] Matthews 1989: 231–5.

For by engraving many kinds of birds and beasts, even of another world, in order that the memory of their achievements might the more widely reach generations of a subsequent age, they registered the vows of kings, either promised or performed.

If we consider these different kinds of evidence together, the Lateran obelisk constitutes a threefold accident of survival: the object itself, with its Middle Egyptian inscription; Constantius' inscription (now physically lost); and Ammianus' text. In this respect its life story is unique among obelisks, its status matched by its preeminent size.[18] Such accidents are central to the narrative of its life.

Obelizing Narrative(s)

Narratives are not neutral. Rather, they bring their own burdens and impose meanings via inclusions, exclusions, and other choices; their perspectives and ideologies, often implicit, require scrutiny. The narrative above focuses on the Roman life of the Lateran obelisk and its movement through geographical space. It is also a "thick description" that brings outs its Roman social context.[19] Even the term "Lateran obelisk," convenient as it is, naturalizes the object in an ancient and modern Roman setting. The narrative omits its Egyptian, pre-Roman history; that is attested by other inscriptions on the flanks, however, enabling a counter-narrative of sorts that focuses on originary Egyptian contexts.

We know from the inscriptions on the flanks that the obelisk was first erected by Thutmose III, and both his grandson Thutmose IV and Ramesses II added further text of their own. Thutmose IV's addition indicates that the already hewn obelisk spent thirty-five years being prepared. This presumably explains why the obelisk was erected on its own, as Thutmose III states in the original inscription. The Unfinished Obelisk of Aswan, left in the ground when a large crack appeared near the top, appears to have been intended as its partner. The "Lateran" obelisk was erected by Thutmose III when it became clear that not enough time remained to him to have a second monolith prepared.[20] Beginning in the Middle Kingdom, normal practice dictated that obelisks would be installed in tandem, which makes this New Kingdom example the exception.

---

[18] Though it is arguably sold short in its present location: though it does stand at a major traffic intersection, its proximity to surrounding streets and buildings does not give it the impact of, say, Saint Peter's or the Piazza del Popolo.
[19] The standard account of obelisk lives is Iversen 1968–80, now partly updated by Curran *et al.* 2009.
[20] Habachi 2000: 67.

To what degree can or should this Egyptian narrative be considered separate from, or else subsumed by the Roman narrative? Should the matter be decided by the extent to which Romans understood their Egyptian pasts? What evidence we have for knowledge about obelisks, especially the late antique *Hieroglyphics of Horapollo*, shows a preference for elaborate metaphysical interpretations over the honorific inscriptions actually made by the pharaohs.[21] It would seem safe to assume that Constantius' inscription imposes new meaning without regard for or even knowledge of the foregoing pharaonic inscription. It is a late Roman appropriative speech act par excellence.

What of the early modern history of the obelisk? Here we can merely gesture in that direction. In 1587 the physician and antiquarian Michele Mercati first alerted Pope Sixtus V to the presence of the obelisk in the Circus Maximus; in his book on obelisks he describes the excavation of its three large surviving pieces, its transportation through the city, then repair and installation at the Piazza San Giovanni in Laterano.[22] Placed on its new base, the obelisk now received a cross at its apex, marking its change of status.[23] It was inaugurated on 3 August 1588.

Pharaonic Egypt and (early) modern Italy thus emerge as the twofold supplement to the ancient history of the Lateran obelisk. What happens if our narrative purview were broadened to include other obelisks? Dare we even ask: What would a world history of obelisks look like? The question is not as frivolous as it might seem. It would be easy to tell an "obelizing" version of the grand narrative of Western Civilization, moving from the Fertile Crescent via classical antiquity and the Renaissance to modern times, and touching on colonialism and the nation-state. For the Romans themselves, obelisks and universal history were both linked to the same circumstance of evolving empire. And further, as we have seen, the lives of individual obelisks, by virtue of their longevity, take us beyond any one people's history. What other histories might be part of such a broader timespan? Here we can merely mention them by way of a *praeteritio*.

The Romans were not the first to take up the Egyptian form. In this they were preceded by the Assyrians; the so-called black obelisk of Shalmaneser III (mid-ninth century BCE), now in the British Museum, comes from Nimrud in northern Iraq. Though different from the obelisk form it represents a creative and unique response to a form that was already ancient and foreign.

---

[21] Boas 1993; Iversen 1993: 38–57; Pope 1975: 11–21. Contrast the modern translations of Ciampini 2004.
[22] Mercati 1589: 277–310.　　[23] Iversen 1968–80: 62.

Axum stelae of the fourth century CE constitute another ancient people's creative response to the obelisk form. The modern history of one Axum stele – imported by Mussolini to Rome in the 1920s, returned in the early twenty-first century in response to lengthy diplomatic and public pressure on the Italian government – provides a telling variant or even alternative to obelisk narratives. It shows, among other things, differences between ancient and modern politics around cultural property.[24]

As Jennifer Trimble discusses in her chapter, Augustus' two obelisks in Rome were evidently intended to mark the establishment of universal empire, deploying cosmological symbolism (p. 119).[25] It is no accident that around the same time universal histories were being written, and the Hellenistic idea of the succession of world empires received a Roman inflection.[26]

When Constantinople was established as the new Rome on the Bosporus an obelisk marked its capital status. Installed in 390–391 CE in the Hippodrome, it honors Theodosius. However, the inscription on its flank points back to Thutmose III, who had it installed as part of a pair at the great temple of Karnak.[27]

No obelisks seem to have been raised in the western Middle Ages, a period when many of Rome's obelisks actually fell down. By contrast, Byzantium reveals several responses to the obelisk form, most famously the so-called Walled Obelisk also in the Hippodrome. This brick structure is associated with the tenth-century ruler Constantine VII Porphyrogenitus but may be older. Constantinople especially shows that obelisks have marked not only empire itself, but also – and this is crucial for us – the possibility of establishing empire anew. To this transhistoric resonance we shall return at the end.

Obelisks would enjoy their second modern heyday in the nineteenth century, after French and British interventions in Egypt. In this period obelisks travelled from the Nile to Paris, London, and New York. In all three cases, the engineering feats of transportation and re-installation attracted much attention.[28] In the case of the London obelisk, sailors temporarily lost control of the barge carrying it, producing a newsworthy story of adventure. The base of the Paris obelisk depicts scenes from its

---

[24] Miles 2008.   [25] Cf. Schneider 2008; Zanker 1988.   [26] Clarke 1999b; Swain 1940.

[27] A frieze at Karnak depicts twin obelisks with comparable inscriptions. Thutmose III is known to have erected at least nine obelisks at Karnak and Heliopolis, of which none still stands in its original location. See further Habachi 2000: 47–9, 85–6.

[28] See esp. D'Alton 1993 on New York's Central Park obelisk.

re-erection at the Place de la Concorde, perhaps recalling Theodosius' frieze on the base of the Hippodrome obelisk. Gifts from the Ottoman pasha, these obelisks participated in the "panda diplomacy" of their time, earning goodwill for their donors and potentially subjecting the recipients to open-ended bonds of obligation. In this respect obelisks may be considered colonial signifiers par excellence, emphasizing power encompassing faraway lands, with universalist overtones, and also marking capital cities for their centrality: senses of both space (open-ended imperial expanse) and place (metropolitan specificity). But this new imperialism was flexible, for the older empires of Britain and France were joined by an emerging one across the Atlantic. It should be no surprise, then, that obelisks would prove attractive to emerging nations, including Argentina and Australia, as articulations of their power. Even without ancient obelisks from Egypt available, the form still proved productive by virtue of its distinctiveness. Newly minted obelisks were much used in US Civil War and World War I cemeteries and other memorials. This process of replication continues into our own times, when the traditional nature of obelisks as monuments has given them a role, via radical adaptation, in abstract expressionist and postmodern designs.[29]

Obelisks thus mark particular moments in the use of power, usually in the context of the state; they are also interventions in memory with the potential for considerable social impact over time.[30] The historical moments highlighted here suggest that obelisks disrupt any easy distinction between micro- and macro-narratives; though they are prone to object biographies, the episodes involved are easily aligned with the broader brush of world history. The materiality of obelisks, their large size and their longevity, have given them this special narrative status. Yet far from plainly marking the grand narrative of Roman power "from village to empire," as a noted textbook of Roman history would have it,[31] obelisks can in fact be a site of fragmented narratives. The episodic nature of these stories is itself telling, valorizing jagged edges over any smoothly linear narrative, to say nothing of the fragmentary, composite nature of many of the surviving obelisks.[32] It is in these senses that obelisks offer heuristic opportunities for thinking about the nature of Roman power.[33]

[29] Rosenberg 1971.   [30] Parker 2003.   [31] Boatwright *et al.* 2011.

[32] An extreme case is the obelisk now at the Piazza di Montecitorio; severely damaged in the early middle ages, its restoration in the eighteenth century was made with surviving fragments of the column of Antoninus Pius. See Iversen 1968: 142–60. The base of that column depicts a reclining Campus Martius, together with a strategically placed obelisk.

[33] Compare the radical idea of "denarration" that Richardson 2001 sees in modernist English fiction.

Before exploring one related opportunity below, we shall take stock of the many senses of appropriation that are already emerging.

Distortion: Variations on a Theme

It is worthwhile to adumbrate the ways in which obelisks have been incorporated into Roman culture by way of an overview; again we compare other surviving monoliths. Such kinds of incorporation inevitably distort prior meanings, even as the objects themselves survive. Here we see a number of contextual resonances, presented as a series of propositions involving obelisks.

Physical movement is here a foundational sense of appropriation, and in this important respect obelisks differ from the otherwise comparable case studies in the current section.[34] We have already glimpsed the mechanics of obelisk transportation, the *cura vehendi* in the inscription above. Constantius' phrase invites comparison with the elder Pliny (*HN* 36.69):

> super omnia accessit difficultas mari Romam devehendi, spectatis admodum navibus.

> On top of everything there came the challenge of relocating the obelisk to Rome on sea. The ships used attracted much public attention.

The last part of Pliny's sentence is stylistically awkward in its compression, but the sense is clear, particularly since Pliny goes on to talk about the tourist appeal of the ships which had brought the first three obelisks to Rome (36.70). Again, river transport from Pozzuoli to the metropolis of Rome was "another challenge" (*alia ... cura*, 36.70). Both Pliny and Ammianus devote much attention to the topic of transportation, giving the impression that obelisks were the most severe test of technologies of mobility and required virtuosic engineering. Both authors give the impression that obelisks are the largest objects that can be moved, in which respect they differ from pyramids, the next topic in Pliny's extended discussion of stones (Book 36). At a different point in the *Natural Histories*, now discussing trees, Pliny describes the fir from which one of the obelisk ships was made; it transported the obelisk that had been commissioned by Caligula for installation in the Vatican Circus and which today stands in Saint Peter's Square (16.201–2).[35] Transportation is thus the most physical sense of appropriation, indeed the baseline from which any more elaborate analysis must proceed.

---

[34] Nichols and Trimble; cf. Nelson (2003).   [35] Compare Suet. *Claud.* 20; Dio Cassius 60.11.

Appropriation sometimes involves the assembly of fragments, or other kinds of reconfiguration whereby something broken is presented as complete. In a sense, this is a subset of the kind of reconfiguration whereby, for example, Bernini integrated obelisks into the virtuoso architecture of the Fountain of Four Rivers (Piazza Navona); or Sixtus had crosses placed atop obelisks he had baptized.[36] Obelisk stories typically involve the movement of whole monoliths, yet closer inspection sometimes shows their integrity is illusory. The Lateran obelisk lost four meters when it was excavated in 1587–88. An unspecified length of Istanbul's Hippodrome obelisk was lost, either in transit or once in Constantinople. The current length of its shaft is 19.80 meters, but some sense of the lost section may be grasped in a frieze depicting this obelisk (or a similar one) at Karnak.[37] The most drastic physical reconfiguration involves the obelisk brought by Augustus to the Campus Martius, now at the Piazza di Montecitorio. It was repaired in 1789–92 by using parts of the column of Antoninus Pius and Faustina (ca. 161 CE). It is telling that the original column base, which still survives, depicts an obelisk as part of a personification of the Campus Martius, a design that seems to foreshadow the act of spoliation some sixteen centuries later. Furthermore, the smaller obelisks from Iseum Campense have undergone several transformations; the one now at Urbino's Piazza del Duomo consists of five segments of at least three different obelisks, whereas only the top 2.68 meters of the Celimontana obelisk comes from an obelisk inscribed by Ramesses II, which found its way to the Iseum Campense, probably in the late first century CE. Its current location and augmented form are linked to the avid sixteenth-century collector, Ciriaco Mattei, and his heirs.[38]

Indeed, collecting is one way to characterize the processes by which objects are appropriated. Neither the small numbers involved nor the large proportions should obscure the fact that obelisks are preeminently collectible objects. According to Pearce's influential study, there are three kinds of collecting: *systematic*, in which objects are collected for ideological reasons, often requiring completeness; *fetishist*, removing objects from their historical and cultural contexts and redefining them to suit new ones; and

---

[36] Likewise, the Vatican obelisk was subject to a ceremonial exorcism and baptism. The inscription on its base reads as follows: "I exorcize you, creature of stone, in the name of God, the all-powerful Father, and in the name of Jesus Christ, his son, and by virtue of the Holy Spirit, that you may become an exorcized stone" (*exorcizo te, creatura lapidis, in nomine Dei patris omnipotentis, et in nomine Iesu Christi, filii eius, domini nostri, et in virtute Spiritus sancti: ut fias lapis exorcizatus*). See further Curran *et al.* 2009: 141–2.

[37] Habachi 2000: 47–9, 85–6. [38] Habachi 2000: 73.

souvenir collecting, in which objects are prized for their power to carry the past into the future.[39] Obelisks would seem to exemplify all three, through primarily their public aspects: we have already seen Roman political ideologies of universal power and the new cultural and spatial contexts of Augustan and late antique Rome; there are hints of a personal connection in Hadrian's inscribing and importation of an obelisk as a memory object for his beloved Antinoos. In any case, the desire of imperial collectors was clearly the momentum that brought obelisks from Egypt to Rome.

Appropriation has ideological dimensions, often linked to individuals. A political sense is summed up in the final word of Constantius' inscription: *triumfis*. This has Augustan precedent, going back to the two obelisks imported by Augustus (now at Piazza di Montecitorio and the Piazza del Popolo) and inscribed as follows (*CIL* 6.701–2 = *ILS* 91):

> Imp(erator) Caesar Divi f(ilius)
> Augustus,
> pontifex maximus,
> imp(erator) $\overline{XII}$, co(n)s(ul) $\overline{XI}$, trib(unicia) pot(estate) $\overline{XIV}$,
> Aegypto in potestatem
> populi romani redacta,
> Soli donum dedit.

> When emperor for the twelfth, consul for the eleventh, and tribune of the people for the fourteenth time, the emperor Augustus, son of the deified Caesar, dedicated this gift to the Sun, once Egypt had been restored to the power of the Roman people.[40]

Especially significant here is the prefix *re-* in *redacta* ("restored").[41] This is misleading insofar as it suggests that Egypt previously belonged to Rome; in practice it was a new conquest. The point is to naturalize Roman conquest, making a claim of legitimacy. The second line of Constantius' inscription makes a comparable gesture with *orbe recepto*, an even more inflated claim to "rightful" world power. In this case, the sense of restoration centers on reaffirming the political order in the wake of an insurrection.

---

[39] Pearce 1995: 32.

[40] Iversen 1968–80: 65, like others, translates the ablative absolute as "when Egypt had been brought under the sway of the Roman people," but this misses the force of *redacta*, i.e., "given *back*" or "*duly*." "Restored" in the sense I have used it does not necessarily have a temporal sense; rather it appears to underline a change of status. For additional discussion of this inscription see Trimble's chapter in this volume.

[41] Cf. Lewis & Short, s.v. "re," esp. II 2: "transition into an opposite state."

As for Constantius, so for Augustus, and indeed for the pharaohs who preceded them, power is personally focused on the ruler; the point is well illustrated by the inscriptions. The most unusual instance of this is surely the obelisk at Piazza Navona, which Domitian had inscribed with his own name, in Middle Egyptian hieroglyphics, to mark his accession. Strikingly, this was erected in Rome itself, rather than in Egypt. The obelisk at Monte Pincio was also inscribed by a Roman emperor, Hadrian, to commemorate his lover, Antinoos, who died in Egypt.[42]

Less obvious but no less significant is an economic sense of appropriation, together with a religious one. The city of Rome had, by the time of Augustus, a high dependency on Egypt as a source of grain.[43] Yet that economic relation made little impression in the artistic sphere, with the partial exception of some coins. In this light, obelisks are an indirect reflection of this crucial trans-Mediterranean link. This kind of spectacular displacement is something we have already seen above, when an obelisk was identified as the effective monument to the defeat of Antony. Of course, obelisks had a religious charge, too. Many of the smaller obelisks found in Rome were once housed in the Iseum Campense, and two survive at the shrine of Isis at Benevento. The cult of Isis, the most widespread Mediterranean cult before Christianity, was thus one context in which Romans encountered and collected obelisks.

The different kinds of value involved are exchangeable. A letter sent by the emperor Julian in 363 CE from Antioch to the people of Alexandria makes this point handsomely. He requests that the Alexandrians send an obelisk to his native city of Constantinople. In exchange Julian offers a colossal bronze statue of himself.[44] Tellingly, Julian asks as follows:

> ...καὶ πέμψαι τῇ ἐμῇ πατρίδι τῇ ξενοδοκούσῃ καλῶς ὑμᾶς, ὅτε εἰς τὸν Πόντον εἰσπλεῖτε, καὶ ὥσπερ εἰς τὰς τροφὰς καὶ εἰς τὸν ἐκτὸς κόσμον συμβάλλεσθαι. πάντως οὐκ ἄχαρι καὶ παρ᾽ αὐτοῖς ἐστάναι τι τῶν ὑμετέρων, εἰς ὃ προσπλέοντες τῇ πόλει μετ᾽ εὐφροσύνης ἀποβλέψετε.[45]

> Please send it to my native city, which always receives you hospitably when you sail into the Pontus, and to contribute to its external adornment, even as you contribute to its sustenance. It cannot fail to give you pleasure to have something that has belonged to you standing in their city, and as you sail towards that city you will delight in gazing at it.

---

[42] Habachi 2000: 83–5.   [43] Scheidel 2001: 231–3.
[44] Presumably the statue would be of himself rather than of Constantius, but this is not clearly specified.
[45] Julian, *Letters* 48.

Not only are the bronze colossus and an obelisk a fair exchange in Julian's mind; the fact that Alexandria feeds Constantinople makes the obelisk an obvious extension of the relation. As it happens, Julian died that same year, his plan not carried out – a variant on a theme seen in Constantius' inscription. Nonetheless, the letter gives a strongly Bourdieuian sense that different kinds of capital are parallel and subject to exchange.[46]

Appropriation can have a competitive edge, particularly in the sphere of collective memory. Constantius' inscription shows him competing, in different senses, with Constantine and Magnentius. Pliny begins his discussion of obelisks on these lines (*HN* 36.64):[47]

> trabes ex eo [lapide] fecere reges quodam certamine, obeliscos vocantes Solis numina sacratos.
>
> Kings constructed beams out of that kind of stone, i.e., marble, in a certain spirit of competition, calling them obelisks, dedicated to the power of the Sun.

There is also a geographical aspect to competition. When obelisks were used in circuses at Caesarea and Arles, provincial centers and their elites were competing with metropolitan Rome through emulation. We have already considered the Hippodrome obelisk as a means by which Theodosius proclaimed Constantinople the new imperial capital. Competitive appropriation sometimes has a ludic side as well. Representations of obelisks have been found on a number of mundane objects – toys, rings, bread molds, and cameo glass – far from the kind of public commemorations and assertions of power we have seen.[48]

At a more abstract level, appropriation involves language. To be sure, the Middle Egyptian inscriptions on some obelisks were prominently displayed in Rome. We have already seen Ammianus' translation of the inscription on the flanks of the Lateran obelisk, as well as the *Hieroglyphics of Horapollo*. Both reveal the crucial mistake that dogged decipherment efforts up to Young and Champollion.[49] These are Roman imperial

---

[46] Parker 2014: 283–4.

[47] Cf. Tacitus' comment that pyramids were "built like mountains in keeping with kings' competitiveness and wealth" (*instar montium eductae pyramides certamine et opibus regum*), *Ann.* 2.61.1. Tacitus expresses no value judgment in this, in contrast to Pliny (*HN* 36.75) and Frontinus (*Aq.* 16): Goodyear 1981: 385.

[48] In such contexts obelisks could also be part of a game of scale. See Schneider 2005.

[49] As Ammianus puts it (17.4.9): "individual characters stood for individual nouns and verbs; and sometimes they meant whole phrases" (*singulae litterae singulis nominibus serviebant et verbis; non numquam significabant integros sensus*). This misconception is developed to the nth degree by Athanasius Kircher in the seventeenth century. See further Iversen 1993: 38–59.

appropriations of Middle Egyptian language, via Greek. Domitian and Hadrian made use of Middle Egyptian without translations, for public display in the city of Rome. Elsewhere there are clear instances of what we might call the hieroglyphic effect: approximations by persons who had clearly no knowledge of the script. This seems to be the same principle as the use of the Hebrew script in inscriptions at Rome "as much for its symbolic and visual effect as for any linguistic reason."[50] One of these is found on an unusually shaped small obelisk now at the Florence; the *Mensa Isiaca* also has fake hieroglyphs.[51] In such cases we encounter various forms of the colonization of language;[52] an exotic language is taken over by the conquerors, and meanings are imposed from the outside.

Still on an abstract level, we may identify some temporal aspects of appropriation, already glimpsed in the episodic obelizing narratives. By temporal appropriation we mean that previous meanings are, at some level, taken over and reconfigured in a new context. This cannot happen without some awareness of earlier contexts on the part of a viewer, even if those are not in our sense objectively accurate: most significant is some awareness that there were indeed previous meanings inherent in the object. Late Antique art has plenty of evidence of a "cumulative aesthetic": the Arch of Constantine makes extensive use of second-century reliefs as *spolia*; second-century statue bodies and bases receive fourth- and fifth-century heads and inscriptions.[53] When it involves obelisks, this phenomenon has an exotic element insofar as Egypt was considered an ancient society par excellence.

Finally, among the many contextual resonances, power is worth emphasizing. It takes different forms: over the object itself, over enemies, and by implication over viewers. In these ways obelisks are the perfect tokens of colonial imperialism. Consider how these aspects come together in the inscription on the Hippodrome obelisk base (*CIL* 3.737 = *ILS* 821):

> Difficilis quondam dominis parere serenis
> iussus et extinctis palmam portare tyrannis
> omnia Theodosio cedunt subolique parenni (sic)
> ter denis sic victus ego domitusque diebus
> iudice sub Proclo su[pera]s elatus ad auras.

---

[50] Noy 2000: 264.

[51] The rudimentary representation of hieroglyphs on mosaics, including the Great Hunt mosaic of Piazza Armerina, provides further evidence, in such a case subject to the limitations of the mosaic medium. Cf. Baines & Whitehouse 2005 on a mysterious small, non-tapering obelisk now at the Museo Archeologico Nazionale, Florence: it is inscribed with unintelligible hieroglyph-like script.

[52] The term is tellingly developed by Mignolo 2003.   [53] Elsner 2004: esp. 279.

> Formerly reluctant, I was ordered to obey the serene lords and
> carry the palm once the tyrants were dead. Everything yields to
> Theodosius and his everlasting offspring. So conquered and
> vanquished in three times ten days I was raised to the lofty sky
> while Proclus was judge.

Here Proclus, prefect of Constantinople in 388–392 CE, is honored for
overseeing the installation at the Hippodrome in 390 or 391. Insofar as it
commemorates Theodosius' victory over Maximus' Italian rising in 389, it
articulates a network of power that links Constantinople with both Egypt
(the origin of obelisks) and old Rome (the established metropolis, marked
with prominent obelisks). *Proclo* reveals erasure and re-inscription, consistent with the murder of Proclus by Rufinus in 392, and his posthumous
rehabilitation in 395 under Arcadius. As in Constantius' inscription, the
term *tyrannus* is used for a usurper.[54] The obelisk speaks of its own
"subjugation" (*victus ego domitusque*) in the course of installation. *Difficilis*
denotes the engineering challenge it presented, glossing over whatever
mishap befell the obelisk on the journey from Thebes to Constantinople,
during which several meters of its lower shaft were lost. In this triumphal
context the inscription speaks, by implication, on behalf of the conquered
enemy. One of the striking features of the Hippodrome obelisk base is that
it depicts not only the emperor at the races, but also the spectators – a
reflection of its own *mise-en-scène* in its new transplanted setting. The
vocabulary of the inscription is a good measure of the power dynamics
involved.

We can begin now to draw some initial conclusions. Inscriptions,
whether of Augustus, Constantius or Theodosius, play a crucial role as
appropriative speech-acts. We have also seen plenty of evidence that time
depth and historical resonance were part of the dynamics whereby the
monoliths were incorporated into their new Roman contexts. This is
especially important for the Late Antique period, in which there is already
a strong sense of tradition about previous Roman pasts, in this case
stretching back to Augustus. Obelisks were and are charismatic objects,
enjoying high status by virtue of their size and an enlarged sense of their
meanings. These meanings were created via metonymy (Egypt symbolized
by objects from Egypt), but also via metaphor. Perhaps increasingly over
time, obelisks came to symbolize power tout court.

---

[54] Cf. Zosimus 2.42.1 and Sextus Aurelius Victor 41.23 on Magnentius; by contrast, Magnentius
represented himself as "restitutor libertatis" (e.g., *CIL* 5.5397); the language of liberation recalls
Augustus' *Res Gestae* 1.1.

Countercurrents: Diocletian's Stele

At this point we digress to consider a monument that has a vivid life story of its own, a monument that invites comparison with obelisks while being also distinctive. Standing in the Serapeum of Alexandria, "Pompey's Pillar,"[55] as it was commonly and mistakenly known, was raised by Diocletian in 298. For eight months Diocletian had besieged the city in response to an insurrection there. This much is evident from an inscription on its flank (*OGIS* 718 = Kayser 1994: no. 15):

> Τὸ[ν τι]μιώτατον Αὐτοκράτορα,
> τό[ν] πολιοῦχον Ἀλεξανδρείας,
> Διο[κλη]τιανὸν τὸν ἀν[ίκη]τον,
> Πού[πλιος] ἔπαρχος Αἰγύπτου

> The most honorable ruler, Alexandria's city protector, Diocletian, the unconquerable – (honored) by Publius, Prefect of Egypt.

This is the sole ancient monument still standing above water in that city today; its survival is improbable, given the precariousness of its original rubble base and the seismic activity in this part of the Mediterranean basin.

The stele stands 30 meters tall, with an elaborate Corinthian capital on top. Like most obelisks, but unlike triumphal columns, it is a monolith made of Aswan granite. Judging from a fifth-century mosaic at Sepphoris that seems to depict it, and also from other columns,[56] it once had a statue of Diocletian on top.[57] This feature distinguishes honorific columns from obelisks. Its modern history, especially after Napoleon, reads like something of a picaresque novel, so many adventures does it survive.[58]

Today Diocletian's Pillar stands on its own, its solitude poignantly depicted by several artists.[59] The solitude of the Lateran obelisk has been rather different. As we have seen, Thutmose III's inscription indicates that it was originally installed on its own, unusually so, probably because of the

---

[55] The misattribution is a telling case of historical memory. European visitors to Ottoman Egypt, even before Napoleon's expedition of 1798, assumed that the monument must have been linked to the famous death and burial of Pompey the Great at Alexandria while fleeing Caesar: Appian 2.86; Dio Cassius 69.11.1; *Historia Augusta, Life of Hadrian* 14.4. Among modern travelers' accounts, see Pococke 1803: 9.

[56] Compare Trajan's Column at the Forum in Rome (113 CE). The tradition of mounted statues goes back at least to the monument of Aemilius Paulus at Delphi (167 BCE).

[57] Thiel 2006 concludes that this would have been one of four such columns, in keeping with the tetrarchic ideology seen for example in the fourfold statue in Ravenna. At the Serapeum in Alexandria the evidence for such replication is not compelling.

[58] E.g., Norry 1800.   [59] E.g., David Roberts 1838.

abandonment of the Unfinished Obelisk. It is all the more interesting to see how obelisks and columns have been combined in different representations. The sketch by Enea Vico (ca. 1542), combining an unidentified, uninscribed obelisk with the Column of Antoninus Pius, shows that the shared vertical aspect has been noticed; the emphasis here is on monuments at Rome. The most striking juxtaposition is found in the *Description de l'Égypte* (1809–1828); in its often reproduced frontispiece, the pillar (partly obscured) is paired with an obelisk, possibly that at Karnak, so that the two frame the picture on its left and right borders. Like the Nile mosaic of Palestrina, the frontispiece offers a representation of the entire Nile basin in flood, looking south from the delta.

Three points deserve emphasis in this brief comparative look at Diocletian's column. First, its life story defies the south-to-north traffic of so many obelisks. It is often remarked that today more obelisks stand in the city of Rome than in Egypt. Though its content is Aswan granite, also used in obelisks, its form is a southward transplant, particularly the Corinthian capital. Second, its modern history of non-removal suggests that it was not considered exotic enough by nineteenth-century plunderers, collectors, and diplomats. Third, it suggests (rather than answers) interesting questions of juxtaposition; its solitary character today, which may or may not have matched its ancient status, corresponds to that of obelisks at Rome today but contrasts with the dual installation of most obelisks by the pharaohs.

Envoi: Theorizing Obelisks from the South

In a controversial recent book, Jean and John Comaroff suggest that developing nations should be seen as a source for theorizing about global trends, and not purely in terms of the impact of those trends. *Theory from the South, or, How Euro-America is Evolving towards Africa* reverses the usual pattern of analysis. Its ethnographic focus on the local contradicts the usual discourse about globalization, which typically regards initiative on the part of industrialized countries as axiomatic. After all, the world beyond the developed west is no mere "reservoir of raw fact."[60] Their goal is no upside down inversion; rather, they suggest that it is worthwhile to find more nuanced ways of conceiving the relations and flows between the global south and north.

---

[60] Comaroff & Comaroff 2012: 1.

On the basis of this thought experiment we may ask of the foregoing material: Where does Egypt fit into the broader picture of the Roman world? Or even, Why Egypt? Did any features make it particularly prone to Roman appropriation? This large question still needs to be broached. Monumental and deep historical time are two elements that fascinated the ancient Egyptians themselves. They also fascinated the Greeks from the time of Herodotus and his *Histories*. For the Romans, an imperial context would prove decisive in the period after Octavian's conquest of Cleopatra and Antony in 31 BCE, just as it would for Europeans from 1798, in the wake of Napoleon's short-lived campaign. Egypt's objects became collectibles par excellence. (Diocletian's pillar, presumably not "Egyptian" enough to merit exportation, is an exception that proves the rule in a nineteenth-century context.) Egypt provided Roman emperors with media and styles of self-presentation.[61] Insofar as Egypt is an early empire of world history, it lends itself to the effect of multiple recession; even as objects survive from the past, contemporary responses are framed by a temporally receding set of responses that include early modern Europeans, Romans, Greeks, and not least the Egyptians themselves. In this light the appropriation of obelisks is a cross-cultural phenomenon, several times over, in the long term. At the same time, a specifically Roman factor was the economic dependence on grain; this appears to underlie Roman Egyptomania more implicitly than explicitly.

Now that long-term dynamics are established, it is important to recognize the problems of continuity and change. Luxury consumption is a social process, involving change over time almost by definition.[62] Yet Romans imported obelisks first in 10 BCE (to Rome) and finally in 390 CE (to Constantinople). Should we consider this repeated Roman engagement with obelisks as persistence or variable recurrence? We are dealing with objects that have survived over considerable time, long enough to match *translatio imperii*, the medieval idea of the succession of world empires; yet their lengthy survival opens up rather than forecloses variations of social meaning. It would be wrong to imagine that ongoing survival implies stability of meanings. On the contrary: in practice, our evidence for excavating meanings over long-term history is limited to specific times and places and not necessarily representative of broader trends. Diocletian's pillar is a prime example, since the evidence for its life history is so concentrated on the nineteenth century.

---

[61] This dual self-presentation goes back to the Ptolemies.   [62] Wallace-Hadrill 2008: 315–55.

Obelisks, with their distinctive form, have different histories. Just as Swetnam-Burland has problematized the distinction often made between Egyptian and Egyptianizing artifacts, so we should seek to compare and contrast, say, the Bankes obelisk at Kingston Lacy, Dorset, with the obelisk-like monument that marks Champollion's grave in the Père Lachaise Cemetery, a reminder of his role in the decipherment. Nonetheless, the long-term attractiveness of obelisks as a form, even within Roman antiquity from Augustus to Theodosius, proves harder to explain than their physical survival. Provisionally, we might suggest that the decisive factor is adaptability to different memorializing purposes, as is suggested by the variety of inscriptions on the obelisk bases.

To focus on the appropriation of obelisks is to emphasize their charisma. Of course Max Weber's influential articulation of this concept focused on persons, yet there is clearly a case to be made for obelisks as charismatic objects. Pliny and Ammianus have emphasized the "awe-arousing centrality" with which people regarded them.[63] To be sure, Romans knew that obelisks were from a land that was itself a source of fascination and importance (Egypt) and were laden with political, economic, and religious meaning. Obelisks seem to create a connection between the exceptional status of Egypt in the ancient Mediterranean and the exemplarity of Rome in later empires. It is important to try to understand this charisma in a way that links in ordinary objects as well, especially the grain supply. So, too, while spatial aspects of appropriation loom large today, underlined by debates about cultural property and heritage, it is important not to neglect temporality. This is especially significant in a Late Antique context, given the high degree of spoliation in late Roman monuments and the appeals to a wide range of pasts – classical, Judaeo-Christian, and certainly also Egyptian.

We have seen much evidence of a meta-level sense that obelisks are in the first instance about other obelisks, something that is visible in the Assyrian basalt columns. Some such instances may be considered replication.[64] Certainly obelisks were used by cities to compete with Rome's prominence, and that process has continued into modern times. Representations of obelisks, particularly those on small and mundane objects, give the impression that the issue of size was as apparent to the ordinary people who might have used those objects as they were to Pliny and

---

[63] Shils 1965.
[64] The principle of replication is still deeply embedded in the scholarly literature on cross-cultural contact ("Romanization"), even though more nuanced approaches are in order: see esp. Woolf 1998.

Ammianus, and even to the emperors who raised obelisks on a competitive basis. Rome's use of Egyptian obelisks has metamorphosed, in modern times, with a profusion of responses to the obelisk form. It is an enduring paradox that emperors, starting with Augustus, chose an Egyptian form to articulate Roman power, and that, further, the power of ancient Rome has been rearticulated by many others via an originally Egyptian symbol.

Finally, is appropriation the best term for all this? There is much to recommend it, and obelisks as a case study do indeed reveal several features of appropriation: the interaction of object and text, aspects of (physical) circulation, and varieties of (metaphorical) distortion. It matters not that the last of these seems intrinsically provisional, subject to ongoing physical and social change by virtue of the objects' sheer longevity. The process continues yet. Diocletian's column is a sobering limit case, for it reminds us of the multilateral aspects of Roman cross-cultural exchange. Its life history has none of the south-to-north, east-to-west momentum of so many obelisks. Exchange in the Roman world was no one-way street; rather, the empire was a network of multiple connections. Everyday commodities such as grain were no less subject to exchange than were huge monuments. At the same time, though obelisks may seem chapter-markers in the grand narrative of the Roman Empire, a more creative approach – emphasizing ruptures, fragments, and happenstance – opens new possibilities for narrating or even "denarrating" Roman power. In a context of obelisks the chapter-divisions of Roman history, and even the Romanness of Rome, prove to be not so clearly defined after all.

CHAPTER 9

Distortion on Parade
Rethinking Successful Appropriation in Rome

Carolyn MacDonald

This volume began with a Roman boasting of his city's unmatched success at matching her rivals. Kaeso's caution to the Carthaginian official articulates one vision of Roman hegemony: Rome is an empire won through the active acquisition and knowledgeable redeployment of foreign goods and social practices. Which is to say, an empire won by successive and, in Kaeso's eyes, successful acts of appropriation. Robert Nelson's seminal discussion, from which we set off in the Introduction and to which this section has returned, presents successful appropriation in a rather different light. Nelson's definition of appropriation as "a distortion, not a negation of the prior semiotic assemblage," is not just a definition; it is also a criterion for judging the success of artistic and cultural takeovers.[1] "When successful," Nelson continues, "[appropriation] maintains but shifts the former connotations to create the new sign and accomplishes all this covertly, making the process appear ordinary or natural."[2] This becomes distinctly sinister in a second formulation, which describes the successful appropriation "silently breaching the body's defenses like a foreign organism and insinuating itself within, as if it were natural and wholly benign."[3] The antidote is knowledge, in particular the expert knowledge of the art historian: "to defeat the working of . . . appropriation, one focuses . . . not on the end product of signification but on any of its prior stages, thereby thwarting the semiotic slide into myth and revealing the occluded motivating forces."[4]

My purpose in rehearsing Nelson's position here is not to point out the rather obvious fact that the modern art historian is less enthused about appropriation than the third-century Roman imagined in the *Apothegmata Romaika*.[5] Nor am I trying to congratulate this volume for answering

[1] Nelson 1996: 163–4.   [2] Nelson 1996: 164.   [3] Nelson 1996: 164.   [4] Nelson 1996: 164.
[5] A negative stance toward appropriation has come more to the fore since Nelson's essay. In Baselitz *et al.* 2012, Ambrose points out although the term "can convey the neutral, albeit fundamental, idea

Nelson's call for appropriation exposés – although many of our contributors do indeed shine new light into the darker corners of Roman appropriative processes. Rather, I return to Nelson because the chapters of this section illustrate and nuance the manifold distortions undergone by spoliated signs and objects, while prompting us to reconsider the play of occlusion, revelation, and knowledge in "successful" Roman appropriations. Kaeso's boasting makes successful appropriation a form of geopolitical theater, in which Rome stages herself and her power not just by taking over but by being seen to do so.[6] The three chapters in this section suggest that experts were key spectators for this performance of imperial power. Learned viewers see the strangeness of *spolia* – their foreign origins, their prior meanings, their incongruity in the urban landscape of Rome – but in so doing collude with rather than thwart Roman myth-making. How, then, are we scholars to defeat the workings of Roman appropriation? I will return to this question at the end of my response, with a brief reflection on where we might look for traces of unsuccessful appropriation in the Roman cargo imaginary.

I will begin, however, with a key point about distortion that emerges from all three chapters. In the case studies they present, appropriation does more than shift former connotations to create a new sign; it also retrojects the new connotations, so that prior and present meanings become intractably entangled. We see this clearly in Vitruvius' explanation of caryatids and *statuae Persicae*. Marden Fitzpatrick Nichols's chapter demonstrates that Vitruvius presents himself as preserving the original Greek meaning and function of these adopted architectural forms. His reader thus learns that caryatids originally signified Caryan women, enslaved and degraded by Athens as revenge for Caryan medizing, and that Persian statues

that all artists borrow from one another ... in recent decades [it] has often signaled the actions of a calculating, even transgressive, individual who uses something old in order to promote a new agenda" (169). In the same article, Mathur speaks of an "essential ambiguity" that hangs over the concept, raising a question of ethics: "Is it a good thing or a bad thing, that is, should its productive aspects – subversion, creative inhabitation, reinvention, and innovation – be understood as outweighing some of its more rivalrous modes, such as violation, co-optation, distortion, and theft?" (181–2). Kinney 2011 notes that the answer "is frequently determined by the direction of the appropriation in relation to perceived distributions of power. Appropriation of tribal or 'primitive' art forms by western cultural institutions generates a strong negative charge, for example, while the appropriation of western industrial artifacts or 'post-consumer items' by artisans on the cultural or economic margins is seen as positive" (8).

[6] Cf. recent work on the triumph, that paradigmatic spectacle of Rome-as-world-power (Brilliant 1999, Beard 2007, Östenberg 2009). Kinney 2011 writes of the late twentieth-century Appropriation artists that their art "represents the practice at its most naked and is an atypical extreme. Unlike the general habit of appropriation, it called attention to itself by testing the limits of permissible taking" (8). *Mutatis mutandis*, might we say the same of Rome?

holding up architraves originally signified Persian soldiers, overcome and captured by Spartan forces at the battle of Plataea. And yet, as Nichols notes, these "original," "Greek" meanings are constructed via markedly Roman retrojections (pp. 99–100). Vitruvius imagines fifth-century Athenians and Spartans holding triumphs, constructing manubial monuments, and memorializing their enemies' subjection in statues subjected to the weight of those very monuments – all of which echoes the semantic function of caryatids and other load-bearing statues in Augustan Rome.

Jennifer Trimble identifies a similar process, which she terms "double appropriation," in her chapter on the Ara Pacis' architectural citation of Egyptian jubilee temples (pp. 119, 129, 132, 134). On the one hand, the Ara Pacis retrojects onto the jubilee temple form all that pharaonic Egypt has come to mean in the first-century Mediterranean: religious solemnity, the conquest of time as well as space, and divine monarchic rule over the *oikoumene*. On the other hand, the cultural synthesis of the monument as a whole shifts and moderates the monarchic connotations, situating Augustus' rule in the context of proper Roman ritual. Trimble concludes, "there was no stable 'original' meaning that was then taken up and distorted for new purposes. . . . Two distortions operated simultaneously: one was the meaning projected back onto the past, and the other was the distortion inherent in the actual appropriation, reshaping that projected meaning for the new context" (pp. 134–5).

The obelisks and obelizing objects discussed by Grant Parker offer a fascinating limit case for this process of double appropriation. We must reckon, as Parker does, with the sheer longevity of the obelisks appropriated from Egypt by Rome and subsequently by newer imperial powers. These are objects that have outlived each specific context in turn, carrying something of the deep past with them into each successive present and future. And yet, Parker reminds us, "their lengthy survival opens up rather than forecloses variations of social meaning" (p. 157): indeed, in the course of Parker's whirlwind tour of space and time, we witness obelisks shifting from signs of individual rulers' power to signs of Egypt, of Rome, of empire, of power *tout court*. The effect becomes one of multiple recessions, as contemporary responses frame and are framed by a "temporally receding set of responses that include early modern Europeans, Romans, Greeks, and not least the Egyptians themselves" (p. 157). But present meanings exert at least as much power over prior meanings as vice versa. Erecting an obelisk lays claim to the deep past, and shifts the meaning of 'obelisk' both now and then. Appropriating an object of such longevity is thus, as Parker puts it, a "colonization of time" (p. 138).

This double distortion of both past and present meanings would seem to naturalize the new signs created by Rome's appropriation of the caryatid motif, the jubilee temple form, and an impressive collection of obelisks. It is far from clear, however, that Roman appropriations from other cultures appeared (or were intended to appear) ordinary or natural – especially to knowledgeable viewers.[7] For all his Roman retrojecting, Vitruvius is clearly concerned that caryatids continue to signify as Greek, and his emphasis upon their Greek origin calls attention to their status as cultural take-overs. This is even more true in the case of the Corinthian *echea* dedicated by Mummius in the Temple of Luna. Nichols shows how Vitruvius underscores "their incongruous fit within both building and cityscape, [which] allows them to serve as markers of geographical and cultural distance" (p. 105). It also allows them to serve as markers of empire. To recognize the Corinthian origin of the *echea* and their incongruity in Rome is to recall, as Vitruvius does, Mummius' brutal conquest and sack of Corinth. Crucially, this abets rather than counters the central Roman myth of the *De archi- tectura*. Nichols explains: "if transferred ... objects lose their otherness, Roman culture loses its self-definition as variegated and appropriative" (p. 96). It is crucial to Vitruvius' vision of imperial culture that foreign elements remain foreign. Appropriations must signify as such, and the expert knowledge of the architect–author works to precisely that end.

We catch glimpses of the strangeness of spoliated objects and motifs in Trimble and Parker's chapters as well. Trimble reminds us that the Ara Pacis, which we take for granted as a crystallization of Augustan ideology, was and is an extremely bizarre little structure.[8] To those viewers ill equipped to recognize the altar's layered references (to pharaonic, Italic, classical Greek, Hellenistic Greek, and Ptolemaic sources), it might have looked simply odd. To the knowledgeable elite viewers whom Trimble posits as the monument's primary audience, might it have looked even odder? Trimble speaks of the Ara Pacis' "synthesis" of different cultures and pasts (p.133, e.g.), but we might equally term the unprecedented juxtaposition of so many distinct elements bricolage or pastiche. As in

---

[7] Edwards 2003, on the reception of plundered statues and statues representing conquered peoples, raises related questions. She wonders, "How comfortably ... did they fit into the topography of the city? Were they invariably seen as emblems of Rome's power? Or might they sometimes seem more problematic, evidence perhaps of Rome's artistic inferiority, or of attempts on the part of individuals to promote themselves in quite un-Roman ways?" (45). Without disputing any of these possibilities, I wish to add that incongruity is not necessarily at odds with being emblematic of Roman power – on the contrary, it might be crucial.

[8] Galinsky 1996 dubs the altar "the most representative work of Augustan art," although he does note that "only that judgement is conventional; the monument itself is not" (141).

Nichols' reading of *De architectura*, moreover, recognizing the strange and foreign within the imperialist monumental landscape of Rome is key to the semantic functioning of that landscape. The Egyptian element of the Ara Pacis must stand out *as such* in order both to celebrate Augustus' conquest of space and time, and to remind the *princeps* that Rome is still not the ordinary or natural place for a pharaoh.

As for obelisks, they are perhaps the ultimate extraordinary object; to transport and erect so great a monolith is to defy the constraints of nature itself. This emerges from Parker's reading of the Latin inscription on the Lateran obelisk and is borne out by the literary sources discussed elsewhere in his chapter. The whole natural world – earth, sky, and ocean – is caught up in the miraculous translation of the Lateran obelisk. The inscription imagines the waves marveling at the boat as it bears the mountainous mass to Rome, where it leaps up and strikes the very poles of heaven.[9] Transportation figures heavily in the obelisk narratives of Pliny the Elder and Ammianus Marcellinus as well; Parkers notes that both authors "[give] the impression that obelisks are the largest objects that can be moved" and are thus "subject to virtuosic engineering" (p. 148). So much so, in fact, that the ships themselves become tourist attractions in Rome. Far from being occluded and naturalized, then, the act of obelisk appropriation is a spectacle in its own right and central to the meaning of the monoliths as they are framed by their inscriptional and literary paratexts.

The three chapters in this section thus paint a picture of successful Roman appropriation as a performance of imperial power that is sustained rather than undermined by the knowledgeable spectators who see the strangeness of spoliated motifs and objects. If one of our goals in studying Roman appropriation is to defeat its workings, this will evidently require more than focusing on the prior meanings of appropriated signifiers – not least because, as we have seen, those prior meanings are themselves distorted, perhaps irrecoverably, by each successive takeover. Appropriation's great virtue as a critical concept is the emphasis it places upon agency: the "active, subjective, motivated" myth-making purposefully perpetrated by identifiable actors and cultural forces.[10] However, when the actors are imperial elites and emperors (as they have been in this section), there is a danger that their openly paraded agency will appear total. To "de-narrate" Roman power, as Parker puts it in his conclusion, might then require an approach that balances agency against contingency, experimentation, and accident (p. 159).

---

[9] *CIL* 6.1163.10–14, 19–20.   [10] Nelson 1996: 162.

In this vein, Parker reminds us that the grand history of obelisks is also one of fragmentation and happenstance: obelisks break, lose length, are pieced together into new monoliths of illusory integrity; pharaohs and emperors die before their obelisks can be hewn, or transported, or erected. While emphasizing the senate's sophistication in crafting the message of the Ara Pacis through multiple appropriations, Trimble also shows this quintessential Augustan monument in a new light – as an experiment in image-making for the new political climate, and not one that was ever repeated. And Nichols offers us a glimpse of Lucius Mummius, that "lightning rod" for Roman debates about conquest and plunder (p. 105). Mummius gets off lightly in Vitruvius' account of his disposition of Corinthian *spolia*, but in other authors his notorious boorishness raises the spectre of unsophisticated, even unsuccessful appropriation.[11]

To be sure, Mummius' spoils reached and adorned Rome (and subject and allied cities across the Mediterranean), but ancient anecdotes about him dilute his agency and expose his appropriations to incident and risk. Velleius Paterculus records the following about Mummius' lack of cultivation (1.13.4):

> Mummius tam rudis fuit, ut capta Corintho cum maximorum artificum perfectas manibus tabulas ac statuas in Italiam portandas locaret, iuberet praedici conducentibus, si eas perdidissent, novas eos reddituros.

> Mummius was so boorish that when, after the capture of Corinth, he was contracting for the transportation to Italy of pictures and statues by the hands of the greatest artists, he ordered for the contractors to be warned that if they lost them, they would have to replace them with new ones.

Back in Rome, Pliny the Elder writes, Mummius almost let a treasure slip through his fingers (*HN* 35.8.24):

> namque cum in praeda vendenda rex Attalus emisset tabulam Aristidis, Liberum patrem, pretium miratus suspicatusque aliquid in ea virtutis, quod ipse nesciret, revocavit tabulam, Attalo multum querente, et in Cereris delubro posuit.

---

[11] Mummius' lack of sophistication is recorded by Vell. Pat. 1.13.3–5; Cic. *Verr.* 2.1.55; *de Off* 2.76; Strabo 8.6.23; Plin. *HN* 35.8.24. This characterization surely belongs in part to the tendentious Roman discourse of lost rusticity; one thinks, inevitably, of Horace *Ep.* 2.1.156–7 or Ovid's description of Ennius as *ingenio maximus, arte rudis* ("very great in talent, rough in his art," *Trist.* 2.1.424). There is much to be said about how this discourse emerged from the age of conquest and subsequently fueled Roman self-fashioning (Wallace-Hadrill 2008: 24–6 provides a helpful summary; see also Gruen 1992). My interest, however, lies in how Mummius' lack of sophistication is tied up with the implication that his appropriations were near misses.

> For when at the sale of the spoils King Attalus had purchased a painting of
> father Liber by Aristides, Mummius – amazed at the price and suspecting
> that the painting must have some value of which he himself was unaware –
> recalled the painting, despite Attalus' strong protests, and placed it in a
> shrine of Ceres.

Mummius is hedged around by a crowd of other actors: the contractors
who transport his spoils, the go-betweens who convey his instructions to
said contractors, the king from the Greek East whose bid defines the value
of Aristides' painting. Between the ocean and the auction, moreover, the
entire process is open to chance. The *Father Liber* dedicated in the shrine
of Ceres – so appropriate! and with that subtle shift in nomenclature, from
the Greek *Dionysus* to the Roman *Liber pater*, so appropriative! – turns out
to be a twofold accident. It survived the voyage; Attalus showed his hand
by bidding so much.

   To be sure, these are still narratives of Roman power. The unequal
standing of Roman general and Hellenistic king, for example, is vividly
enacted when Mummius recalls the painting from Attalus. Nonetheless,
Mummius' near disasters provide some counterbalance to Kaeso's vision of
Roman appropriation and hegemony as knowledgeable, unfettered, and
inevitable. The chapters in the next section will continue to tip the scales,
calling attention to the improvisations of sub-elite actors (merchants,
middlemen, soldiers, and slaves) implicated in the circulation of all kinds
of cultural cargo in the ancient Mediterranean.

PART III

Circulation

CHAPTER 10

The Traffic in Shtick

Amy Richlin

After Alexander, war shipped out across the Mediterranean. Trade followed the flag (or vice versa, as in the First Illyrian War), although the slave trade had always trafficked in the fruits of war. Writing in the mid-100s CE, the jurist Gaius says of the origins of enslavement: "They considered those things to be most absolutely theirs that they had taken from the enemy" (*iusto dominio ea maxime sua esse credebant quae ex hostibus cepissent*, *Inst.* 4.16). At about the same time, Aulus Gellius has the sophist Favorinus say, "The word *praeda* is used for the very bodies of the things which have been taken, while the word *manubiae* is properly affixed to the money realized by the quaestor from the sale of *praeda*" (*Nam 'praeda' dicitur corpora ipsa rerum quae capta sunt, 'manubiae' vero appellatae sunt pecunia a quaestore ex venditione praedae redacta*, 13.25.26–7). *Corpora* are fungible. The paths across the water, in time, created the Roman Empire, so that one day a Roman soldier might write down a poem in Latin on papyrus in southern Egypt, or Hercules in his travels might put on Roman clothing. But at the earliest point at which we can read the story in Latin, the paths across the water are traced by jokes, *corpora* light and changeable as coins, carried, with comedians, on the trading ships, the slave ships, from Sicily to mainland Greece, around the islands, to Alexandria, up and down the coast of Asia Minor, along the coast of North Africa, and, finally, to central Italy.[1]

---

[1] On the luxury trade, see Chapter 13 of this volume, as well as Chapter 1 on its relationship to the Plautine audience; on Gallus in Egypt and Hercules in Spain, see Chapters 11 and 12. For *manubiae* in the 200s BCE, cf. Naevius 4 *TrRF*, *manubias suppetat/pro me*, implying, whatever the text said, the equivalency of *manubias* and *me*. This chapter began at the "Cargo Culture" conference at Stanford University, March 2014; many thanks to the editors, and to C. W. Marshall and Timothy Moore for commenting on drafts. The text of Plautus used here is Lindsay's OCT, except for the fragments, which follow de Melo in adopting Monda's numbers. Translations are my own except as noted.

Human Cargo and the Circulation of Art

The playwright Terence died at sea, coming back from Greece with 108 plays translated from Menander, according to one late-Republican authority. Others say he died in Arcadia, out of grief and aggravation over his lost luggage, sent ahead on shipboard, and, lost with it, the new plays he had made. Or so says Suetonius, writing almost three hundred years later (*Life of Terence* 5). This is the story everyone remembers about Terence: he was carrying plays like cargo back to Rome with him. But Suetonius' *Life* begins with another part of Terence's story: "Publius Terentius Afer, born at Carthage, was a slave at Rome belonging to Terentius Lucanus," who had him educated "like a free person" (*liberaliter*) because of his "talent and beauty" (*ingenium et formam*). Others say Terence was a captive, sold out of Africa into slavery. That is, Terence himself started out as cargo.[2]

If Roman art and literature were cargo – appropriated from elsewhere – we should bear in mind that some of the cargo was human, and that armies looted not only Greek art but also Greeks. Nor was looting limited to Greece; nor were Romans the only looters, as is vividly clear from Menander's *Aspis*. The slave trade was transnational, and the ships that carried home the statues carried home the sculptors and the masons, the quarrymen and the models, while other ships carried enslaved Roman soldiers to Greece after Cannae. The slave craftsmen might be understood as "commodifying commodities" – objects that produced other objects – like the *Sonderkommando*; but, as will be seen, they were not mute.[3] That a Greek speaker, Livius Andronicus, "invented Latin literature" has excited attention, but perhaps it matters more that he was (probably) a freed slave, and that he came from Tarentum, not Athens, at a time when Tarentum was embroiled in the big wars. Certainly he was not the inventor of the *palliata* but the first to win official notice and so become visible, long afterward, to Roman antiquarians.[4] And so, eventually, to us. Others are still invisible.

---

[2] On the Suetonius *Life*, see Goldberg 1986: 9 n. 12, 95. For the circulation of Greek intellectuals through the slave trade, see Yarrow 2006a: 37–44, largely focusing on the first century BCE, but including observations on Terence.

[3] On Messala's painter and Marcellus' triumph, see Richlin forthcoming a and Chapter 4 herein; on the *palliata* as telling the woes and voicing the desires of slaves in central Italy in the 200s, see Richlin 2014, forthcoming b, and cf. Forsdyke 2012 on slave voices in Greek popular culture.

[4] Sander Goldberg's dictum, "the beginning of the evidence was not necessarily the beginning of the story" (2005: 3), is fundamental to this chapter. Feeney 2016 largely excludes the *palliata* from his account of the invention of Latin literature.

It takes a troupe to make a play, and as best we can tell these plays were produced and acted by slaves and lower-class men. Moreover, as C. W. Marshall argues, "the verses our manuscripts preserve include improvisatory expansions and variants that originated in the collective of the theatrical troupe" (2006: 268–9). The audience, too, must have included many people newly enslaved or newly freed, for Italy, like the whole Mediterranean after Alexander, was at war, and mass enslavements and forced movements of populations were common (see Eckstein 2006, Rosenstein 2004, 2012).[5] At the same time, theater historians like Brigitte Le Guen have been able to document an explosion in the travel of actors in Alexander's wake. She sums up (2014: 367): "The festivals held across this huge territorial expanse involved performers of every sort of national origin." These Greek-speaking professional troupes did not go everywhere, however; Le Guen says definitively, "we have no document that mentions travels on the part of any association of *tekhnitai* to the western areas" (371). She adds that this does not rule out the "arrival of performers from the Greek east"; indeed not. Travel in the 200s BCE was more chaotic and, for many, less voluntary than theater historians generally take into account. Human trafficking must be a factor in any model for understanding how Greek comedies reached Latium and morphed from Greek into Latin.

The Circulation of Comedians

Understanding of the circulation of performance genres now tends to be grounded in a consciousness of performers as agents of transmission. The Freiburg school, led by Eckard Lefèvre, has spent over thirty years arguing for Italian oral performance genres as the chief source of the fabric of the extant plays. An important tenet of this school has been its emphasis on the status of Italian forms as improvisatory performance (*Stegreifspiel*), which would explain the paucity of contemporary traces.[6] John Barsby observes that "it cannot be accidental that no authors' names or texts survive for Atellan farce or mime for this early period" (1995: 58); Gregor Vogt-Spira notes that "ad-libbing actors do not possess the dignity of an

---

[5] Rarely dealt with by historians of the *palliata*; see Benz 1995: 145–9, and esp. Leigh 2004. Le Guen mentions war as the backdrop for acting troupes' travels (2014: 364) and as a possible cause for the absence of Sicily from the festival circuit (373). Richlin 2014 maps the development of the *palliata* against wars and mass enslavements in the Mediterranean from 321–184 BCE.

[6] Of many contributions, Wallochny 1992 is most directly pertinent here. See Marshall 2006: 263–6 for a critique and overview.

epic or lyric bard," and hence have not been the subject of study in themselves (2001: 95).[7] To the performance forms commonly cited, we can usefully add the *thaumata* that show up in Theophrastus' *Characters* (probably datable soon after 319 BCE); Theophrastus describes not the show but the audience, as the "shameless" man circulates among the crowd to collect money (*Char.* 6.4), a suggestion of the way troupes supported themselves outside state sponsorship. Jeffrey Rusten translates *thaumata* as "street fairs," and certainly the "shameless" man frequents the marketplace (cf. 6.9).[8] At the other end of the social scale, comedians performed at the courts of Hellenistic kings, especially at banquets (Panayotakis 2014: 379–81), and characteristically traveled from court to court (Richlin 2016: 83–92). Each of these performance venues and types implies performers, each with his own skill set, all vulnerable to enslavement. Fraenkel took the circulation of human cargo for granted as part of his model of how Plautus made his plays: "Finally one must not forget that the numerous Greek slaves and freedmen in Rome had brought with them the wondrous tales of their people and undoubtedly found eager listeners" (2007: 67).

The element of oral performance suggests several things about the texts that we have. First, it is unlikely that the first plays on record, credited to Livius Andronicus, were invented from scratch as bare translations. As will be seen below, even the few shreds of his plays now extant include an expression that is typical of joke formulas in plays credited to Naevius as well as to Plautus, and the extant *palliata* is full of jokes marked as corny, couched in a vigorously Latin comic language. Before Livius, the plays of the *Nea* had a good fifty years to circulate northward into Latium, carried by performers too low on the social scale to register on the historical record. The bilingualism or multilingualism of the first adapters was characteristic of the hybrid populations produced by war. The ground they traversed, from Latium to Sicily, put them in contact with all kinds of performance; indeed, Plautus and Caecilius Statius, if their legendary origin stories are even vaguely true, push the geographical range northward into Umbria and Cisalpine Gaul. The *palliata* from 300 to 200 BCE belongs to a period before the writer as *auteur* really gets going in

---

[7] As will be seen later in the chapter, the comparison is apt, since formulae inform comedy as well as epic performance; just as Vogt-Spira would expect, however, no comedians appear in Hunter & Rutherford 2009.

[8] Rusten & Cunningham 2002: 68–9, 130–1. See also on Xenophon *Symposium* 2.1, 4.55 later in the chapter.

central Italy, a period when plays were a form of trade goods, and, in Latium, so were the actors.

The jokes, the techniques, the routines, and the scenarios, then, traveled with the actors, much as theatrical images on painted pottery circulated from Greece to Sicily to southern Italy to Campania before 300 BCE. Some art historians have treated the "native" versions of such paintings as inept knockoffs (see discussion in Green 2012: 325–7); rather, context makes meaning, as E. G. D. Robinson argues (2004: 207):

> it is perhaps time . . . to consider the perspectives that some decades of post-colonial theory may offer for the general situation in South Italy. Two factors emerge very clearly. Firstly, a colonial society (such as the Greeks in South Italy) is inevitably changed in its transferral to foreign shores. . . . And . . . [w]hen it comes to their neighbours, recent studies have demonstrated that those aspects of Greek culture which appeared amongst the Italians were extremely unlikely simply to have been passively accepted. Material culture does not work like that. Foreign objects and concepts tend to be brought into existing value systems and are reinterpreted and used for the benefit of the adopters, usually to send messages to others within their own societies.[9]

A fortiori, when the objects are human, they change not only the content they bear, but also the reception of that content. As the roads pushed through Italy from the 310s through the 190s, they served military goals, imposing, as Emma Dench remarked, a Roman meaning on an Italian landscape (2003: 306–7); slaves and displaced persons moved down these roads through central Italy, and actors and the *palliata* went along with them, imposing meanings of their own. The constant wars produced multiple hybrid identities, nor is the subject position onstage in this period necessarily Roman, although our knowledge of the outcome has led us to take Rome as central (Dench 2003, 2005: 167–72).

The voluntary circulation of comedians and their work around the Mediterranean is well attested, and not only among the *tekhnitai*. Nor was the traffic one-way. Sophron, the Syracusan mime writer, is said to have influenced Plato, who certainly could have acquired the taste in Syracuse, if his sojourns there are not fictitious; in any case Sophron's reputation reached the wider world (see Kutzko 2012). The fictional Philippos, the *gelōtopoios* in Xenophon's *Symposium* (late 360s), tells jokes much like those later found in both the *Nea* and *palliata* (*Symp.* 1.11–6, cf. Corbett 1986: 6–7), exploiting what Lefèvre, following Andreas

---

[9] I am indebted to Sander Goldberg for drawing my attention to this article.

Thierfelder, calls in Plautus "*die Technik der bedeutungsvollen Pause*" (2001: 116, 117), as in "Take my wife . . . please!" Long before Xenophon, a joke resembling one of Philippos' appears in a *parasitos* speech attributed to the Syracusan Epicharmus (480s BCE; *Elpis*, or *Ploutos*, fr. 32.1–2, Ath. 6.235f).

Conversely, as Xenophon imagines Philippos, he shares the limelight with entertainers from the west: a man from Syracuse who provides a music girl, a dancing boy, and an acrobatic dancing girl. The man is free, the young performers probably slaves, and the man shows them for money ὡς ἐν θαύματι (2.1); he also does puppet shows (4.55), a staple of the *thaumata*. Philippos mimics a dance by the boy and girl, getting into the act, appropriating their performance form through parody (2.21–2) – a classic mode of circulation. The playwright Philemon is also said to have come to Athens from Syracuse, likewise Alexis from Thurii in southern Italy; Menander famously refused to leave Athens for Alexandria, but Herodas came to Alexandria from Kos. Characters onstage ricochet around the map, in step with the times. The Ionic dance steps, the *cinaedi* who shimmy through Plautus, traveled to Latium from Ionia and Alexandria as juba dance traveled to the Americas from West Africa. How far a joke could travel is suggested by a vividly obscene metaphor for female genitalia among the fragments of Sophron (24 = Athenaeus 3.87a), based on κόγχαι, "mussels"; a dragged-in one-liner joke about *conchae* at *Rudens* 704 taps the same vein (unique in Plautus in this sense, and I doubt he was translating it from the *Nea*). *Concha* is here common parlance, as indeed it is now in Spanish (still very obscene).

Although there were clearly non-Greek performance forms in the east (viz. the sambuca players in *Stichus*, below), it is mainly in Italy that we can see a lot of evidence for the passage of verbal performance through a language membrane, and in Italy that we have stories of performers moved by enslavement and war. A comparison with vaudeville may be useful. Italy north of Capua was like the Sullivan-Considine and Pantages vaudeville circuits in the Pacific northwest – a place far off the beaten track, but not barren; Groucho Marx first saw Charlie Chaplin perform in a theater in Winnipeg.[10] Vaudeville was divided into big-time and small-time, in a system where management companies owned theaters strung out across defined regions (Bernstein 1984[1923]). In a similar way, burlesque was divided into two major "wheels," and Andrew Davis explains how "stock variety thrived in the areas that the touring shows did not visit," which

---

[10] On the Sullivan-Considine circuit and Pericles Pantages, see Stewart 2005: 153–5; on the Pantages circuit and Chaplin, see G. Marx 1959: 133–5.

included everything west of Kansas City (2011: 33–5). The rules were different outside the wheels: more freedom onstage, but the life was brutal, with long hours and low pay. In 1910, the Marx Brothers' mother moved the family to Chicago, "the hub of the small-time vaudeville circuits and wheels, where an act like ours would have a fighting chance" (H. Marx 2000[1962]: 97), but what Harpo called "the Road of One-Night Stands" was lower than small-time. If they had to, the brothers walked from town to town, "lugging two bags apiece, crammed with posters, props and costumes," in all weather, sleeping in bug-infested hotels, eating bug-infested food, enduring anti-Semitic taunts, performing in cheap outdoor theaters (98–101). Even worse, then, was the life of a *grex* in Italy in the 200s BCE, where war, debt, poverty, and hunger were certainly more extreme than they were south of Chicago in 1910, and where some of the actors were bought in the slave market. The Syracusan impresario in Xenophon's *Symposium* affirms as a matter of course that he sleeps with his boy dancer every night (4.54); perhaps, then, actors were picked out as boys, like the Syracusan's, for their sex appeal, along with their vocal or acrobatic skills. Or like Terence. Inasmuch as the actors came from Italy or Sicily rather than Athens, and to the extent that their training was picked up locally or resumed after the catastrophe of enslavement, they were lucky to be alive – tough survivors of hard times. Anyone onstage in 200, one year in which we know Plautus' *Stichus* was performed, had lived through Hannibal's fifteen-year-long invasion, as had everyone in the audience but the babies. As a slave woman says of the *parasitus* Gelasimus in *Stichus*, "Nobody's funnier, when he's hungry" (*ridiculus aeque nullus est, quando essurit, St.* 217).

I take as a paradigm for the circulation of comedy through human trafficking a scene from *Stichus* in which Gelasimus is made to realize that he is himself a commodity. The slave Pinacium reports to him that his patron's ship has arrived from Asia, loaded with luxury goods: gold, silver, wool, purple, ivory and gold furniture, and Babylonian tapestries (*St.* 367–79). But also with human cargo (*St.* 380–3):

> PI. poste, ut occepi narrare, fidicinas, tibicinas,　　　　　　　　380
> sambucas advexit secum forma eximia. GE. eugepae!
> quando adbibero, adludiabo: tum sum ridiculissumus.
> PI. poste unguenta multigenerum multa. GE. non vendo logos.

> PI. And then, as I was telling you, he's brought with him　　　　380
> lyre-girls, flute-girls, sambuca-girls, of outstanding beauty. GE. Awesome!
> When I get drunk, I'll fool around; then I'm at my funniest.
> PI. And then, also, all kinds of perfume. GE. I'm not selling my jokes.

Gelasimus, before Pinacium arrived with the good news, has been auctioning off his possessions, including his jokes, because he is starving; now he looks forward to entertaining at dinners, where he will be fed.

Then Pinacium ruins Gelasimus' happiness: "And then, though, he's brought *parasiti* with him" – Gelasimus cries, "Oh, no! I'm dead!" And Pinacium finishes, "The funniest" (PI. *poste autem advexit parasitos secum* – GE. *ei, perii miser!*/ PI. *ridiculissumos, St.* 388–9). Gelasimus, crushed, vows that now his jokes are for sale again, the ones he said he would not sell (*venales logi sunt illi quos negabam vendere*, 393). He goes inside to consult his books (*libros*), in search of his better jokes (*de dictis melioribus*, 400) that will help him compete with this cargo of comedians.

Aristophanes stages a similar commodification in *Acharnians*, where a *sukophantês* is packaged up like crockery for sale at Dikaiopolis' market (*Ach.* 910–58). This scene balances an earlier one in which a starving Megarian sells his young daughters as *khoiroi* ("pigs"/"pussies," *Ach.* 729–836). The difference in point of view between Old Comedy and the *palliata* is instructive; the daughters in *Acharnians*, embodying their own genitals, say only "Oink oink!" and "We want to be sold," and the *sukophantês* has it coming, whereas the *parasitus'* daughter who is sold onstage in Plautus' *Persa* has plenty to say for herself, and Gelasimus in *Stichus* tells the audience at length how it feels to be a commodity. The difference in staging underscores the difference in meaning: the *sukophantês* is packaged onstage, in a typically surreal sight gag, and the daughters are made to put on little hooves and snouts and climb into a sack, little visual puns; the shipload of musicians in *Stichus* are actual (onstage, in drag) imported slaves, and the parasite's daughter in *Persa* is sold as an actual (fake, onstage, in drag) enslaved girl. Notably, the daughter in *Persa* is sold to a pimp, just as the imported music girls belong to the sex trade. Unlike the imported *parasiti*, they show up onstage with the merchant and his slave Stichus, as Gelasimus exits, and stand there mute while owner and slave make plans; Stichus is told to take them inside (418, 453).[11] They are soon requested as a gift for sexual use (539–73): the female equivalent of the *parasitus*. Both are trafficked, and, as the audience can see, both are played by comic actors, some of whom were, in real life, imported slaves.

Moreover, in several plays the *parasitus* has jokes, even jokebooks, as part of his personal capital. Ergasilus in *Captivi* complains that times are

[11] On mute characters and their effect, see Klein 2015. Among the commonest mute characters (a category largely servile) are baggage carriers, producing the visual equation of slaves *with* baggage.

hard, and he cannot buy himself dinner with his jokes the way he used to: "I tell a funny joke, one of my better jokes, / with which I used to get dinners with commenstrual regularity before; / nobody laughs" (*dico unum ridiculum dictum de dictis melioribus, / quibu' solebam menstrualis epulas ante adipiscier. / nemo ridet, Capt.* 482–4). Gelasimus, setting up his auction, lists the kinds of jokes he has in stock, his *logos ridiculos* (*St.* 221; specified, 226–31):

> vel unctiones Graecas sudatorias
> vendo vel alias malacas, crapularias;
> cavillationes, adsentatiunculas,
> ac peiieratiunculas parasiticas;
> robiginosam strigilim, ampullam rubidam,   230
> parasitum inanem quo recondas reliquias.

> For sale: my Greek rubdowns that make you sweat,
> or some that are foo-foo, good for a hangover,
> my teasy sneers, my smarmy little flatteries,
> my little white lies like all the parasites tell,
> a rusty strigil, a wrinkly reddish pouch,   230
> an empty *parasitus* to store the leftovers in.

His jokes are a joke on himself, and he sells his body into the bargain, first in the form of his beat-up, phallic, parasitic accessories, then as a food-storage jar. Later, when his patron comes home, Gelasimus takes a look at his *libri* and decides they will enable him to hang onto his meal ticket (*St.* 454–5).

The fungibility of this cultural cargo is underscored by a speech made by the *parasitus* Saturio to his daughter, the unnamed Virgo, whom he is about to sell to the pimp (just a scam; but she is worried). She will pretend to be a slave woman trafficked from Arabia to Persia to here – marketable, as is enacted onstage, for both her former untouchability and her distance from home. This faux slave comes from the land of spices and other high-priced commodities, just as Plautus' plays slap a "Made in Attica" label on themselves in their prologues.[12] Meanwhile, her father assures her that he has a dowry ready for her – another kind of price tag in the traffic in women (*Per.* 388–96):

> VI. ergo istuc facito ut veniat in mentem tibi
> me esse indotatam. SAT. cave sis tu istuc dixeris.

---

[12] On sex trafficking in New Comedy, see Marshall 2013. With the Virgo's disguise, compare Libanus in *Asinaria*, whose name means "Frankincense." On trafficking in slaves and luxury goods between Italy and Asia in the 200s BCE, see Richlin 2016: 79–83; on luxury and claims to Greekness in the *Menaechmi* prologue, see Chapter 1 in this volume.

pol deum virtute dicam et maiorum meum,   390
ne te indotatam dicas quoi dos sit domi:
librorum eccillum habeo plenum soracum.
si hoc adcurassis lepide, quoi rei operam damus,
dabuntur dotis tibi inde sescenti logei
atque Attici omnes; nullum Siculum acceperis: 395
cum hac dote poteris vel mendico nubere.

VI. Just see to it that you keep this point in mind –
I have no dowry. SAT. Watch out, don't say such a thing.
Jeeze, thanks to the gods, I'll tell you, and my ancestors,   390
so you shouldn't say you have no dowry when your dowry's to hand:
look, I've got a storage basket full of books.
If you take care of this nicely, the deal we're doing,
you'll have a dowry from here of six hundred *logei*,
and all Athenian, you won't get a single Sicilian: 395
with this for a dowry you could even marry – a beggar.

Like other *parasiti* and slaves in Plautus, Saturio lays claim to ancestry,
which in his case is a long line of comedians to whose jokes he is heir. He
keeps them in a *soracus*, a loanword from Greek comedy; a rare word in
Latin, it had to be glossed by Festus as "something in which theatrical
costumes are carried" (*quo ornamenta portantur scenicorum*, 382L, reconstructed from Paulus): a guess.[13] Saturio counts the jokes out like coinage
and identifies them with the high-prestige Athenian stage, the big time, as
opposed to Sicily, here the small time; of course his hybrid *logei* are actually
in Latin, which puts them off the theatrical map altogether. The specter of
beggary haunts a lot of punch lines in the plays. The joking speeches
of Ergasilus, Gelasimus, and Saturio depend on the audience's recognition
of the poverty of a comic who would sell his daughter, or himself, for a
meal; on a sense that jokes are commodities; and on the knowledge that
comedy and comedians travel.[14] The title character of the play *Stichus* is
the slave who returns with his owner on the trading ship, and the slave is
the line, or the joke: the στίχος, the shtick. This name seldom appears in

[13] Pollux, at about the same time, made the same guess, based on Aristophanes frg. 259 K–A; the word
is rare in Greek and shows up later in Babrius in the fable of the town mouse and the country mouse
(108.18), full of dates, in the larder (appropriate for a *parasitus*? Translate "food-bin"? Or, meta-
theatrically, "theater trunk"?).

[14] On the *parasitus* and the comic tradition see Corbett 1986: 5–26; Damon 1997; Tylawsky 2002; and
Vogt-Spira 1991 on Gelasimus' role in *Stichus*. On the *parasitus* and poverty see Pansiéri 1997:
419–33. For an argument on jokebooks as Roman rather than Greek, and their commodification as
characteristic of Roman patron-client relationships and imperialist tendencies, see Beard 2014:
201–9; qualified in Richlin 2016: 85 n. 28.

the *palliata*, and in Latin literature only once otherwise, as the name of one of Trimalchio's slaves (Petronius *Sat.* 77.7–78.2); it is rarely attested in Latin inscriptions.[15] But "Stichus" is the generic slave name in Gaius *Institutes* and Justinian *Digest*, appearing over two hundred times. He would become the epitome of the slave as chattel. In *Stichus*, he is fresh off the boat, along with a cargo of comedians, each carrying a jokebook.

Shtick

What was in the jokebooks? Andrew Davis, writing on American burlesque as oral tradition, explains that "most scenes were passed on orally. Young comics learned them by watching more experienced performers at work. The scripts that exist were aids to the rehearsal process" (2011: xii). He illustrates with Gypsy Rose Lee's account of her rapid preparation for a stage routine. The comic asks her if she has ever done the "Illusion" scene before; when she says no, he says it does not matter, because he will be doing a "rehash" of it anyway (Davis 2011: 29):

> "I go right inta the switch on the Joe the bartender bit. . . . And after the yok yok with Stinky, the second banana, the lights come up and you're lying stage left in front of a grass hut. I give you a skull, then a slow triple, and you get up and start giving me the business." . . . "What finish?" I asked faintly. "Him and me clinching – the old tried and true." [= Lee 1957: 192]

Davis explains (2011: 30):

> [the comic's] run-down . . . contains terminology and jargon that Gypsy, having grown up in vaudeville, would be expected to know. To do a "switch" on a bit is to create an alternate or topical version of the joke, writing a new set-up or punch line for the joke. . . . A "yock" was a loud laugh or a belly laugh. The "second banana" refers to the number two comic in the cast. A "skull" was the burlesque term for a "take," as in the expression "double take," while a "slow triple" is a delayed reaction or take, often involving more than one turn of the head.

---

[15] In Plautus, only at *As.* 433, 437, the name of an imaginary slave's slave; and the possibly Plautine frg. inc. 173 (Lindsay 149), in a list of house slaves. Only four times in Clauss-Slaby: *CIL* 6.33791 (Rome, slave name); 6.38853a (Rome, cognomen); 10.290 (Tegianum on the Lucania-Campania border, cognomen of a freeborn man); 10.4780 (Teanum Sidicinum in Campania, cognomen of a freeborn man). The name is extremely rare in the extant Greek epigraphic record, with only five occurrences in the seven volumes of the *Lexicon of Greek Personal Names* (Fraser & Matthews 1987–): none from Attica, though several are from the 200s BCE. See Tordoff 2013: 23–7 on slave onomastics in Greek comedy and the relation, or not, of stage to extant attested slave names.

The scripts now in archives, as Davis presents them, include scenarios along with stage business and jokes – the "yocks" (Doc. "Do you stutter often?" 1st W[oman]: "No, only when I talk." Doc. "I see, and what business are you in?" 1st W: "I work in a bird store." Doc. "A bird store? What could you do in a bird store?" 2011: 225). This exchange illustrates the dynamics of one of the basic structures of vaudeville: the "two-act," playing a straight man off against a funny man (or, in this case, what is thought-provokingly called in the business a "talking woman"). The straight man, as here, sets up the jokes (asks questions, linked by repetition of the comic's line and by neutral transitions like "I see, and"); his reactions to the comic's jokes form part of the joke. This balance permeates comedy down to (or up to) the level of clowning, as Eric Idle shows in his satirical analysis of the White Face clown and the Red Nose clown (1999: 6), along with a list of comedians who fit one or the other profile (145–6).

Barsby cautions against reasoning backward about the *palliata* from *commedia dell'arte* or vaudeville as if all comedy worked by the same rules (1995: 59), but there are elements in the *palliata* that strongly resemble some structural elements in comedy as we know it. Scholars working with the Freiburg school have put together examples of elements that arguably demonstrate the oral or improvised nature of the *palliata*, frequently with comparison to the *lazzi* of *commedia*.[16] Marshall, in a detailed analysis of a routine he labels the "double aside," argues for the elastic construction of scenes that pile one yock on another (1999: 127): "Strings of *lazzi* drag the audience from one routine to the next, and the audience is drawn along from shtick to shtick, a technique I am tempted to call 'shtickomythia.'"[17] A *shtick*, in Yiddish, is a "bit," a "piece," and indeed routines are made up of bits, as in the burlesque script sampled earlier; Eckard Lefèvre calls it the "box-of-bricks principle" (*Baukasten-Prinzip*, 2001: 113). For present purposes, it does not matter whether what is now printed in the Oxford Classical Text of Plautus is based on a script or a transcript, as long as it represents a group product; what matters is where it came from, or, what did you get when you bought a comedian? Answer: a walking jokebook.

---

[16] See, for example, Barsby 1995: 65–70, esp. 67 on dialogues; Blänsdorf 1995: 8–16, who shows the cutoff lines in a half-dozen scenes; Lefèvre 2001 (later in the chapter); Marshall 1999, esp. the catalogue of cues at 124–5; Marshall 2006: 192–202, on shtick, and 245–79 on improvisation; Wallochny 1992: 72–7 on openers and cutoffs in verbal dueling.

[17] Cf. Fraenkel 2007: 282 (on *Epid.* 1–6), where "untrammeled impulsive forward movement" translates "*ungehemmten elastischen Vorwärtsbewegung*"; Vogt-Spira 2001: 101.

With shtick, audience reaction is what tells the comedians how many bits to string together. So Marshall (1999: 111): "the constant interplay between performance and audience is continually gauged by the actors, and successful routines can be expanded or contracted (either through the rehearsal process or on the spot) to suit audience tastes." Vaudevillians' memoirs note the way performers constantly retooled their routines based on what worked and what flopped.[18] This implies that similar content will show up with different meanings at different times and places, and indeed this can be demonstrated for the comic traditions of the ancient Mediterranean.

I take as Exhibit A a short bit that exists in closely similar form in the *Mimiambi* of Herodas and in *Stichus*. Shorter than the commonly mentioned *lazzi* (door-knocking scenes, running-slave scenes), longer than a Q & A, this entrance speech appears to be a shtick complete in itself. Here it is at the opening of *Mim.* 6, as the housewife Koritto asks her slave woman to get a chair for a guest (2–6):

> ... πάντα δεῖ με προστάσσειν
> αὐτήν, σὺ δ' οὐδὲν ἄν, τάλαινα, ποιήσαις
> αὐτὴ ἀπὸ σαυτῆς. μᾶ, λίθος τις, οὐ δούλη
> ἐν τῆι οἰκίηι <κ>εῖς'. ἀλλὰ τἄλφιτ' ἢν μετρέω   5
> τὰ κρίμν' ἀμιθρεῖς ...[19]

> ... I have to see to everything
> myself, you wouldn't do a thing, you wretch,
> yourself on your own initiative. Fie! A stone, not a slave-woman,
> that's you, lying around the house. But if I'm measuring your grain
>   ration,   5
> you reckon up the bits of meal ...

And here it is in *Stichus*, as the mean old man enters from his house. His opening lines show just how mean he is (*St.* 58–61):

> qui manet ut moneatur semper servos homo officium suom
> nec voluntate id facere meminit, servos is habitu hau probust.
> vos meministis quotcalendis petere demensum cibum: 60
> qui minu' meministis quod opus sit facto facere in aedibus?

> A slave person who always waits to be told his duty
> and doesn't remember to do it voluntarily, that slave is not
>   worth owning.

---

[18] See numerous examples collected in Stein 1984. For an in-depth study of rapport between actors and audience in Plautus, see Moore 1998.

[19] Text from Rusten & Cunningham 2002: 246.

You all remember on the first of the month to look for your food
    ration;   60
Why can't you remember to do what needs doing in the house?

How are we to account for the resemblance? The *Stichus* didascaliae say
that "the Greek [play was] Menander's *Adelphoe*," and Walter Headlam
reasoned that "the two passages may derive from that common origin"
(2001[1922]: 282) – a stemmatic model. But Herodas scholars take the
Mimiambi to be street mimes recast in what Headlam called "an antique
and unfamiliar dialect" (ix), a highly literary production (now often
demonstrated) based on an original both low and oral (necessarily conjectural, and rarely discussed).[20] Writing around 1913, Headlam was not at a
loss to explain the vast difference in delicacy between Menander and
Herodas: "Alexandria, with its huge mob of mixed races, its Hellenistic
tongue, its passion for shows of tawdry finery, its commercial crowd, was
not the place for the flowers of Attic wit" (xv). Writing probably around
270 BCE, Herodas stands roughly halfway between the death of Menander
(290) and the birth of Plautus (c. 254). Menander alone is said to have
written over one hundred plays, of which we have substantial fragments of
fewer than twenty; the playwrights of Middle Comedy are credited by
Athenaeus with over eight hundred plays. Over against the stemmatic
model, then, it seems equally probable that this single bit of shtick was
something floating around in the comic soup – something Menander
could have picked up at the *thaumata*, and Herodas could have picked
up at a street mime, and the *palliata* could have picked up along with a
couple of comedians fresh off the boat from anywhere.[21]

The point is that this joke does different work in Herodas and in
Stichus, just as Aristophanes' packed-for-shipping *sukophantês* means something different from the cargo of *parasiti* in *Stichus*. Even in the limited
remains of Herodas (only eight more-or-less complete mimes, most well
under 150 lines), this entrance speech has cousins; Herodas likes to show
owners scolding slaves, especially at the door, especially women owners
(cf. 1.1–2; 5.10, 23–4, 40–1, 47–51; 6.12–17, 98–9; 7.4–15; 8.1–15; Hunter
1995: 156–7). Similar complaints appear in Menander, where house slaves

---

[20] See esp. Kutzko 2012; Panayotakis 2014: 381–2. Mastromarco 1984 has a useful discussion of class
   issues in Herodas, with an overview of Russian and Polish scholarship, and a brief review of ideas
   about possible performance venues (74–80, 87–97). See also Hunter 1993, arguing that the
   (common and harsh) abuse of slaves in Herodas derives from performed mime.

[21] See Hunter 1995 on Herodas as "para-comedy" and on the "repertoire . . . available for more than
   one kind of 're-performance'" (162). For more on the circulation of comedians through Alexandria,
   and their commodification through theatrical anecdotes and terracottas, see Richlin 2016: 84–6.

are sometimes abused from the doorway (*Sam.* 440–3, by the owner; cf. *Dys.* 459–64, a slave knocking). In Plautus, this speech is one of several in which an owner enters while abusing the help (cf. *Per.* 731–2, a pimp); in *Stichus*, the old man's mean character from this scene is maintained in a later scene where he asks to be given a music girl – along with her rations, so he does not have to pay to feed her (553–4, 563). Plautus' stingy owners are almost all male, and the males are not lead characters (Phronesium is the exception); the fact that the slave Stichus is the title character in this play is significant for the play's point of view (multiple; slaves have a big voice). In Herodas, the scolding is done by the main, perhaps the solo, performer, and if Herodas is imitating an oral form, that is the performer he is imitating. In *Stichus*, the speech belongs to a negative character, and the Latin vocabulary of the speech as a whole, extending through line 67, is deeply rooted in the large-scale response the *palliata* makes to the organization of power in contemporary Latium.[22]

Shtick, then, was portable, easily broken down into modules for *ad hoc* reuse, as it was in burlesque (Davis 2011: 87). Many have noticed that there are cues embedded in Plautus' text; Fraenkel, commenting on the *locus classicus* in *Asinaria*, "I want to cut this verbal skirmish short" (*verbivelita-tionem fieri compendi volo, As.* 307), said, "Often Plautus sets a limit to his digressions with a 'basta' of this kind" (2007: 97).[23] In fact the plays are full of formulaic phrases that, like the setup and cutoff lines used by the straight man and the funny man in a two-act, help the performers move through a sequence of jokes. Vogt-Spira posed a challenge: "If one examines Plautus' text ... it becomes clear that it is full of signals for segmentation and transition in which communication between actors becomes a component of the spoken text; these reflections of the dramaturgy of a nonliterary theory have not yet been systematically examined" (2001: 101–2).[24] Here I can only give some examples that illustrate important aspects of how these cues worked. In what follows, the setup lines are in **boldface type**, the jokes are in {curly brackets}, and the cutoff lines are in *italics*.

The opening scene of *Poenulus*, after the prologue, introduces a typical pair in which the owner acts as straight man and the slave acts as funny

---

[22] On violence against slaves in Menander, see Konstan 2013; for critique of harsh owners in Plautus, see Richlin forthcoming b.

[23] See Lefèvre 2001: 121, applying this observation in relation to *Epidicus* 39–40. On the military connotations of *verbivelitatio* and the relation of Plautine comedy to the lower ranks of soldiers – another commodifying commodity – see Richlin forthcoming a.

[24] In the 2001 translation and abridgment of this 1995 essay, "these reflections ... have not yet been systematically examined" appears to be an inserted update (compare 1995: 84).

man. This is the unmarked situation in the plays; owners, especially old
ones, are often the butt of jokes, the dupe. Clueless young men also serve
this purpose, as in *Curculio, Miles,* and *Pseudolus*; so Agorastocles in
Poenulus sets up for his slave Milphio, as here (410–4):

> AG. **Quid nunc mi es auctor, Milphio?** MI. {ut me verberes   410
> atque auctionem facias: nam inpunissume
> tibi quidem hercle vendere hasce aedis licet.}
> AG. **quid iam?** MI. {maiorem partem in ore habitas meo.}
> AG. *supersede istis verbis.* MI. **quid nunc veis tibi?**

> AG. **What do you authorize for me now, Milphio?** MI. {You should beat me
> and hold an auction: for you can surely by God
> sell this house here, with total impunity.}
> AG. **What, now?** MI. {Mostly you're living in my face.}
> AG. *Cut it out with your jokes.* MI. **What do you want now?**

A normal flow. Coming off a dialogue with his beloved and her sister,
Agorastocles turns to Milphio and asks for instructions, feeding Milphio
the setup for his joke (*auctor*); Milphio responds with a play on *auctor/auctio*,
followed by a riddle in which he points to Agorastocles' house (*hasce aedis*).
Agorastocles (*quid iam?*) sets him up for the punch line (answer to the riddle –
literally a punch, "you're living in my face"); after it lands, Agorastocles signals
that the joke is over. Milphio's question then triggers a move into lines that
move the action forward. As is often observed of these routines, they function
as loops in the action, which stands still while they are going on, and they
constitute a large percentage of the lines in any given play. Many of these lines
take the form of a two-act – identifiable, in some versions, as verbal dueling of
a particularly Italian kind, but always in performance terms a team act.

The cutoff lines are particularly formulaic. At the end of a run of "take
my wife" jokes in *Trinummus* – unusually for a two-man routine, between
a pair of old men rather than an owner-slave pair – the first one cuts off
with, "But pay attention to this, and away with the funny business" (*sed
hoc animum advorte atque aufer ridicularia, Trin.* 66). In *Asinaria*, at the
end of one of their spectacular insult matches, Leonida and Libanus sign
off (*As.* 576–8):

> [LI.] num male relata est gratia, {ut collegam collaudavi?}
> LE. {ut meque teque maxume atque ingenio nostro decuit.}
> LI. *am omitte istaec,* **hoc quod rogo responde**...

> [LI.] I hope I returned the favor nicely {when I read the eulogy for my
>   colleague?}
> LE. {Just the way it's proper for me and you and our special gifts.}
> LI. *Now stop all this,* and **answer me this, what I'm asking you** ...

Not only *omitte* and *aufer*, and the metatheatrical "pay attention" (*animum advorte*, often a direction to the audience by the prologue speaker), but also the command *responde* have a technical sense in the plays. The verb *respondere* in particular is used in verbal dueling to mean "take one's turn," and between a pair of performers it refers to what they are doing, the give and take in the Q & A.[25] Libanus' *responde* signals his partner that a setup is coming, or a changeup. Does this come from Atellan farce? There is no way to tell, since oral forms are *ipso facto* ephemeral and we have no observers' reports. It does not come from Menander, at any rate, where the two-act exists only in rudimentary form.[26]

Where you do see more of a two-act in Greek is in Old Comedy, though mostly in lines involving Xanthias in *Frogs* (but not Kariôn in *Wealth*), and in Middle Comedy, especially in Antiphanes.[27] Athenaeus was not interested in shtick *per se*, so that examples show up only by chance, and, considering the sheer volume of lines he quotes, rarely. Based on a survey of books 6–10, most of his excerpts are monologues, and of those that do incorporate exchanges between two or more characters, only some exhibit the features of shtick discussed here. Notable is Antiphanes' *Stratiôtês* fr. 200 (Ath. 6.257d–f), a tall tale about doves on Cyprus, perhaps told by a soldier to an interlocutor, ~ Plautus *Poenulus* 470–89, a tall tale about flying men in Pentetronica, told by a soldier to a pimp. The straight man's cues in *Poenulus* include *quo modo, quoi rei, quid postea*; Antiphanes has εἰπέ μοι, ἐν τίνι τόπῳ, λέγε γάρ, ποῖον, πῶς (picked up by ὅπως). Antiphanes' *Kouris* (fr. 127, Ath. 7.303f–304a) again has a straight man who sets up for speakers to say (somewhat) funny things, as does another three-way exchange in his *Boutalion* (fr. 69, Ath. 8.358d–f) and an exchange between a straight man and a Cynic in his *Kôrukos* (fr. 132,

---

[25] *Respondere*: e.g., *Cas.* 141, *Per.* 417, and note *Men.* 620–1, *num ancillae aut servei tibi| responsant? . . . impune non erit*. Cutoff lines: with *omitto*, *Mer.* 942, *quin tu istas omittis nugas?*; *Trin.* 1074, *omitte alia: hoc mihi responde*; with *aufero*, *Aul.* 638, *aufer cavillam, non ego nunc nugas ago*; probably *Cist.* 52, *aufer istaec verba*; *Cur.* 245, *aufer istaec . . . atque hoc responde quod rogo*; *Poen.* 1035, *maledicta hinc aufer*; *Truc.* 861, *aufer nugas, nil ego nunc de istac re ago*. For formal analysis of Roman verbal dueling conventions, see Richlin forthcoming.

[26] For an overview, see Wallochny 1992: 30–58, 82–8. For some brief two-act exchanges in Menander, see *Sam.* 295–6, cook and slave; *Epitrep.* 166–8, music girl and young man. There are plenty of setup lines in Menander, but they are not usually followed by jokes; the one joke structure that appears in both Menander and Plautus is the "bedeutungsvolle Pause" (earlier in chapter), especially the type in which a speaker starts a line and then changes course to form an insult, often in the form of a wish or prayer. With *Epid.* 23–4, cf. *Dys.* 661, *Epitrep.* 575–6. See also Scafuro 2014: 208–14, who illustrates what she calls a "patter pattern" in a half-dozen writers of *Nea*: clearly shtick, but not a common structure in the *palliata*.

[27] See the comprehensive discussion in Wallochny 1992: 13–29.

Ath. 9.366b–c). And in general the hapless interlocutors of cooks act as straight men, rarely getting a word in edgewise except "What do you mean?" Teamwork is not well developed; in a long excerpt from Strato's *Phoenicides* (fr. 1.1–47, Ath. 9.382b–383b) the cook does both parts as a monologue. Tellingly, a similar tactic appears in prose anecdotes about jokers, where a collector like Lynceus provides a joker like Dorion with an interlocutor whose only job is to set up the joke: πῶς; (Ath. 8.337d–e).[28]

The key point is that Greek shtick that shows up in Plautus in the form of single jokes does not come from the play's ostensible Greek original (or, could have come from multiple precursors). *Poenulus*, for example, is said in its prologue to come from Καρχηδόνιος, author unspecified (*Poen.* 53), but, as seen earlier, the tall tale about flying men is a variant of the tall tale in Antiphanes' *Stratiôtês*, while Plautus *Poen.* 1260–2 ~ Menander *Dys.* 700–2 (but see Arnott 2004). Jokes, to a much greater extent than plotlines, are detachable.[29] As for the skill set, it seems safe to assume that, whatever training an actor might have had in Greek comedy on the revival circuit, that is not where he learned to do the kind of rapid-fire, joke-to-joke shtick we see in the early *palliata*.

It is important, then, that formulae in Latin show up very early among the fragments of the *palliata*. One of the (maybe) six comic fragments attributed to Livius Andronicus, from his *Gladiolus* (1 R), is this: *Pulicesne an cimices an pedes?* **responde mihi** ("Fleas or bedbugs or lice? **Answer me**"). A list of insect pests comes up in a rant in Plautus, too – "flies, gnats, bedbugs and lice and fleas" (*muscae, culices, cimices pedesque pulicesque, Cur.* 500) – and we might compare Harpo Marx's heartfelt list (2000[1962]: 99): "Fleas, ticks, bedbugs, cockroaches, beetles, scorpions, and ants." Dionysus himself, as an experienced trouper, brings up "landladies with the fewest bedbugs" (*Frogs* 114–5, trans. Henderson). But it is *responde mihi* that marks this single line in Livius as part of a run of shtick, and probably not something invented for the first time in Latin by this Greek-speaker from Tarentum (see Wright 1974: 15–8, and 28–9 on the meter). Similarly in one of the fragments of Naevius (from his *Agitatoria*, 11–2 R):

---

[28] See also Timocles *Dionysus* (fr. 7, Ath. 9.407e), a riddle involving Syrian slaves, in a section of Athenaeus on bean soup and farting; and, to some degree, Alexis *Stratiôtês* fr. 212, Ath. 6.223e–f; Antiphanes *Turrênos* fr. 209, Ath. 7.329e; Antiphanes *Agroikos* fr. 1, Ath. 9.396b; Antiphanes *Akestria* fr. 21, Ath. 9.402d–e; Heniochus *Trochilus* fr. 4, Ath. 9.408a–b, also from the bean soup discussion.

[29] Also evidently true *within* Middle Comedy. Athenaeus' narrative voice at 7.304a–b remarks that some of the lines in Antiphanes' *Kouris* on tuna fish are also in his *Akestria* and *Boutalion*; the Cynic/sophist Cynulcus at 8.358d identifies *Boutalion* as a διασκευή of one of several plays Antiphanes wrote titled *Agroikos*. See above on the "switch" in burlesque.

eho an vicimus?
#Vicistis. #Volup est. **quo modo**? #{dicam tibi.

Whoa, did we win?
#You've won. #That's delightful. **How?** #{I'll tell you.

Dicam tibi is very often the lead-in for a punch line or a big lie in Plautus (see Wright 1974: 58 n. 47 on its usual position at line end). Here it is set up by the straight man's question, "How?" This usage must, like tickling fingers, have made audiences laugh before anything funny had been said, in a conditioned reflex; perhaps it is connected with the common use of *dicta* to mean "jokes" (so Gelasimus and Ergasilus, earlier). *Dicta* appear as jokes in connection with Livius five centuries later, in an often-quoted account from the *Life of Carus* in the *Historia Augusta* (13.4–5). Here the *HA*-writer tells a story in which Diocletian, then an officer, quotes the *Aeneid*. Expressing surprise, the *HA*-writer explains that soldiers often appropriate old poetry, "comic or some such"; then he adds that comic poets themselves make soldiers appropriate old jokes (*vetera dicta usurpare*); he cites as an example the famous punch line about the bunny – "You're a bunny, and you're looking for meat?" – as "a joke of Livius Andronicus" (*Livi Andronici dictum est*). The implicit analogy to his own praxis should give pause. It would be entirely in keeping with the *HA*-writer's sense of humor to have made the whole thing up (the *HA* is full of bogus allusions), especially since it forms part of a passage of classic baloney about the stories his grandfather told about Diocletian, building up to an exchange of jokes (14.2–3).[30] He may well be thinking of Terence, as is generally thought. Alternatively, the *HA*-writer may mean that it was an old joke when a soldier in Livius Andronicus told it, too – that the whole "old joke" shtick is just that: a joke even more in keeping with the *HA*-writer's sly, self-reflexive sense of humor. He never mentions Terence or the *Eunuchus* scene in which the soldier claims he invented the bunny joke and the *parasitus* tells the soldier the joke is old (*Eun.* 419–33). After all, Terence says the characters in this scene come from Menander's *Colax* (*Eun.* 30–4), in a prologue in which he famously defends himself against the charge that he cribbed from the *Colax* of Naevius and an old play of Plautus (25); he argues that it is impossible to be original in comedy: "there's nothing now said that hasn't been said before" (*nullumst iam*

---

[30] Ribbeck, at least, took the *HA*-writer's word for it, and lists the joke as Livius *com. inc.* 8. Fraenkel, who initially went along with Ribbeck (2007: 33), later changed his mind ("For some time I have regretted my credulity," 2007: 392). See Fraenkel's remarks on the possible prehistory of this joke in both Greek and Latin (33).

dictum quod non dictum sit prius, 41), or, "there's no joke now that wasn't a joke before."[31] Already Aristophanes' *Frogs* begins with a run of jokes about old jokes. Livius, born (maybe) in 284, and (if so, if really from Tarentum) sold into a Latin-speaking area at any time from the age of four onward, could have been producing plays when Plautus was in knee pants, and John Wright long ago demonstrated the unity of content in the *palliata* (1974), including Livius and Naevius; they must have worked with a *grex* that already knew how to do a two-act in Latin.

A straight man vs. funny man exchange also comes up in one of the few comic fragments of Ennius – "**Where are you taking me?**" #"{Where you'll hear the noise of the millstones most clearly}" (*quo nunc me ducis? #{ubi molarum strepitum audibis maximum}*, *Pancratiastes* 4 R) – here probably, then, with the roles reversed, as the slave sets up and the owner launches into a comic threat (see Wright 1974: 63–4). This happens between Agorastocles and Milphio in *Poenulus* during their long runs of shtick in the first part of the play, and is marked as a switch within the joke itself (*Poen.* 279–80):

[AG.] **Milphio, heus, Milphio, ubi es?** MI. **assum apud te eccum.** AG. {at ego
    elixus sis volo.}
MI. enim vero, ere, *facis delicias*. AG. {de tequidem haec didici omnia.}

[AG.] **Milphio, hey, Milphio, where are you?** MI. **I'm here with you, look.**
    AG. {But I wish you were boiled.}
MI. Shazam, boss, *you're making jokes*. AG. {I learned it all from you.}

Agorastocles sets up for Milphio to make a joke; instead, Milphio feeds him a straight line, setting up for a pun on *assum* "I'm here" and *assum* "roasted." Agorastocles obliges.[32] Then Milphio can comment on the switch while cuing that this bit is over (a metatheatrical comment is another common cutoff), and Agorastocles can credit him while setting up for the next joke ("learn" and "teach," *doceo* and *disco*, are also technical terms used of rehearsing, as at *Poen.* 552–4; and also of giving and taking orders).[33] The joke itself is a groaner, an example of what Michael Fontaine

---

[31] For discussion of the passage in Terence, see Beard 2014: 8–14; Fraenkel 2007: 32–40, who takes the joke to be of a type derived from "the speech of the people" (35); Wright 1974: 24–7, on Livius Andronicus and this line.

[32] See *Mos.* 1115 for another joke on *elixus / assus*; most likely also in the probably Plautine *Frivolaria*, frgs. 80, playing on *assunt* and *accensi*.

[33] Metatheatrical cutoffs: with *delicias facis*, *Cas.* 528, *nimias delicias facis*; with *iocor*, *Poen.* 163, *eundem me dato . . ./ #iocare*; with *ludis* and *ludificas*, *Mer.* 307, *Mil.* 324–5, *Ps.* 24; with *nugas agis*, *As.* 91, *Aul.* 651, and esp. *Men.* 621, 622, 623, 624, 625, where it is used as a refrain (cf. Barsby's comments, 1995: 67); *nugas blatis*, *Am.* 626, *Cur.* 462 (both closely preceding an exit), and similarly *Bac.* 569, *loqueris*

isolates as a "rimshot" (2010: 41). In line 281, the funny lines return to Milphio, but there is a rapid-fire set of switches at 295, so that Milphio closes out this run at 296 with "Really, boss, you're beating me [ow] at my own game and making jokes" (*enim vero, ere, meo me lacessis ludo et delicias facis*), an expansion of his part of line 280.

Expansion is a key property of shtick and shows up in a classic run in *Mostellaria* in which both performers play slaves and the straight-man role also goes back and forth. Here the two *pueri* Pinacium and Phaniscus insult each other (*Mos.* 887a–98; extra cues are here <u>underlined</u>):

PI. manesne ilico, {inpure parasite?}
PHA. **qui parasitus sum?** PI. <u>ego enim dicam</u>: {cibo perduci poteris quovis.}
    PHA. {mihi sum, lubet esse.} **quid id curas?**
PI. {ferocem facis, quia te erus amat.} PHA. <u>vah!</u>   890
{oculi dolent.} PI. **qur?** PHA. {quia fumu' molestust.}
PI. *tace sis*, {faber, qui cudere soles plumbeos nummos.}
PHA. <u>non <pol> potes tu cogere me ut tibi male dicam.</u>
novit erus me. PI. {suam quidem culcitulam oportet.}   894–95
PHA. {si sobriu' sis, male non dicas.} PI. {tibi optemperem, quom tu mihi
    nequeas?}
at tu mecum, {pessume,} *ito advorsus.* PHA. *quaeso hercle apstine*
iam sermonem de istis rebus. PI. faciam et pultabo fores.

PI. Won't you wait right there, {you dirty *parasitus*}?
PHA. **How am I a *parasitus*?** PI. <u>Well, I'll tell you</u>: {by food you can be led
    anywhere.}
PHA. {I belong to myself, I like to be/eat.} **What do you care?**
PI. {You're acting tough, because the owner loves you.} PHA. <u>Fooey!</u>   890
{My eyes hurt.} PI. **Why?** PHA. {Because the smoke is annoying.}
PI. *Shut up*, {you counterfeiter, you're always forging plugged nickels.}
PHA. <u>You can't make me insult you.</u>
The owner knows me. PI. {He ought to know his own mattress.}   894–95
PHA. {If you were sober, you wouldn't insult me.} PI. {I should be sober for you,
    when you can't do it for me?}
But you, {bad boy,} *should go meet him with me.* PHA. *Please, God, stop*
gabbing about that already. PI. I'll do it, and I'll knock on the door.

Phaniscus sets up for Pinacium at 888 and 889, and again at 894–5; he is usually the straight man, but at 891 Pinacium sets up for him.

---

nunc nugas; with *nugas garris, Cur.* 604, a Groucho-like joke about comedians: PL. *nugas garris.* CU. {*soleo, nam propter eas vivo facilius*}. This format underlies the vocative and deictic use of *nugator* (*Mil.* 1078, *Trin.* 936, and esp. *Trin.* 972, *abi sis, nugator. nugari nugatori postulas*), and can also be used to express incredulity or accuse someone of insanity (*Capt.* 628, 877, *Cur.* 326, *Men.* 381, 825, *Mer.* 942, *Mos.* 1080, 1081).

At 888 Pinacium uses the boosting cue *ego enim dicam*; at 890 Phaniscus buys time with *vah*, a placeholder; at 893 Phaniscus uses the metatheatrical *non <pol> potes tu cogere me ut tibi male dicam* as a teasing feigned breakoff, a straight man's *praeteritio*. Pinacium's *tace sis* (892) is usually an attempted cutoff, but he launches back into an insult; the "forging plugged nickels" line, literally "forging lead coins," is taken to mean that jokes about smoke (891) are old and tired (note the use of *faber*, "(metal) worker," as an insult, and the equation of jokes with coinage).[34] Once Pinacium has the cutoff cue, he can go on and knock on the door, but the two of them make it look as if they could have kept it up indefinitely; here, as elsewhere, being insulted for hunger and for sexual use by the owner is a standard part of shtick.

Similarly elastic is the cooks scene in *Aulularia*; cooks were famously funny back to Middle Comedy, but this scene, in which two cooks interact with the slave Strobilus, provides a meta-comment on elasticity. Strobilus has been making jokes about the neighbor ("How stingy *is* he?," *Aul.* 294–319), but now he cues the cooks Anthrax and Congrio to go into the finale of the shtick (320–7):

[STR.] **sescenta sunt quae memorem, si sit otium.**   320
sed uter vostrorum est celerior? memora mihi.
AN. {ego, ut multo melior.} STR. {coquom ego, non furem rogo.}
AN. {coquom ergo dico.} STR. **quid tu ais?** CO. {sic sum ut vides.}
AN. {coquos ille nundinalest, in nonum diem
solet ire coctum.} CO. {tun, trium litterarum homo,   325
me vituperas? fur.} AN. {etiam fur, trifurcifer.}
STR. *Tace nunciam tu...*

[STR.] **There are six hundred I could tell you, if we had time.**   320
But which of you is faster? Tell me.
AN. {I am, just like I'm much better.} STR. {I'm looking for a cook, not a thief.}
AN. {So I mean "as a cook."} STR. **What about *you*?** CO. {I'm just as you see.}
AN. {He's a nine-day [= market-day] cook – every nine days
he cooks the books.} CO. {You, you three-letter person,   325
you insult me? F-U-R (thief).} AN. {Thief yourself, triple thief in a yoke.}[35]
STR. *Shut up now, you. ...*

---

[34] Counterfeiting jokes are of particular interest due to the late arrival of local coinage in Rome and the generally accepted late date for the monetization of the Roman economy; see Richlin forthcoming b on the circulation of coins and comedy up from southern Italy into Latium in the 200s BCE.

[35] For the spelling joke, and the play on *fur* and *trifurcifer* ("three times a person deserving to be punished by wearing a yoke"), see Jones 1987: 153, who takes this to be a rare reference in the *palliata* to punitive facial tattooing (less rare in Greek, cf. Herodas *Mim.* 5.65–8).

Strobilus sets up for the cooks (321, 323), by instigating an insult match and cuing for speed (*celerior*); their lines at 322 and 323 must be sight gags, and they rattle on until he cuts them off. He ends his own run of jokes with a meta-comment on their number, recalling Saturio's promise to his daughter of *sescenti logei* (*Per.* 394). Like Jimmy Durante's "I got a million of 'em," this is both a professional boast and a placeholder (cf. *Per.* 410, *trecentis versibus*); here it emphasizes the relation between the rapid-fire construction of the scene and the comedian's knowledge.

So far these runs of shtick do look as if they could have been improvised onstage. But in fact the dialogue from *Mostellaria* is a song and probably could not have been; it is a song made to look like improvised verbal dueling. Closely comparable is the opening scene in *Epidicus*, thoroughly analyzed by Eckard Lefèvre (2001), who divides the scene into "rounds" in a verbal duel. Again, this *Epidicus* opener looks like a run of jokes that could be expanded or shortened ad lib., but it cannot be so; as Timothy Moore demonstrates in his analysis of the scene, the rhythms are extremely complex, and two sequences (1–24, 25–47) fall roughly into strophe-like units (2001: 317–8). This is not only a song, but also quite possibly a song and dance (see Moore 2012: 126–7 on "antiphonal choreography"). Instead of Burns and Allen, then, or Key and Peele, we have something more like Milton Berle and Ethel Merman, in a 1949 performance, singing Cole Porter's song "Friendship," from *Anything Goes*. Based on a mixture of buddy songs and the two-act, this song involves the singers in clever lyrics, mutual insults, upstaging each other, and escalating threats of violence. It is hard to sing, and in their duet Berle (trained in vaudeville) flubs a line, while Merman (trained in musical comedy) sails on (conversely, in the two-act lead-in, she steps on his lines). The choreography is loose, and some of the business looks improvised, as when Berle pulls Merman's hat over her face. But the flub might well have been part of the show (although Berle looks nonplussed, and Merman laughs); when Sutton Foster and Joel Grey performed the song on TV sixty years later, they built in a flub, and Foster at times sang like Merman, marking her debt to her comic ancestor.[36] The intentional flub plays with the performance as performed, whereas the lyrics dress up the two-act format with

[36] Berle & Merman: *Texaco Star Theater* (*The Milton Berle Show*), episode #1.42, 22 March 1949; the whole episode can be seen sporadically on YouTube, and on 3 October 2016 was available in the public domain at https://archive.org/details/TexacoStarTheater22March1949. Foster & Grey: *The Rosie Show*, 25 January 2012: http://www.youtube.com/watch?v=YXMlv0raIXM (accessed 3 October 2016).

rhyme, repetition, and a silly chorus, and the music makes the audience bounce along and leaves them with the tune stuck in their heads for days.

This is where orality hits a limit. It takes a lot of skill to pull off a two-act, but it takes multiple skills to pull off a song and dance – extreme skills that demand physical strength and coordination, years of training, and unusual talent, all extra difficult for the chronically malnourished. It also takes rehearsal, and improvisation becomes too risky. In this respect, Plautus stood in relation to the *palliata* as Cole Porter stood to vaudeville: smarter, with better lyrics. No Yale degree for Plautus, though. But just because people are poor doesn't make them stupid.[37]

A Sea Change

When Gayle Rubin wrote "The Traffic in Women," she drew on Lévi-Strauss's dicta on the structural foundations of kinship systems in order to explain the world historical oppression of women (1975: 169–77). In this model, "the exchange of women is a profound perception of a system in which women do not have full rights to themselves" (177). What does it mean, then, when comedians are exchanged? In *Stichus*, the ship's cargo carries "the funniest *parasiti*" along with music girls and luxury goods. Comedy and jokes are bound onto the body of the comedian, shipped along with him around the Mediterranean, and he becomes a tool for pleasure, just like the music girls and the perfume; all performers hold the bottom position, *a fortiori* slave performers, *a fortissimo* comedians and female slaves. Slave artists in a slave society were commodities just as art was – no question. But they could speak, and in the *palliata* they often speak about what it means to be a slave. They were not exactly testifying, however; they were performing, and through masks. Their jokes were compounded of skill, training, and tradition, as well as experience. Like the *parasiti* they played, they sang for their supper, so their audiences must have wanted to hear about slavery – not in any monolithic way, but strongly enough to affect what was onstage. Our idea of the playwright as *auteur* puts Plautus in the spotlight and erases the *grex* that made the plays. In any case, the whole phenomenon is visible to us only until the

---

[37] Here I differ from Fontaine 2010: 183–7, who argues that Plautus' audience was mainly elite, interested in Greek comedy as part of their advanced education. See Richlin 2014: 217 n. 52 on this argument (with reference to Livy 34.44.4–5 and 34.54.3–8), and 216–9 on the audience.

death of Terence, after which it disappears from our view: sinking out of sight, along with Terence's ship, under a wave of money.

For, as Roman armies crossed the sea to Greece and points east, a silver tide flooded back to Italy, and now literature had wealthy patrons; now the voices of slaves in their thousands, paradoxically, can no longer be heard. The slave trade was an essential part of the ancient world; slaves, as Page duBois pointed out in *Slaves and Other Objects* (2003), were invisible to elite writers in Greek because they were ubiquitous, and so they have often been invisible to readers who came later. They were not invisible to each other; as human cargo, some of them had made the art transported with them, or made new art when they reached their point of sale, and they left that art for us to see – unsigned, however. In central Italy, for a while, they joked onstage about their lives, and their lines by chance survived. Walter Benjamin used Roman conquest to describe the historian's dilemma (1968: 256):

> All rulers are the heirs of those who conquered before them. Hence, empathy with the victor invariably benefits the rulers. Historical materialists know what that means. Whoever has emerged victorious participates to this day in the triumphal procession in which the present rulers step over those who are lying prostrate. According to traditional practice, the spoils are carried along in the procession. They are called cultural treasures, and a historical materialist views them with cautious detachment. For without exception the cultural treasures he surveys have an origin which he cannot contemplate without horror. They owe their existence not only to the efforts of the great minds and talents who have created them, but also to the anonymous toil of their contemporaries. There is no document of civilization which is not at the same time a document of barbarism.

Rome after Plautus fades into something rich and strange.

CHAPTER II

Agents of Appropriation
Shipwrecks, Cargoes, and Entangled Networks in the Late Republic

Carrie Fulton[*]

Introduction

In the early first century BCE, a large freighter was cruising along the tip of the Peloponnese when it sank off the island of Antikythera, Greece. Since its discovery in 1900, this shipwreck has been used to illustrate the types of luxury goods that Romans were importing from Greece and the Near East at the end of the late Republic: finely made glassware; gold and silver cups; wooden couches with bronze decorations; marble and bronze statues; and various ceramics, including amphorae from Kos, Rhodes, and Ephesus.[1] On the one hand, these remains represent a snapshot of trade, encompassing the various components involved in the production and consumption of objects within a formal economy. On the other hand, this shipwreck also preserves objects lost in the process of being transported between the contexts that scholars usually rely upon to provide an interpretative framework. But instead of interpreting the remains of the Antikythera shipwreck according to where they were produced or headed, we can also evaluate them as the material vestiges of the agents who were responsible for circulating goods, people, and ideas around the Mediterranean at the end of the late Republic.

In this chapter, I contextualize late Republican and early Imperial shipwreck remains within broader networks of production, transportation, and consumption in order to address processes of appropriation. So far, prior models have largely been consumer-driven, crediting consumers with the agency for selecting objects that were then used to construct a social

---

[*] This manuscript has been much improved by discussions with friends and colleagues. In particular, I thank Dan-el Padilla Peralta, Carolyn MacDonald, and Matthew Loar for helpful comments on prior versions of this manuscript. I am grateful to Verity Platt, Annetta Alexandridis, and Sturt Manning for their feedback not only on this manuscript, but also the overall project. Any errors are my own.

[1] See Kaltsas *et al.* 2012 for a monograph and catalogue of the Antikythera shipwreck. For the discussion of shipwrecks as indicators of the trade in luxury goods, see Hölscher 1994, Wallace-Hadrill 2008: 361–2, and Bouyia 2012a. Assigning objects to a category of "luxury" without social and economic contextualization is problematic: e.g., Berry 1994: 3–10, Wallace-Hadrill 2008: 338–45, and Zanda 2011: 1–6.

discourse.[2] Although consumers and producers certainly figured prominently in these selections, multiple agents acted to facilitate and determine the transportation and circulation of objects. Moreover, these agents spanned a range of geographical and chronological contexts. In addition to material goods, items such as religious cult, poetry, and slaves traveled within and beyond Italy – as other chapters in this section show.[3] Thus, a model of appropriation needs to highlight the people and objects that were transported, the people who assembled and shipped the cargoes, and the geographies that were traversed.

In order to integrate these various components and different stages, this chapter first develops a heuristic framework based on the concept of a *chaîne opératoire* that emphasizes the production of an object's form as well as meaning. Next, it uses this framework of an enchained sequence to untangle the appropriation of luxury goods at the end of the late Republic. When adapted for analysis of ancient shipwrecks, this model underscores the people, things, and landscapes intertwined in the processes of sailing a ship, arranging a cargo into a temporary assemblage for shipment, and creating social meaning for the objects. This approach moves away from a consumer-driven model of appropriation that centers on how Romans used or displayed foreign items in their villas, temples, or civic spaces, and it instead emphasizes the multiple Roman and non-Roman agents acting across different temporal and geographical scales. Late Republican and early Imperial shipwrecks provide a primary source of evidence for understanding which cargo assemblages were shipped across which maritime routes. This evidence shifts our focus from a top-down, elite consumer-driven model of appropriation to one that involves individuals across multiple social, economic, and cultural categories. Shipwrecks, such as the one at Antikythera, are not merely illustrations of economic trade; they are also evidence for the social processes that compelled the production, circulation, and consumption of objects around the Mediterranean.

Appropriation, Logistics Networks, and *Chaînes Opératoires*

As ships transported goods to Rome to satiate the growing desire for foreign imports, many of these cargoes met their demise while at sea.[4]

---

[2] For consumer-centered approaches, see Wallace-Hadrill 2008, Rutledge 2012, and Walsh 2014.

[3] See Daniels, Myers, and Richlin in this volume.

[4] For example, in addition to the archaeological evidence, Lucian, writing in the second century CE, also notes that a ship had wrecked off Cape Malea while transporting some of Sulla's *spolia* back to Rome (*Zeuxis* 3). For more on the Roman social commentary for displaying booty and *spolia*, see p. 203.

Reconstructing shipwrecked remains into what was once a ship is not always straightforward: organic materials such as textiles, food stuffs, or people are rarely preserved except in traces recovered through analyzing remains such as residues, botanical or faunal remnants, or impressions in semipermanent objects.[5] Although statistically quantifying this transport can be problematic due to the factors influencing archaeological recovery, the number of known shipwrecks peaks in the first century BCE and first century CE.[6] The majority of these ships were transporting amphorae filled with wine, olive oil, and fish sauce, but several included cargoes of furniture, statues, building materials, glassware, animals, and slaves from Greece, Africa, Asia Minor, and the Near East.[7]

Within a broader logistics network, ships connect nodes of production and consumption in interregional and localized systems; any resulting shipwrecks illuminate the connections between these nodes, albeit by preserving what were meant to be transient associations between objects.[8] For example, the Antikythera shipwreck that opened this chapter was transporting glassware of Syro-Palestinian and Egyptian production, ceramic vases (*lagynoi*) commonly produced in Asia Minor, and marble statues possibly quarried on Paros and carved on Delos.[9] These various regions of production in the Eastern Mediterranean are linked by the routes of traders who brought raw materials to the craftsmen and who then transported finished objects to a location where they could be loaded

[5] Because of the lack of preservation of many organic remains (e.g., textiles, timber, grain, spices, books, and slaves, among others), scholars turn to literary and epigraphic sources for details about their shipment. See Murphy 1983 and Stewart 1999 for discussions of preservation in shipwrecks.

[6] The quantification of known shipwrecks is presented, most notably, in Parker 1992a. For the discussion of shipwrecks as proxies of economic growth see Gibbins 2001, Scheidel 2009, and Wilson 2009: 219–29. Patterns from shipwreck data can be skewed by preservation, variances in long-distance and regional trade, types of cargoes, precision in dating shipwrecks, and survey methods: Wilson 2011: 33–9.

[7] These objects are not meant to be a comprehensive list of luxury cargoes but have been found among the first-century BCE shipwrecks at Le Grotticelle, Italy (Mocchegiani Carpano 1986: 178–9); Spargi, Sardinia (Beltrame 2000; Lamboglia 1961a, 1971); Fourmigue, France (Baudoin *et al.* 1994); Mahdia, Tunisia (Hellenkemper Salies *et al.* 1994); and Antikythera, Greece (Kaltsas *et al.* 2012). For the acquisition of slaves, see Bradley 1994: 31–56, Harris 1999, and Scheidel 2005.

[8] The term "network" refers to connections between entities, not only as geographic regions, but also systems of physical and social environments (see Latour 2005, Ingold 2008, and Knappett 2011a). The analysis of networks has a long bibliography: for useful discussions of trade networks see Sherratt and Sherratt 1993, Davies 1998, Brughmans 2010, and Knappett 2011a.

[9] Though it seems likely that the glassware originated in Syro-Palestine and Egypt given its form and material compositions, it is difficult to determine a workshop since similar glassware has been found throughout the Eastern Mediterranean and Greece (Avronidaki 2012). *Lagynoi* are common throughout Greece and the eastern Aegean; similar types have been identified in workshops in the Aegean, Asia Minor, and Cyprus (Vivliodetis 2012). The marble for the statues has been sourced to Paros, but the statues may have been sculpted on Paros, Delos, or at Pergamon (Vlachogianni 2012).

onto the Antikythera vessel. Each node in this network is produced by the interaction between people, goods, and actions not only at that specific node, but also at other nearby nodes in a highly interconnected system.

In order to more fully explore the link between these actions and interactions at each node, I will use the concept of a *chaîne opératoire* (an operational sequence) to emphasize the technical actions that transform raw materials into fabricated objects as well as the production of social and ideological concepts.[10] Analysis of an object extends beyond manufacture to incorporate behavioral interactions between people, objects, and actions throughout an entire sequence of material acquisition, production, distribution, consumption, repair, reuse, and discard.[11] For example, in the course of manufacturing ceramics, a potter performs a series of technical actions informed by social and technical knowledge in order to produce a vase, such as an amphora. For this ceramic sequence, interactions include knowledge of what type of clay to use, how to form the amphora, what shape to render it in, what wine to fill it with, which consumers to sell to, and how to seal, refill, and repair it as needed.[12] Understood in this way, a *chaîne opératoire* addresses not only the activity at the discrete nodes in a network – the individual steps – but also the connections between the nodes – the exchange of information that influences an object's physical form and imbues it with meanings.

Emphasizing this social component of a *chaîne opératoire* allows us to follow the behavioral and technical actions crucial to interpreting an object's changing meanings throughout appropriations. Within this framework of interpretation, objects derive meaning from their materials (objective physical properties) and from their materiality (subjective social qualities).[13] Over the course of an operational sequence, just as materials undergo a series of actions to produce technical forms, so too are materialities transformed when distinct social meanings are produced at each step. The elements of this enchained process are far from prescriptive; links can be manipulated as situations arise, according to the evolving sequential production (and reproduction) of social patterns and depending on access to resources.[14] Rather than following a single linear progression through

---

[10] On the development of *chaîne opératoire* for conceptualizing production sequences, see Leroi-Gourhan 1964, Inizan *et al.* 1999: 14–7, and Bar-Yosef & Van Peer 2009.

[11] Skibo & Schiffer 2008: 10–22 and Hodder 2012: 54–8.

[12] For Roman patterns of ceramic manufacture, use, and reuse see Peña 2007.

[13] For defining materiality, see Ingold 2007.

[14] On the manipulation of links, see Leroi-Gourhan 1964: 231. Knappett 2011b argues against the prescriptive nature of a *chaîne opératoire*. For agencies of social reproduction see Dobres and Robb 2005.

discrete steps, an enchained framework incorporates iterative feedback
loops in a nonlinear sequence to accommodate the continuous circulation
of materials for which new social meanings were produced. These meanings shifted across different geographic and temporal scales.[15] Through this
modified view of a *chaîne opératoire*, we can strive to recreate the voices
within a sequence of distribution that are not usually represented in
scholarship. These voices are the result of the agencies present within
interactions between objects, people, and landscapes – aspects that are
explored in the remaining sections of this chapter.

Agency of Objects: Ships and Cargoes

With the ability to influence actions and mediate social relationships,
objects possess an agency that is relational as well as context dependent.[16]
Therefore, though goods may reflect the social norms of those who *produce*
them, they are also agents that actively mediate relationships for those who
acquire them. Within the context of transportation, the material agency of
objects influenced a cargo's assemblage, which was shaped both by the
objects' physical qualities and by their positions within prevailing economic, political, and social structures of trade.

As objects were loaded onto a ship, their physical properties determined
assemblage compositions, since their mass and arrangement in the hold
influenced how the ship sailed.[17] For instance, because a cargo of wine-
filled amphorae required a different arrangement in the hold than baskets
of grain, a captain had to consider what other goods could be added to a
cargo while still maintaining a proper displacement and distribution to
allow the ship to sail safely. Thus, cargoes were determined by the physical
constraints of sailing and by the technological sophistication of ships. By
the second century BCE, advances in ship technology and in the

[15] See discussion in Knappett 2011a: 26–33, 2011b: 47. This approach incorporates Igor Kopytoff's
proposed biographical life history of an object in which the life history of commodities is regarded as
a cultural biography (1986).
[16] For the social agency of objects, Alfred Gell (1998: 17–23) outlines a relational agency in which there
is an active participant who confers agency and a passive recipient onto whom this agency is
conferred. These categories of agent and recipient are by no means absolute but can shift as the
context changes across a *chaîne opératoire*.
[17] The weight of the goods and the distribution of that weight (the lading of a vessel) impact the trim
and balance of a vessel (Marsden 1994). If the cargo is too heavy, the ship will sink; if too light, it will
be unstable and difficult to sail, essentially sliding over rather than gliding through the water. Ballast
was brought on board in order to add weight to certain areas, and heavier objects were loaded along
the keel (the centerline) of the ship in order to provide an appropriate center of gravity (McGrail
1989).

construction and design of port facilities that could safely harbor larger ships enabled an increase in trading activity.[18] Although this activity included specialized transport and a proliferation of small ships moving cargoes under 75 tons, it also meant the development of large freighters over 100 tons: the first-century BCE wrecks at Madrague de Giens in France and at Albenga in Italy were carrying 6,000–7,000 and 11,500–13,000 amphorae, respectively.[19]

Economic, political, and social motivations also shaped cargo assemblages, as evidenced by tax laws and regulations. Most notably, the Roman state instituted reforms in 218 BCE with the passing of the *lex Claudia*, which prohibited any senator from possessing a vessel capable of transporting more than three hundred amphorae.[20] This law expresses a desire to regulate the size of ships and scale of commercial activity for senators, while still permitting senators to own ships for circulating products from their villas.[21] Additionally, tax laws show that once a ship reached port, captains had to distinguish which objects on board their ships were circulating as commodities, private possessions, or property of the state. A collection of tax laws at Ephesus (dated between 75 BCE and 62 CE) reveals that commodities had to be declared and taxed, but items for private (ἴδιος χρῆσις) and state use (δῆμος Ῥωμαίων) had the import tax (τέλος) waived.[22] However, it can be difficult for modern researchers to identify and distinguish these different economic categories from only

---

[18] On the correlation between advancements in technology and increases in maritime trade, see Wilson 2009: 226–7, 2011: 39 and Harris 2011: 257–87. Small ships engaged in local trade, sailing in shallow waters that required low draft (Houston 1988). Hull constructions were modified to include wells for transporting live fish (Boetto 2006, Beltrame *et al.* 2011) and accommodate *dolia* for transporting liquids (Heslin 2011). Ships likely were also modified to transport live animals, although their transport is visible primarily in iconography and has been inferred from references to exotic animals used in *venationes* and other *munera*: Jennison 2005: 137–53 and Friedman 2011: 134–6.

[19] For the wreck at Madrague de Giens, see Tchernia *et al.* 1978 and for the wreck at Albenga see Lamboglia 1961b. Ships carrying this many amphorae would have a capacity upward of 250 or 500 tons, respectively (see Parker 1992b).

[20] Livy 21.63.3–4.

[21] See discussion in Wallinga 1964: 20–2 and Tchernia 2011: 199–228. By 70 BCE, it seems that the *lex Claudia* was among those laws that Cicero considered ancient and dead, perhaps because senators found loopholes that enabled them to benefit from maritime trade (Kay 2014: 14, 150), among which were the opportunities for backing maritime loans (Rougé 1980, Rathbone 2003, and Aldrete & Mattingly 2010). For a discussion of the connection between politically influenced economic control and social standing at the end of the late Republic, see D'Arms 1981: 20–47. For a discussion of the *lex*'s interface with Plautine comedy, see Dufallo in this volume (p. 22).

[22] The *lex portorii Asiae* distinguishes between items needed for the journey (such as the ship and the equipment of a ship); those imported for private use; and those carrying anything for the public purpose of the Roman people, including those set aside for religious functions (*lex portorii Asiae* 58–63, 74, 81, 84 [Cottier & Corbier 2008]).

material remains: whereas the size and type of a ship determined the maximum quantity of a cargo, the assemblage could include goods belonging to different types of exchange, such as spoils of war, gifts, state-owned materials, or items traded in an open market.[23]

An example of different economic categories aboard one ship is visible in Cicero's correspondences about acquiring sculptures for his villas. In one acquisition, Cicero requests that Atticus select herms and other statues appropriate for certain rooms and send them to Italy on a suitable ship.[24] Though Cicero initially mentions that Atticus may export the statues on ships belonging to Lentulus, he later instructs his friend to find an appropriate vessel if Lentulus' ships are unavailable.[25] What other items might have been transported along with Cicero's statues aboard Lentulus' ships? Although there are several individuals named Lentulus who may have owned these ships, John D'Arms makes a case that they were likely transporting wine from Italy to Athens because Dressel 1B amphorae stamped with "L. Lentu P.f." have been found in the Athenian Agora.[26] If this was the case, then on the return trip to Italy, Lentulus' ships likely transported slaves, Greek wine, tablewares, or luxury items.[27] Despite traveling with other artifacts, which could have been destined for the open market, Cicero's statues would have belonged to a different category of trade.

The types of trade in which a ship engaged resulted in either homogeneous or heterogeneous cargoes, as defined by the material nature of the goods contained in the assemblages.[28] In heterogeneous cargoes, luxury items were moved alongside goods such as wine, olive oil, and tablewares.[29] As discussed previously, the cargo from the early first-century BCE shipwreck at Antikythera, Greece, contained a mixture of luxury and utilitarian items from the Near East and Greece.[30] Because of this diversity

---

[23] The classification of goods into economic systems has a long bibliography associated with it: e.g., Appadurai 1986, Kopytoff 1986, and Horden & Purcell 2000: 342–400.

[24] Cic. *Att.* 1.9.2 with discussions in Leen 1991, Zimmer 1994, Miles 2008, and Bouyia 2012a.

[25] Cic. *Att.* 1.8.2.

[26] D'Arms 1981: 68. Filippo Coarelli (1983: 52–3) suggests that this "Lentulus" possibly refers to P. Cornelius Lentulus Spinther *cos.* 57 BCE or Lucius Cornelius Lentulus Crus *cos.* 49 BCE. Shackleton Bailey (1965: 284) argues that Lentulus was returning from his governorship of Cilicia in the East, whereas Coarelli (1983: 45–6) insists these ships were part of a commercial venture because there is no evidence that anyone with the name of Lentulus was in the eastern province in the years preceding Cicero's letter in 67 BCE.

[27] On discussions of trade, see Kay 2014: 189–213.

[28] For different definitions of cargoes see Parker 1992b and Nieto Prieto 1997: 149.

[29] See Brun & Castelli 2013 for an economic definition of the term "luxury"; see Wallace-Hadrill 2008: 329–38 for a discussion of a Roman social discourse of luxury.

[30] See the catalogue on the Antikythera shipwreck: Kaltsas *et al.* 2012.

of objects from different regions, researchers propose that the cargo was assembled at a large entrepôt that served as a major shipping hub and redistribution center, such as Delos, Ephesus, or Pergamum.[31] The mixed cargo of the Antikythera wreck contrasts sharply with the homogeneous cargoes of the first-century BCE shipwrecks at Madrague de Giens and Albenga; these ships were carrying large quantities of wine-filled amphorae with only some space left for additional goods.[32] Homogeneous cargoes originated from one node of production; mixed cargoes linked together multiple regions and different social, cultural, historical, and economic frameworks.

Since items in a mixed cargo were manufactured according to various material sequences and at different times, the remains of a shipwreck often represent different stages in multiple, intersecting *chaînes opératoires*. For example, the cargo of the shipwreck at Antikythera contained finished works of late Classical and Hellenistic bronze statues and first-century BCE Parian marble statues; these statues were neither the sole component of the cargo nor do they seem to have been selected for transport according to material, size, or type.[33] This diverse group includes marble and bronze statues of gods, Homeric heroes, philosophers, and athletes, to list a few thematic categories.[34] Though the statues' material dictates different *chaînes opératoires*, the timelines of production also showcase intersecting sequences. The Parian marble statues were likely produced by a single workshop in the first century BCE, during the years or decades immediately preceding the shipment.[35] In contrast, some of the bronze statues were cast in the fourth century

---

[31] The discussion of possible homeports of the Antikythera shipwreck takes into consideration the ship's construction as well as the marble sources for the statues on board (see discussions by Kaltsas 2012: 15–6, Bouyia 2012b: 38, and Vlachogianni 2012: 70).

[32] Most of the amphorae on the Madrague de Giens were one of three variations on the type of Dressel 1B, which likely held wine; a different amphora type was stamped with Q.MAE ANT and was loaded on top of the Dressel 1B amphorae. In addition to the amphorae, the ship was also transporting several hundred examples of black-gloss pottery and coarseware (Tchernia *et al.* 1978: 33–59). The Albenga wreck also had Dressel 1 amphorae (Lamboglia 1952), whereas other ceramic items seem to have been for use while on board (Lamboglia 1965). For the transport of Italian wine and Dressel 1 amphorae, see Laubenheimer 2013.

[33] For an analysis of the statues in the Antikythera shipwreck, see Vlachogianni 2012. Additionally, single statues have been discovered in several shipwrecks and were found as solitary items on the seabed, perhaps jettisoned purposefully or accidentally by a passing ship (Tzalas 1997 and Arata 2005). In accordance with the Roman law for jettison, the captain, crew, and passengers decided what was thrown overboard in order to lighten the ship, but legally they would need to reimburse the owners of any cargo that was lost (Chevreau 2005 and Aubert 2007).

[34] Even within these thematic categories, there are variations, such as multiple sculptural types of Aphrodite (see analysis in Bol 1972: 43–7, Vlachogianni 2012: 65).

[35] Vlachogianni 2012: 64–9.

BCE and show signs of use in previous contexts.[36] Since the bronze statues already had undergone a series of distributions and reuses before being loaded on board the Antikythera ship, the *chaînes opératoires* of the bronze and marble statues differed not only in technical actions, but also in the sociohistorical frameworks according to which they were produced. On the one hand, the forms of the marble statues were produced in dialogue with consumers' tastes, which had been shaped by prior engagement with similar objects; the statues were newly sculpted for immediate consumption within a contemporary cultural milieu.[37] For the bronze statues, on the other hand, new social values were created through their displacement; their original form and prior contexts of display had been chosen according to sociohistorical frameworks in place during the fourth century BCE.

Having both fiscal worth as well as social value, an object was commoditized throughout multiple steps in a *chaîne opératoire* according to the temporal, cultural, economic, and social frameworks of those who engaged with it at each step.[38] As objects were moved around the Mediterranean, new assemblages and relations were frequently produced, thereby aiding in transforming the objects' social meanings and commoditization. When luxury objects were transported on board the Antikythera ship in a first-century BCE market, they entered into dialogue with prior shipments and distributions of *spolia* and *praeda*, objects that had been taken from conquests of Sicily, Greece, and Asia Minor during the third and second centuries BCE.[39] As a result of the conquests, foreign artifacts such as statuary and paintings flowed into Rome and reached private ownership, a development that many ancient authors saw as responsible for the eventual corruption of Roman values.[40] Within one system of Roman appropriation of luxury objects, what were once spoils of war switched between different social and economic frameworks when they were openly traded as luxuries; their meanings were transformed not only by geographic

[36] Although the bronze statues from the Antikythera shipwreck are heavily fragmented, several bronze statues have patches; whereas some patches are remnants of the casting process, others seem to be indicative of prolonged use due to their locations on the statues: Vlachogianni 2012: 80–5.

[37] For this chapter, I am setting aside the question of whether the statues from the Antikythera shipwreck were commissioned specifically by a consumer (or middleman) or sculpted generally for trade in an open, public market. See Harris 2015 for a discussion of Roman art within different markets.

[38] For a discussion of the general process of commoditization, see Appadurai 1986: 13–28.

[39] See Holz 2009. Definitions of *spolia* include things that pertain specifically to weapons, armor, and trophies from war as well as the general reuse and appropriation of objects (Greenhalgh 2011).

[40] See, e.g., Livy 39.6.9 and Plin. *HN* 24.5, with discussion by Carey 2003: 77, McDonnell 2006, and Miles 2008: 156.

displacement, but also by commoditization.[41] The dynamics of importation and cultural integration entailed changes in the significations of captured objects from their initial triumphal display as *spolia* in the third and second centuries BCE to their subsequent repurposing as commodities.[42]

The movement of these imported items from registries of *spolia* meant for public display to commodities that were part of private collections opened up a transitional dialogue between public magnificence and private wealth.[43] With the tension between public and private display contexts raising questions of legal ownership and audience, the objects become instrumental in negotiating identities – both of Rome as a collective entity and of individual owners. For example, when commenting on Marcellus' return with spoils from Syracuse in 211 BCE, Polybius cautions against claiming the objects of conquered foes for oneself and imitating their habits.[44] Cicero, however, would qualify Marcellus' use of spoils by stating that Marcellus limited himself to the *public* display of captured booty; Cicero structures Marcellus as a foil to Verres, who is characterized as rapaciously plundering Syracuse for his private benefit.[45] According to Cicero, Verres had plundered art that served specific purposes in public settings and violated this art by removing it to private settings for his own personal use.[46] In disparaging Verres as a *mercator* (merchant) who travels to provinces to buy and bring back statues and paintings, Cicero implies that Verres abuses statues by disregarding their social meaning and focusing only on financial gain.[47] Verres turns these objects into commodities – in

[41] At the end of the third and beginning of the second century BCE, the volume of booty flowing into Rome from military ventures altered the commoditization of these items and the economy within which they circulated (see, e.g., Kay 2014: 21–42).

[42] The economic value of spoliated objects figured prominently in their triumphal display, with Roman authors commenting on material and numbers of paraded booty; display in turn created a demand, satisfied not only through acquisition in war, but through purchase in commercial markets (Östenberg 2009: 79–119 and Harris 2015).

[43] See discussion by Gruen 1992: 111–12. The tension had to do not only with displaying spoliated objects in private settings, but with moving spoliated statues of the gods into the house – thereby treating them as furniture, according to Cato (*ORF*⁴, fr. 98 = Cugusi *OR* 72).

[44] Polyb. 9.10.2–3, 5–6, 13. See Holliday 2002: 195–219, Miles 2008: 218–84, Östenberg 2009: 262–92, and Zarmakoupi 2014: 17–23 for the incorporation of spoils into Roman commemorative and architectural practices.

[45] Cic. *Verr.* 2.1.55, 2.2.4, 2.4.115–6, 2.120–3; see Cic. *Rep.* 1.21 for mention of Archimedes' globe, which Marcellus took for himself out of the booty from Syracuse. According to Livy (26.31.9), Marcellus recounts that he took his *spolia* in accordance with the law. For more on Marcellus' spoliation of Syracuse and Fabius Maximus' spoliation of Tarentum, see Dufallo in this volume (p. 19).

[46] See Miles 2008: 154–5 for a discussion of how Verres not only wronged the objects, but also the communities in which they had been displayed.

[47] Cic. *Verr.* 2.1.22, 2.4.4; cf. Weis 2003 on Verres' role as an art dealer. For the semantics of *mercator*, see Broekert 2013: 150–3.

the manner of a *mercator* – and is criticized for displacing them into a *chaîne opératoire* in which their economic and commercial aspect is paramount.

In contrast to Verres, Cicero portrays himself as actively engaging with the social value of these objects, while still participating in the art market; he is aware of their ability to lend a particular meaning to the space in which they are displayed and to reflect upon their owner's character. Cicero's perspective on how art, space, and agents work together is evident in his own acquisition of statues. In a letter to Marcus Fadius Gallus (Cic. *Fam.* 7.23), Cicero mentions having asked Gallus to select some statues for him through a dealer, Arrianus Evander. Gallus, however, has chosen pieces that Cicero deems unworthy, an outcome for which Cicero blames his freedman and a certain Julius (a friend of Arrianus).[48] Cicero is astonished not only at the agreed-upon price, but also at Gallus' selection, namely statues of the Bacchantes and Mars. Although Gallus had defended his selection of the Bacchantes by comparing them to a group of the Muses, Cicero remarks that while the Muses would have been better suited at least for his library, there is no place in his house for Bacchantes, the frenzied followers of Dionysus. Likewise, Cicero questions why he, a supporter of peace, would want a statue of Mars, the god of war.[49] For Cicero, statues inform a viewer about the nature of the space in which they are displayed as well as about the character and status of their owner.[50] In Cicero's Verrine orations and in his private correspondence, the agency of objects inflects not only their display, but also their pathways of acquisition – routed through middlemen such as Arrianus Evander and Julius.[51]

Throughout this process, the Romans tried to control the social ramifications of incorporating foreign objects into their cultural frameworks. This incorporation was not simple or straightforward, as reflected in changes to Roman sumptuary legislation. When viewed diachronically, sumptuary laws show a loosening of restrictions on expenditure in reaction to the increasing availability of luxury items.[52] As Tacitus notes, the senate stopped attempting to formally regulate consumption in 22 CE because this legislation was disregarded so frequently.[53] However, while sumptuary legislation may have been abandoned in part because it was difficult to

---

[48] Cic. *Fam.* 7.23.3.   [49] Cic. *Fam.* 7.23.2.
[50] For sculptural programs in villa display, see Neudecker 1998. See also Marvin 2008 for the intricate dialogue between differing classifications of Greek and Roman sculpture.
[51] The cast of middlemen and other people involved in the acquisition of statues and other luxury objects is explored in the next section.
[52] Zanda 2011: 49–71.   [53] Tac. *Ann.* 3.52–4.

uphold, the shift from the Republic to the Principate also opened up new frameworks for regulating imported luxuries (one of which was emulation of the Imperial family).[54] The vogue in Corinthian bronzes during the first centuries BCE and CE is suggestive of such a process.[55] By the end of this period, Corinthian bronze seems to have fallen out of fashion, since few sources still mention its elevated status. To understand why, we should consider not formal restrictions – those emanating from the Roman rhetoric that imports were to blame for the burgeoning expression of luxury – but the informal constraints stemming from changes in the availability of foreign resources and luxury goods.[56] Perhaps the market had become oversaturated, at which point Corinthian bronze ceased to be pursued as a marker of elite status and was replaced by other luxury objects. Ships such as the one that wrecked at Antikythera were importing assemblages of foreign luxury goods; these imports could lead to the saturation of the market and of consumer demand for those imports as markers of elite identity.

Human Agents in Distribution

Whereas Roman elites (such as Cicero) are present in the literary record as consumers of foreign luxuries, agents of diverse statuses and backgrounds were involved in the processes of consumption, production, and distribution. Acting across all steps of the *chaînes opératoires* of these objects, both Roman and non-Roman agents arranged specific cargo assemblages and moved between different regions. Our analyses of macro-level sociocultural constructions and of micro-level formations of personal identities will need to differentiate agents according to their geographical and temporal spheres of action.

In Cicero's correspondence, the names of certain individual agents at various steps of the *chaîne opératoire* are only occasionally recorded; more often the specific identities of other agents are omitted and known merely through references to roles or (implied) actions. When Cicero instructs his

---

[54] For more on integration and recreation of social order in the early Principate, see Winterling 2009: 9–33. For the role of images in the process, see Zanker 1988 and Eder 1990.

[55] The term "Corinthian bronze" may refer to a particular alloy rather than production in Corinth (see Mattusch 2003). Roman authors suggest that Antony or Augustus included some people in the proscriptions just to acquire their Corinthian bronzes and that its inflated price in the marketplace had to be regulated by the Senate: e.g., Plin. *HN* 34.6 and Suet. *Aug.* 70.2, *Tib.* 34.1. For a general discussion on the Roman obsession with Corinthian bronzes, see Jacobson and Weitzman 1999: 239.

[56] Wyetzner 2002 and Silver 2007.

friend Atticus to acquire *ornamenta* or *signa* for his villa, he suggests certain sculptural subjects, but the selection, freight, and movement of the objects are out of his control.[57] Decisions about each of these procedures are allocated to other agents in the network. Cicero is informed of the movement and arrival of the sculptures in Italy, but he does not personally receive them. When Cicero eventually confirms that the statues had arrived at Caieta, he had not yet seen them, only having had time to send a man to pay freight costs and to move the statues to his house at Formiae. In this form of private acquisition, Atticus (or perhaps one of his slaves, freedmen, or associates) selected the statues for Cicero in Athens and arranged for their transport to Italy. In the previously mentioned example of Cicero's displeasure with Gallus' choice of the Bacchantes, Gallus had selected these from an inventory belonging to a dealer, Arrianus Evander.[58] Gallus had to rely on the objects that Arrianus had previously acquired or imported. The procurement and final installation of specific objects thus fell to different agents within a logistical and communicative hierarchy: Cicero (who received the statues); Atticus or Gallus (who selected the statues); and various freedmen, art dealers (such as Arrianus Evander), and merchants who acquired, moved, or transported the statues.

The intermediaries who acquired goods for redistribution also transported them to market spaces for selection by consumers or their assistants. Within Rome, spices, statues, jewelry, and other luxury goods were sold in established markets like the *Horrea Piperataria* along the Via Sacra or in multifunctional spaces such as the Saepta Iulia in the Campus Martius.[59] By the first century CE, the Saepta had become synonymous with luxury and entertainment, with the sale of these objects regarded as its own spectacle; according to Martial, it was a place where golden Rome ostentatiously displayed her wealth.[60] Consequently, for a potential buyer who visited the Saepta, many of the prior decisions in the network had already narrowed his or her choices regarding which object could be acquired.

The many agents responsible for narrowing these choices worked at harbors, sailed aboard ships, or had an invested economic interest in

---

[57] Cic. *Att.* 1.3, 1.4.   [58] Cic. *Fam.* 7.23.

[59] On the *Horrea Piperataria*, see Pollard 2009: 329–36 and Holleran 2012: 246. For the spice trade, see Miller 1969.

[60] Martial 2.57, 9.59. The Saepta was first used as a place for voting (e.g., Livy 26.22) and then monumentalized and transformed (Cic. *Att.* 4.6.14, Cass. Dio 53.23.2, 55.8.5, and Suet. *Claud.* 21, *Ner.* 12): *LTUR* IV: 228–9 s.v. "Saepta Iulia." In the Campus Martius, the activities of viewing, buying, and selling luxuries occurred against the backdrop of foreign import reflected in the marble imports and paintings adorning the Saepta (Plin. *HN* 36.29) and in the adjacent Iseum Campense with its sanctuary for the Greco-Egyptian cult of Isis (Lembke 1994).

circulating cargoes. Roman law specified responsibilities for the agents who managed a ship and arranged for the cargoes: the *exercitor* (business manager), *magister* (shipmaster), *nauclerus* or *navicularius* (ship captain), and *dominus* (ship owner).[61] Those who worked aboard the ship included the *gubernator* (helmsman), *proreta* (first mate), and *nautae* (sailors).[62] Administrative duties fell to the clerks, magistrates, and tax collectors who shared bureaucratic duties once a ship reached a harbor, or even accompanied the ship during its voyage.[63] Additional agents would be involved in the offloading and loading of a cargo, such as *geruli* (stevedores) and *lenuncularii* (boatmen of smaller craft).[64] Middlemen such as *mercatores* (merchants), *negotiatores* (businessmen), and other specialized traders would link those on board the ship to those who produced the goods and transported them to harbors.[65]

As owning and operating a ship would have been expensive, merchants eased the risk and financial burdens of trade by engaging in joint ventures and seeking loans for financing cargoes.[66] In the first century BCE, social networks that connected elites and non-elites were also repositioned and rebuilt through the use of *collegia*; membership in these formal associations offered a chance to forge a social identity that was separate from a civic hierarchy, as showcased in the funerary inscriptions and honorary dedications through which members constructed and communicated their

[61] The legal responsibilities of these roles are preserved in Justinian's *Digest*: *exercitor* (*Dig.* 14.1.1.15), *magister* (*Dig.* 14.1.1.1), *dominus* (*Dig.* 14.1.1.15). For discussions of these terms: Casson 1995: 314–21, Rauh 2003: 146–51, and Broekaert 2013: 216–22.

[62] Casson 1995: 316. The role of a *gubernator* could either be subordinate to or performed by the captain or owner, as in a Ciceronian example in which the owner of the ship is also the helmsman (*Inv. Rhet.* 2.154). For *proreta*, see Casson 1995: 319; for *nautae*, see Broekaert 2013: 175–7.

[63] On state magistrates and tax collectors in particular, see Badian 1972, Rathbone 2007, and Broekaert 2008.

[64] On these terms, see Sirks 1991: 256, Casson 1995: 369–70, Rauh 2003: 151–2, and Blackman 2008: 653. Inscriptions record several groups of *lenuncularii* at Ostia, with the largest having 258 members in 192 CE; among these members were several Roman senators (see, e.g., CIL 14.251, 341, 352 and Aldrete and Mattingly 2010: 205–6). For specialized and general roles involved in loading and off-loading cargo, see Sirks 1991: 256 and Aldrete and Mattingly 2010: 207.

[65] These roles are discussed by Rauh 2003: 135–45; for *negotiatores* and *mercatores*, see Broekaert 2013: 15–23, 150–3. On the *institores* in charge of the business side of trade arrangements, see Aubert 1994.

[66] On the risks undertaken by merchants, see Hasebroek 1933, D'Arms 1981: 48–71, 154–9, and Cartledge 1983: 2–5. Joint ventures by multiple merchants are shown by the names of multiple merchants in *tituli picti* on Spanish amphorae (Rodríguez Almeida 1989 and Remesal Rodríguez 2004). According to Plutarch, Cato the Elder entered into a *societas* of fifty people to finance a maritime trade venture (Plut. *Cat. Mai.* 21). Such a *societas* not only mitigated risks by spreading out the amount of investment, but also ensured that one person would not profit immensely, as discussed by Verboven 2002: 275–86.

personal and group identities.[67] A *collegium* could be beneficial for moni-
toring different steps in the process, decreasing the economic risk of losing
goods, and gathering market information.[68] Not only did members of
collegia come from diverse backgrounds, but so too did those individuals
who owned, contracted, or operated a ship. There were no legal restrictions on the basis of status, gender, or freedom: roles were open to male or
female, *paterfamilias* or youth, and free or slave.[69] More than working as
mere operators, however, individuals in these roles were directly responsible for the cargoes being transported, as exemplified by a late second- or
early third-century CE tax receipt in which a woman named Sarapias is
named as the owner (*naukleros*) of a ship and as the person in charge of
arranging for a cargo of wheat to be transported down the Nile.[70]

Throughout the various steps of production, distribution, and consumption in a *chaîne opératoire*, individuals of different social statuses acting in
different economic markets and different geographic regions made choices
that shaped patterns of distribution. In the example of the Parian marble
statues from the Antikythera shipwreck, quarriers targeted specific blocks of
stone with a view to the final product's integrity, sculptors selected those
blocks for particular forms, merchants acquired the finished sculptures for
transport, dealers and other intermediaries chose specific statues for acquisition, and members of the elite displayed these statues in their villas.[71]

The individuals making these selections belonged to different social,
cultural, and economic groups – not only members of the elite such as
Cicero, but also individuals (usually anonymous) whose agency is evident
in traces of their actions. At the same time, individual decisions concerning
acquisition, consumption, and distribution were actively being worked out
in a macro-level debate over cultural norms, if the angst expressed in
Cicero, Livy, and Pliny about the incorporation of foreign objects into
Rome's social fabric is any guide.[72] This social discourse was mediated and

---

[67] Broekaert 2013, 20. For *collegia*, see Tran 2006, Verboven 2007: 872, and Liu 2009: 4–11. On
constructions of identity with regards to inscriptions and dedications, see Joshel 1992 and Petersen
2006: 114–6, and e.g., for sailors at Lyon: Bérard 2012.

[68] Broekaert 2008: 232–3.   [69] *Dig.* 14.1.1.4, 14.1.1.16, 14.1.1.21, with Aubert 1994: 58–64.

[70] *P Teb.* II 370, with van Minnen 1986 and Hauben 1993.

[71] This sequence represents just one pathway: marble objects were also shipped as roughly finished goods,
and some quarries were under Imperial control (Maischberger 1997 and Russell 2015). The early
second-century CE Şile shipwreck provides evidence for marble objects that were transported as
roughly carved objects (Beykan 1988). See Trimble 2011 for the social and economic factors
underlying the production, acquisition, and display of a marble sculptural type during the second
century CE.

[72] For this social tension see p. 203. For discussions of acquired material within the Roman villa and
creation of an elite identity, see Hölscher 1994, Neudecker 1998, and Rutledge 2012.

propelled by actions on an individual level: people initiated and maintained their social relationships through the manipulation and transport of objects. By placing the transportation of objects within a broader *chaîne opératoire*, we can observe not only the numerous conversations among multiple interlocutors who were living and working in different eras and across different regions, but the types of agency that are often omitted from the discussion of appropriation.

Agency of Natural and Built Environments

Within *chaînes opératoires* of cargoes, the mobility and circulation of humans and objects actively shape and structure appropriation. However, mobility does not merely encompass the movement of objects across geographical distances and between nodes; it includes movements through landscapes that are webbed with distribution patterns.[73] For this reason, the Mediterranean seascape and littoral landscape are more than merely backdrops for a logistical network of exchange. The winds, currents, and coastlines influenced the pathways of travel and routes between certain regions, but the natural elements by no means prescribed voyages; merchants and sailors weighed environmental conditions against their knowledge of the route and the potential economic benefits of travel.[74] Although in antiquity it was preferable to sail from March through November due to more predictable weather patterns and calmer seas, some routes could have been sailed year-round or favored during different seasons depending on shifting wind patterns and knowledge of particular landscapes and weather patterns.[75] Sailors acquired a familiarity with coastlines and conditions by repeating journeys between ports, as shown by narratives in several *periploi* and by the example of Flavius Zeuxis – who boasted on his tomb at Hierapolis that he had safely rounded Cape Malea seventy-two times in his lifetime.[76] This boast was a testament to his knowledge and ability as a seafarer to navigate around a dangerous part

---

[73] On mobility and transit as features of appropriation, see Sponsler 2002 and Hahn & Weiss 2013.

[74] See discussions of the maritime environment by Arnaud 2011, Whitewright 2011, and Tartaron 2013. Tim Ingold (1993) discusses the construction of landscape through repeated engagements. For an example of the integrated nature of the natural environment with sailing routes, see the web-based geospatial model ORBIS project (Scheidel & Meeks 2014).

[75] Arnaud 2005: 16, 26–7. For discussion of the sailing season, see Rougé 1975, 24; cf. Beresford 2013: 79–90.

[76] *Syll.*³ 1229 = *IGRR* IV 841 and Rathbone 2007: 314. These *periploi* include a fourth-century BCE *periplus* by Pseudo-Scylax (Shipley 2011), the first-century CE *Periplus Maris Erythrae* (Casson 1989), and Arrian's second-century CE *Periplus Ponti Euxini* (Liddle 2003).

of the Peloponnese; he chose to use his conquest over this landscape to permanently showcase his identity on his tomb.

Ports and harbor facilities also played an important role in connecting maritime trade to land-based distribution by furnishing ships with the necessary facilities for trade and with protection from rough weather. With the Roman invention of a hydraulic form of concrete in the late third or early second century BCE, port cities were able to provide an extensive interface – through the construction of moles, quays, and breakwaters – to protect ships from harsh winds and seas while cargoes were offloaded and reloaded.[77] If space was unavailable for a ship to dock or if conditions restricted close access, smaller boats shuttled goods between larger freighters and the shore, and buildings such as warehouses facilitated trade and the redistribution of goods.[78] These warehouses, which lined the quays in Roman harbors, served only as intermediary holding places for goods to be distributed to other markets by wagons, pack animals, or boats along paths, manufactured roadways, and rivers.[79] Although these various components of infrastructure were necessary for the movement of goods, they represent only the potential nodes in the network; sailors and merchants decided the actual routes and composition of cargoes transported around the Mediterranean.

Changes to the size and type of ships reflect alterations in the availability of cargo and harbor facilities, directly connecting types of trade and sailing routes in a *chaîne opératoire*. When traveling between two ports, ships could either travel over open water in a type of direct sailing, or they might travel along the coastline in a type of segmented sailing that moved from cape to cape.[80] In either sailing pattern, the type of trade could be coordinated in advance between merchants at two emporia; alternatively, the ship captain could engage in an opportunistic type of trade in which goods were offloaded or picked up as necessary. A ship, however, would not need to adhere to one mode of sailing or trade; actual cargoes represented a spectrum of possibilities and could connect a hierarchy of ports.[81] For a ship to engage in segmented sailing, its hull had to have an

---

[77] For more on the harbor installations, see Blackman 2008: 644–8, Rickman 2008: 6–7, 14–15, and Oleson *et al.* 2011.

[78] Blackman 2008: 649–50. For survey of small craft used in harbors, see Casson 1995: 335–7.

[79] On pathways of transportation, see Laurence 1999: 11–26, 95–108 and van Tilburg 2007: 68–74. Strabo (5.3.8) emphasizes the continuity of moving goods by ship and by wagon, noting that paved roads were cut through the countryside so that wagons could take on a shipload (*phortia*).

[80] See Horden & Purcell 2000: 368–72 and Wilson 2011: 53.

[81] On hierarchies of ports, see Nieto Prieto 1997, Arnaud 2011, and Boetto 2012.

appropriate draft to dock at proper facilities or be able to exchange cargoes in shallow waters.[82] These qualities were characteristic of smaller ships built for localized trade but were not as conducive to open-water voyages.[83] In contrast, larger ships would have been constructed for long-distance direct sailing, able to handle rougher seas, and equipped with space to carry survival necessities such as food and freshwater.

Whereas large ships moved goods between large ports, smaller ships were able to sail much more varied routes between both large and small ports. The cargo of a first-century BCE wreck (referred to as Fourmigue C) off Golfe-Juan, France, provides an example of trade between large distribution and redistribution centers. In addition to the one hundred Dressel 1B amphorae produced near Cosa in Italy, the ship was transporting elaborately decorated couches (*klinai*) produced at Delos and various bronze vases likely produced at Athens; the raw material for the latter is likely to have come from Cyprus.[84] Based on the ship's smaller size, the *klinai* and vases would have been shipped first to a larger trading port in Italy (such as Puteoli or Ostia), where the Fourmigue C vessel would have acquired them.[85] This smaller ship would have been more suitable for sailing on the Tyrrhenian Sea (where it could travel along the coastline and seek shelter from winds and storms), rather than across the open sea of the Mediterranean (where it would be susceptible to large swells and sudden storms). The Fourmigue C shipwreck also provides evidence that not all imported luxury items were being consumed in Italy; many luxuries were being shipped to consumers in the provinces.[86] A closer look at these networks of provincial distribution through the study of the *chaîne opératoire* of a cargo can bring into clearer focus the transformation of consumption patterns in regions outside of Rome.[87]

By considering interactions across an object's life history, we eliminate polarized models of consumer- or producer-driven systems of exchange that provide only partial views of appropriation. Instead, a biographical

---

[82] For the approximate tonnage of the Mahdia wreck, see Coarelli 1983: 48–9. The remains for the Mahdia suggest a ship approximately forty meters in length and fourteen meters in breadth (Höckmann 1994).

[83] For the relationship between the hull shape, construction techniques, ship size, and maneuverability of the ship, see Dell'Amico 2011 and Pomey 2011. See Steffy 1994: 8–10 for sailing mechanics.

[84] Baudoin *et al.* 1994: 13–21. For the *klinai*, vases, and bronze *situla* from Fourmigue C, see Baudoin *et al.* 1994: 50, 61–87, 123. The bronze decorations for the *klinai* were similar to those from the Mahdia shipwreck (Faust 1994).

[85] The Dressel 1B amphorae were likely acquired at Cosa; for the transport of Italian wine and Dressel 1 amphorae, see Laubenheimer 2013.

[86] See Dietler 2010: 133–8 for a discussion of shipwrecks off the southern coastline of France.

[87] See Myers in this volume for a case study that emphasizes a network focused outside of Rome.

view allows for interactions across multiple time scales, among different geographies, and throughout every stage of production, consumption, and distribution. Previous models of appropriation have used the term "contact zone" to refer to an area in which goods and appropriators interact, yet areas of contact change as an object moves through different geographical regions and different stages of appropriation.[88] For example, contact zones for a bronze statue from the Antikythera shipwreck would have encompassed public civic spaces in Greece, marketplaces or warehouses in Athens and Italy, cargo holds on board ships, and display spaces in Roman villas. At each stage and each contact zone, a statue would have meant different things to the individuals who came into contact with it. These context-dependent meanings were intertwined all throughout the *chaînes opératoires* of specific objects and collective assemblages.

Conclusions

A scalable model built around the concept of a *chaîne opératoire* links human and nonhuman agents across multiple contact zones and chronological time frames, simultaneously emphasizing the broader dynamics of trade and the role of the individual. By illuminating and differentiating various agents within circulation networks, this detailed and context-specific model replaces a homogeneous view of the processes of cultural formation and change. Agencies are not only ascribed to those people who were involved in assembling, transporting, and distributing a cargo, but also are extended to goods and landscapes. Such an approach shifts our model of appropriation away from one that is driven primarily by elite consumption and toward one that underlines the role of the intermediaries within the process of appropriation; in doing so, it gives a voice to those nameless individuals whose instrumental roles in the process are overlooked by literary testimonies. It also shifts our view of *where* appropriation occurs.

When an object changes context through appropriation, the object's semiotic ability to evoke an intended meaning also changes. In order to study these semiotic shifts, Robert Nelson has suggested that scholars look at the active agents within a particular historical context, abandoning the "privileged autonomy of the art object" in favor of a focus on the construction of an object's meaning.[89] This focus is at the heart of the *chaîne*

---

[88] For discussions of "contact zone," see Hahn 2012 and Huck & Bauernschmidt 2012: 238, 245.
[89] Nelson 2003: 172.

opératoire approach. For objects such as the marble statues from the Antikythera shipwreck, the agents involved in the construction of meaning included not only the stone quarriers and sculptors working the marble into forms recognized and desired by consumers, but also the material itself, which imposed parameters on its sculpted size and shape and the decisions made concerning its transportation. On the one hand, the physical properties of the objects dictated which goods were selected for a particular transport, as heavy marble and bronze statues or bulky *klinai* would have limited the volume of other goods that a merchant could transport on board one ship.[90] On the other, the selection of goods for transport was driven by potential economic profits and social demands. Thus, both the physical properties and the social qualities of an object play a role in ultimately influencing the construction of meanings over time.

If we concentrate primarily on the conversations between objects and their final consumers (thus attributing agency only to specific individuals, the broader class of "elites," or even "Romans"), we at best can only gain a partial perspective on appropriation. Though Cicero's requests for acquiring statues from Athens are preserved through his letters and orations, he was not the only one determining which objects were to be imported. As noted earlier, the selection of specific statues occurred in different stages and was contingent upon the availability of statues, the suitability of ships, and the aesthetic and logical choices of middlemen, freedmen, and slaves. Highlighting these roles within the *chaîne opératoire* of an object opens up to scrutiny the full network of agents – middlemen, merchants, sailors, and harbor workers – responsible for an object's shifts in contexts and in meaning.

By using the notion of *chaîne opératoire* as a heuristic device for thinking through the process of appropriation, we move beyond treating shipwrecks as isolated examples of trade. Instead, these shipwrecks illuminate selective processes occurring on local and global scales within which various agents acted to determine a cargo's composition and the meanings of the objects it contained. Cargoes such as those represented in the Antikythera and Fourmigue C shipwrecks were products of entwined networks of multiscalar exchange in which people, objects, and landscapes assumed active roles. Through these networks, objects and humans circulated constantly. As cargoes underwent reconfigurations, they were instrumental in instigating, mediating, and transforming social engagements across the Mediterranean.

---

[90] For the special case of obelisk transport, see Parker in this volume.

CHAPTER 12

Import/Export
Empire and Appropriation in the Gallus Papyrus from Qasr Ibrim

Micah Y. Myers

Robin Nisbet concludes the *editio princeps* of the Gallus papyrus discovered at Qasr Ibrim (P.QasrIbrim inv. 78–3–11/1 [L1/2]) by noting the coincidence between the papyrus' discovery in a Roman military context in Lower Nubia, Gallus' role as the first equestrian prefect of Egypt, and Ovid's prediction that Gallus' poetic renown would be disseminated far and wide:

> If the Romans at Carrhae transported Milesian tales in their baggage (Plut., *Crass.* 32.3), a lonely officer might treasure romantic elegies on love and war, written in his youth by the Prefect of the province . . . It is deeply satisfying that the Egypt Exploration Society should have recovered this papyrus, two thousand years after it was jettisoned, from the limits of the province which the poet conquered and ruled. His literary fame, said Ovid, would reach as far as his military commands, and last longer:
>> Gallus et Hesperiis et Gallus notus Eois,
>> et sua cum Gallo nota Lycoris erit [= *Am.* 1.15.29–30].[1]

The present chapter explores further aspects of the relationship between the Gallus papyrus and the circulation of soldiers, poets, and poems, as well as other individuals and objects. I shall consider ways in which the papyrus, as a literary text and as a material artifact, evokes a variety of intertwined processes of importation, exportation, and circulation during the late Republic and early Principate.[2] These processes of circulation were facilitated by networks that were fundamental to the administration and expansion of Roman *imperium* as well as to other sorts of travel, trade, and transport, including the diffusion of literary culture and other writing practices. Roman networks were complex, multidirectional, and highly interconnected, with different networks, such as military or commercial,

---

[1] Anderson *et al.* 1979: 155.
[2] For the analysis of papyri as both texts and artifacts: Fearn 2010. Fearn also highlights how the links between imperial power and the circulation of papyri extend to nineteenth-century Britain and other contemporary European powers. See also Cuvigny 2009, Keenan 2009.

composed of distinct as well as overlapping nodes, routes, and agents.[3] I follow this model of multidirectional Roman networks, although my discussion of the Gallus papyrus focuses especially on circulation from the periphery to Rome and from the Roman Empire's core and its provinces to the frontier zone of Lower Nubia (Figure 12.1).[4]

The verses on the papyrus (Gallus fr. 2 Courtney) point to the importation toward Rome of triumphal spoils, humans, literature, and literary traditions, whereas the papyrus itself is an example of the exportation and circulation of texts and writing practices along with the expansion of Roman military power. The Gallus papyrus is by no means unique in reflecting the phenomenon of texts circulating together with the Roman military; compare, for example, the diffusion of Vergil's poetry to far-flung military contexts such as Vindolanda, Mons Claudianus, and Masada. Yet the papyrus' discovery at Qasr Ibrim, a distant and apparently briefly occupied outpost of the Roman empire, makes it an exceptional case study for the broader phenomenon of the circulation of literature, especially in Roman military contexts, as well as for the ways that Roman poetry is dependent upon the circulation toward Rome of texts, objects, and individuals.

The first two sections of the chapter review the life of Gallus and introduce the papyrus. I turn to the content of Gallus fr. 2 in the third section, focusing on themes of importation into Rome in Gallus' verses, which manifest themselves through references to triumphal display, literary appropriation, reading, viewing, and human trafficking. This combination of imports evokes the manifold ways in which the imperial process brings the *orbis* to the *urbs*. While the third section explores how Gallus fr. 2 engages with aspects of Roman importation, the fourth section, split into three parts, argues that the circulation of Gallus' poetry to Qasr Ibrim is indicative of how Roman literary culture was exported along with Roman military power, even if the precise circumstances that led to the deposit of the Gallus papyrus cannot be known. The first two parts situate the Gallus papyrus within the broader context of Roman-period Qasr Ibrim by reviewing the historical and archaeological evidence, including other papyri, inscriptions, and nonliterary finds from the site. The third part surveys other examples of the circulation and

---

[3] Cf. Rathbone 2009. For the elements that comprise networks: e.g., Malkin 2011: 17.

[4] My concept of networks, connectivity, circulation, and mobility is especially influenced by Horden & Purcell 2000, Adams & Laurence 2001, Morris 2003, Malkin 2003 and 2011, Barchiesi 2005a, Malkin *et al.* 2009: 1–11, Purcell 2012 and 2013, De Angelis 2013. The editors of this volume inform me that circulation and "circuits" will feature prominently in Horden & Purcell's forthcoming *Liquid Continents*; cf. Grenier 1997: 397–400. Greenblatt 2009: 7–12 sets Roman cultural mobility within a broader historical perspective. In this volume see Fulton's discussion of Roman commercial networks and *chaînes opératoires* (p. 195).

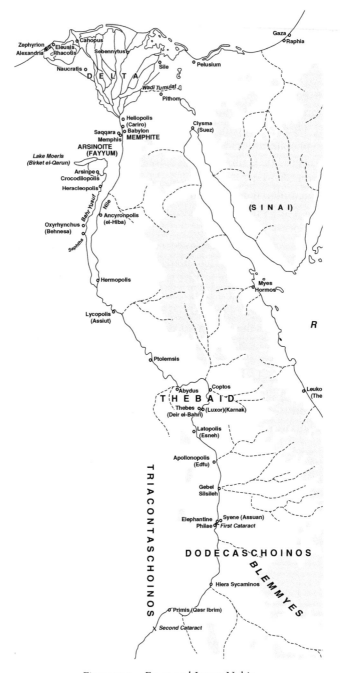

Figure 12.1.   Egypt and Lower Nubia

composition of literature around the empire, especially in military contexts. In sum, I argue that the Gallus papyrus, as a literary text and as a material artifact, exemplifies the power of circulation in the Roman world.

C. Cornelius Gallus

The *testimonia* for the life of Gallus are well known and will not be rehearsed at length here.[5] In the context of the present chapter – the Gallus papyrus as a case study for literary, material, and human circulation in the Roman world – two points are worth emphasizing:

1. The *testimonia* suggest that Gallus himself circulated around the Mediterranean as a military officer and imperial administrator, although we only have notices of a few of his posts. From 30 until sometime before his death in 27/26 BCE, Gallus, first as Octavian's *praefectus fabrum* and later as *praefectus Alexandreae et Aegypti*, campaigned throughout Egypt at least as far south as Philae, in the first cataract region (Figure 12.1).[6] Earlier in the 30s Gallus likely also played an important part in Octavian's military and political activities around the empire, given his leading role in the decisive Egyptian campaign.[7] In addition he may have served under Asinius Pollio in Spain in 44 and in Cisalpine Gaul in 41–40.[8]

2. My interpretation of the papyrus is informed by scholars who argue, contrary to the assertions of some ancient sources (Dio Cass. 53.23.5–6, Amm. Marc. 17.4.5, Serv. on *Ecl.* 10.1), that Gallus' disgrace and suicide was not the result of gross misbehavior or disloyalty while Egyptian prefect, but rather because Gallus in some way offended (Suet. *Aug.* 66) – or was falsely accused of offending (Ov. *Am.* 3.9.63–4) – the *princeps*.[9] By extension, I am also persuaded that the loss of much of Gallus' poetry and the reuse of the monuments he erected in Egypt was most likely not due to memory sanctions.[10] Thus, while I shall suggest that the circulation of the Gallus papyrus to Qasr Ibrim should be considered in relation to

---

[5] See esp. Boucher 1966: 5–65, Crowther 1983: 1623, Courtney 1993: 259–62, Manzoni 1995: 3–55, Faoro 2007, Hollis 2007: 225–30, Myers 2015.

[6] *CIL* 6.882, *CIL* 3.14147[5], Strabo 17.1.53, Suet. *Aug.* 66, Plut. *Ant.* 79, Dio Cass. 51.9 and 53.23, Amm. Marc. 17.4.5, Serv. on *Ecl.* 10.1, Jer. *Chron.* ann. Abr. 1990, Oros. 6.19.15.

[7] Faoro 2007: 33.

[8] Pollio: *Ad Fam.* 10.32.5 and 10.31.6. Gaul: Syme 1932: 252. Cf. Serv. on *Ecl.* 6.64 and on *Ecl.* 9.10, on which see Broughton 1951–2: 2.377.

[9] See esp. Boucher 1966, Hoffmann *et al.* 2009.

[10] Flower 2006: 2 prefers "memory sanctions" to *damnatio memoriae*, asserting that the latter often implies a more standardized system of penalties than the historical record supports (xix). Hirschfeld 1896: 482, Skutsch 1901: 142 already conjecture that Gallus suffered *damnatio memoriae*; but cf. Boucher 1966: 57, Jacobsen 1984, Manzoni 1995: 53–5, Hoffmann *et al.* 2009: 40.

Gallus' own activities in Egypt, I do not approach the fragments on the
papyrus as verses from a banned book.

The Papyrus

The discovery of P.QasrIbrim inv. 78–3–11/1 (L1/2) in 1978 expanded our
access to Gallus' poetry beyond the single verse preserved via the manuscript
tradition. It comprises five papyrus fragments that form a single piece of a
bookroll. The elegant script and wide margins suggest that it is a good
professional copy, although definitive assessment of the quality is elusive
since it is among the oldest extant MSS of Latin poetry.[11] Col. i of the papyrus
contains fragments of eleven verses and evidence of several more. Only three
letters are extant in col. ii (*Qui*), although there are traces of six lines. After
lines 1, 5, and 9 in col. i and line 4 of col. ii there are H-shaped marks in the
right and left margins and blank gaps between the lines.[12] The gaps and
marks, which are without a definite parallel, have been variously interpreted
as indicating that the fragments are a series of epigrams, excerpts from a longer
poem or poems, or breaks within a single work, such as a change of speaker in
an amoebaean poem.[13] The first verse addresses Gallus' *puella*, Lycoris. In
addition, scholars have noted many apparent allusions to these verses by other
Roman poets. Taken together, these elements provide strong evidence for
identifying the author as Gallus, with the verses possibly coming from the
beginning or end of a book of poetry.[14] The text of col. i of the papyrus is
presented here with the supplements and translation of Adrian Hollis:[15]

> tristia nequit[ia fact]a, Lycori, tua.
>
> Fata mihi, Caesar, tum erunt mea dulcia, quom tu
>   maxima Romanae pars eri<s> historiae
> postque tuum reditum multorum templa deorum
>   fixa legam spolieis deivitiora tueis.   5
>
>   .....]..... tandem fecerunt ç[ar]mina Musae

---

[11] Anderson *et al.* 1979: 126–7, 138, Capasso 2003: 16–22. See these sources for a full physical
description and images of the papyrus.

[12] Anderson *et al.* 1979: 129–31, Heyworth 1995: 121–2.

[13] Epigrams interpretation (the most common): e.g., Anderson *et al.* 1979: 140–9, Putnam 1980,
Ballaira 1993: 33, Hollis 2007: 250–1. Excerpts interpretation: Heyworth 1984, Courtney 1993: 264.
Single poem interpretation: Newman 1980, Miller 1981. Amoebaean poem interpretation:
Fairweather 1984, O'Hara 1989, Miller 2004: 75–80.

[14] See esp. Anderson *et al.* 1979: 140–55, Barchiesi 1981, Van Sickle 1981, Cairns 2006: 404–44, Hollis
2007: 250–1.

[15] Hollis 2007: 224. The translation includes minor modifications.

quae possem domina deicere digna mea.
...........]. atur idem tibi, non ego, Visce
..]........ !. Kato, iudice te vereor.

    ]...[   ].   10
    ]...[   ]. Tyria
                            ].

<?made> sad, Lycoris, by your wantonness.

My fate, Caesar, will be sweet to me at that time when you become the greatest part of Roman history, and when, after your return, I survey [or: "read about"] the temples of many gods, richer for being fixed with your spoils.

...Finally the Muses have made <?these> poems <?for me> that I could call worthy of my mistress. .... the same to you, I do not, Viscus, I do not, Cato, fear ... with you as judge.

... Tyrian ...

The publication of the papyrus brought renewed interest in Gallan studies.[16] Yet there was more than a little handwringing over whether the unearthed verses live up to the portrait of Gallus that Vergil and the Augustan elegists paint in their poetry.[17] I am in large part persuaded, however, by scholars who have offered a more positive reception of the fragment, arguing, for example, that the word patterning in Gallus fr. 2 reflects the stylistics of Alexandrian and Hellenistic-Roman epigram,[18] and that features of the verses that have been judged as inferior are in some cases well paralleled and in other instances merely reflect what we might have expected about Gallus: namely, that he falls between Catullus and the Augustans in the development of Latin metrics and stylistics.[19] Yet rather than dwelling on the literary merit of Gallus fr. 2, I will turn to considering the fragment as evidence of a variety of intertwined processes of importation, exportation, and circulation during the late Republic and early Principate, processes that were facilitated by multidirectional networks that were fundamental to travel, trade, transport, and the administration and expansion of Roman *imperium*.

---

[16] As of September 2016, *L'Année Philologique* returns 234 results for a search of the term "Gallus (C. Cornelius)." Fewer than forty of the results are from prior to the papyrus' publication; ninety appeared in the decade after publication alone.

[17] E.g., Heyworth 1984: 64, Parsons 1980, Kennedy 1982. Cf. Anderson *et al.* 1979: 149. Van Sickle 1981: 122–3 reports expressions of disappointment at a panel on the papyrus at the Annual Meeting of the American Philological Association in December 1979.

[18] Van Sickle 1981.   [19] Somerville 2009. Cf. Hollis 2007: 251–2.

Importation and Circulation in Gallus Fr. 2

The Gallus papyrus was deposited at Qasr Ibrim in Lower Nubia at the southern edge of the Roman world. Yet the verses on this "exported" fragment of Latin literature describe processes of triumphal, literary, and human importations into Rome. Military triumph and the display of foreign spoils is the topic of the most well-preserved section of the fragment, verses 2–5. The quatrain addresses a Caesar and anticipates his triumph upon return from campaign:

> Fata mihi, Caesar, tum erunt mea dulcia, quom tu
>   maxima Romanae pars eri<s> historiae
> postque tuum reditum multorum templa deorum
>   fixa legam spolieis deivitiora tueis.

> My fate, Caesar, will be sweet to me at that time when you become the greatest part of Roman history, and when, after your return, I survey [or: "read about"] the temples of many gods, richer for being fixed with your spoils.

Whether Gallus addresses Julius Caesar or Octavian here is uncertain, as is the campaign to which he refers. Most scholars conclude that Gallus is writing about Julius Caesar and his planned offensive against the Parthians, the undertaking of which was prevented by his assassination.[20] Whichever campaign and Caesar is mentioned, the verses unmistakably evoke a triumphal context through the description of Roman temples hung with foreign *spolia*, an image that points to the importance of the importation to Rome of military booty won at the empire's periphery.[21]

Why does Gallus focus on *spolia*? A triumphal procession was an ephemeral event. Yet a major goal of a triumph was for the procession to be succeeded by enduring memorials to the victory and the victor.[22] Such triumphal memorials were an important way for Rome's elite to exhibit their political power and lay claim to its permanence.[23] This cultural context is perhaps reflected in the way that Gallus' verses in anticipation

---

[20] See Hollis 2007: 243, Gagliardi 2009.

[21] Anderson *et al.* 1979: 152 and Putnam 1980: 49 observe that the verses must refer to a foreign enemy for Gallus to speak with pride of *spolia* enriching temples. On triumphal spoils in temples: Aberson 1994, Orlin 2002: 135–9, Beard 2007: 21, Rutledge 2012: 132–6. Östenberg 2009: 19–127 and Rutledge 2012: 123–57 discuss spoils in a variety of contexts. Representations of triumph have a long tradition in Latin poetry, likely going back to Ennius; see Hardie 2007; cf. Hinds 1998: 52–63 on the association between Ennius' Muses in the *Annales* and Fulvius Nobilior's importing of Muse statues as spoils from Ambracia.

[22] Beard 2007: 18–31.   [23] Rutledge 2012: 124, Holliday 2002: xxiii.

of Caesar's victory emphasize not the campaign itself, nor even the triumphal procession, but the future memorialization of the triumph through the display of *spolia* in temples. Gallus' emphasis on foreign *spolia* as a triumphal memorial, moreover, stresses how, within the *urbs*, Roman glory and memorialization were dependent upon projecting military power at the empire's peripheries as well as upon the military and administrative networks that facilitated the transport of foreign objects to Rome. In addition, the verses' description of imported triumphal memorials may have come to have added resonance for a Roman reader once they were brought to Qasr Ibrim, as the text and the reader himself had circulated to the edge of empire via the same networks that Gallus' *spolia* evoke.[24]

Though the verses clearly employ triumphal imagery, the manner in which Gallus represents his poetic persona experiencing the triumphal memorial hinges on the interpretation of *legam* in the phrase *multorum templa deorum | fixa legam spolieis deivitiora tueis* (4–5). Some take this use of the verb as a rare sense of *legere*, meaning to "scan" or "survey" the temples and the *spolia*.[25] Others suggest that the phrase *templa legere* is a concentrated way of expressing "to read inscriptions" on temples or on the *spolia*.[26] A third possibility is to take *legere* in its most common sense, meaning "read of" or "read about." According to this interpretation, *legam* resonates with the potentially textual valence of *historia* in verse 3, setting up a reading theme in relation to the triumph.[27] Whereas in the *editio princeps* Parsons and Nisbet advocate for the meaning of *legam* as "I will read about," most scholars have subsequently adopted either the epigraphic or the "survey" interpretation.[28] Yet it is far from a settled matter; for example, in his discussion of the fragment, Hollis notes "without great confidence" that he follows the interpretation of *legam* as "scan" or "survey."[29]

One objection to the interpretation of *legam* as "I will read about" is: why would Gallus need to read about the temples when he could see them himself?[30] This objection only holds, however, if Gallus' poetic persona anticipates that he will be at Rome to see the temples. Yet, as discussed

---

[24] This speculation does not imply that Gallus' poetry was brought to Qasr Ibrim because of this quatrain, although the possibility that Gallus fr. 2 comes from the beginning or end of a book of poetry, as well as the frequent allusions to the verses by other poets (see earlier in the chapter), may suggest that they are programmatic.

[25] Putnam 1980: 51–2 is the first to advocate for this interpretation.

[26] Proposed first by Mazzarino 1980: 39 n. 61.

[27] *Historia*, however, has been interpreted as either a reference to historiographical texts or to historical events themselves; see Hollis 2007: 245. Capasso 2003: 55 and 58 offers an extensive catalogue of how various critics have interpreted *legam* and *historia*.

[28] Anderson *et al.* 1979: 142.   [29] Hollis 2007: 246.   [30] West 1983: 92.

earlier, the extraliterary Gallus spent time away from the city serving in various military and administrative capacities. If the Caesar in fr. 2 is Octavian, Gallus could represent his poetic persona as remaining abroad, either in Egypt or in one of the other roles in which Gallus presumably served during the 30s in order to earn the role of prefect.[31] If, as the majority of critics conclude, the Caesar in fr. 2 is Julius, with the poem dating to the mid-40s, Gallus may nonetheless represent his poetic persona as abroad. As noted earlier, *Ad Fam.* 10.32.5 may indicate that in 44 Gallus served under Pollio in Spain.

Eclogue 10 provides material for further speculation about the manner in which Gallus anticipates experiencing the *spolia* in fr. 2.2–5. In Vergil's poem Gallus is represented as away from Rome. In his absence he must learn from Apollo about events elsewhere in the empire, in this case Lycoris following another man on campaign (21–3). Moreover, in Gallus fr. 1 the description of the Hypanis river dividing Asia from Europe may also derive from an elegy describing Gallus' separation from Lycoris and absence from Rome, since Propertius (1.12.3–4) and Ovid (*Her.* 18.125–6 and 19.142) employ allusions to the verse when discussing the geographical separation of lovers.[32] If one imports the Gallus from *Eclogue* 10 and possibly from fr. 1 (i.e., the poet-lover-soldier who regrets leaving Rome and his *puella*) into the collection of elegies from which fr. 2 derives, the image of Gallus reading about events at Rome from some other location in the empire becomes a plausible interpretation of the verses. Moreover, the image of Gallus reading about the triumphal *spolia* juxtaposes Caesar's importation of foreign spoils into Rome with the exportation to the provinces of reports about his triumph. Admittedly, theories about the itineraries of the extraliterary Gallus or where Gallus' poetic persona in fr. 2 is located must remain speculative. If the fragments anticipate the traffic of information around the empire, however, this is yet another type of circulation reflected in the Gallus papyrus.

Whatever the valence of *legam,* the *spolia* of Caesar's triumph are not the only imports that Gallus fr. 2 evokes. The first line addresses Gallus' *puella*, Lycoris. As Alison Keith notes, Lycoris, as well as her putative inspiration Volumnia Cytheris – regardless of their actual relationship to one another – are representative of female imports from the Greek East, women brought

---

[31] Faoro 2007: 33. Anderson *et al.* 1979: 151–2 consider Octavian's Illyrian campaigns of 35–33 as well as the wars of 31–30 as the context for the fragments. Hutchinson 1981 advocates for the Illyrian campaigns or the invasion of Egypt. West 1983 favors Octavian's departure from Egypt.
[32] Barchiesi 1981: 164, Knox 1985, Cairns 2011.

to Rome through the conquest and domination of the Greek world.[33] Thus, Lycoris is an elegiac symbol of the human trafficking facilitated by imperial networks of travel and transport and representative of "the sexual spoils of military conquest."[34] The words *tristia* and *nequitia* in the first verse of the fragment (*tristia nequit[ia fact]a, Lycori, tua.*) suggest that, for Gallus, Lycoris is a more problematic import than Caesar's *spolia* that will enrich Roman temples. Indeed, *nequitia . . . tua* resonates with the use of *nequitia* to describe amatory disappointments in the poetry of Gallus' elegiac successors as well as with Vergil's depiction of the faithless Lycoris in *Eclogue* 10. The word *tristia*, whatever lost word it modifies (*Carmina? Tempora? Fata?*), together with *nequitia* indicates that Gallus' attempts at triumphs in the amatory realm do not compete with Caesar's in the military sphere. Yet along with that contrast, which Gallus highlights by juxtaposing *tristia* in verse 1 with *dulcia* in verse 2, Lycoris nonetheless evokes the imported human spoils of empire analogous to Caesar's military ones.[35]

At the same time as Lycoris is a symbol of Roman human trafficking, the Greek cultic and literary origins of her name recall the dynamics of cultural appropriation as well as the tradition of transferring Greek poetics into Roman contexts. The etymology of Lycoris may also point to her courtesan status through bilingual wordplay. Keith notes that the Greek *lyk*- root in the name evokes the Latin word *lupa*, slang for "prostitute."[36] Thus, the name Lycoris signals her Greek identity and her status as a sex worker. The appellation Lycoris also points to Apollo's cult name Λυκωρεύς as well as to the use of that title by Greek poets, perhaps especially Euphorion (fr. 80.3 Powell).[37] A reference to Euphorion in the name Lycoris is significant because the ancient Vergilian commentators, and perhaps Vergil as well (*Ecl.* 10.50–1), indicate that Gallus translated and transferred Euphorion's poetry into his own.[38] Gallus' role in the translation and transference of Greek literature is also reflected in Parthenius'

---

[33] Keith 2011.   [34] Keith 2011: 25–6.

[35] Keith 2011: 35–8. I am grateful to the editors for pointing out that the contrast that Gallus fr. 2 creates between Caesar and Gallus' poetic persona parallels the contrast between Octavian and Vergil in the *sphragis* of the *Georgics*.

[36] Keith 2011: 29. Cf. Fabre-Serris 2008: 68.   [37] Hollis 2007: 243.

[38] Serv. on *Ecl.* 6.72, on *Ecl.* 10.1, and on *Ecl.* 10.50, Probus on *Ecl.* 10.50; cf. Diom. *G. L.* 1.484.22. Quintilian (10.1.56) already interprets *Ecl.* 10.50–1 (*Chalcidico . . . versu*) as a reference to Euphorion via his hometown, Chalcis. Cicero may include Gallus among the *cantores Euphorionis* he refers to at *Tusc. Disp.* 3.45. On Gallus and Euphorion, see Keefe 1982, Lightfoot 1999: 57–64, Hollis 2007: 230–4. Some scholars, however, troubled by the fact that Euphorion apparently wrote primarily in hexameters rather than elegiacs, question Gallus' links to Euphorion; see esp. Courtney 1990: 105–9.

dedication of the *Erotika Pathemata*, which Parthenius presents as a catalogue of Greek literary material for Gallus to appropriate for his own Roman poetic production. As it happens, like the female imports that Lycoris evokes, Parthenius himself was also a spoil of war, brought to Rome as a prisoner during the Third Mithridatic War, likely by Gallus' poet-imperial agent predecessor, Helvius Cinna.[39]

The themes of importation, appropriation, and display in Gallus fr. 2.1–5 continue in the third quatrain. In addition, whether *legam* in verse 5 describes "reading about the triumph," "reading inscriptions," or "surveying the temples," the presence of the verb *legere* sets up a reading theme that carries over to verses 6–9:

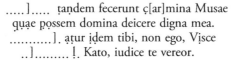

    .....]..... tandem fecerunt ç[ar]mina Musae
quae possem domina deicere digna mea.
    ....]. atur idem tibi, non ego, Visce
    ..].........[. Kato, iudice te vereor.

... Finally the Muses have made <? these> poems <? for me> that I could call worthy of my mistress ... the same to you, I do not, Viscus ... I do not, Cato fear ... with you as judge.

Although the interpretation of these fragmentary verses is uncertain, Gallus may again signal his debt to Greek poetics with the phrase *fecerunt ç[ar]mina Musae*.[40] Parsons and Nisbet note that *fecerunt* "is unconventional in such a context, and to a Roman reader would inevitably suggest ποιητής."[41] Moreover, it appears that in these verses Gallus, after proclaiming that the Muses have fashioned poems worthy of his mistress, addresses a Viscus and a Cato. The former is linked to the Visci who appear in Horace as literary critics.[42] The latter is perhaps the scholar and poet P. Valerius Cato.[43] The two are presented as judges and, by implication, readers of Gallus' poetry. When this quatrain is taken together with the previous one, multiple readers and exhibiters of different varieties of Roman appropriation emerge: Gallus as the reader of Caesar's imported

[39] *Suda* s.v. Parthenius; Hollis 2007: 19. Cinna's epigram (fr. 11 Courtney) on transporting a copy of Aratus from Bithynia points to the poet's participation in literary importation as well: Hinds 2001: 224–36. See Richlin's discussion of the Roman trafficking of comic actors in this volume (p. 171) and Yarrow 2006a: 37–44 on the enslavement and importation of Greek intellectuals.
[40] See Capasso 2003: 59–74, Hollis 2007: 246–50.
[41] Anderson *et al.* 1979: 144. Keefe 1982: 237–8 sees an allusion to Euphorion fr. 118 Powell in the phrase.
[42] *Sat.* 1.10.83, 1.9.22, 2.8.20. See Verducci 1984: 127 n. 16.
[43] See Hollis 2007: 429. Capasso 2003: 65–70, following Hutchinson 1981, argues for reading *plakato* instead of the personal name *Kato*; cf. Hollis 2007: 249–50.

triumphal spoils; Viscus and Cato as the readers of Gallus' elegies, with its imported Greek poetics and *puella*.

Export and Circulation

The elegiac verses in Gallus fr. 2 evoke Roman processes of importing foreign military spoils as well as women and literary culture from the Greek world. Yet the papyrus bearing these verses was found at Qasr Ibrim in the southern frontier zone of Roman Egypt. This section of the chapter argues that, although the precise circumstances surrounding its deposit at Qasr Ibrim are unknown, the papyrus is nonetheless indicative of how Roman literary culture was exported and circulated along with Roman military power. The first part reviews the archaeological and historical evidence for Roman-period Qasr Ibrim in order to explore the conditions in which the papyrus circulated to a periphery of the empire. The second part contextualizes the papyrus in relation to the other papyri, inscriptions, and non-textual finds from Qasr Ibrim. The third part zooms out even further, comparing the Roman textual practices at Qasr Ibrim to examples of the composition and circulation of literature around the empire, especially in military contexts. Through these comparisons I demonstrate how a papyrus that happened to survive at Qasr Ibrim, and which bears verses describing military, human, and literary importations, is also symptomatic of the multidirectional networks of exportation and circulation that were fundamental to Roman society and its empire.

Qasr Ibrim: Archaeological and Historical Contexts for the Gallus Papyrus

The find site for the papyrus, Qasr Ibrim (ancient Primis or Premnis), was a fortified settlement set on a hilltop above the Nile 235 km south of Aswan (Figure 12.1).[44] The Egypt Exploration Society conducted excavations at the site from 1961 to 2006. The site shows evidence of near continuous occupation from at least the late second millennium BCE until the nineteenth century CE. It was an important military, religious, and administrative center in the region between the first and second cataracts of the Nile, i.e., the frontier zone between Egypt and Nubia that in the Ptolemaic and Roman contexts was called the Triacontaschoinos and now

---

[44] Primis: Plin. *HN* 6.180 and Ptol. *Geog.* 6.35. Premnis: Strabo 17.1.54. For the identification of Qasr Ibrim with ancient Primis/Premnis: Capasso 2003: 8 n. 18.

is referred to as Lower Nubia.[45] The dry desert climate facilitated the preservation of a wide variety of organic and inorganic materials. In addition to the Roman-period documents in Greek and Latin discussed later, texts written in languages and scripts ranging from Egyptian (hieroglyphic, demotic, Coptic) to Meroitic (hieroglyphic and cursive) to Arabic and Turkish have been discovered.[46] Publication of the results of the excavations is ongoing.

Gallus, while serving as the first equestrian prefect of Roman Egypt, brought Rome into its initial political contact with the Triacontaschoinos in 29 BCE when he marched an army at least as far as the Nile island of Philae at the northern end of the region. As the inscriptions on the stele Gallus erected at Philae assert (*CIL* 3.14147[5]), his activities in the region included meeting with ambassadors from the Meroitic empire to the south (referred to as Aethiopians in the inscriptions) and establishing a local governor for the Triacontaschoinos.[47] Gallus' arrangement was short-lived. According to an account by Strabo, parts of which are corroborated in the *Res Gestae,* Pliny, and Cassius Dio, in 25 BCE the Meroites invaded the first cataract region while Roman military power in Egypt was diminished due to Aelius Gallus' expedition into Arabia Felix.[48] C. Petronius, the prefect of Egypt in 25, drove the Meroites back, storming Qasr Ibrim as he advanced. The ancient sources assert that Petronius went as far as Napata, 800 km south of the first cataract, although whether he would have had time to march that distance in a campaign lasting seven months at the longest is debated.[49] Strabo reports that on Petronius' return journey to Egypt in 25 or 24 BCE, he improved the defensive fortifications at Qasr Ibrim and installed a garrison of 400 men with supplies for two years. The Meroites launched a second attack in c. 22 BCE, advancing against Qasr Ibrim. Petronius returned once again in advance of the Meroitic incursion and fortified the citadel with military armaments. When the Meroitic army arrived at Qasr Ibrim, Petronius resolved this second conflict by convincing the Meroites to send envoys to negotiate directly with Augustus. The envoys met the *princeps* at Samos in 21/20 BCE, with Augustus acceding to

---

[45] Rose 2011, Adams 2013b: 45. For these toponyms: Adams 1983: 93. On the Triacontaschoinos, see also Török 1997: 420, 432–48, Locher 1999: 252–6. On Lower Nubia as a frontier zone: Adams 1977, 2013a, Török 2009, van der Vliet 2013.

[46] Anderson *et al.* 1979: 125, Rose 2011.　　[47] See Hoffmann *et al.* 2009: 154–60.

[48] Strabo 17.1.54, *RG* 26.5, Plin. *HN* 6.35, Dio Cass. 54.5.4–6. Strabo indicates that taxation was the major source of the Meroitic uprising. Török 1997: 452–4 reasonably conjectures that the taxation issue is related to the *tyrannus* of the Triacontaschoinos whom Gallus appointed. For the chronology of these events see Jameson 1968, Burstein 1979, Stickler 2002: 88–92.

[49] See Eide *et al.* 1996: 166 with further references.

all their requests, according to Strabo. Although the sources are not definitive, at this point the Romans appear to have withdrawn from Qasr Ibrim. Hiera Sycaminos at the southern frontier of the Dodecaschoinos became the furthest Roman outpost in Nubia.[50]

The archaeological evidence for the Roman occupation of Qasr Ibrim appears generally in accord with the literary sources, which imply that Romans occupied the site during the second half of the 20s BCE.[51] Excavations confirm that the Romans added to the site's fortifications, as Strabo mentions.[52] Excavations of rubbish deposits immediately within the citadel's girdle wall between the Northwest Bastion and South Rampart Street during the biennial field seasons from 1974 to 1982 yielded large quantities of Roman material, such as pottery, textiles, footwear, belts, satchels, lamps, coins, ballista balls, other projectiles, and papyri, including the Gallus papyrus.[53]

The papyrus bearing Gallus' poetry was found in level 3 of the deposit on South Rampart Street.[54] Although the deposit was not properly stratified, material found in close association with the Gallus papyrus supports the hypothesis that it was deposited in the first century BCE. In the *editio princeps* Anderson notes a coin from level 3 struck by Cleopatra VII that he concludes would not have remained in circulation longer than the reign of Augustus. In addition, in the same level of the deposit there were three lamps of a style that dates to the first century BCE through early first century CE. There were also other Latin and Greek documents found in levels 3 through 8 (these two levels were separated by approximately one meter). Anderson assigns the Greek documents on paleographic grounds to the first century BCE or early first century CE. In addition, there were three Greek letters from levels 7 and 8 bearing dates of 22 and 21 BCE.[55] Moreover, material from the top of level 3 has a carbon-14 date of 45 BCE–25 CE (67.5% probability) and 100 BCE–70 CE (95.4% probability).[56] Anderson judges that the most likely period for the Gallus papyrus' deposit

---

[50] See Eide *et al.* 1998: 188. Adams 1983 and 1985, Alexander 1988: 78, however, argue that the Roman occupation of Qasr Ibrim lasted longer, perhaps until c. 100 CE, based on the extensive Roman era fortifications and the large amounts of Roman material. Burstein 2004 reassesses the evidence for relations between Rome and Meroe after the meeting at Samos.

[51] Rose 2011: 5–6. N.B. the previous note, however.

[52] Adams 1983 and 1985. The Roman-period walls may have enclosed the entire hilltop: Wilkins *et al.* 2006 (with site plan at 66 pl. 3).

[53] Frend 1976, Weinstein & Turner 1976, Anderson & Adams 1979, Anderson *et al.* 1979: 125–7, Adams *et al.* 1983, Adams 1983 and 1985.

[54] Anderson *et al.* 1979: 125–6. For further analysis and diagrams of the deposit see Anderson & Adams 1979: 33–5, Adams 1983: 95–8 and 1985, Rose 1998: 61–4, Wilkins *et al.* 2006: 68–9.

[55] Anderson *et al.* 1979: 126–7, Derda & Lajtar 2012 and 2013a.   [56] Wilkins *et al.* 2006: 68.

is between 25 and 20 BCE, which corresponds with the brief Roman military occupation of the area described in the ancient sources.[57] In his section of the *editio princeps* Parsons reaches a similar conclusion. He considers the possibility that the papyrus could have been deposited as late as c. 25 CE, yet he prefers a *terminus ante quem* of c. 20 BCE, stating that he assumes, "that the Gallus-papyrus ... arrived at Ibrim in the baggage of a Roman officer."[58]

As noted at the opening of this chapter, Nisbet, who reaches the same conclusion as his coauthors about the date of deposit, remarks on the coincidence between the papyrus likely finding its way along with a Roman officer to Qasr Ibrim and Gallus' activities in Egypt.[59] Similarly, Santo Mazzarino observes, when considering the geographical coincidence of Gallus' poetry having been discovered in the Triacontaschoinos, the same region over which Gallus claimed to have established a local governor in the inscriptions at Philae: "*Politica culturale e politica estera vanno insieme.*"[60] I concur that it appears significant that Gallus' poetry found its way to Qasr Ibrim – that is, into the Egyptian frontier zone that Gallus himself, as the first prefect, helped define – even if the circumstances surrounding the deposit of the papyrus cannot be known with certainty. Regardless of the disgrace that Gallus had fallen into earlier in the 20s BCE, perhaps for at least one Roman at Qasr Ibrim, Gallus' poetry was especially suitable reading to accompany him as he traveled through Egypt and into Lower Nubia, just as Gallus had a few years earlier. Perhaps his poetry also seemed appropriate to read while stationed at a frontier outpost in "Aethiopia," which Gallus had brought into political contact with the Roman Empire for the first time. The fact that the fragments of Gallus' poetry that survive on the papyrus also happen to evoke many aspects of circulation toward Rome makes them all the more interesting as a case study for the phenomenon of the circulation of texts and writing practices along with Roman military power. I will now consider this broader phenomenon, looking first at other texts and writing at Qasr Ibrim, then at examples of the circulation of literature in military contexts across the empire.

Texts and Writing at Roman-Period Qasr Ibrim

The Gallus papyrus is only one example of the exportation of texts and writing practices from the Roman world to Qasr Ibrim concomitant with

---

[57] Anderson *et al.* 1979: 126–7.   [58] Anderson *et al.* 1979: 127–8.   [59] Anderson *et al.* 1979: 155.
[60] Mazzarino 1982: 321.

the expansion of Roman *imperium* into Lower Nubia. The excavators found hundreds of fragments of textual material in the refuse deposits within the girdle wall. The majority are administrative documents and letters written in Greek, but dozens are in Latin; there were also documents in demotic script and a handful in Meroitic.[61] Only a fraction of the papyri have been published. Tomasz Derda and Adam Lajtar are currently undertaking the publication of the remaining Roman-period material.[62]

A refuse deposit south of the Northwest Bastion excavated in the 1974 season yielded Greek and Latin papyri, including fragments of *Iliad* Book 8 and *Odyssey* Books 2 and 5, as well as additional scraps that may be literary, based on the hand.[63] The Homeric fragments appear to come from a bookroll, suggesting the reading of Greek poetry for recreation at Ibrim.[64] Another papyrus may be evidence that a member of the garrison reflected upon Roman martial activities at Ibrim by writing out a verse from the *Iliad*; P.QasrIbrim inv. 80/11, found in 1980 in a dump outside the Northwest Bastion, bears fragments identified as a Homeric verse describing Ares as "man-destroying, bloodstained, wall-smiting (Ἄρες Ἄρες βροτολοιγὲ μιαιφόνε τειχεσιβλῆτα)." The verse, which appears at *Iliad* 5.31 and 5.455, is repeated six times on the papyrus fragment in an elegant book hand similar to the hand from the *Odyssey* 5 fragments. Despite the repetition of the verse, Derda and Lajtar conclude that this papyrus is not a typical school exercise fragment, since it is written in a specialized hand, and it is unlikely that individuals were learning Greek at Qasr Ibrim. Rather, they speculate that the writer may have used the bookroll from which the *Odyssey* 5 fragments come as a model for writing Homeric verse. They also note that the reference to Ares is appropriate for the military context of Qasr Ibrim, an idea that finds a parallel in the fragments on *P.Masada* 721 of *Aeneid* 4.9, in which Dido tells Anna of her terrifying dreams. The editors of that papyrus also speculate that it is not a simple school exercise, but that it may reflect the writer's feeling of horror at the violence that he had witnessed at Masada.[65]

---

[61] Adams *et al.* 1983: 58, Adams 1985: 15 fig. 3. For Demotic and Meroitic texts from Qasr Ibrim, see Ray 2005, Hallof 2011, 2014.

[62] Derda & Lajtar 2012: 184. In addition to Gallus fr. 2, Weinstein & Turner 1976 published forty papyri, Parsons 1983 published a Latin letter (P.Rain.Cent 164 = P.QasrIbrim inv. 78–3–21/24), and Derda & Lajtar have published a Greek letter without an inventory number (2013a) and a Homeric fragment (P.QasrIbrim inv. 80/11) (2013b). They also discuss the contents of several other unpublished papyri (2012).

[63] Weinstein & Turner 1976: no. 1–3 and 23–9.   [64] Derda & Lajtar 2013b: 78.

[65] Derda & Lajtar 2013b. See also Cotton & Geiger 1989: 34.

As mentioned previously, the Greek papyri found at Ibrim include several letters with dates ranging from June 22 to March 21 BCE, dates that fit within the period of occupation described in the historical sources.[66] There are also military provision lists (Weinstein & Turner 1976: no. 4 and P.QasrIbrim reg. 80.2.5.7), a scrap that refers to a *beneficiarius* (Weinstein & Turner 1976: no. 12), and lists of names, presumably soldiers (e.g., P.QasrIbrim reg. 80.2.6/51). The Greek documentary papyri repeatedly indicate a Roman military context through their subject matter and through the use of Latin loan words and Roman numerals. Latin documentary fragments include a possible military roster (Weinstein & Turner 1976: no. 34) and a letter that refers to a century and that may be addressed to its commander (P.QasrIbrim inv. 78–3–21/24).[67]

Papyri are only one medium in which the textual practices of the Roman world present themselves at Ibrim. L. P. Mahaffy reported that he observed a Roman mile marker inscribed on the south cliffs of Ibrim.[68] In addition, several hundred ballista balls were found at the site, especially along the West Rampart. Their relatively good condition suggests that they were never used but rather discarded when the Romans withdrew. Many of the balls are inscribed or painted with their century and their weight in Roman *librae*, the latter written both in Greek and Latin. Ballista ball 4F also bears a fragmentary inscription that the editors reconstruct as "Just right for you, Kandaxe! (ΚΑΝΔΑΞΗ ΊΚΑΝΟΝ)." "Kandaxe" is a variation on Kandake, which Strabo (17.1.54) asserts is the personal name of the queen of the Meroites, although it in fact derives from the Meroitic title for royal wives, *kdke*.[69] The editors compare the inscription to Allied airmen during WWII writing, "Here's one for you, Adolf!" on bombs.[70] We may also compare the ball with other inscribed projectiles from Roman contexts, such as the sling bullets from the siege of Perusia in 41/40 BCE bearing inscriptions addressing Octavian, L. Antonius, and Fulvia.[71] Thus, ballista ball 4F is a vivid example of the convergence of writing culture and Roman military power at the southernmost frontier of Roman *imperium*.

The non-textual finds from the excavations at Qasr Ibrim show that the exportation of texts and writing practices from the Roman world was just one facet of how Roman occupation linked the site to networks that

---

[66] See Derda & Lajtar 2012 and 2013a.   [67] See Parsons 1983.
[68] *CIL* 3.13585[4]. See, however, the discussion of foot outlines and graffiti in Rose 1996: 102–17.
[69] Török 1997: 455–6.
[70] Wilkins *et al.* 2006: 67–74. I am aware of no other inscription that can be dated with certainty to Roman-period Qasr Ibrim.
[71] See Hallett 1977.

stretched across the Mediterranean basin. In particular, in the Roman levels of the site excavators found a considerable number of potsherds and textiles imported from outside of Egypt, including at least one amphora from Cos, polished black ware of possible northern European origin, and woolen fragments from northern Roman provinces, possibly Gaul.[72] Taken as a whole, the Roman-period material from Qasr Ibrim demonstrates that the papyrus bearing Gallus' poetry is not just an extraordinary find, but also indicative of the ways in which Roman objects and textual practices were exported and circulated along with the expansion of Roman military power, even at a site as far-flung and apparently as briefly occupied as this one.

Writing and Imperium *across the Roman World*

The presence of Roman texts and writing practices at Qasr Ibrim is by no means unique. Evidence from other sites and sources demonstrates that the Gallus papyrus and the other Roman-period writing at Qasr Ibrim are examples of a broader phenomenon: across the Roman world, writing practices, texts, and even the papyrus paper essential for the production of texts circulated concomitantly with imperial power.[73] Although a complete catalogue is beyond the scope of the present chapter, several examples will prove illustrative and offer further context for the Gallus papyrus.

The circulation of papyri, in military contexts and otherwise, is fundamentally linked to Egypt, since throughout antiquity Egypt held a monopoly on the production of paper derived from the papyrus plant.[74] Thus, texts written on papyrus that circulated through the Roman world were the product of the networks that linked Egypt's papyrus plantations and manufacturing sites to the Mediterranean basin.[75] Although evidence suggests that papyrus cultivation and production became more privatized under Roman rule than it had been under the Ptolemies,[76] Octavian-Augustus' special relationship to Roman Egypt meant that the dependence

---

[72] Anderson & Adams 1979: 39–40, Adams 1983: 96–7 and 1985: 13–15, Adams *et al.* 1983: 57, Adams 2013: 65. See also the suggestion of Török 1997: 452–3 n. 246 that the bronze head of Augustus found buried in the threshold of a chapel in Meroe City (British Museum inv. 1911.9.1.1) may have come from Qasr Ibrim.

[73] On the circulation of literature in the Roman world, see esp. Starr 1987, Fantham 1996: 10, Parker 2009: 214 and 217. Lucian's description of a stele on a distant island bearing the inscription "Heracles and Dionysus reached this point" (*Ver. hist.* 1.7) also reflects the link between writing and geographic margins, a tradition that stretches back to the *Odyssey*: Romm 1992: 211–14.

[74] Lewis 1974: 3–4. I am grateful to an anonymous referee for the following point.

[75] Lewis 1974: 89–90, 103–34.   [76] Lewis 1974: 121–2.

upon that region for papyrus was another way that textual practices were connected to imperial power during the early Principate, when the Gallus papyrus was likely deposited. In addition, Isidorus (*Etym.* 6.10.5) attributes the development of a certain grade of paper called *Corneliana* to Gallus, which may indicate that Gallus was himself involved not only in producing literature, but also in the papyrus trade upon which the production of texts depended.[77]

Vegetius attests to another aspect of the link between empire and writing in his discussion of the Roman military's widespread predilection for bureaucratic record keeping (*Mil.* 2.19). Moreover, papyri from Roman military sites where environmental factors permit preservation are well known, e.g., in Egypt, Dura-Europos, and elsewhere in Lower Nubia.[78] As noted at the opening of the chapter, the writing tablets from Vindolanda (late first and early second century CE) offer a particularly suitable parallel to the textual finds from Qasr Ibrim, as they come from a military outpost in Rome's British frontier zone and include not only documentary texts, but also tablets bearing verses of Vergil's *Aeneid* and *Georgics,* and possibly Catullus.[79] Although these fragments appear to be writing exercises, they nonetheless reflect the diffusion of elite literary culture via the Roman military. Moreover, A. K. Bowman speculates that Tablet 2.118 (= *A.* 9.473) may indicate that a text of Vergil was present at Vindolanda, since the verse derives from the more rarely quoted second half of the *Aeneid.*[80] Tablets like 2.118 are one example of how Vergil, of all the Latin poets, realized most fully the ambition expressed by Ovid to be read wherever Rome's empire extended (*Met.* 15.877–8).[81] The editors of Tablet 2.118 note in particular quotations and references to Vergil from other military contexts in Egypt and the Levant.[82] In addition, Nicholas Horsfall discusses papyrological and epigraphic examples of Vergil's poetry

---

[77] Cf. Lewis 1974: 42–4 on the possibility that the Isidorus' sources for the names of grades of papyrus were corrupted, however.

[78] See Fink 1971, Adams 2003: 527–641 on Egypt, Millar 1993: 467–71 on Dura-Europos, Speidel 1988 and Welsby 1998 on Lower Nubia. See also Adams 1999 on two verse inscriptions from a military context at Bu Njem.

[79] Tablet 2.118 = *A.* 9.473, Tablet 3.452 = *A.* 1.1, Tablet 4.854 = *G.* 1.125, Tablet 2.119 = Catull. 86.1 (?). Birley 2009 and Scappaticcio 2009 suggest that Tablets 855–6 may also be attempts at Vergilian lines; cf. *Tab. Vindol. IV.*

[80] Bowman 1994: 91–2. The reference to *libros* in Tablet 2.333 may also reflect literary culture at Vindolanda. See also *Tab. Vindol.* II 65–8 and 315 *Tab. Vindol.* III 160, *Tab. Vindol. IV* 191–2, Parker 2009: 214 n. 120.

[81] Cf. *Am.* 1.15.29–30, quoted earlier, where Ovid predicts worldwide poetic fame for Gallus. See also Nisbet & Hubbard 1978: 344–5.

[82] *Tab. Vindol.* II 66 and http://vindolanda.csad.ox.ac.uk/TVII-118.

from the Italian peninsula to the Iberian one, from the Danube frontier to Dura-Europos.[83] Vergil is thus the prime example of the extent to which elite literature circulated through networks like the ones that may have resulted in the exportation of Gallus' verses to Qasr Ibrim.

In the *editio princeps* Nisbet compares the transport of Gallus' poetry to Ibrim with other references to members of the Roman military bringing literature on campaign, including, as mentioned previously, Plutarch's report that a Roman officer had Aristides' Milesian tales in his possession at Carrhae (*Crass.* 32.3).[84] For my discussion this comparison is all the more apt because it is also linked to a frontier zone, in this case the Parthian one, just as the Gallus papyrus is from the frontier zone of Lower Nubia. In a similar vein, Pliny notes that Metilius Nepos brought Pliny's own writings in his baggage while governor of a province (*Ep.* 4.26).[85] Meanwhile, Martial, who describes *libelli* of his poetry being produced in travel editions (1.2), asserts that he has an avid reader who is a centurion on campaign in Moesia Superior (11.3). Martial also sends his poems to imperial administrators in Vindelicia (9.84) and Salona (10.78). Centuries later Sidonius Apollinaris sends copies of Varro and Eusebius to a naval officer stationed on the Atlantic coast (*Epist.* 8.6.18).[86] Nisbet also draws a comparison with the activities ascribed to the *comites* of Tiberius in Horace *Epistles* 1.3, a poem that describes not just literary consumption, but also composition.[87] 1.3 opens with Horace addressing Julius Florus while he is on campaign. Horace inquires about Tiberius' *studiosa cohors*, whom he expects may be composing in a variety of literary genres while in military service (6–21). Horace points to the *cohors'* role as military officers as well as *literati* with the phrase *quid studiosa cohors operum struit* (6), since *operum struit* evokes the terminology of military engineering of the sort that *praefecti fabrum* would engage in, as well as suggesting the composition of literature.[88]

Nor is Horace's linking of campaigns and literary composition unique. Exchanges between Cicero and his brother Quintus in 54 BCE, while the latter was with Julius Caesar in Gaul and Britain, also reveal the connections between military activity on the periphery and the composition and circulation of literature. Quintus writes four tragedies in sixteen days while with Caesar, as if conquering the tragic genre with Caesarian speed. Marcus asks Quintus to send his tragedies back to him at Rome (*ad Quint.* 3.5.7).

---

[83] Horsfall 1984: 49–51. See also Hoogma 1959, Scappaticcio 2010.   [84] Anderson *et al.* 1979: 155.
[85] See Starr 1987: 217, Sherwin-White 1985: 305–6.   [86] See Starr 1987: 217–18 and Adams 1999: 127.
[87] Anderson *et al.* 1979: 155, who also note that Catullus' depiction of Memmius' *comites* evokes literary interests in a military context.
[88] Hubbard 1995: 219–20.

In addition, both brothers write – or at least begin – poems on Caesar's
British campaign: Marcus from Rome, Quintus while on the campaign
(2.14.2, 2.15.4, 3.1.11).[89] Quintus also encourages Marcus to send poetry
abroad to him and Caesar (2.16.4, 3.5.3, 3.7.6). Although Marcus complains repeatedly that he lacks the leisure and inspiration to write (3.4.4,
3.5.4, 3.6.3), he eventually agrees to finish his poem about Caesar's campaign (3.7.6). He also inquires about Caesar's opinion on another of his
poems, *De Temporibus Suis*, which Caesar apparently had with him on
campaign (2.14.2, 2.16.5). The Cicero brothers, as well as the previous
examples, demonstrate the links between military campaigns, literary
consumption, and literary composition, while also attesting to texts similar
to the Gallus papyrus circulating between Rome and its military frontiers.

The epistolary exchanges between Cicero and his brother also point to
the connections between military activity and another facet of the circulation of literary texts: acquisition through purchase and appropriation.
Quintus writes to his brother asking for help in expanding his personal
collection of Greek and Latin texts at the very moment that he is with
Caesar expanding Roman *imperium* abroad (3.4.4, 3.5.6). Quintus' interest
in adding to his personal collection offers a modest parallel to the tradition
of Roman generals acquiring libraries as military plunder and transporting
the texts back toward Italy, a circulation that must have affected the
development of Roman literary and intellectual culture.[90] For the purposes
of this chapter, however, the most interesting instance of circulation which
Cicero's letters attest to occurs in an epistle mentioned earlier, *ad Famil-
iares* 10.32. This letter, written at Cordoba by Asinius Pollio to Cicero
while the former was governor of Spain reveals Gallus' own participation
in the circulation of texts between the imperial periphery and its center;
Pollio concludes his letter by telling Cicero to ask Gallus for a *praetexta*
that Gallus has apparently brought with him back from Spain.

Just as Q. Cicero wrote prolifically while on campaign in the service of
Julius Caesar, Caesar's own writing is closely linked with his military

---

[89] See Allen 1955, Shackleton Bailey 1980 *ad loc.*
[90] Plut. *Aem.* 28.6 reports that Perseus' royal library was the only booty from the Macedonian War
that Aemilius Paullus kept for his family's personal use. Sulla brought Apellicon's so-called library of
Aristotle to Rome after he conquered Athens (Plut. *Sul.* 26, Strabo 13.1.54. Strabo also describes the
earlier circulation of the library of Aristotle from Athens to the Troad and back after the death of
Theophrastus, as well as an incident where the scrolls were hidden to protect them from agents of
the Attalids who were looking for texts for the library that they were establishing at Pergamum).
Pompeius Strabo looted texts from Asculum (Plut. *Pomp.* 4.1). Lucullus expropriated the library of
Mithridates (Isid. *Etym.* 6.5.1). Antony was accused of promising the libraries of Pergamum to
Cleopatra (Plut. *Ant.* 58.5). See Barnes 1997, Dix 2000, Yarrow 2006a: 38.

activities in the provincial peripheries. The texts he wrote in military contexts include his *commentarii* as well as *De Analogia*, which Suetonius reports was written while crossing the Alps to return to his army in Gaul, and a poem entitled *Iter*, written on a journey to Spain in 46 BCE (*Jul.* 56.5). In a letter to Marcus Aurelius, Fronto cites the example of Caesar composing *De Analogia* on campaign, depicting Caesar writing about declensions and aspirations as arrows fly and bugles sound, in order to encourage Marcus Aurelius to read while in the field (*Parth.* 9). We also hear of Caesar's opponents engaging in literary activities: Plutarch relates that while Brutus was on campaign with Pompey he spent his free time reading and writing, even working on an epitome of Polybius directly before Pharsalus (*Brut.* 4).

The sources also point to Octavian-Augustus' desire to read literature while on campaign. During the Cantabrian war, he wrote Vergil from Spain imploring him to send some verses of the unfinished *Aeneid* (Suet. *Vit. Verg.* 31). Similarly, on the *princeps'* victorious return journey from the East in August 29 BCE, Vergil recited the entire *Georgics* to Octavian at Atella, with Maecenas taking over when the poet's voice would give out (Suet. *Vit. Verg.* 27). This anecdote about Vergil's performance of the *Georgics* following Octavian's military victory over Antony and Cleopatra, as the *princeps* made his way back to Rome to celebrate a triple triumph, encapsulates the link between Roman imperial power and the composition and circulation of literature, even though in this instance it is Octavian, rather than the text of the *Georgics,* that had just circulated around the empire.[91] Moreover, Octavian was not traveling alone when he stopped at Atella. In addition to his army he must have been accompanied by the vast amounts of spoils, especially from Egypt, that he displayed in his triple triumph upon his return to Rome (Dio Cass. 51.21.7–8; cf. Vell. Pat. 2.89.1). Octavian and his triumphal spoils were traveling along networks which this chapter has argued that the Gallus papyrus evokes both as a text and as a material artifact: networks of trade and transport, of import and export, of literary circulation, and of imperial expansion and administration.

Conclusion

In discussing circulation in the Roman world, Nicholas Purcell draws on an understanding of the concept by three scholars of south Asian history:

---

[91] See again the *sphragis* of the *Georgics,* with its image of the *princeps* hurling lightning at the Euphrates, while Vergil writes poetry at Naples.

Circulation is different from simple mobility, inasmuch as it implies a double movement of going forth and coming back, which can be repeated indefinitely. In circulating, things, men, and notions often transform themselves. . . .The totality of circulations occurring in a given society and their outcomes could be viewed as defining a "circulatory regime" susceptible to change over time. The "circulatory regime" in turn tends to shape society, which can be seen as an ensemble of criss-crossing circulatory flows.[92]

This description presents circulation and "circulatory regimes" as powerful forces transforming and giving meaning to individuals, objects, ideas, and societies. The verses on the Gallus papyrus offer a case study for the importance to Roman society of the circulation toward the imperial center of military spoils, literature, Greek literary traditions and *literati*, as well as women like Lycoris/Volumnia Cytheris. In addition, the papyrus, as a material artifact, reflects how Roman networks of circulation exported texts to military frontiers, where, as in the case of Gallus fr. 2, literature might have gained new meanings for readers in peripheral contexts. Though Gallus' own activities in Roman Egypt's southern frontier zone make Gallus fr. 2 a spectacular example of poetry circulating along similar networks as the poet himself, the Gallus papyrus is also one instance of a much broader phenomenon: the circulation of texts and writing practices around the Mediterranean world together with Roman military power.

---

[92] Markovits *et al.* 2003: 2–3, quoted in Purcell 2012: 383–4.

CHAPTER 13

Annexing a Shared Past
Roman Appropriations of Hercules-Melqart in the Conquest of Hispania

Megan Daniels*

The materialization and dissemination of a political ideology by dominant elites as a means of asserting social power has long been recognized as a major component of the superstructure of ancient empires.[1] In the case of the Roman Empire, scholars have traced the circulation of an ideologically inflected symbolism that legitimized its leaders by tying the cultural productions of its far-flung subjects back to Rome and to the agencies of its ruling classes.[2] As Clifford Geertz observed, symbols of legitimate leadership "mark the center as the center and give what goes on there its aura of being not merely important but in some odd fashion connected with the way the world is built."[3] Yet such symbolism was not created solely in the center (i.e., Rome), nor solely under the Empire, but rather evolved in dialogue with long-standing "globalized" ideas concerning sovereignty and divinity that stretched back to the Iron Age. Symbols of legitimate leadership constituted a "long conversation," not only between Rome and the provinces, but also between a globalized past and an imperial present.[4] From the Iron Age onward, Romans appropriated symbols of legitimate leadership and divine sovereignty that had already been circulating among the diverse cultures of the Mediterranean and Near Eastern world; any attempt to analyze the symbolic strategies employed by Roman *imperium* must therefore engage with this *longue durée* of past appropriations. In appropriating this symbolic language, Roman imperial power thus

---

* The author would like to thank Alicia Jiménez and Carolina López-Ruiz for their helpful comments and inspiration on earlier drafts, as well as the anonymous reviewers and especially the volume editors for their tireless and patient work in editing. All mistakes in this chapter of course are mine alone.

[1] E.g., DeMarrais *et al.* 1996. See also Mann 1986: 22–4.   [2] E.g., Ando 2000.
[3] Geertz 1983: 124.
[4] To use Malinowski's term, elaborated by Maurice Bloch (1977): the "long conversation" denotes the continual interplay between the past and present within the human cultures that the anthropologist studies.

entered into a fluctuating conversation with Mediterranean cultural groups, such that chasing after a "pure" (Roman or other) cultural original is a quixotic endeavor. A much more fruitful avenue of investigation is to scrutinize how the shared symbolic discourse on social power so vital to imperial unity came to be produced and propagated.

The symbolic repertoire linked to the figure of Hercules – and the development of this repertoire over centuries of prior engagement by Mediterranean peoples – illuminates the operations of this shared discourse. This chapter focuses on the development of Hercules as a symbol of leadership, concentrating on southern Spain, a province populated prior to the Roman takeover by a host of indigenous groups and Greek and Phoenician settlers from the Levant and North Africa. In situating the rise of Hercules' worship in Spain against the long history of Mediterranean appropriations of this god as a symbol of leadership, I argue that the evolution of Herculean symbolism in this region was driven by the continuous interaction between the contingencies of the imperial present and the durability of a globalized past. With this framework in mind, we move beyond debates that argue for or against Rome's direct appropriation of the earlier Phoenician worship of Melqart in southern Spain, and instead see the interactions between different cultural groups in the wake of conquest as part of a much longer dialogue about power and legitimacy.

I first briefly outline what I mean by symbolic power. After this theoretical overview I then consider Hercules as a recurring symbol of leadership, highlighting both his global associations with leadership and world conquest across different cultural groups and his early appearance in the city of Rome. Next, I explore the cultural milieu of southern Spain from the third to first centuries BCE, focusing on the symbolism of Melqart/Hercules as it appears in the numismatic record and its appropriations and reappropriations in the period of Rome's conquest. Finally, I analyze the Roman employment of the Hercules motif in Spanish contexts from the first century BCE to the second century CE, focusing especially on numismatic and epigraphic sources from the Augustan and early Antonine periods. Here I contend that the usage of Hercules as a symbol of leadership in southern Spain interacted both with the previous presence of Melqart and the Romans' own conceptions of Hercules – and that both were based on centuries' worth of engagement with the god and his movements within the global Mediterranean system.

Symbolic Power, the *Longue Durée*, and Hercules

I begin with an explanation of what I mean by symbolic power, how it operates over the long-term, and what implications its operation holds for our analysis of Hercules in Hispania. Symbols are storehouses of meaningful information and social values.[5] Focusing on their connections to power, Pierre Bourdieu has defined symbols as "the instruments *par excellence* of 'social integration': as instruments of knowledge and communication . . . they make it possible for there to be a consensus on the meaning of the social world, a consensus which contributes fundamentally to the reproduction of the social order."[6] To Bourdieu, symbolic power pervades all dimensions of social life as an essential component of *habitus*: symbols are thus part of the tacit infrastructure operating over the long-term that aids in indoctrinating individuals to legitimate and sustain the social system. At the same time, symbolic power does not merely form an inert backdrop to human development; even though such power remains constrained by meanings and structures operating over the *longue durée*, it is brought into being by the ruling class through communicative efforts and contested by different social groups through a variety of means.

Symbolic power is thus entrenched within longstanding and widespread mental and spiritual frameworks – what Fernand Braudel characterized as *"prisons de longue durée."*[7] It is this very entrenchment within longstanding meanings, however, that lends uses of symbolic power their legitimacy in relation to particular events and ensures their future transmission. Situating the usage of Hercules as a symbol of political power under the Roman Empire against its long history of Roman – and wider Mediterranean – appropriations helps to clarify this god's appearance and function in provincial contexts: the association of emperors and local leaders with Hercules in Spain reflected the success of a long-enduring meme that had become intelligible to different cultural groups in the context of a globalized and globalizing Mediterranean.[8]

The abundance of material and literary representations of Hercules from all over the Mediterranean repeatedly disclose the extent to which elites striving to consolidate and legitimize their power had recourse to the god-hero. The symbolic language of Hercules as conqueror, king, and god

---

[5] Turner 1968: 2.   [6] Bourdieu 1991: 166.   [7] Braudel 1987 [1958]: 15.
[8] On globalization as applied to the Mediterranean world: Horden & Purcell 2000; Morris 2003; Broodbank 2013. See also Sommers 2014 for a *longue-durée* approach to globalization in the Mediterranean world with reference to the Roman Empire.

shares roots with the Iron Age worship of the Phoenician god Melqart, the royal city god of Tyre.[9] Along with his consort Astarte, he guaranteed the prosperity of the city as embodied in the figure of the king.[10] With the overseas movements of both Phoenicians and Greeks, Melqart came to be equated with the Greek Herakles, whom Greek colonists worshipped as *archegetes* of heroic and genealogical lines.[11] As such, Herakles often served as a focal point for dynastic legitimacy and irredentist contestation between Greeks and their neighbors during overseas expansions.[12]

Peoples of the Italian peninsula worshipped some form of the deity: the excavations around the church of Sant'Omobono in the Forum Boarium in the mid-twentieth century recovered a life-size terracotta statue dating to the sixth century BCE of a god in a lion skin with a female consort, identified by most scholars as Minerva/Athena.[13] Patricia Lulof has interpreted this Hercules and Minerva group within the broader contexts of elite political competition through ostentatious, propagandistic display and suggests that early Romans were engaging with this god in ways similar to their Greek and Phoenician neighbors.[14] The placement of the site of Sant'Omobono on the fordable part of the Tiber was conducive to interactions with a wider Mediterranean world – whether through stylistic and iconographic exchange (the Hercules/Minerva statue) or commerce (attested by the quantities of East Greek, Attic, Corinthian, and Laconian pottery uncovered in the area of the sanctuary).[15] Hercules enjoyed several

---

[9] Melqart appears to have no known antecedents in the second millennium BCE. He appears in the early first millennium BCE, possibly under Hiram I of Tyre (tenth century BCE) (Aubet 2001: 152). See also Bonnet 1988; Lipiński 1995: 226–43.

[10] The earliest secure iconographic evidence for Melqart (late ninth or early eighth century BCE), showing his ties to kingship, is a stele from Bureij in northern Syria with an image of Melqart and an inscription indicating that a king named Bir-Hadad had dedicated it to the god (Bonnet 2007; Pitard 1988; Nitschke 2013: 259–60). Josephus (*AJ* 8.5.3), quoting Menander, recounts how King Hiram I of Tyre built temples to Melqart ("Hercules") and Astarte.

[11] A bilingual inscription on a cippus from the second century BCE on the island of Malta makes this conflation clear (*KAI* 47; *AO* 4818; with Nitschke 2013: 258 n. 20; Bonnet 1988: 244–7). A series of bronze hatchet razors dating to the third century BCE from the cemetery of Sainte-Monique in Carthage fuse Hellenistic and Phoenician iconographies: Bonnet 1986: figs. 1 and 3–4; also Bonnet 1988: 399–415; Rawlings 2005: 159–60.

[12] Malkin 2005; 2011. See Herodotus 5.43 on Doreius in Sicily (Malkin 2011); cf. Isocrates (*Philip.* 76–7, 111–14), who, in his speech to Philip II, alluded to the Macedonian king's Heraklean ancestry and encouraged him to reconcile the Greek cities to conquer the Persian Empire through allusions to Herakles' unification of the Greeks and the conquest of Troy.

[13] Other suggestions include Venus and Fortuna Virilis: see Holloway 1994: 78.

[14] Lulof 2000. Augustan-era mytho-histories of Rome would link religious activity in the vicinity of Sant'Omobono to Rome's kings as well, particularly Servius Tullius (so, e.g., Ov. *Fast.* 6.479–80).

[15] Earlier scholars postulated that the Hercules of the Forum Boarium was originally introduced by the Phoenicians (e.g., Rebuffat 1966; Van Berchem 1967), but there is really no evidence for this: Holloway 1994: 167 and 196 n. 12.

other prominent cult places in the Forum Boarium, most notably the *Ara Maxima* and the temple to Hercules Victor *ad portam trigeminam*.[16] We find evidence of his worship throughout Latium, Campania, Etruria, Umbria, the Veneto territory, Abruzzi, Apulia, Lucania, and the Adriatic.[17]

Such associations, of course, only seemed to intensify into the Hellenistic period, under Alexander the Great and the Diadochoi, as well as the Carthaginian rulers in Sicily, North Africa, and Spain.[18] At Rome, the conception of Hercules as a victorious god connected to Rome's triumphant rulers is already evident from at least the late fourth century BCE.[19] Numerous generals dedicated to Hercules in gratitude for their victories, notably L. Mummius after his Achaean conquests, as well as Sulla, Pompey, and Julius Caesar.[20] An exhaustive exposition of the long history of Hercules and his relations to Herakles and Melqart is unnecessary given the already substantial number of comprehensive discussions on this topic; but we should keep in mind the god-hero's continuing associations with political and military power, specifically for Roman leaders who became increasingly adept at manipulating this globalized discourse in the period of the Republic's rise to Mediterranean hegemony. Bearing in mind Hercules' long history as a charged symbol of contested claims to power, we can now proceed to contextualize his appearance in Hispania before and after the Roman conquest.

---

[16] See *LTUR* III: 15–17. Mythical accounts claim that Hercules and Evander founded the *Ara Maxima*, after Hercules arrived at the site of the future Forum Boarium from Gades (Livy 1.7; Ovid, *Fast.* 1.554; Virgil, Aen. 8.184–279; Propertius 4.9; Dionysius of Halicarnassus, *Ant. Rom.* 1.39–44; Aurelius Victor, *De Orig. Gent. Rom.* 6). The temple of Hercules Victor, known from a dedication of the Mummius who conquered Corinth, was dedicated from Achaean war booty (*CIL* I².626 = *CIL* 6.331 = *ILLRP* 122). On the debates over the precise identification of this temple see now Loar 2017.

[17] In Etruria the name Hercle first appears on an Attic red-figured kylix from the early fifth century BCE at his sanctuary in Caere. Hercle, like Hercules, had important connections with transhumance, trade, water, initiation, and triumph; discussion and bibliography in Schwarz 2009.

[18] On Alexander the Great's association with Herakles see Weinstock 1957: 214–15. In Sicily, the Carthaginians minted coins around 300 BCE with the head of Melqart in his lion-skin, a clear allusion to the Alexander prototype; on these issues and the cultural contexts informing their production see Nitschke 2013, building on Jenkins 1978 and Prag 2011.

[19] See Livy 9.44.16 with Oakley 2005 *ad loc*. Rome claimed a "Herculean legacy" in part by minting a series of coins commemorating the Roman victory over Tarentum with Romulus and Remus suckling the she-wolf on the obverse and a Greek Hercules in lion skin on the reverse: Miles 2011: 268–9. For the *Heraklesschalen* ceramics see the exhibition catalogue *Roma medio repubblicana* (1977).

[20] On Sulla: Plut. *Sull.* 35. On Pompey: Appian *BC* 2.76; Plut. *Pomp.* 1.1. with Santangelo 2007: 228. On Caesar: Suet. *Iul.* 7 and Dio 37.52.2; cf. Plut. *Caes.* 11.5–6.

Numismatics and Symbolic Communication

Before moving on, however, it is worth considering the utility of the main source of evidence put to use in this chapter, namely numismatics, in gauging patterns of symbolic communication. There has been considerable debate over the power of coinage in forming (and informing) public opinion among Roman subjects.[21] A. H. M. Jones argued in 1956 that coin imagery did not lend itself to wide readership in the Roman world; M. H. Crawford, relying primarily on written sources, similarly expressed doubt that programmatic messages in imperial coinages ever had much impact on Roman viewers, reasoning that "the diversity, imaginativeness and often great beauty of Roman imperial coin types" resulted from a holdover of competitive Republican oligarchic sentiments coupled with an independent artistic tradition.[22] Yet how doubtful should we be of the communicative potential of numismatic symbolism? Christopher Ehrhardt has disputed the "excessive skepticism" of Crawford's claims, noting – among other trends – the multiplicity of types and messages that surfaced in coins whenever political upheaval took place. Ehrhardt ascribes far more communicative importance to Republican oligarchical and subsequent imperial use of a symbolic language that was encapsulated in numismatic imagery from the Late Republic until at least the Tetrarchy. Moreover, Ehrhardt cites the presence of enduring symbols on coins – some of whose encore appearances occurred many decades after their first documented usage – as proof that upper-class Romans not only read and understood the imagery on coins (both old and new) but assumed others could do so as well.[23]

Ehrhardt sought to prove the communicative power of coins largely through the timing and circumstances surrounding their issuance. Another method scholars have adopted is to examine the interaction of numismatic symbolism with other visual media, a trend spurred by the works of Tonio Hölscher and Paul Zanker. Barbara Levick – who originally argued that imperial coinage was struck with the primary intention of flattering the emperor – later conceded that "[i]n this shell world of texts and discourses, verbal and pictorial, in which buildings, death, even vestal virginity can be 'read,' the products of Roman imperial and civic mints also have to be found a place."[24] Recently, Carlos Noreña has emphasized the interchangeability of the messages on imperial coinage with other visual

---

[21] See Levick 1982 and 1999a for discussion and bibliography of twentieth-century literature.
[22] Crawford 1983: 59.   [23] Ehrhardt 1984: 52.
[24] Levick 1999a: 44. See Levick 1982 for the original article.

media – particularly inscriptions – in contexts of official communication. These symbolic messages, which evolved and matured during the Hellenistic period, saturated the public sphere with images and virtues associated with imperial rule. But "official" communication inevitably interfaced with a host of other agents, both official and unofficial, to create a dynamic "symbolic system": "And it is really this dynamism and fluidity of communications, focused on the Roman emperor, that constitutes the circulation of imperial ideals in its fullest sense."[25]

Building on Noreña, I suggest that (a) by following the manifestation and evolution of Roman numismatic images out of much deeper historical contexts and (b) by cross-referencing these symbols with messages gleaned from other contemporary media (literary sources and inscriptions), we can reanimate the imperial and aristocratic messages concerning power and legitimacy that the visual deployment of Hercules in Spain was meant to convey.

Coinage and Heterogeneous Traditions in Southern Spain, Third to First Centuries BCE

Our best evidence for conceptualizing the symbolic associations of Hercules, as well as Melqart, his earlier counterpart in Spain, is to be found in the numismatic record. Indeed, the heterogeneity in numismatic traditions in southern Spain before and after the Roman conquest has important implications for considering the evolution of Hercules' worship in an increasingly interconnected and culturally intermixed region (Figure 13.1). For about thirty years, in the late third century, the Barcids stimulated the circulation of money in southern Spain; the coinage minted went to support the Carthaginian military effort. Whereas Gades had started minting coins before the Second Punic War, other cities began during or after.[26] On the basis of metrologies, typologies, and inscriptions, Francisca Chaves has suggested that the coins of the third to first centuries BCE were minted by indigenous magistrates but often fell in line with Roman metrological standards

---

[25] Noreña 2011: 199–200.

[26] Chaves 1998: 165. On the dates of Iberian coin issues see Alfaro Asins 1997; López Castro 2007: 109; Ripollès 2007: 80. Malaca and Sexs may also have started at the end of the third century: Campo & Mora 1995; Jiménez 2014: 235. The *Corpus nummum Hispaniae ante Augusti aetatem* identifies around 160 cities in the Iberian peninsula as minting coins before the arrival of Augustus: Gozalbes 2012: 17. It is difficult to know to what extent the emergence of Spanish mints around the time of the Second Punic War resulted from the need to finance armies. Though Livy (28.34.11) vaguely refers to army payments during the Second Punic War in Spain, cultural factors may have played into the increase of minting as well. Cf. Burnett 1989.

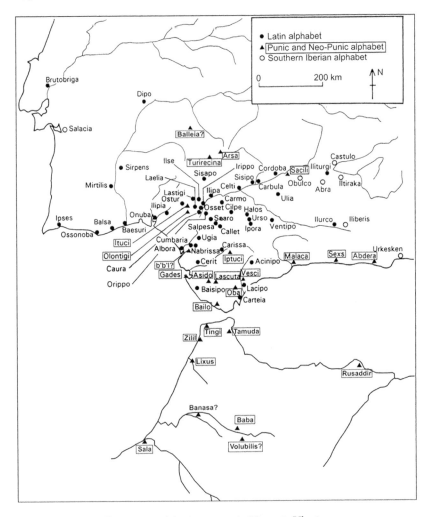

Figure 13.1.   Minting towns in Hispania Ulterior

and utilized symbols, deities, and control marks that were recognizable across cultural boundaries.[27] In the third and second centuries BCE

---

[27] Of the seventy known names on coins, most from Carteia, Obulco, and Castulo, around 30 percent are personal names of indigenous/Phoenician origin, while 70 percent are of Latin origin: Chaves 1998: 155. In most cases, the legends always name the city or ethnic group but sometimes also give personal names of the civic elite: Ripollès 2007: 82–3. The weight systems are also mixed: while most areas around Gades followed a Punic weight system, some mints, including Arsa, Lascuta, and Turirecina used Roman metrologies: Jiménez 2014: 226; see also Mora Serrano 2006 on the metrological systems employed by Spanish mints.

these mixed issues were largely due to Roman entrepreneurs and families penetrating the southern Peninsula rather than to the exercise of official Roman control over specific regions.[28] Coinage issues were generally sporadic and do not seem representative of any systematic demand for currency, however.

What is especially interesting about these coins is that they reflect not only Roman and indigenous iconographies but also traditional Levantine aniconism, with astral signs, animals, or vegetation symbolizing specific deities.[29] Included with these symbols were scripts in Punic and neo-Punic dialects, sometimes paired with Latin.[30] Overall, these issues were clearly intended for a heterogeneous society whose members came from Iberian, Italian, and North African backgrounds.[31] Of all cult figures on coins, Melqart was the most popular. He was especially attested on coins from Gades and the settlements in the Baetis Valley, including Carteia, Asido, Lascuta, Baelo, Carissa, Carmo, Caletus, Iptuci, and Detuma. In the oldest coin issues of the third century BCE he is represented in a Hellenizing manner, possibly resonating with the Barcids' mythologizing self-representation.[32] Alongside these Hellenizing traits, however, were Phoenician themes: the head of Eshmun, Tanit with wings, and Tanit as a warrior, as well as a palm tree and horse symbolizing Tanit.[33] Thus from at least the third century BCE we see a mixture of Hellenistic and Phoenician traits incorporated into the iconography of Melqart and Tanit in southern Spain. Following the collapse of the Barcids, Melqart continues to show up on coins in a number of locales and is most often depicted

---

[28] Chaves 1998: 169; 1999; Ripollès 2007: 81; Keay 1998: 65–7. These smaller-scale activities as drivers of cultural transformation: Chaves 1998: 166–7. The cultural impact of colonies such as Italica, established by Scipio after the Second Punic War: Chaves 1998: 166.

[29] García-Bellido 1990: 371–5.

[30] This phenomenon is attested especially on coins from the hinterland of Gades from the mid-second century to the mid-first century BCE, originally attributed by Zóbel de Zangróniz to an ethnic group he termed "Libyphoenicians." On coins associated with these so-called Libyphoenicians and the problems of labeling ethnic groups in Spain see Jiménez 2014: esp. 236–7. The growing use of the Latin language in Hispania in the late second and early first centuries BCE: Untermann 1995.

[31] On the cultural and economic relationships between southern Spain and Mauretania see Gozalbes Cravioto 1994; Callegarin 2008.

[32] Livy 21.21.9 specifies that Hannibal visited the sanctuary of Melqart in Gades before starting his march to Italy in order to consult the god's oracle and to obtain protection. Hannibal – or the Greek intellectuals who sympathized with his cause – may have modeled his journey over the Alps to Italy after Herakles' journey from Spain to Rome: Rawlings 2005; Miles 2010: 241–55. On Hannibal's use of propaganda, see Miles 2011.

[33] García-Bellido 1991: 42. The palm tree was a popular icon in Iron Age Syro-Palestine: for the palm tree in Phoenician coinage as a riff on the Greek *phoenix* and its expression of a type of pan-Phoenician, Mediterranean-wide identity see Frey-Kupper 2014: 103; López-Ruiz 2015.

with maritime fauna such as tuna and dolphins – allusions to some of the major industries of coastal southern Spain (Figure 13.2).[34]

It is of course impossible to pinpoint how or when this god is identified with or as Hercules on the coinage, or whether he was consistently conflated with Hercules.[35] The Roman exploitation of these associations of the iconographic and religious connections of these two gods, however, is most pronounced in Baetica, and in particular Gades, to which I turn next.

Rome Infiltrates Gades, Late Republic and Early Empire

The material traces of Roman – and Herculean – penetration into the cultures of Hispania picked up pace in the first century BCE with the foundations of *coloniae* and *municipia* under Pompey, Caesar, and Augustus: these developments enabled the native aristocracy to attain Roman citizenship, fostered the euergetism of Rome's ruling class, and altered the political geography of Spain.[36] In Hispania Ulterior, the increasing production of coinage from the mid-second century BCE onward and the intensifying exploitation of mines reflect the imposition of more systematic forms of taxation; beginning in the late second century, Baetican mints also furnish evidence of metrological accommodation to Roman standards.[37] But local mints remained in the hands of local magistrates up until Claudius' time, and as a result we cannot interpret the infiltration of Roman ideological power without reference to the symbolisms and identities these magistrates chose to express through numismatic

---

[34] García-Bellido 1991: 51. On the issues from Salacia in western Lusitania, Melqart is shown with the lion skin and with tuna or dolphins on the reverse: marine fauna evoked the rich fishing grounds of cities such as Gades, and possibly also Melqart's role in navigation and colonization: Marín Martínez 2011: 585–6; García-Bellido 1991: 51; Alfaro Asins 1988: 41; Aubet 2001: 278; Malkin 2005. The name "Salacia" may allude to the connection between salt production and fishing: cf. Purcell (1996: 192, citing Kolendo 1970) on how Romans made use of these lucrative industries, first exploited by the Phoenicians in Spain. On Melqart's connection to vegetation, note a sheaf of wheat next to Melqart's head in the *as* and semi-*as* issues of Baelo from the first century BCE: García-Bellido 1985–1986; 1990; 1991; Marín Martínez 2011: 589.

[35] The final coinage issues from Salacia seem to show Neptune on the obverse with tuna or dolphins on the reverse, whereas in previous phases the obverse held images of Melqart (see previous note): García-Bellido 1990: 378.

[36] Chaves 1999: 297–9; Ripollès 2007: 88. Despite this increasing political consolidation, there is evidence that enduring Phoenician cultural practices in Iberia persist despite these developments: some Baetican towns, for instance, continue using metrological systems similar to those of North Africa (Chaves 1998: 162; Chaves 1999: 299); on the presence of rock-cut tombs outside Gades in use until at least the first century CE see my following discussion.

[37] Keay 2001: 129; Richardson 1986: 122–3. Note the testimony of Strabo 3.2.10 on the revenue extracted through mining at New Carthage to pay tribute to Rome.

Figure 13.2. Coins from Gades featuring Hercules, first century BCE

iconographies. The use and modification of these iconographies entered into dialogue with preexisting, trans-Mediterranean traditions concerning Melqart and Hercules; the issues from Gades, the most powerful city in southern Spain and western North Africa by the time of the Second Punic War and home to a famous sanctuary to Melqart, offer the best evidence for this dialogue.[38]

To contextualize this evidence, it is necessary to sketch briefly what the Roman takeover of Gades and Melqart's sanctuary during the Second Punic War meant for Roman leaders, and how their subsequent exploitation of this god vis-à-vis their own worship of Hercules tapped into *longue durée* appropriations of his symbolic power. The agreement between Rome and Gades following Gades' surrender in 206 BCE had both political and sacred connotations. The stipulation of a *foedus* and the *deditio* of Gades were sacred acts: the surrendering community gave up their gods and cults but was allowed to receive them back as a sign of Rome's magnanimity.[39] Yet the religious fervor surrounding the cult of Melqart afforded the latter special status in the articulation and representation of Roman power. One significant consequence of this surrender was the merging of Carthaginian and Roman conceptualizations of imperialism against the backdrop of Hellenistic traditions embodied in Gades' sanctuary.[40] The pact between these powers enabled the Roman state to employ, through Gades and its patron god, models of political legitimacy recognized across ethnic and civic groups in Gades and the surrounding region.[41]

The symbolic "takeover" of Gades and Melqart would become especially pronounced under the rule of Augustus, when the persona of the emperor was explicitly tied to traditional Mediterranean myths involving Hercules.[42] Coins minted in Gades linked the victorious god to the

---

[38] This sanctuary, on the eastern end of a long narrow island adjacent to the mainland and just outside the Straits of Gibraltar, is known only through literary sources. Strabo's discussion in Book 3 of his *Geography* draws on Posidonius' ethnographic account; generally on the literary sources see García y Bellido 1963 and Mierse 2004. In 1984, dredging operations off the island discovered a votive deposit containing bronze figurines of a type of deity known as the "Smiting God," possibly associated with the warlike capacities of Melqart and his traditional Tyrian consort Astarte: Sánchez 2004: 37–8.

[39] See Cicero, *Balb.* 32–5, who suggests that this particular treaty was one that recognized the superiority of Rome over Gades. Broadly on *fides, foedus,* and *deditio* see Hölkeskamp 2000.

[40] López Castro 1995: 105; López Castro 1998.

[41] The distribution of Gaditan coins, metrologies, and coin imagery – particularly Melqart's imagery – in Baetica and Mauretania as markers of Gades' political and economic influence: Jiménez 2014: *passim.* Gaditan coins amount, in weight, to 80 percent of the total foreign coins found in Mauretania: Callegarin 2008: 302.

[42] Even if, as Weinstock 1957 notes, Augustus and other Julio-Claudian emperors resisted association with the epithets Victor and Invictus.

emperor by showing Augustus as DIVI F. on the obverse and what is likely Melqart's temple on the reverse framed by a laurel crown. Other issues displayed the words DIVI F. on the reverse but instead used the image of the head of Hercules with lion skin and club that had been popularized on pre-Augustan Gaditan coinages (whose reverses had formerly depicted dolphins or tunas) (Figure 13.3).[43] Other issues from Gades presented the laureate heads of Augustus, Agrippa, Tiberius, and Gaius and Lucius as emblematic of the Julio-Claudian dynasty.[44] The promotion of legitimate rule and dynastic stability was a major component of establishing *consensus* within the provinces, as Clifford Ando outlines in his 2000 monograph. Certainly, Gades was an appropriate showground, and Hercules was an appropriate medium, for the elucidation of this *consensus*. Writing in the early Principate, Strabo claims that the Phoenicians had settled Gades by divine omens, erecting the temple to Melqart before the colony was laid out; this mythical positioning of this city, civilized by its patron god at the ends of the *oikoumene*, would have been particularly resonant under a *princeps* who, in the prophetic words of Virgil's Jupiter, would "circumscribe empire with ocean," and who would be likened by Horace to Hercules upon his return from campaigning in Spain.[45]

Roman leaders and local oligarchs perpetuated these associations by appropriating for use on the obverse of their issues the same head of Hercules with lion skin and club that had appeared on pre-Augustan coins. Cornelius Balbus and Marcus Agrippa were named on several coin issues from Gades that featured this Herculean iconography. Marcus Agrippa is termed MVNICIPI PARENS and MVNICIPI PATRONUS PARENS on the reverse of these coins, while Cornelius Balbus' distinction of PONT(ifex) is accentuated through priestly symbols such as the axe and *simpulum*.[46] This Cornelius Balbus is likely the Younger, who was admitted to the pontifical college under Augustus and undertook numerous building projects in Gades, including the construction of a new harbor.[47] Several decades later, Nero's coins would feature the same head of

---

[43] See Vives y Escudero 1924–6: plates LXXVI.1–4 and LXXVII.4–5.

[44] Mierse 1993. See Vives y Escudero 1924–6: plates LXXVI–LXXVII.

[45] Strabo 3.5.5; Virgil *Aen.* 1.286–8; Horace *Odes* 3.14.1–4 (cf. *Odes* 3.3.9–36 and *Epistles* 2.1.1–17). See also Pompon. 3.46, on the Tyrian foundation of the temple of "Aegyptian Hercules" and the consecration of Hercules' bones at Gades.

[46] See Vives y Escudero 1924–6: plate LXXV for Cornelius Balbus and plate LXXVI.5–7 for Marcus Agrippa. In LXXVI.5, the legend clearly indicates Agrippa: M AGRIPPA COS III MUNICIPI PARENS.

[47] Strabo 3.5.3.

Figure 13.3. Coins from Gades featuring Hercules on obverse with symbols of pontifical college on reverse (nos. 1–3); a tetrastyle temple on obverse and rayed symbol on reverse (no. 4); Augustus's head on obverse and a tetrastyle temple encircled with a laurel wreath on reverse (no. 5); and coins referencing both Augustus and Gaius and Lucius (nos. 6 and 7)

Hercules on the obverse and an image of a *simpulum* together with the phrases TI. CLAVDIUS or TI. CLAVDIUS NERO on the reverse.[48]

Some scholars see these actions as a direct appropriation of the Phoenician god Melqart by Roman leaders in the guise of Hercules Gaditanus – but this name is not attested until Hadrian.[49] Others prefer to speak of a Hercules who arrived under the Romans and had little to do with a Roman appropriation of Melqart. Such a claim is based mainly upon the use of his name in epigraphic dedications by individuals with Latin names; in these dedications Hercules is either named without epithets or is titled Augustus, Primigenius, or Invictus.[50] But by juxtaposing Roman leaders' usage of Hercules in Spain during the early Empire against the long-term discursive conception of this god as a symbol and guarantor of legitimate leadership, we can place this debate on a new footing. Taking the longer view, we do not have to decide for or against a complete reappropriation of Melqart from the Augustan period onward; instead, we can articulate in more nuanced forms how the repeated usage of a trope enabled leaders to display and legitimize political power among various ethnic and civic groups.[51]

Carrie Fulton's deployment of *chaîne opératoire* in this volume to uncover the multiple, nonlinear scales of appropriation reflected in shipwrecks is instructive: rather than focusing solely on the end point of Roman "consumption" of Hercules (or Melqart), we can examine the Roman adoption of this god within networks of Herculean symbolism iterated and reiterated over time. The Roman consumption – or appropriation – of Hercules in Spain was thus a result of centuries of prior appropriation and reappropriation by Mediterranean and Near Eastern peoples, a long conversation whose cross-cultural symbols of power and legitimacy were put to effective use by Rome in its interactions with Greek, Punic, and Iberian groups in southern Spain. Whereas religious syncretism was hitched to various social, political, or economic purposes, the long-term "globalized" significations attached to a deity such as Hercules illustrate how and why symbolic power functioned as part of a conceptual *lingua franca* that pervaded the Mediterranean world.

---

[48] See Vives y Escudero 1924–6: plate LXXVII.1–3.
[49] For example, García y Bellido 1963 and 1967, interpreting the other epithets associated with Hercules in Spain as rooted in the Phoenician Melqart.
[50] For example, Mangas Manjarrés 1996; Oria Segura 1989; 1993; 1997. The only dedication to Hercules with an indigenous name (Tongo) comes from Galicia, where Hercules is named along with Jupiter Optimus Maximus: *ILER* 78 with Oria Segura 1989: 271.
[51] Similar situations occurred in other imperial arenas: see Melliti 2006 on how the aristocracy of Hellenistic Carthage played a pivotal role in spurring religious change for political ends.

The Long Conversation Continued: Trajanic and Hadrianic Appropriations of Hercules

By the late first century CE, when local mints in Spain were no longer in the hands of local magistrates, the global Hercules trope would be reappropriated and re-articulated under different circumstances. The emperor Trajan (born in Italica, a colony in Baetica) and particularly his successor Hadrian (likely born in Rome but of the same family as Trajan) brought the "Spanish Hercules" back to Rome, so to speak, in a celebration of both the military and civilizing facets of the Empire at its greatest extent.[52] Though not as explicit as Hadrian in connecting Spain and Rome through this deity, Trajan fostered a close relationship with Hercules.[53] Imperial coins of 101–104 CE do show on the reverse a statue of Hercules, which Paul Strack originally considered to be a representation of Hercules Gaditanus.[54] Olivier Hekster argues, however, that this is likely a statue of Hercules from the Ara Maxima, a monument which Trajan is known to have restored between 100 and 104 CE. It was Hadrian, instead, who introduced the persona of Hercules Gaditanus, named explicitly on Hadrianic coins.[55]

Whereas Trajan tended to invoke the military aspects of this god, Hadrian emphasized the wandering characteristics of Hercules – a nice fit for an emperor who traveled extensively under mostly peaceful circumstances to the boundaries of the empire. Hadrian's mother, Domitia Paulina, was from Gades, the city at the end of the *oikoumene* from which Hercules had set out to reach the Forum Boarium after slaying Geryon and taking his cattle. At the western extreme of the inhabited world, Gades was also believed to be the place where Hercules collected the apples of eternal

---

[52] Hadrian's birthplace is somewhat obscure. Although the *Historia Augusta* (*Hadr.* 1.3) states that he was born at Rome on 24 January 76 CE, his tribe, the "Sergia," is associated with Italica. As Syme notes (1964: 142), however, one's birthplace is not always the same as the *origo* of one's family.

[53] Pliny the Younger compared Trajan's military exploits under Domitian to the labors of Hercules (*Pan.* 14.5); Dio Chrysostom presented Hercules as Trajan's prototype (*Or.* 1.56–84): Braund 2012: 99; Hekster 2005: 205; Garzón Blanco 1988: 257. The emperor gave one of his new legions, the *Legio Secunda Traiana*, the emblem of Hercules on the regimental standard and linked himself to Hercules through his coins (*RIC* 3, Trajan, nos. 581; 695; 702). In addition, Trajan may even have appeared as Hercules on a statue now on display at the Palazzo Massimo in Rome: Hekster 2005: 205–7.

[54] *RIC* 3, Trajan, nos. 37, 49–51; Strack 1931: 95–105. In 1955, J. Beaujeu suggested that this statue of Hercules represented Hercules Gaditanus on the basis of comparisons with the depiction of Melqart on Tyrian coin issues from 98–99 CE: Garzón Blanco 1988: 257–8.

[55] Hekster 2005: 215–6 n. 18. Garzón Blanco (1988: 257) reads the olive tree in the panel on Trajan's Arch at Beneventum in which Trajan is depicted facing a young Hercules draped in the lion skin as a reference to Hispania.

Figure 13.4.   Hadrianic aureus featuring laureate and cuirassed bust of Hadrian (obverse) and Hercules Gaditanus with water god reclining below and prow on left (reverse)

youth: the apples of the Hesperides.[56] Hadrianic *aurei* show Hercules standing within a distyle or tetrastyle temple holding apples in one hand and his club in the other; one issue displays two female deities (likely the Hesperides) standing on either side of Hercules as he holds the apples.[57] In another variation on the theme, Hercules appears standing (not in a temple this time) with club and apples in hand as a water god reclines at his feet and the title HERC GADIT splashed across the center, making explicit the emperor's link with Gades and (as Hekster suggests) with the deity who had obtained immortality through his travels (Figure 13.4). And on another issue, a fish appears together with the water god – reminiscent of the earlier issues from Gades that had shown Melqart in the company of dolphins or tuna.[58]

The binding of Spain to Rome through Hadrian's iconographic affiliation with Hercules makes manifest how the explicit appropriation of

[56] Hesiod *Theogony* 215–6 has the Hesperides guarding their apples "beyond glorious Ocean" (*perēn klutou Ōkeanoio*). One of the Hesperides was named Erytheia ("the red one"), a name Strabo equates with Gades (3.2.11) and the home of Geryon (3.5.4), citing the fifth-century BCE mythographer Pherecydes of Leros *BNJ* 3 F 18b). Pliny the Elder (*NH* 4.120) states that Ephorus and Philistides called Gades Erytheia, whereas the natives supposedly called it the Isle of Juno (cf. Strabo 3.5.3), after the goddess who had appointed the nymphs to guard the apples. An alternative tradition places the Hesperides in Libya, however: see e.g., Varro *RR* 2.1.6.

[57] *RIC* 3, Hadrian, nos. 57–60. Hekster 2005: 207; Barry 2011: 22; Garzón Blanco 1988: 258. Garzón Blanco takes the flat roof of the temple to denote a building designed according to Phoenician customs. Hadrian seems to have shown great reverence to Melqart at Gades: Ulpian the jurist mentions that this temple was one of the few allowed to receive inheritances (*Frag.* 22.6), an enactment which Mangas Manjarrés 1989 dates to Hadrian.

[58] For HERC GADITANUS: *RIC* 3, Hadrian, no. 125. For Hercules with fish and water god: *RIC* 3, Hadrian, no. 61. Hekster 2005: 207; Garzón Blanco 1988: 258.

Figure 13.5.   Hadrianic aureus featuring laureate and cuirassed bust of Hadrian (obverse)
and Hercules standing in a tetrastyle temple holding club and apples;
the face of a god (Oceanus?) and ship's prow appear below (reverse)

these long-term motifs of Hercules and their connotations of rulership and
world dominion related to the circumstances of a particular emperor's rule:
in this case, the Hadrianic emphasis is not on Hercules' military prowess
but on Hercules' valor in traversing (and thereby delimiting) the *oikoumene*. Certainly the myths of Hercules' slaying of Geryon, his journey to
the site of the future Forum Boarium, his combat with Cacus and
foundation of the Ara Maxima – all stories popularized under Augustan
authors – provided a ready-to-hand link between the epicenter of Rome's
mytho-history, the figure of Hercules Gaditanus, and the deeds of the
emperor. Also implicated in Hadrian's Herculean projection is the water
god who, on four of the Hadrianic *aurei*, is depicted as reclining immediately below the hero-god; on a fifth issue, instead of an entire god, there is
simply a frontal face.[59] Fabio Barry has proposed that this water god, both
in full form and as disembodied face, represents Oceanus, which Hercules
crossed to reach the Hesperides and kill Geryon, Oceanus' grandson.
Hadrian was the only emperor to mint coins combining these two deities
(Figure 13.5).[60] Furthermore, Barry argues that the Oceanus of the famous

[59] *RIC* 3, Hadrian, no. 61. Another issue shows the bodiless face in profile: *RIC* 3, Hadrian, no. 57;
    Barry 2011: 35 n. 133.
[60] Barry 2011. Other scholars have argued for an identification of this deity with Oceanus as well: e.g.,
    García y Bellido 1963. See Hesiod, *Theog.* 287–94 and 979–83; Pherecydes (*apud* Ath. *Deipn.* 470c–
    d: *BNJ* 3 F 18a) claimed that Hercules had had to subdue Oceanus on his way to Gades.

Bocca della Verità was set up on the Ara Maxima under Trajan or Hadrian so as to bring into closer rapport the god's aspect of martial courage (as embodied in the Hercules Victor of the Forum Boarium) with his identity as wandering civilizer whose power extended to the outermost extent of Ocean. A similar representation of a frontal-facing water god appears on the cuirass of a monumental bronze statue thought to be Trajanic or Hadrianic in date that was found in the Bay of Cadiz.[61] The mythologized conquest of hostile waters would continue to appeal in Romano-Iberian settings well after Hadrian: a late third-century CE milestone from Spain records the repair of a road, in part, through a thorough taming of an antagonistic river.[62]

Although Barry's reading rests on multiple tiers of speculation – both the Ara Maxima and the Bocca della Verità will likely remain fraught with uncertainties – this emphasis on Hercules as a victorious hero, whose pacification of the farthest-flung reaches of the *oikoumene* made him into an admirable prototype for sovereignty, brings out the extent to which the "Hercules" meme interfaced with the cultural and physical geographies of the Mediterranean world. Although scholars categorize Hercules Gaditanus in particular as the Roman equivalent of the original tutelary god of Gades, he was not a direct replacement of Melqart: he represented, instead, the reappropriation of a long-enduring cultural trope anchored in Roman conceptions of their own past and developed through interactions with neighboring Mediterranean peoples over several centuries.

Beyond Gades: Hercules in Southern Spain, First and Second Centuries CE

In Gades, the association of the emperor and other Roman officials with Hercules – in some cases evocative of the Punic Melqart – is clear. Elsewhere in southern Spain, the Roman conceptualization of Hercules

---

[61] Barry compares the Bocca with numerous drain covers that featured the frontal face of water gods such as Triton and Acheloös. On the bronze statue, the face of the water god replaces what is usually a Gorgon on the cuirass. The statue was dredged up in 1925 around the island where the Temple of Melqart stood; on the dating see Barry 2011: 35 n. 135. A similar statue of Trajan or Hadrian that displays a water god on the chest, but this time placed above a Triton wrestling two sea monsters, has been found at Terracina: Barry 2011: 22.

[62] *CIL* 2.4911 = *AE* 1960 with Purcell 1996, 199. The link between Hercules and roads has a long history: ancient writers report a semi-mythical *via Herculis* through the Alps, along which the hero-god drove his cattle to Rome: Strabo 4.1.7; Diod. Sic. 4.19; Ps.-Aristot. *Mirab.* 85; Amm. 15.10.9. On the famous Vicarello Goblets and their representation of the mythical journey from Gades to Rome, see Schmidt 2011.

and its relation to preexisting Punic cultural traditions are murkier. Much of our evidence consists of a few dozen inscriptions from Lusitania, Baetica, and Tarraconensis.

In a 1989 study, Mercedes Oria Segura reviewed a total of 42 Iberian inscriptions mentioning Hercules, dated with varying levels of confidence from the early first to the third century CE. Most of the inscriptions (thirty-four) record *ex voto* dedications to Hercules; two mention priests, one is a dedication by a *collegium*, and three are inscribed roof tiles from Carteia; finally, two are of doubtful function and attribution.[63] Excluding inscriptions from the last two categories, Oria Segura counts thirty-seven total known Spanish dedications to Hercules over two centuries, as compared to 186 to Jupiter, 39 to Mars, and 37 to the Nymphs. Since her study, one more *ex voto* inscription from the area of San Esteban de Gormaz has come to light, pushing the number up to thirty-eight.[64] Most inscriptions (twenty-four) come from Tarraconensis, but the densest concentration occurs in Baetica, whose fourteen inscriptions are spread out over an area three times smaller than Tarraconensis. Only four come from Lusitania. The find-spots of the inscriptions are grouped around river basins – not all that surprising given the proximity of Iberian settlements and economic centers to rivers. Also noteworthy is the concentration of inscriptions in the south, specifically near coastal regions. Baetica and southern Tarraconensis were of course areas where the original Phoenician cities had been established; these areas had witnessed the circulation of coins featuring Melqart during the third to first centuries BCE, and under the Romans these same areas became the most heavily populated in Iberia.[65] Finally, Baetica has the highest number of inscriptions to Hercules accompanied by an epithet: Invictus (three), Augustus (three), or Primigenius (one). In southern Tarraconensis, there is one inscription to Hercules Augustus from Ilici and another to Hercules Gaditanus from Carthago Nova.[66]

---

[63] Oria Segura 1989. One of the doubtful fragments, from the Ebro Valley, reads O ... / ... CIDAE ...; some have proposed restoring a form of Alcides. The other, found in the theatre at Segóbriga, has only the name of the dedicator preserved, but Oria Segura notes that the excavator considered it to be dedicated to Hercules by analogy with three other confirmed inscriptions to Hercules from the same location.

[64] See Gómez-Pantoja & García Palomar 2001, who discuss *CIL* 2.2814 in connection with *CIL* 2.2815 and 2816 from San Esteban de Gormaz (the latter two discussed in Oria Segura 1989).

[65] Oria Segura 1989: 267–8.

[66] *CIL* II *Suppl.* 5950 and *CIL* 2.3409 with Rodríguez Cortés 1991: 62–5 for discussion. Two of the three *Invictus* inscriptions come from Tucci, a Roman military colony: one was dedicated by the emperor Tiberius (*CIL* 2.1660= *ILER* 205); another, dating to the first half of the second century CE, came from L. Cornelius Ianuarius, possibly a freedman (*ILER* 204 with Rodríguez Cortés 1991: 64).

What, if anything, do these inscriptions tell us about Roman interactions with past appropriations of Hercules in the imperial cultural milieu
of southern Spain? Inscriptions to Hercules in the south are concentrated
in the area southeast of the Guadalquivir River where the original
Phoenician cities issued coins displaying Melqart: that is, the original
conventus of Gades.[67] This distribution, when compared to the strikingly
low number of inscriptions to Hercules from another area heavily populated under the Romans – the Ebro River basin (although this low number
may reflect preservation issues) – indicates that the worship of Hercules in
Baetica and southern Tarraconensis corresponded to earlier patterns in
Melqart's worship. The entire region southeast of the Guadalquivir, from
the Mediterranean coastline up to Hispalis and Italica, generally displays
strong evidence for the continuation of Punic cultural practices well into
the Roman Empire. At Carmo, tombs employed Punic-style architecture
(shafts with either handholds and footholds or sloping stairs) but Roman
burial practices (the use of cinerary urns, one containing the Punic name
Urbanival).[68] Other burial forms represented throughout the region
include Phoenician-style tower tombs as well as *cupae*, semicylindrical
tombs with roots in North African commemoration. The temple to
Melqart at Gades was described by several authors as having retained its
Punic roots.[69] Epigraphic evidence indicates that a mixed population
inhabited some of the cities: at Ostippo, for instance, where the inscription
to Hercules Primigenius was found, other inscriptions preserve names
alluding to North African – though not necessarily Punic/Phoenician –
origins, such as Fulvia Maura and L. Mummius Maurus.[70]

This Hercules Primigenius inscription is held by A.T. Fear to be intelligible only if the name was applied to Melqart (without elaborating as to
why); A. García y Bellido has posited that the Hercules worshipped
throughout the region stemmed directly from Melqart.[71] On the other
hand, since all the dedications to Hercules we have noted are dedicated

---

[67] García y Bellido 1967 assumed that each city issuing a coin showing Melqart's image also had a
temple and cult dedicated to this deity, but this remains conjectural; see Oria Segura 1989: 268.
[68] Fear 1996: 242.
[69] According to Strabo – who never visited the peninsula but consulted the firsthand accounts of
Pytheas, Artemidorus, Asclepiades of Myrleia, Polybius, and Posidonius – there were two bronze
pillars in front of the temple, perhaps representing the mythical Ambrosial Rocks that led to the
founding of Tyre (3.5.5 with Mierse 2004: 547).
[70] *CIL* 2.1453 and *CIL* 2.1462 with Fear 1996: 246. The Hercules Primigenius inscription: *CIL* 2.1436.
For further discussions on the mixed populations of Spain see Strabo 3.2.13; Pompon. 2.96; 3.3 (on
this last author, see Batty 2000).
[71] Fear 1996: 237; García y Bellido 1963.

only to the Roman deity (with or without epithets) by individuals with Latin names and never explicitly identify him with Melqart, Julio Mangas Manjarrés has insisted on a strictly Roman Hercules in his reading of these inscriptions; he credits the worship of Hercules in Baetica not to the existence of a pre-Roman Melqart but to the population's increasing familiarization with Roman cultural and ideological forms.[72]

Instead of siding with either of these interpretations, we can instead emphasize Hercules' standing as an elastic symbol already woven into Rome's past and into the pasts of Iberia that could be appropriated and reworked within provincial settings. This process is most pronounced in Gades, of course, but elsewhere we can see the troping of Hercules as a model for dynastic leadership. At Munigua, one hundred kilometers to the north of Gades, in the province of Seville, an inscription on a statue base set up by L. Quintius Rufus as a dedication to Hercules Augustus dates to the second half of the second century CE.[73] Two other inscriptions to Hercules Augustus (now lost) hailed from Jerez, about forty kilometers from Gades.[74] Collectively these three inscriptions connect Hercules to the practice of the imperial cult: although in general Mars is more often invoked as "Augustus" in Spain (twelve attested instances as compared to Hercules' four), the fact that Hercules is worshipped with this epithet in the greater vicinity of Gades speaks to the successful dissemination of the ideal propagated by Augustus and the Roman emperors through their identification with the Hercules/Melqart at Gades.[75] In the case of the Munigua text, Hercules shares the title "Augustus" with the goddess Fortuna in Munigua – commemorated in another dedication as "Fortuna Crescens Augusta." These were likely the deities worshipped in the giant terraced sanctuary built at Munigua during the Flavian period that was modeled after the Sanctuary of Fortuna Primigenia in Praeneste and that of Hercules Victor in Tivoli.[76] Darius Arya has detailed how the deified personification of Fortune and the *sacra* of her cult at Praeneste were incorporated into the discourse of dynastic succession cultivated under the emperors. Hercules is rarely worshipped alongside Fortuna, who is

---

[72] Mangas Manjarrés 1996: 292, 296.

[73] Collantes de Terán & Chicarro de Dios 1972–4: 345 no. D-4; see also Oria Segura 1989: 264; 1997; Rodríguez Cortés 1991: 65. L. Quintius Rufus came from one of the most prominent families in Munigua; his name is seen in two other dedications from Munigua, one of which dedicates a monument to his father, L. Quintius Rufinus: *CIL* 2.1074 with Rodríguez Cortés 1991: 65.

[74] *CIL* 2.1303 (= *ILER* 197) and *CIL* 2.1304 (= *ILER* 196).

[75] The other inscription to Hercules Augustus is a dedication by a *sevir suā pecuniā* at Ilici in southern Tarraconensis: *CIL* 2 *suppl.* 5950.

[76] Coarelli 1996.

most often associated with Mars in imperial symbolism; her connection to Hercules at Munigua thus becomes all the more exceptional and significant.[77] The use of the enduring symbolism associated with both deities within the framework of the imperial cult reflected imperial ambitions that were first articulated on Spanish shores by Roman leaders in Gades but, indeed, had much deeper roots.

The existence of these deeper roots means that we should not be looking for a purely Roman model when it comes to Hercules, either in Spain or Rome. All reincarnations of Hercules drew on past appropriations of this roving god to address the contingencies of the present. We might think of C. Cornelius Gallus' reference in the Qasr Ibrim papyrus – as explicated in Micah Myers's chapter in this section – to the importation of the *orbis* to the *urbs* through *spolia*, artifacts infused by Rome's elite with claims to military power and political eminence. Although material *spolia* made their way to Rome along military and commercial networks created and maintained by Empire (and accrued new social, cultural, and technical significations within *chaînes opératoires*, as Carrie Fulton observes), this chapter has stressed, with its case study of Hercules' symbolism, the preexisting conceptual networks along which notions of Roman power traveled. Symbols gained new life and greater longevity not only through the continuous circulation of people and ideas but through the multiple rounds of reiteration and improvisation that this circulation provoked. The circulation of Herculean iconography involved people and their cultural backdrops as much as texts and objects and resulted in cultural and social discourses that were adapted to suit changing circumstances: improvisations not at all dissimilar to those of Amy Richlin's comic troupes.

Conclusion: The Statics and Dynamics of Appropriation

In this chapter, I have laid out a long-term approach to the Roman appropriation of Hercules, reading it as an adoption of a long-standing

---

[77] Arya 2002: esp. 351–3. On Fortuna in Spain, see Baílon García 2012. Connections with Tivoli are evident in the transformation of the local college of *Herculanei* to *Herculanei Augustales* under Augustus or Tiberius: Mierse 1999: 256. For engagement with the iconographies of Hercules and Oceanus at Hadrian's villa at Tivoli – in particular the *Teatro Marittimo* – see Barry 2011. On the possibility that the Sant'Omobono statues paired Hercules and Fortuna Virilis, see n. 13. Though Hercules' Primigenius epithet at Ostippo may have been intended to evoke an association with the Fortuna Primigenia at Praeneste, a Hercules Primigenius was also worshipped in Rome: see *CIL* 6.7655 and 9645.

form of symbolic power grounded in a globalized and globalizing Mediterranean world. Through this approach, I have tried to reframe the debate of Hercules in Hispania, moving away from the question of whether or not he was a Roman appropriation of Melqart and focusing instead on how the employment of the Hercules trope in a provincial setting replicated centuries' worth of Mediterranean peoples' engagement with symbols of power and conquest. As Rome evolved within this globalized Mediterranean, its symbolic repertoire inevitably became entwined with that of other cultural groups – as evidenced early on at Sant'Omobono – thus paving the way for strategically felicitous syncretisms in other times and places.

A monolithic, centralizing notion of "appropriation" will not fly given the Mediterranean world presented in this chapter and the other chapters in this section – a world of multidirectional networks along which people, goods, ideas, and meanings were always on the move. Appropriation, the act of "making something one's own," may imply to some a static end point or insinuate unidirectional power dynamics, yet it is clear that the cargoes appropriated by Rome never ceased to be a part of the mobile Mediterranean. Hercules never stops wandering, even after he is made one of Rome's founding heroes and linked to the emperors: not only his mongrel origins but his constant movement across cultural boundaries invest him with resonance as a symbol of dynastic leadership across the Roman world. What Roman appropriation does in the case of Hercules, then, is refocus the conversation of power and legitimacy embodied by this god (in his many cultural guises) toward Rome. Can we say the same for other dynamic processes in the Mediterranean – the *chaîne opératoire*, for example, or the shticks of Roman comedy? Should we be thinking of Roman appropriation less as a co-option of specific objects, customs, and styles and more as a tapping of long-term cultural and social processes? Such a change of perspective would inspire new scholarly conversations and recalibrate our understanding of Roman political and ideological power as it was staged in the perpetually globalizing Mediterranean.

CHAPTER 14

Circulation's Thousand Connectivities

Dan-el Padilla Peralta

> Objects in motion tend to stay that way.
> – Jim White

But what keeps them in motion? Well before Jim White's drawling and Isaac Newton's laws of motion, Lucretius invoked desire and attraction as the name of the game.[1] My title for this response registers the gravitational pull exerted on the rubric of cargo by two scholarly enterprises: at one end, Peregrine Horden and Nicholas Purcell's celebration of connectivity in *The Corrupting Sea*; at the other, Gilles Deleuze and Félix Guattari's *Thousand Plateaus*, and poststructuralist and postcolonialist investigations of commodification and culture more generally.[2] Although the "circulations of signs and commodities" in the Mediterranean under Roman rule did not derive from the capitalist structures whose "vicious circuits of surplus value" are often scrutinized by these investigations, each of our contributions directly or indirectly positions the circulation of cargoes – ideas and objects, humans, humans as objects – within the matrices of the Roman imperial system whose specter haunts modern empires.[3] In this response I will pair summary and amplification of each contribution with an attempt to tease out some of the conceptual and thematic connectivities activated by application of the circulation paradigm; then, as *sphragis* to this section and the volume as a whole, I will offer some parting thoughts on possible directions for future research into the circulation of Roman cargo.

---

[1] *DRN* 1.1–20.

[2] This response was drafted prior to the publication of Concannon & Mazurek 2016, whose introductory overview of approaches to Mediterranean connectivity also takes inspiration from Deleuze and Guattari (see esp. pp. 13–14).

[3] For the quoted phrases in this sentence and at the beginning of the next paragraph: Bhabha 2004: 285–6 and 283. "Circulation" as conceptual rubric: Purcell 2012 and 2013, drawing from Markovits *et al.* 2003 (see discussion in Myers); cf. the "circulatory urbanization" paradigm for Princeton's digital humanities project *Designing Empire* (https://digitalhumanities.princeton.edu/designing-empire/).

Amy Richlin's opening chapter takes up the challenge of historicizing what we may term "the event of the dehistoricized": the traffic in human cargo through which Greek comedy came to be appropriated into Roman culture. The knowledge of the shtick performance routines that animated Greek New Comedy was embodied; many of those who carried and perfected this comic expertise were enslaved as a consequence of Rome's centuries of warfare against its Hellenistic adversaries. That Roman comedy routinely mines the tensions between slave(ry) and free(dom) for gold has been explored elsewhere;[4] what is distinctive about Richlin's piece is her reading of the *palliata* as a genre whose formal techniques were shaped by circulation on the backs of the unfree. In a world of constant enslavements and ceaseless movement, improvisation was king.[5]

Far from simply enhancing our reading of Plautus, Richlin's approach brings out striking continuities between the emergence of Roman comedy in the time of the Punic Wars and the explosion of specialized literary and scientific pursuits during the last few decades of the Roman Republic. In both periods, slaves and freedmen swept up by the dragnet of Roman power proved to be indispensable cultural interlocutors and virtuosos.[6] Her contribution's insights into the interrelation of artistic strategies and human circulation also push us to reassess – and here I quote from a contemporary writer's recent diagnosis of aesthetic production in the age of globalization – "the implications of this idea that important art always travels."[7] In locating the development of shtick within the welter of bodies and artifacts commandeered by Roman power, Richlin reminds us that art traveled under conditions, not infrequently violent and ex/appropriative ones. Reliant on joke routines that repeatedly alluded to and/or derived their full force from the traffic in traumatized human bodies, the *palliata* exemplifies the "migratory subjectivity" whose traces are apparent in other genres of early Latin literature.[8] Republican Rome thus has an important place in the global history of captives as culture brokers, recently the focus of transcultural and borderlands research.[9]

---

[4] E.g., McCarthy 2000.   [5] On these points, see also Richlin 2014 and 2016.

[6] The late republican intellectual revolution: Rawson 1985. For the importance of enslaved bodies to this revolution see the story of the *grammaticus* Daphnis: Pliny *NH* 7.128 and Suet. *De gramm.* 3.5 on the price paid for his purchase; Flower 2014 on his literary collaboration with the hellenophile Q. Lutatius Catulus.

[7] Parks 2015: 75.

[8] For the quoted phrase and detection of these traces, see Sciarrino 2011: 114–15 and 204–6.

[9] This global history is the subject of Cameron 2016, esp. 133–62 on captives and cultural transmission.

The traffic in bodies is approached from a different angle in Carrie Fulton's chapter, which examines through the lens of *chaîne opératoire* theory how humans and objects in circulation entered new circuits of meaning as they shifted hands and contexts. With this model, Fulton seeks to redirect the conversation about agency away from the imperial center and toward the enterprising middlemen who oversaw commercial traffic and grappled directly with this traffic's physical properties. In many cases, these properties themselves dictated the specifics of transport; nowhere is this more evident than with the supersized commodities such as megafauna and obelisks that required technical and infrastructural adaptations to facilitate their shipping and exhibition.[10] And whereas Fulton's model is initially conceived around the ruin of the shipwreck, its elaboration over the course of the chapter brings the agents and spaces responsible for the organization of shipments to the fore. With great individual responsibility came great individual perks – exemption from public service, citizenship[11] – but of course individuals did not act alone; civic and corporate entities (teams of magistrates, networks of trading towns, merchant *collegia*) collaborated to assemble, disassemble, inspect, and reassemble cargoes.

In its emphasis on agency and individual initiative, Fulton's exposition of the interlinked chains of commerce strongly stresses the role of correspondence. Cicero's exchanges with Atticus over the requisitioning of statues underscore how and to what ends members of Rome's elite exercised control (through intermediaries) over the choice of significance-laden goods being circulated their way.[12] Cicero's epistolary exchanges are the tip of the iceberg: public and private correspondence during the Hellenistic and Roman periods was crucial to the coordination of commerce and politics; and the movement of letters along with the brokering of commercial transactions through letters loom especially large in the literary genre so sensitively attuned to vectors and habits of material circulation – Roman comedy.[13] Among the most valuable cargoes speeding

[10] See, in addition to Fulton, Parker in this volume on obelisk transport. The technological watershed of ferrying elephants to Rome for the First Punic War triumph of Lucius Caecilius Metellus: Pliny *NH* 8.6.16.

[11] Exemption from public service for merchants who provisioned the city of Rome with grain: *Digest* 50.6.6. Admission to citizenship of Latins who built ships with a minimum capacity of 10,000 *modii* and imported grain to Rome for six years: Gaius *Institutes* 1.32c with Tchernia 2016: 212–9.

[12] Fulton's reading of Ciceronian anxiety about the significations of particular types of statues neatly complements Bodel 2009: 25–6 with n. 34.

[13] The traffic in letters: Ceccarelli 2013 and Bencivenni 2014 on Hellenistic royal correspondence; Corcoran 2014 on the prolific output of imperial correspondence during the Roman Empire. Pliny

across the Roman Mediterranean were words themselves, and by the time of the Empire storage infrastructure had evolved in tandem with transport technology to handle this traffic. Galen's account (styled as a letter) of the manuscript losses he suffered when the warehouses on the Sacra Via burned to the ground in 192 CE illuminates with striking clarity both the sophistication of imperial Rome's storage systems and the options available to those seeking to safeguard rare texts. The choice of a building material less vulnerable to fire, the construction of the warehouses at a remove from private houses, the assignment of a military unit to stand guard, and the levying of higher rents for their use were all decisions undertaken by different agents acting to ensure that commodities such as Galen's irreplaceable books were protected from the prospect of damage or destruction.[14]

Even though circulating commodities had to be protected from violence, these commodities were often themselves the product of violence. In her reading of Cicero's animadversions against Verres, Fulton joins Richlin in underlining the role of force in Rome's appropriation of goods. This thread in the Verrines resurfaces in Cicero's correspondence with his brother: specified as unbecoming to a Roman magistrate of Quintus' distinction are pried-away statuary, paintings, vases, textiles, and human bodies.[15] This last item gestures to the grim reality visible beneath the lightheartedness of a contemporary's quip about a sexy provincial wife, namely the trafficking of provincials for the sexual exploitation of Roman elites.[16] Even when the libidinous overdrive of these men leaves its imprint in textual form – by incurring the satirical wrath of a Catullus, whose polymetrics swarm with the spoils of imperial violence[17] – any attempt to recover the voices and agencies of those on the dagger end of Roman imperial power will need to range

the Younger's letters to Trajan as "postcards from the edge of empire": Woolf 2015. Letters in Plautine comedy: Barbiero 2014.

[14] Galen Περὶ Ἀλυπίας, esp. §§ 8–9; read with Nicholls 2011: 125–30.

[15] *Ad Q. fr.* I.I.7–8: *praeclarum est enim summo cum imperio fuisse in Asia biennium sic ut nullum te signum, nulla pictura, nullum vas, nulla vestis, nullum mancipium, nulla forma cuiusquam, nulla condicio pecuniae, quibus rebus abundat ista provincia, ab summa integritate continentiaque deduxerit.* Cf. the Varronian fragment in next note and Juv. *Sat.* 8.144–5.

[16] Varro *Men.* fr. 176 Cèbe: . . . *habet quiddam enim* ἑλκυ[ι]στικὸν *provincialis formonsula uxor;* Cèbe renders ἑλκυ[ι]στικὸν as "sex appeal." The late republican traffic in slave women "often bought as breeders": Betzig 1992. Hellenistic Greek literature – e.g., the character in Herodas who boasts of having brought *pornai* from Tyre (*Mim.* 2.16–8; cf. Plautus *Truc.* 530 *ancillas tibi . . . ex Syria duas*) – taps into this social reality; discussion of sex slaves in Greek New Comedy and its Roman heirs in Marshall 2013.

[17] Argued with nuance in Young 2015: 52–88.

beyond the literary evidence. Structured around the archaeological record, Fulton's recreation of the temporally and geographically dispersed nodes at which middlemen and women (such as the stevedores and dockworkers, many formerly and currently enslaved themselves) performed the work of organizing and funneling the movement of goods and bodies is a necessary first step in this recovery. Remaining to be reckoned are the other handlers that populated the *chaîne opératoire* of enslavement, from the slave trader who boasted of his profession on stone to the pimps, pirates, and bandits whose recurring roles in Roman comedy mirrored their importance to Mediterranean commerce.[18]

If Verres the bandit stands at the apex of one system of Roman provincial (mis)administration, Cornelius Gallus the poet-administrator stands at the apex of another. Micah Myers' reading of the Gallus papyrus from Qasr Ibrim puts flesh on the multidirectional networks along which material goods and literary practices flowed from center to periphery and back again. At the heart of Myers's analysis is the fragmentary papyrus itself, with its evocation of multiple – and multiply layered – forms of circulation: the movement of spoils toward Rome; the movement of texts and writing from Rome; and the synchronization of these two types of movement to organize, systematize, and in time commemorate human and nonhuman traffic into and out of Egypt. By redirecting our gaze to the fragment (anticipated in our volume introduction's opening reflections on the fragmentary *Ineditum Vaticanum*), Myers provides a timely reminder of what can be done with a literary-artifactual category whose disciplinary history is intimately bound up with the transit of texts and scholars alike.[19]

The integration of Egypt's monopoly on paper production into the economic machinery of the Principate is indispensable to any contextualization of Gallus' life in relation to imperial circuits of cargo: Myers comments on the existence of *Corneliana*, the high-grade paper whose invention was credited to the *eques* himself (Isid. *Etym.* 6.10.5). Whatever the precise reasons for the veil drawn over Gallus' memory in Augustan

---

[18] The funerary inscription of Aulos Kapreilios Timotheos: Finley 1977; Bodel 2005. Pimping and prostitution in the Roman world: McGinn 2004. Pirates in the Greek and Roman Mediterranean: Ormerod 1924; de Souza 1999. Bandits in the Roman Empire: Shaw 1984.

[19] Histories of classical fragments and the scholarship devoted to them: Brunt 1980; Dionisotti 1998, especially 4–5 on how the bio-bibliographical tradition – itself derived from fragments – has molded interpretations of the Gallus papyrus. For the category of the fragment and the fragmentary in the history of modern museological and curatorial practice, see O'Neill 2012.

literature, his name continued to circulate long after his death as a
descriptor for a specific and valuable commodity. Among the products of
empire, papyrus occupied a privileged place: under Tiberius a shortage of
charta brought state operations to a standstill and led to the implementa-
tion of a temporary rationing scheme. Even as production of papyrus was
ramped up to accommodate imperial needs (chief among these the
epistolary industry through which the empire was governed), special
precautions were taken to protect and repair papyrus sheets already in
use, the most preferred one being their anointment with cedar oil.[20]
Though the branding of a class of papyrus after Gallus falls perfectly in
line with the practice repeatedly attested in Pliny the Elder's exhaustive
catalogues of commodities – the regular nicknaming of valuable goods
after those individuals credited with first importing them into Italy – there
is one final wrinkle to the story of Gallus' afterlife as imperial commodity:
a Greek-language silverware inventory from Egypt preserved on papyrus
and dated to the first century CE states that some of the items were stored
in a chest marked "property of Gallus" (ἐχούσηι Γάλλου).[21]

By repositioning the papyrus fragment from Qasr Ibrim within circuits
of import and export, Myers (echoing Richlin and Fulton) reminds us to
keep an eye out for the intermediaries whose life stories played out along
these circuits. Why the poet Gallus fell so precipitously from agent and
arm of Augustus in Egypt to renounced *amicitia* and forced suicide
remains murky. Less murky but equally suggestive is the fate of Eros,
Augustus' (freedman?) procurator in Egypt, whom the *princeps* ordered
crucified on a ship's mast after learning that Eros had not only bought a
(presumably costly) prize-fighting quail but cooked and eaten it. If this
Eros is the same person as the C. Numidius Eros who returned to Egypt
from a sea voyage to India in 2 BCE, Augustus will have staged his
punishment as an allusively macabre joke: affixed to the ship's mast, Eros
the seafarer could finally relish the Siren call of luxury.[22] However outland-
ish, Augustus' punishment aligned with his interest in regulating certain
types of consumption, an interest conditioned by and responsive to the

---

[20] The Tiberian papyrus shortage: Pliny *NH* 13.89 with Swetnam-Burland 2015: 2. The coating of
papyrus with cedar oil to protect against worms and rot: Vitr. 2.9.13; Pliny *NH* 16.197 and 16.212,
commenting on cedar oil's properties; Varro *De bibliothecis* fr. 54 *GRF* Funaioli with Hendrickson
2015.

[21] Naming as imperial (f)act in Pliny: Swetnam-Burland 2015: 22–3. For the "Property of Gallus"
silverware see *BGU* III 781 with Oliver & Shelton 1979.

[22] The punishment of Eros: Plut. *Apophtheg. Rom.* 207B. Epigraphic testimonies for C. Numidius
Eros' trip: Bernand 1977: 161–2 offers text and commentary.

long history of sumptuary legislation at Rome. What differentiated republican patterns of circulation from imperial ones was not merely the change
in scale, or the expansion of geographic catchment areas, or the diversifi-
cation of commodities, but the figure of the *princeps* – working through a
legal-political apparatus and with the aid of an emergent imperial bureau-
cracy (managed in part by correspondence on papyrus) to exert control
over practices of appropriation.

How the apparatus of empire nourished itself on *longue durée* discourses
of ideological legitimation is the theme of Daniels' chapter, which studies
the traffic in Hercules in the Iberian Peninsula before and after the Roman
conquest. Daniels trains her sights on the traffic of iconographies on coins,
the single most ubiquitous and quantitatively prolific medium of communication to circulate in the Greco-Roman Mediterranean.[23] Her contribution posits that Roman imperial appropriations of Hercules intersected
with a "long conversation" about the god reaching back to the Early Iron
Age. Well before the consolidation of Roman power in what became
Hispania, the region had seen the rise of a hybridizing cultic discourse
centered on Herakles/Melqart, with indigenous populations as well as
Greek and Punic merchants and soldiers all responsible for the discourse's
shaping. After Hispania's incorporation as a Roman province, the cities of
southern Spain remained steeped in this discourse, but Roman forces and
concepts traveling to the province now interacted with it and enriched its
contents. Rome's own lengthy history of Herculean mythopoiesis would
come to inflect the significations attached to imperial-era Spanish coin
issues: further proof of the fact, stressed in the contributions and response
for Part I of this volume, that Rome's appropriation of the subordinated
Other not infrequently entailed the reappropriation of its own past.

Throughout her exploration of how an idiom (Hercules-speak) and a
medium (the coin) came to collaborate in the formulation of imperial
identities, Daniels steers clear of container thinking – a move that puts this
contribution in the company of recent work on globalization and circulation.[24] Another strength of Daniels' contribution is its (de)territorialization
of the divine under the sign of empire; from itinerant hero-god of an
expansionist city-state, Hercules is repurposed to accommodate a globalizing imperial system, at the head of which stood a *princeps* whose ability to

---

[23] By the early first century BCE, hundreds of millions of Roman silver coins were in circulation:
Hopkins 1980: 109 fig. 2 (extrapolating from the work of Michael Crawford); large-scale production
continued well into the High Empire. Noreña's (2011) study of imperial messaging on coins – cited
by Daniels – relies on a database of over 185,000 coins minted between 69 and 235 CE.

[24] E.g., Pitts' (2015) study of globalization and circulation in the Roman world.

travel and govern vast spaces was figured in Herculean terms.[25] This figuration did not come about strictly through a top-down process, as Daniels reminds us; it was local magistrates who minted coins, local residents who set up inscriptions to Hercules. Lest these individual decisions be construed as mere foam on the Braudelian sea, Daniels's exposition of statics and dynamics shows how thinking with the notion of circulation can yield a more satisfying perspective on the relation of the micro- to the macro-historical; and her conclusion articulates and problematizes the tension – regularly on display in the preceding three chapters – between the fantasies of cultural stability and the realities of constant (even vertiginous) movements of cargo.[26] Bearing in mind Marshall McLuhan's insistence on the medium as message, we might add that the extraction of the precious metal minted to create the medium structured connectivities as well, with political and economic destinies both in Rome and in Spain yoked to the production and transfer of metallic wealth.[27]

If, as I suggested earlier in connection with Myers, circulation was a process over and through which imperial power was exercised, it is crucial to acknowledge the pushback that circulation triggered. Roman bodies circulated in the face of military resistance: between indigenous opposition, the rebel operations of Sertorius, and the campaigns of the civil wars and early Principate, Hispania would drain blood and money for two centuries.[28] Romanizing commemorative practices circulated in the face of local adaptation and resistance: Daniels' Punicizing south Iberian tombs on one side of the Straits of Gibraltar, Libyan and Numidian funerary architecture on the other.[29] At the opposite end of the great pond, even the circulation of cheap items such as fir cones and broken pottery could become a flashpoint for contention among religious and ethnic groups striving to articulate their identities in deliberate counterpoint to Helleno/Romanization.[30] The global circulation of cargo spurred investment in and intensification of the *local*,[31] sometimes defended to the death.

[25] My use of "deterritorialization" here has in mind not so much Deleuze and Guattari's original application in *Anti-Oedipus* but its afterlife in cultural anthropology.

[26] On a microhistorical approach to the study of cargo note Loar's response in this volume.

[27] For the wealth generated by precious metal extraction in Spain and the unique career of Sextus Marius, see Champlin 2015.

[28] Plut. *Sert.* 9.3–5 on the rebel's Herculean gesture: a journey to Antaeus' tomb.

[29] Reading the latter as "resistance": Benabou 1974.

[30] The evidence of the Mishnah: *Abodah Zarah* I.5–9 on prohibitions against selling fir-cones and other materials to Gentiles (for fear that they might be used in sacrifice); 2.3 on the banning not only of wine but of "Hadrianic earthenware" (shards used to flavor water); generally on the Mishnah's treatment of artifacts, see Balberg 2015.

[31] Local Greek identities in a globalized Roman world: Whitmarsh 2010.

Where do we go from here? Much like Tennyson's Ulysses, cargo will not rest – it must drink life to the lees. Although the lines of argument plotted by each of the contributions could be pursued along several different tracks, I will close with some thoughts on the liquid and aromatic vectors of circulation through which the cargoes under discussion in this unit were transformed into new forms.[32] Let us take water, the *sine qua non* for the shipping of goods across the Mediterranean. Following in the footsteps of their Greek and Near Eastern predecessors, Romans exhibited an imperializing obsession with manipulating water's circulation; hydraulic engineering (and its extravagant demands on manpower) went hand in hand with discourses of hydrological mastery. Under the late Republic and early Empire, the waters of the Mediterranean and adjacent seas were exploited with accelerating intensity, and the results of that exploitation – fish, shellfish, coral, salt, sea silk, pearls – routed directly into commercial and literary circulation.[33] Another liquid has something to offer us as well: blood, especially as metaphorized to signify relations of kinship. Long studied for their aetiological and political premises, claims of lineage and consanguinity in Greek and Latin literature readily lend themselves to being read through the lens of circulation.[34] Legible through this same lens is the sacro-medical complex through which menstrual blood came to be disciplined and its significations renegotiated. With an eye to the modern semantics of blood – and in a different methodological vein – the circulation paradigm could incorporate recent applications of DNA analysis and isotope testing, which have greatly enhanced our understanding of human migration in the Roman Mediterranean.[35]

Not only liquids but vapors and odors circulated throughout the Roman *oikoumene*. At Rome itself among the most pervasive smells was that of urine, wafting from tanned hides; but the smell might even emanate from

---

[32] For which we await *Liquid Continents*, the follow-up to Horden & Purcell 2000: Liquids in the "savage biology" of Roman culture: Bettini 2016.

[33] The metaphorization of water in connection with discourses of literary appropriation is explored by Nichols in this volume. Synthesizing history of Greco-Roman waterworks: Mithen 2012: 75–149. The discursive articulation of hydraulic engineering to hydrological mastery at Rome: Purcell 1996. For the ecological devastation of this engineering note (purely, e.g.) the report that Lucius Licinius Lucullus had a mountain near Naples removed for the tidal irrigation of his fishponds: Varro *RR* 3.17.9. Technologies of marine exploitation: Marzano 2013.

[34] Anidjar 2014 assigns a medieval origin to the notion of kinship as blood, but I am skeptical. For the status of blood in Roman gentilician discourse, see Smith 2006: 32–3 and *passim*.

[35] Menstrual blood in Roman culture: Lennon 2014: 81–8. Ancient Italy's population genetics: Brisighelli *et al.* 2009; Di Gaetano *et al.* 2009; see now Killgrove & Montgomery 2016 on the evidence for human migration to Rome culled from isotope analysis of Roman skeletons.

the mouth of some parvenu provincial applying it as mouthwash.[36] Likewise ubiquitous was the stench of feces, whose proper routing through and disposal beyond the city earned a place in law and whose proper movement through and expulsion from the body earned a place in medical and religious texts.[37] The Romans had "mobility aids": for Cato the Elder, some homegrown cabbage sufficed (no surprise), and its consumption facilitated the discharge of medicinally valuable urine; but by the time of Pliny the Elder, bowel discomfort was being alleviated with Cyprian *ladanum* and powdered gentian – items snared in the web of Rome's ecological imperialism.[38] In the century after Pliny, anxieties about the proper circulation of fecal matter would be documented in Artemidorus' analysis of dreamscapes; the *Oneirocritica* reports a positive outcome for those who dream of defecating in riverine or marshland environments, since such dreams signified that the defecator would "unload (his) cargo without shame" (χωρὶς αἰσχύνης ἀποφορτίσασθαι).[39]

In the spirit of Sarah Silverman's deadpan rendition of the infamous "Aristocrats" joke, we might say that cargo is all about timing; for Hellenistic Greeks and for the imperializing Romans who conquered them, the circulation of excrement left an indelible mark on all kinds of daily and seasonal rhythms.[40] But the more consequential point is that Rome's continuous circulation and consumption of cargo cannot be decoupled from circuits of waste. To adapt one of Lacan's most arresting juxtapositions, Rome was its spoils – the Cloaca Maxima.[41]

---

[36] Hide tanning: Juv. *Sat.* 14.201–5 for fullers and Suet. *Vesp.* 23.3 on the *urinae vectigal*, with discussion in Flohr & Wilson 2011: 153–4; for these and other "disreputable professions" see Bond 2016. The notorious (Celtiberian) dental regimen satirized in Catullus 39: Katz 2000.

[37] On smells in antiquity see the chapters in Bradley 2015, especially Morley on Rome. The regulation of feces disposal: *CIL* I² 838–9 and 2981; 4.7038 and 10488; 6.3823; 9.782. *Q(uando) St(ercum) D (elatum) F(as)* on the *fasti*: Varro *LL* 6.32; Festus 466L.; cf. Ov. *Fast.* 6.713–4. Sewage infrastructure: Hodge 2002: 270–2.

[38] I borrow the term "ecological imperialism" from Crosby 2004. On cabbage consumption and good urine see Cato *De agricultura* 156–7, with Courtney 1999: 68–9 on Catonian appropriation of Greek medical literature. *Ladanum* and gentian: Pliny *NH* 26.47; *NH* 25.34 on the derivation of gentian's name from the Illyrian King Genthius who was defeated in 168 BCE and subsequently paraded in Rome; for botanical imperialism in the *NH* see Pollard 2009 and now Manolaraki 2015.

[39] Artemidorus *Oneir.* 2.27, with Harris-McCoy 2012 *ad loc.* on the cargo resonances of the verb ἀποφορτίσασθαι.

[40] A *hetaira*'s wittily phrased refusal to offer anal sex in the morning: Machon fr. 16 327–32 Gow with Brioso 1991. "Dung therapy" in ancient medical texts: von Staden 1992. The commodification of pigeon droppings: *IG* XI² 161 and 162 on their sale in Hellenistic Delos; repeated references to the quality of pigeon guano in Roman authors (e.g., Cato *De agricultura* 36; Varro *RR* 1.38.1–2); cf. O'Donnell 1993 on nineteenth-century American and British "guano imperialism."

[41] Quotation and elaboration in Laporte 2000: 56. For illustration of Laporte's aphorism "the State is the Sewer," see Gowers 1995 on the representation of the Cloaca Maxima in Latin literature.

Bibliography

Aberson, M. (1994). *Temples votifs et butin de guerre dans la Rome républicaine*, Rome: Institut Suisse de Rome.

Adams, C. & Laurence, R., eds. (2001). *Travel and Geography in the Roman Empire*, London: Routledge.

Adams, J. N. (1999). "The poets of Bu Njem: language, culture and the centurionate." *JRS*, 89, 109–34.

(2003). *Bilingualism and the Latin Language*, Cambridge University Press.

Adams, N. K. (2013). "Influences from abroad: the evidence from textiles." In J. van der Vliet & J. L. Hagen, eds., *Qasr Ibrim: Between Egypt and Africa*. Leuven: Peeters, pp. 65–81.

Adams, W. Y. (1977). *Nubia: Corridor to Africa*, Princeton University Press.

(1983). "Primis and the 'Aethiopian' frontier." *JARCE*, 20, 93–104.

(1985). "Ptolemaic and Roman occupation at Qasr Ibrim." In F. Geus & F. Thill, eds., *Mélanges offerts à Jean Vercoutter*. Paris: Editions Recherche sur les Civilisations, pp. 9–17.

(2013a). "Nubian history in global perspective: an anthropological view." In J. van der Vliet & J. L. Hagen, eds., *Qasr Ibrim: Between Egypt and Africa*. Leuven: Peeters, pp. 23–44.

(2013b). "Qasr Ibrim: connecting the dots." In J. van der Vliet & J. L. Hagen, eds., *Qasr Ibrim: Between Egypt and Africa*. Leuven: Peeters, pp. 45–63.

Adams, W. Y., Alexander, J. A., & Allen, R. (1983). "Qasr Ibrim 1980 and 1982." *JEA*, 69, 43–60.

Albèri Auber, P. (2011–2). "L'obelisco di Augusto in Campo Marzio e la sua linea meridiana. Aggiornamenti e proposte." *RendPontAcc*, 84, 447–579.

Aldrete, G. & Mattingly, D. (2010). "Feeding the city: the organization, operation, and scale of the supply system for Rome." In D. S. Potter & D. J. Mattingly, eds., *Life, Death, and Entertainment in the Roman Empire*, 2nd edn. Ann Arbor: University of Michigan Press, pp. 195–228.

Alexander, J. A. (1988). "The Saharan divide in the Nile Valley: the evidence from Qasr Ibrim." *African Archaeological Review*, 6, 73–90.

Alfaro Asins, C. (1988). *Las monedas de Gadir–Gades*, Madrid: Fundación para el Fomento de los Estudios Numismáticos.

(1997). "Las emisiones feno-púnicas." In C. Alfaro Asins, A. Arévalo González, & M. Campo Díaz, eds., *Historia monetaria de Hispania antigua*. Madrid: Jesús Vico, pp. 50–115.

Allen, R. E. (1983). *The Attalid Kingdom: A Constitutional History*, Oxford: Clarendon Press.

Allen, W. (1955). "The British epics of Quintus and Marcus Cicero." *TAPA*, 86, 143–59.

Anderson, B. (2006). *Imagined Communities: Reflections on the Origin and Spread of Nationalism*, 2nd edn, London: Verso.

Anderson, R. D. & Adams, W. Y. (1979). "Qasr Ibrim 1978." *JEA*, 65, 30–41.

Anderson, R. D., Parsons, P., & Nisbet, R. (1979). "Elegiacs by Gallus from Qasr Ibrim." *JRS*, 69, 125–55.

Anderson, W. S. (1993). *Barbarian Play: Plautus' Roman Comedy*, University of Toronto Press.

Ando, C. (2000). *Imperial Ideology and Provincial Loyalty in the Roman Empire*, Berkeley and Los Angeles: University of California Press.

Anidjar, G. (2014). *Blood: A Critique of Christianity*, New York: Columbia University Press.

Appadurai, A. (1986). "Introduction: commodities and the politics of value." In A. Appadurai, ed., *The Social Life of Things: Commodities in Cultural Perspective*. Cambridge University Press, pp. 3–63.

Arata, F. P. (2005). *Opere d'arte dal mare: testimonianze archeologiche subacquee del trasporto e del commercio marittimo di prodotti artistici*, Rome: Istituto poligrafico e Zecca dello Stato, Libreria dello Stato.

Armstrong, R. (2009). "Against nature? Some Augustan responses to man-made marvels." In P. Hardie, ed., *Paradox and the Marvellous in Augustan Literature and Culture*. Oxford University Press, pp. 75–95.

Arnaud, P. (2005). *Les routes de la navigation antique: itinéraires en Méditerranée*, Paris: Errance.

(2011). "Sailing 90° from the Wind: Norm or Exception." In W. V. Harris & K. Iara, eds., *Maritime Technology in the Ancient Economy: Ship-Design and Navigation*. Portsmouth: JRA Supplementary Series No. 84, pp. 147–60.

Arnold, D. (1999). *Temples of the Last Pharaohs*, Oxford University Press.

(2003). *The Encyclopedia of Ancient Egyptian Architecture*, N. & H. Strudwick, eds., S. H. Gardiner and H. Strudwick, trans., Princeton University Press.

Arnott, W. G. (2004). "Alexis, Greek New Comedy and Plautus' *Poenulus*." In T. Baier, ed., *Studien zu Plautus' Poenulus*. Tübingen: Gunter Narr, pp. 61–92.

Arya, D. (2002). "The goddess Fortuna in imperial Rome: cult, art, text," PhD diss., The University of Texas at Austin.

Asso, P., ed. (2011). *Brill's Companion to Lucan*, Leiden: Brill.

Aubert, J.-J. (1994). *Business Managers in Ancient Rome: A Social and Economic Study of Institores, 200 BC–AD 250*, Leiden: Brill.

(2007). "Dealing with the abyss: the nature and purpose of the Rhodian sea-law on jettison (*Lex Rhodia de Iactu*, D 14.2) and the making of Justinian's

Digest." In J. Cairns & P. du Plessis, eds., *Beyond Dogmatics: Law and Society in the Roman World.* Edinburgh University Press, pp. 157–72.

Aubet, M. E. (2001). *The Phoenicians and the West: Politics, Colonies and Trade,* 2nd edn, M. Turton, trans., Cambridge University Press.

Avronidaki, C. (2012). "The glassware." In N. Kaltsas, E. Vlachogianni, & P. Bouyia, eds., *The Antikythera Shipwreck: The Ship, the Treasures, the Mechanism; National Archaeological Museum, April 2012–April 2013.* Athens: Kapon Editions, pp. 132–45.

Badian, E. (1972). *Publicans and Sinners: Private Enterprise in the Service of the Roman Republic,* Ithaca: Cornell University Press.

Baílon García, M. (2012). "El culto a *Fortuna Dea* en *Hispania.* Contribución a la romanización del territorio." *Antesteria,* 1, 51–61.

Baines, J. & Whitehouse, H. (2005). "Ägyptische Hieroglyphen in der Kaiserstadt Rom." In H. Beck, P. Bol, & M. Bückling, eds., *Ägypten, Griechenland, Rom. Abwehr und Berührung.* Frankfurt: Das Städel, pp. 405–15.

Balberg, M. (2015) "Artifact." In C.M. Chin & M. Vidas, eds., *Late Antique Knowing: Explorations in Intellectual History.* Oakland: University of California Press, pp. 17–35.

Baldwin, B. (1990). "The date, identity and career of Vitruvius." *Latomus,* 49(2), 425–34.

Ballaira, G. (1993). *Esempi di scrittura latina dell' età romana.* Vol. I: *Dal III–II secolo a.C. al I secolo d.C.,* Turin: Edizioni dell' Orso.

Barbiero, E. (2014). *"Reading between the lines: letters in Plautus,"* PhD diss., University of Toronto.

Barchiesi, A. (1981). "Notizie sul 'nuovo Gallo.'" *A&R,* 23, 153–66.
  (1999). "Representations of suffering and interpretation in the *Aeneid.*" In P. Hardie, ed., *Virgil, Critical Assessments.* Vol. III: *The Aeneid.* London: Routledge, pp. 324–44.
  (2005a). "Centre and periphery." In S. J. Harrison, ed., *A Companion to Latin Literature.* Malden: Blackwell, pp. 394–405.
  (2005b). "Learned eyes: poets, viewers, image makers." In K. Galinsky, ed., *The Cambridge Companion to the Age of Augustus.* Cambridge University Press, pp. 281–305.

Barkan, L. (2001). *Unearthing the Past: Archaeology and Aesthetics in the Making of Renaissance Culture,* New Haven: Yale University Press.

Barnes, J. (1997). "Roman Aristotle." In J. Barnes & M. Griffin, eds., *Philosophia Togata II: Plato and Aristotle at Rome.* Oxford University Press, pp. 1–69.

Barresi, M. (1989). "Vitruvio e Plinio il Vecchio: per una lettura comparata." *Quaderni di storia dell'archittetura e restauro,* 1, 43–50.

Barry, F. (2011). "The mouth of truth and the Forum Boarium: Oceanus, Hercules, and Hadrian." *The Art Bulletin,* 93(1), 7–37.

Barsby, J. (1995). "Plautus' *Pseudolus* as improvisatory drama." In L. Benz, E. Stärk, & G. Vogt-Spira, eds., *Plautus und die Tradition des Stegreifspiels.* Tübingen: Gunter Narr, pp. 55–70.

Bartman, E. (2002). "Eros's flame: images of sexy Boys in Roman ideal sculpture." In E. K. Gazda, ed., *The Ancient Art of Emulation: Studies in Artistic Originality and Tradition from the Present to Classical Antiquity*. Memoirs of the American Academy in Rome, Supplementary Vol. I. Ann Arbor: University of Michigan Press, pp. 249–71.

Bar-Yosef, O. & Van Peer, P. (2009). "The chaîne opératoire approach in Middle Paleolithic archaeology." *CurrAnthr*, 50, 103–31.

Baselitz, G. *et al.* (2012). "Notes from the field: Appropriation: back then, in between, and today." *The Art Bulletin*, 94 (2), 166–86.

Batty, R. (2000). "Mela's Phoenician geography." *JRA*, 90, 70–94.

Baudoin, C., Liou, B., & Long, L. (1994). *Une cargaison de bronzes hellénistiques: l'épave "Fourmigue C" à Golfe–Juan*, Paris: CNRS.

Beacham, R. C. (1991). *The Roman Theatre and Its Audience*, London: Routledge.

Beard, M. (2007). *The Roman Triumph*, Cambridge, MA: Harvard University Press.

  (2014). *Laughter in Ancient Rome: On Joking, Tickling, and Cracking Up*, Berkeley: University of California Press.

Beck, D. (2007). "Ecphrasis, interpretation, and audience in *Aeneid* 1 and *Odyssey* 8." *AJP*, 128(4), 533–49.

Beck, H. (2005). *Karriere und Hierarchie: Die römische Aristokratie und die Anfänge des cursus honorum in der mittleren Republik*, Berlin: Akademie Verlag.

Beck, H., Bol, P., & Bückling, M., eds. (2005). *Ägypten, Griechenland, Rom. Abwehr und Berührung*, Frankfurt: Das Städel.

Beltrame, C. (2000). "A review of the Roman wreck of Spargi (Sassari/Italy): an evidence of the commerce of luxurious furniture during Late-Republican age." In H. von Schmettow, ed., *Schutz des Kulturerbes unter Wasser: Veränderungen europäischer Lebenskultur durch Fluß- und Seehandel: Beiträge zum Internationalen Kongreß für Unterwasserarchäologie (IKUWA '99), 18–21. Februar 1999 in Sassnitz auf Rügen*. Lübstorf: Archäologisches Landesmuseum für Mecklenburg-Vorpommern, pp. 155–62.

Beltrame, C., Gaddi, D., & Parizzi, S. (2011). "A presumed hydraulic apparatus for the transport of live fish, found on the Roman wreck at Grado, Italy." *IJNA*, 40(2), 274–82.

Benabou, M. (1974). "Résistance et romanisation en Afrique du Nord sous le Haut Empire." In D.M. Pippidi, ed., *Assimilation et résistance à la culture gréco-romaine dans le monde ancien*. Bucharest/Paris: Belles Lettres, pp. 367–75.

Bencivenni, A. (2014). "The king's words: Hellenistic royal Letters in inscriptions." In K. Radner, ed., *State Correspondence in the Ancient World: from New Kingdom Egypt to the Roman Empire*. Oxford University Press, pp. 141–71.

Benjamin, W. (1968). "Theses on the philosophy of history." In H. Arendt, ed., H. Zohn, trans., *Illuminations*. New York: Schocken Books, pp. 253–64.

Benz, L. (1995). "Die römisch–italische Stegreifspieltradition zur Zeit der Palliata." In L. Benz, E. Stärk, & G. Vogt-Spira, eds., *Plautus und die Tradition des Stegreifspiels*. Tübingen: Gunter Narr, pp. 139–54.

Béranger, J. (1953). *Récherches sur l'aspect idéologique du principat*, Schweizerische Beiträge zur Altertumwissenschaft 6, Basel: Friedrich Reinhardt.

Bérard, F. (2012). "Les corporations de transport fluvial à Lyon à l'époque romaine." In M. Dondin-Payre & N. Tran, eds., *Collegia: Le phénomène associatif dans l'Occident romain*. Bordeaux: Ausonius Éditions, pp. 135–54.

Beresford, J. (2013). *The Ancient Sailing Season*, Boston: Brill.

Bergmann, B. (1995). "Greek masterpieces and Roman recreative fictions." *HSCP*, 97, 79–120.

Bernand, A. (1977). *Pan du désert*, Leiden: Brill.

Bernstein, A. L. [1923] (1984). "The facts of vaudeville." In C. W. Stein, ed., *American Vaudeville as Seen by its Contemporaries*. New York: Alfred A. Knopf, pp. 124–30. Orig. pub. *Equity News* 9: 33–40.

Berry, C. (1994). *The Idea of Luxury: A Conceptual and Historical Investigation*, Cambridge University Press.

Bettini, M. (2016) "Per una 'biologie sauvage' dei Romani. Prime proposte." *EuGeStA*, 6, 66–85.

Betzig, L. (1992). "Roman polygyny." *Ethology and Sociobiology*, 13, 309–49.

Beykan, M. (1988). "The marble architectural elements in export-form from the Şile shipwreck." In N. Herz & M. Waelkens, eds., *Classical Marble: Geochemistry, Technology, Trade*. Boston: Klewer Academic Publishers, pp. 127–37.

Bhabha, H. (2004). *The Location of Culture*, 2nd edn, London: Routledge.

Biggs, T. (2017). "*Primus Romanorum*: Origin Stories, Fictions of Primacy, and the First Punic War." *CP*, 112 (3), 350–67.

Birley, A.R. (2009). "Some writing-tablets excavated at Vindolanda in 2001, 2002 and 2003." *ZPE*, 170, 265–9.

Bispham, E. (2008). Review of *Appius Claudius Caecus. La République accomplie*, by M. Humm, *JRS*, 98, 188–9.

Blackman, D. (2008). "Sea transport, part 2: harbors." In J. Oleson, ed., *Oxford Handbook of Engineering and Technology in the Classical World*. Oxford University Press, pp. 638–70.

Blänsdorf, J. (1995). "Reste der Improvisation in den plautinischen Eingangsszenen." In L. Benz, E. Stärk, & G. Vogt-Spira, eds., *Plautus und die Tradition des Stegreifspiels*. Tübingen: Gunter Narr, pp. 3–21.

Bleckmann, B. (2002). *Die römische Nobilität im Ersten Punischen Krieg: Untersuchungen zur aristokratischen Konkurrenz in der Republik*, Berlin: Akademie Verlag.

Bloch, M. (1977). "The past and the present in the present." *Man*, New Series 12(2), 278–92.

Boas, G., trans. (1993). *The Hieroglyphics of Horapollo*, new edn, Princeton University Press.

Boatwright, M. T. *et al.* (2011). *The Romans: from Village to Empire: A History of Rome from Earliest Times to the End of the Western Empire*, 2nd edn, New York: Oxford University Press.

Bodel, J. (2005). "*Caveat emptor*: towards a study of Roman slave-traders." *JRA*, 18(5), 181–95.

(2009). "'Sacred dedications': a problem of definitions." In J. Bodel & M. Kajava, eds., *Dediche sacre nel mondo greco-romano. Diffusione, funzioni, tipologie.* Rome: Institutum Romanum Finlandiae, pp. 17–30.

Boetto, G. (2006). "Roman techniques for the transport and conservation of fish: the case of the Fiumicino 5 wreck." In L. Blue & F. Hocker, eds., *Connected by the sea. Proceedings of the Tenth International Symposium on Boat and Ship Archaeology, Roskilde 2003.* Oxford: Oxbow, pp. 123–9.

(2012). "Les épaves comme sources pour l'étude de la navigation et des routes commerciales: une approche méthodologique." In S. Keay, ed., *Rome, Portus, and the Mediterranean.* London: British School at Rome, pp. 153–73.

Bol, P. (1972). *Die Skulpturen des Schiffsfundes von Antikythera*, Berlin: Gebr. Mann.

Bond, S. (2016). *Trade and Taboo: Disreputable Professions in the Roman Mediterranean*, Ann Arbor: University of Michigan Press.

Bonnet, C. (1986). "Le cult de Melqart à Carthage. Un cas de conservatisme religieux." In C. Bonnet, E. Lipiński, & P. Marchetti, eds., *Religio Phoenicia: Studia Phoenicia 4.* Namur: Peeters, pp. 209–22.

(1988). *Melqart: cultes et mythes de l'Héraclès tyrien en Méditerranée*, Leuven and Namur: Peeters. – (1992). "Héraclès en Orient: interpretation et syncrétismes." In C. Bonnet & C. Jourdain-Annequin, eds., *Héraclès: D'une rive à l'autre de la Méditerranée. Bilan et perspectives.* Brussels: Institut Belge de Rome, pp. 165–98.

(2007). "Melqart." In *Iconography of Deities and Demons in the Ancient Near East: electronic pre–publications.* Zurich: Swiss National Science Foundation. www.religionswissenschaft.uzh.ch/idd/prepublications/e_idd_melqart.pdf. Last accessed August 2014.

Bonnet, C. & Bricault, L. (2016). Quand les dieux voyagent: cultes et mythes en mouvement dans l'espace méditerranéen antique, Genève: Labor et Fides.

Bonnet, C. & Jourdain-Annequin, C., eds. (1992). *Héraclès d'une rive à l'autre de la Méditerranée: Bilan et perspectives*, Brussels: Institut Belge de Rome.

Borbein, A. (1975). "Die Ara Pacis Augustae: Geschichtliche Wirklichkeit und Programm." *JdI*, 90, 242–66.

Borchardt, L. (1938). *Ägyptische Tempel mit Umgang*, Beiträge zur Ägyptischen Bauforschung und Altertumskunde, Heft 2, Cairo: Selbstverlag.

Boucher, J. P. (1966). *Caius Cornélius Gallus*, Paris: Les Belles Lettres.

Bounegru, O. (2006). *Trafiquants et navigateurs sur le bas Danube et dans le Pont Gauche à l'époque romaine*, Wiesbaden: Harrassowitz.

Bourdieu, P. (1991). *Language and Symbolic Power*, G. Raymond and M. Adamson, trans., Cambridge, MA: Harvard University Press.

Bouyia, P. (2012a). "Maritime commerce and luxury in the age of Cicero." In N. Kaltsas, E. Vlachogianni, & P. Bouyia, eds., *The Antikythera Shipwreck: The Ship, The Treasures, The Mechanism; National Archaeological Museum, April 2012–April 2013.* Athens: Kapon Editions, pp. 287–92.

(2012b). "The ship." In N. Kaltsas, E. Vlachogianni, & P. Bouyia, eds., *The Antikythera Shipwreck: The Ship, The Treasures, The Mechanism; National Archaeological Museum, April 2012–April 2013.* Athens: Kapon Editions, pp. 36–49.

Bowditch, P. L. (2011). "Tibullus and Egypt: a postcolonial reading of Elegy 1.7." *Arethusa*, 44(1), 89–122.

Bowersock, G.W. (1998). *Roman Arabia*, Cambridge, MA: Harvard University Press.

Bowman, A. K. (1994). *Life and Letters on the Roman Frontier: Vindolanda and its People*, London: British Museum Press.

Bowman, A. K. & Rathbone, D. (1992). "Cities and administration in Roman Egypt." *JRS*, 82, 107–27.

Boyd, B. (1995). "*Non enarrabile textum*: ecphrastic trespass and narrative ambiguity in the *Aeneid*." *Vergilius*, 41, 71–90.

Bradley, K. (1994). *Slavery and Society at Rome*, Cambridge University Press.

Bradley, M. (2010). "Introduction: approaches to classics and imperialism." In M. Bradley, ed., *Classics and Imperialism in the British Empire*. Cambridge University Press, pp. 1–25.

ed. (2015). *Smell and the Ancient Senses*, London and New York: Routledge.

Braudel, F. [1958] (1987). "Histoire et sciences sociales: la longue durée." *Réseaux*, 5(27), 7–37. Orig. pub. *Annales. Histoire, Sciences Sociales*, 13(4), 725–53.

Braund, S. M. (2012). "Praise and protreptic in Early Imperial panegyric: Cicero, Seneca, Pliny." In R. Rees, ed., *Latin Panegyric*. Oxford University Press, pp. 85–108.

Bravi, A. (2012). *Ornamenta urbis. Opere d'arte greche negli spazi romani*, Bari: Edipuglia.

Brenk, B. (1987). "*Spolia* from Constantine to Charlemagne: aesthetics versus ideology." In *Dumbarton Oaks Papers 41, Studies on Art and Archaeology in Honor of Ernst Kitzinger on His Seventy–Fifth Birthday*. Washington, D.C.: Dumbarton Oaks Research Library and Collection, pp. 103–9.

Bricault, L., Versluys, M. J., & Meyboom, P. G. P., eds. (2007). *Nile into Tiber: Egypt in the Roman World*, Leiden and Boston: Brill.

Bright, D. (1980). *Elaborate Disarray: The Nature of Statius' Silvae*, Meisenheim am Glan: Hain.

Brilliant, R. (1982). "I piedistalli del giardino di Boboli: spolia in se, spolia in re." *Prospettiva*, 31, 2–17.

(1999). "'Let the trumpets roar!' The Roman triumph." In B. Bergmann & C. Kondoleon, eds., *The Art of Ancient Spectacle*. Washington, DC: National Gallery of Art, pp. 221–30.

(2011). "Authenticity and alienation." In R. Brilliant & D. Kinney, eds., *Reuse Value: Spolia and Appropriation in Art and Architecture, from Constantine to Sherrie Levine*. Farnham: Ashgate, pp. 67–177.

Brilliant, R. & Kinney, D. (2011). *Reuse Value: Spolia and Appropriation in Art and Architecture, from Constantine to Sherrie Levine*, Farnham: Ashgate.

Brink, C. O. (1972). "Ennius and the Hellenistic worship of Homer." *American Journal of Philology*, 93(4), 547–67.

Brioso, M. (1991). "Machon, fr. XVI 327–332 Gow." *Quaderni Urbinati di cultura classica*, 39(3), 115–8.

Brisighelli, F., *et al.* (2009). "The Etruscan timeline: a recent Anatolian connection." *European Journal of Human Genetics*, 17, 693–96.

Broekaert, W. (2008). "*Creatio ex nihilo*? The origin of the *corpora nauiculariorum* reconsidered." *Latomus*, 67, 692–706.

(2013). *Navicularii et negotiantes: A Prosopographical Study of Roman Merchants and Shippers*, Rahden/Westfalen: Verlag Marie Leidorf

Broodbank, C. (2013). *The Making of the Middle Sea: A History of the Mediterranean from the Beginning to the Emergence of the Classical World*, London: Thames and Hudson.

Broughton, T. S. (1951–2). *The Magistrates of the Roman Republic*, 2 vols., New York: American Philological Association.

Brown, P. G. McC. (2002). "Actors and actor-managers at Rome in the time of Plautus and Terence." In P. Easterling & E. Hall, eds., *Greek and Roman Actors: Aspects of an Ancient Profession*. Cambridge University Press, pp. 225–37.

Brughmans, T. (2010). "Connecting the dots: towards archaeological network analysis." *OJA*, 29(3), 277–303.

Brun, A. & Castelli, C. (2013). "The nature of luxury: a consumer perspective." *International Journal of Retail & Distribution Management*, 41(11/12), 823–47.

Brunt, P. A. (1980). "On historical fragments and epitomes." *CQ*, 30(2), 477–94.

Buchner, E. (1982). *Die Sonnenuhr des Augustus: Nachdruck aus RM 1976 und 1980 und Nachtrag über die Ausgrabung 1980/1981*, Mainz: Philipp von Zabern.

Budge, E. A. W. (1926). *Cleopatra's Needles and Other Egyptian Obelisks: A Series of Descriptions of All the Important Inscribed Obelisks, with Hieroglyphic Texts, Translations, etc.*, London: Religious Tract Society.

Burnett, A. (1989). "The beginnings of Roman coinage." *AIIN*, 33, 33–64.

Burstein, S. M. (1979). "The Nubian campaigns of C. Petronius and George Reisner's Second Meroitic kingdom of Napata." *ZÄS*, 106, 95–105.

(2004). "Rome and Kush: a new interpretation." In T. Kendall, ed., *Nubian Studies 1998*. Boston: Northeastern University Press, pp. 13–23.

Cairns, F. (2006). *Sextus Propertius: The Augustan Elegist*, Cambridge University Press.

(2011). "C. Cornelius Gallus and the river Hypanis." *RFIC*, 139, 326–38.

Callebat, L. (2003). "La notion d'*auctoritas* dans le *De architectura* de Vitruve." *Voces*, 14, 113–20.

Callebat, L. & Fleury, P., eds. (1986). *Vitruve: De l'architecture, Livre 10*, with trans. and comm., Paris: Les Belles Lettres.

Callebat, L. & Gros, P., eds. (1999). *Vitruve: De l'architecture, Livre 2*, with trans. and comm., Paris: Les Belles Lettres.

Callegarin, L. (2008). "La côte Mauretanienne et ses relations avec le littoral de la Bétique (fin du IIIe siècle a.C. –1er siècle p.C.)." *Mainake*, 30, 289–328.

Cameron, C. M. (2016). *Captives: How Stolen People Changed The World*, Lincoln: University of Nebraska Press.

Campbell, D. A. (1982). *Greek Lyric Poetry*, 2nd edn, London: Bristol Classical Press.

Campo, M. & Mora, B. (1995). *Las monedas de Malaca*, Madrid: Museo Casa de la Moneda.

Capasso, M. (2003). *Il ritorno di Cornelio Gallo: Il papiro di Qaṣr Ibrîm venticinque anni dopo*, Naples: Graus.

Carey, S. (2003). *Pliny's Catalogue of Culture: Art and Empire in the Natural History*, Oxford University Press.

Carradice, A.I. & Buttrey, T.V. (2007). *The Roman Imperial Coinage, Vol. II part. I. Second Fully Revised Edition. From AD 69 to AD 96, Vespasian to Domitian*, London.

Cartledge, P. (1983). "'Trade and Politics' Revisited: Archaic Greece." In P. Garnsey, K. Hopkins, & C. R. Whittaker, eds., *Trade in the Ancient Economy*. Berkeley: University of California Press, pp. 1–15.

Casson, L. (1989). *The Periplus Maris Erythraei: Text with Introduction, Translation, and Commentary*, Princeton University Press.

(1995). *Ships and Seamanship in the Ancient World*, rev. edn, Baltimore: Johns Hopkins University Press.

Castriota, D. (1995). *The Ara Pacis Augustae and the Imagery of Abundance in Later Greek and Early Roman Imperial Art*, Princeton University Press.

Cébeillac-Gervasoni, M. (2014). "*Quaestor Ostiensis*: une fonction ingrate?" In M. Chiabà ed., *Hoc quoque laboris praemium. Scritti in onore di Gino Bandelli* (Polymnia. Studi di Storia romana, 3). Trieste: Edizioni Università di Trieste, pp. 53–62.

Ceccarelli, P. (2013). *Ancient Greek Letter Writing: A Cultural History (600 BC–150 BC)*, Oxford University Press.

Chassinat, E. & Daumas, F. (1978). *Le Temple de Dendara, 8*, Cairo: Institut Français d'Archéologie Orientale du Caire.

Chaudhuri, P. (2014). "Classical quotation in *Titus Andronicus*." *ELH*, 81(3), 787–810.

Chaves, F. (1998). "The Iberian and Early Roman coinage of Hispania Ulterior Baetica." In S. Keay, ed., *The Archaeology of Early Roman Baetica*. Portsmouth: JRA Supplementary Series No. 29, pp. 145–70.

(1999). "El papel de los 'itálicos' en la amonedación hispana." *Gerión*, 17, 295–315.

Chevreau, E. (2005). "La *lex Rhodia de iactu*: un exemple de la réception d'une institution étrangère dans le droit romain." *The Legal History Review*, 73, 67–80.

Christenson, D. M., ed. (2000). *Plautus: Amphitruo*, Cambridge University Press.

Churchill, J. B. (1999). "*Ex qua quod vellent facerent*: Roman magistrates' authority over *praeda* and *manubiae*." *TAPA*, 129, 85–116.

Ciampini, E. M. (2004). *Gli obelischi iscritti di Roma*, Rome: Poligrafico dello Stato.

Citroni, M. (2006). "The concept of the classical and the canons of model authors in Roman literature." In J. I. Porter, ed., *Classical Pasts*. Princeton University Press, pp. 204–34.

Clarke, K. (1999a). *Between Geography and History: Hellenistic Constructions of the Roman World*, Oxford University Press.

(1999b). "Universal perspectives in historiography." In C. S. Kraus, ed., *The Limits of Historiography: Genre and Narrative in Ancient Historical Texts*. Leiden: Brill, pp. 249–80.

Clauss, J. J. (2010). "From the head of Zeus: the beginnings of Roman literature." In J. J. Clauss & M. Cuypers, eds., *A Companion to Hellenistic Literature*. Chichester, UK: Wiley-Blackwell, pp. 463–78.

Clay, D. (1988). "The archaeology of the temple to Juno in Carthage." *CP*, 83(3), 195–205.

Cleary, V. (1982). "To the victor belong the *spolia*: a study in Vergilian imagery." *Vergilius*, 28, 15–29.

Coarelli, F. (1970–1). "Classe dirigente romana e arti figurative." *DialArch*, 4–5, 241–65.

(1983). "Il commercio delle opere d'arte in età tardo-repubblicana." *DialArch*, 3(1), 45–53.

(1985). *Il Foro Romano*. Vol. 2, *Periodo repubblicano e augusteo*, Rome: Edizioni Quasar.

(1988). *Il Foro Boario: Dalle origini alla fine della repubblica*, Rome: Edizioni Quasar.

(1990). "La *pompé* di Tolomeo Filadelfo e il mosaico nilotico di Palestrina." *Ktema*, 15, 225–51.

(2014). "I quaestores classici e la battaglia delle Egadi." In M. Chiabà, ed., Hoc quoque laboris praemium. *Scritti in onore di Gino Bandelli* (Polymnia. Studi di Storia romana, 3). Trieste: Edizioni Università di Trieste, pp. 99–114.

ed. (2009). *Diuus Vespasianus, il bimillenario dei Flavi*, Rome: Electa.

Coffee, N. (2013). "Intertextuality in Latin poetry." *Oxford Bibliographies*, doi: 10.1093/OBO/9780195389661-0113.

Coleman, K. M. (1986). "The emperor Domitian and literature." *ANRW*, 2.32(5), 3087–115.

Collantes de Terán, F. & Chicarro de Dios, C. (1972–4). "Epigrafia de Munigua (Mulva, Sevilla)." *Archiva Español de Arqueología*, 45–7, 337–409.

Comaroff, J. & Comaroff, J. L. (2012). *Theory from the South, or, How Euro-America Is Evolving Toward Africa*, Boulder: Paradigm Publishers.

Concannon, C. & Mazurek, L. A. (2016). *Across the Corrupting Sea: Post-Braudelian Approaches to the Ancient Eastern Mediterranean*, London and New York: Routledge.

Conlin, D. A. (1997). *The Artists of the Ara Pacis: The Process of Hellenization in Roman Relief Sculpture*, Chapel Hill: University of North Carolina Press.

Cooley, A. E. (2009). *Res Gestae Divi Augusti: Text, Translation, and Commentary*, Cambridge University Press.

Corbett, P. (1986). *The Scurra*, Edinburgh: Scottish Academic Press.

Corcoran, S. (2014). "State correspondence in the Roman Empire: imperial communication from Augustus to Justinian." In K. Radner, ed., *State Correspondence in the Ancient World: from New Kingdom Egypt to the Roman Empire*. Oxford University Press, pp. 172–209.

Cottier, M. & Corbier, M., eds. (2008). *The Customs Law of Asia*, Oxford University Press.

Cotton, H. M. & Geiger, J., eds. (1989). *Masada II: The Yigael Yadim Excavations 1963–1965: Final Reports: The Latin and Greek Documents*, Jerusalem: Hebrew University of Jerusalem Press.

Courrént, M. (2004). "'*Non est mirandum.*' Vitruve et la résistance à l'étonnement." In O. Bianchi, P. Mudry, & O. Thévenaz, eds., *Mirabilia: conceptions et représentations de l'extraordinaire dans le monde antique: actes du colloque international, Lausanne, 20–22 mars 2003.* Bern: Peter Lang, pp. 265–78.

(2011). *De architecti scientia: idée de nature et theorie de l'art dans le De architecture de Vitruve,* Caen: Presses Universitaires de Caen.

Courtney, E. (1990). "Vergil's sixth *Eclogue.*" *QUCC,* n.s. 34(1), 99–112.

(1993). *The Fragmentary Latin Poets,* Oxford: Clarendon Press.

(1995). *Musa Lapidaria: A Selection of Latin Verse Inscriptions,* Atlanta: Scholars Press.

(1999). *Archaic Latin Prose,* Atlanta: Scholars Press.

Crawford, M. H. (1974). *Roman Republican Coinage I,* Cambridge University Press.

(1983). "Roman Imperial coin types and the formation of public opinion." In C.N.L. Brooke *et al.,* eds., *Studies in Numismatic Method Presented to Philip Grierson.* Cambridge University Press, pp. 47–63.

Croisille, J.-M., ed. (1985). *Pline l'Ancien: Histoire naturelle, Livre XXXV,* with trans. and comm., Paris: Les Belles Lettres.

Crosby, A. (2004). *Ecological imperialism: the biological expansion of Europe, 900–1900,* 2nd edn, Cambridge University Press.

Crowther, N. (1983). "C. Cornelius Gallus: his importance in the development of Roman poetry." *ANRW,* 2.30(3), 1622–48.

Cuomo, S. (2011). "Skills and virtues in Vitruvius' book 10." In M. Formisano & H. Böhme, eds., *War in Words: Transformations of War from Antiquity to Clausewitz.* Transformationen der Antike, Bd. 19. Berlin: de Gruyter, pp. 309–32.

Curran, B., *et al.* (2009). *Obelisk: A History,* Cambridge, MA: MIT Press.

Cuvigny, H. (2009). "The finds of papyri: the archaeology of papyrology." In R. Bagnall, ed., *The Oxford Handbook of Papyrology.* Oxford University Press, pp. 30–58.

D'Alton, M. (1993). *The New York Obelisk, or, How Cleopatra's Needle Came to New York and What Happened When It Got There,* New York: Metropolitan Museum of Art.

Daly, L. J. (1979). "The Gallus affair and Augustus' *lex Iulia maiestatis*: a study in historical chronology and causality." *Studies in Latin Literature and Roman History,* 1, 289–311.

Damon, C. (1997). *The Mask of the Parasite: A Pathology of Roman Patronage,* Ann Arbor: University of Michigan Press.

D'Arms, J. (1981). *Commerce and Social Standing in Ancient Rome,* Cambridge, MA: Harvard University Press.

Dart, C. J. & Vervaet, F. J. (2011). "The significance of the naval triumph in Roman history (260–229 BCE)." *ZPE,* 176, 267–80.

Davies, J. (1998). "Ancient economies: models and muddles." In H. Parkins & C. Smith, eds., *Trade, Traders, and the Ancient City.* New York: Routledge, pp. 225–56.

Davies, P. J. E. (2011). "*Aegyptiaca* in Rome: *adventus* and *Romanitas.*" In E. S. Gruen ed., *Cultural Identity in the Ancient Mediterranean.* Los Angeles: Getty Research Institute, pp. 371–87.

282 *Bibliography*

Davis, A. (2011). *Baggy Pants Comedy: Burlesque and the Oral Tradition*, New York: Palgrave Macmillan.

De Angelis, F. (2013). "Introduction: approaches to the movement of ancient Phenomena through time and space." In F. De Angelis, ed., *Regionalism and Globalism in Antiquity*. Leuven: Peeters, pp. 1–12.

de Certeau, M. (1984). *The Practice of Everyday Life*, S. Rendall, trans., Berkeley: University of California Press.

Deichmann, F. W. (1975). *Die Spolien in der spätantiken Architektur*, Munich: Beck.

DeLaine, J. (2002). "The temple of Hadrian at Cyzicus and Roman attitudes to exceptional construction." *PBSR*, 70, 205–30.

Deleuze, G. & Guattari, F. (1987). *A Thousand Plateaus: Capitalism and Schizophrenia*, trans. B. Massumi. Minneapolis: University of Minnesota Press.

Dell'Amico, P. (2011). "Osservazioni riguardanti alcune innovazioni in ambito navale di epoca classica: pregi e difetti." In W. V. Harris & K. Iara, eds., *Maritime Technology in the Ancient Economy: Ship-Design and Navigation*. Portsmouth: JRA Supplementary Series No. 84, pp. 57–82.

DeMarrais, E., Castillo, L. J., & Earle, T. (1996). "Ideology, materialization, and power strategies." *Current Anthropology*, 37(1), 15–31.

Dench, E. (2003). "Beyond Greeks and barbarians: Italy and Sicily in the Hellenistic Age." In A. Erskine, ed., *A Companion to the Hellenistic World*. Oxford: Blackwell, pp. 294–310.

(2005). *Romulus' Asylum: Roman Identities from the Age of Alexander to the Age of Hadrian*, Oxford University Press.

Derda, T. & Lajtar, A. (2012). "Greek and Latin papyri from the Egypt Exploration Society excavations at Qasr Ibrim: a testimony to the Roman army in Upper Egypt and Lower Nubia in the first years of Augustus." In P. Schubert, ed., *Actes du 26e Congrès international de papyrologie, Genève, 16–21 août 2010*. Geneva: Librairie Droz, pp. 183–6.

(2013a). "The Roman occupation of Qasr Ibrim as reflected in the Greek papyri from the site." In J. van der Vliet & J. L. Hagen, eds., *Qasr Ibrim: Between Egypt and Africa*. Leuven: Peeters, pp. 105–10.

(2013b). "P. Qasr Ibrim inv. 80/11: a testimony to Zenodotus' Edition of the *Iliad*?" In R. Ast *et al.*, eds., *Papyrological Texts in Honor of Roger S. Bagnall*. American Studies in Papyrology 53. Durham: The American Society of Papyrologists, pp. 75–8.

Description de l'Égypte, ou recueil des observations et des recherches qui ont été faites en Égypte pendant l'expédition de l'Armée Française (1809), Paris: Imprimerie Imperiale.

de Souza, P. (1999). *Piracy in the Graeco-Roman World*, Cambridge University Press.

De Vos, M. (1980). *L'Egittomania in pitture e mosaici romano-campani della prima età imperiale*. *EPRO* 84, Leiden: Brill.

Dietler, M. (2010). *Archaeologies of Colonialism: Consumption, Entanglement, and Violence in Ancient Mediterranean France*, Berkeley: University of California Press.

Di Gaetano, C., *et al.* (2009). "Differential Greek and Northern African migrations to Sicily are supported by genetic evidence from the Y chromosome." *European Journal of Human Genetics*, 17, 91–9.

Dillon, S. & Welch, K., eds. (2006). *Representations of War in Ancient Rome*, Cambridge University Press.

Dionisotti, A.C. (1998). "On fragments in classical scholarship." In G. W. Most, ed., *Collecting fragments – Fragmente sammeln*. Göttingen: Vandenhoeck & Ruprecht, pp. 1–33.

Dix, T. K. (2000). "The library of Lucullus." *Athenaeum*, 80, 441–64.

Dobres, M. and Robb, J. (2005). "'Doing' agency: introductory remarks on methodology." *Journal of Archaeological Method and Theory*, 12, 159–66.

D'Onofrio, C. (1992). *Gli obelischi di Roma: storia e urbanistica di una città dall'Età Antica al XX Secolo*, Rome: Romana Società Editrice.

duBois, P. (2003). *Slaves and Other Objects*, University of Chicago Press.

Dufallo, B. (2013). *The Captor's Image: Greek Culture in Roman Ecphrasis*, New York: Oxford University Press.

Eckstein, A. M. (2006). *Mediterranean Anarchy, Interstate War, and the Rise of Rome*, Berkeley: University of California Press.

Eden, P. T. (1975). *A Commentary on Virgil: Aeneid VIII*, Leiden: Brill.

Eder, W. (1990). "Augustus and the power of tradition: the Augustan Principate as binding link between Republic and Empire." In K. Raaflaub, M. Toher, & G. W. Bowersock, eds., *Between Republic and Empire: Interpretations of Augustus and His Principate*. Berkeley: University of California Press, pp. 71–122.

Edwards, C. (1996). *Writing Rome: Textual Approaches to the City*, Cambridge University Press.

  (2003). "Incorporating the alien: the art of conquest." In C. Edwards & G. Woolf, eds., *Rome the Cosmopolis*. Cambridge University Press, pp. 44–70.

  ed. (1999). *Roman Presences: Receptions of Rome in European Culture, 1789–1945*, Cambridge University Press.

Edwards, C. & Woolf, G., eds. (2003). *Rome the Cosmopolis*, Cambridge University Press.

Ehrhardt, C. T. H. R. (1984). "Roman coin types and the Roman Republic." *Jahrbuch für Numismatik und Geldgeschichte*, 34, 41–54.

Eichholz, D. E., trans. (1962). *Pliny. Natural History, Volume X: Books 36–37*, Cambridge, MA: Harvard University Press.

Eide, T., *et al.*, eds. (1996). *Fontes Historiae Nubiorum: Textual Sources for the History of the Middle Nile Region Between the Eighth Century BC and the Sixth Century AD*, Vol. II. University of Bergen Press.

  (1998). *Fontes Historiae Nubiorum: Textual Sources for the History of the Middle Nile Region Between the Eighth Century BC and the Sixth Century AD*, Vol. III. University of Bergen Press.

Elliot, J. (2014). *Ennius and the Architecture of the Annales*, Cambridge University Press.

Elsner, J. (1991). "Cult and sculpture: sacrifice in the Ara Pacis Augustae," *JRS*, 81, 50–61.

(2000). "From the culture of spolia to the cult of relics: the Arch of Constantine and the genesis of Late Antique forms." *PBSR*, 68, 149–84.

(2004). "Late Antique art: the problem of the concept and the cumulative aesthetic." In S. Swain & M. Edwards, eds., *Approaching Late Antiquity: The Transformation from Early to Late Empire.* Oxford University Press, pp. 271–309.

(2006). "Classicism in Roman art." In J. I. Porter, ed., *Classical Pasts.* Princeton University Press, pp. 270–97.

Erren, M. (2003). P. Vergilius Maro: *Georgica. Band 2:* Kommentar, Heidelberg: Universitätsverlag Winter.

Esch, A. (1969). "Spolien. Zur Wiederverwendung antiker Baustücke und Skulpturen im mittelalterlichen Italien." *Archiv für Kulturgeschichte*, 51, 1–64.

(2011). "On the reuse of antiquity: the perspectives of the archaeologist and of the historian." In R. Brilliant & D. Kinney, eds., *Reuse Value: Spolia and Appropriation in Art.* Farnham: Ashgate, pp. 13–32.

Etienne, R. & Braun, J. P. (1986). *Ténos I: Le sanctuaire de Poseidon et d'Amphitrite.* BEFAR 263, Athens: École Française d'Athènes; Paris: Diffusion de Boccard.

Fabre-Serris, J. (2008). *Rome, l'Arcadie et la mer des Argonautes*, Villeneuve d'Ascq: Presses Universitaires du Septentrion.

Fairweather, J. (1984). "The 'Gallus Papyrus': a new interpretation." *CQ*, 34, 167–74.

Fane-Saunders, P. (2016). "Pliny the Elder: an early reader of Vitruvius." In P. Sanvito, ed., *Vitruvianism: Origin and Transformations.* Berlin: de Gruyter, pp. 65–81.

Fantham, E. (1996). *Roman Literary Culture: From Cicero to Apuleius*, Baltimore: Johns Hopkins University Press.

Faoro, D. (2007). "Sull'origo e sugli esordi politici di Cornelio Gallo." *Forum Iulii*, 31, 27–38.

Farney, G. D. (2007). *Ethnic Identity and Aristocratic Competition in Republican Rome*, Cambridge University Press.

Farrell, J. & Nelis, D. P. (2013). *Augustan Poetry and the Roman Republic*, Oxford University Press.

Faust, S. (1994). "Die Klinen." In G. Hellenkemper Salies, H-H. von Prittwitz und Gaffron & G. Bauchhenss, eds., *Das Wrack: der antike Schiffsfund von Mahdia.* Köln: Rheinland Verlag, pp. 573–605.

Fear, A. T. (1996). *Rome and Baetica: Urbanization in Southern Spain, c. 50 BC–AD 150.* Oxford: Clarendon Press.

Fearn, D. (2010). "Imperialist fragmentation and the discovery of Bacchylides." In M. Bradley, ed., *Classics and Imperialism in the British Empire.* Oxford University Press, pp. 158–85.

Feeney, D. (1998). *Literature and Religion at Rome: Cultures, Contexts, and Beliefs*, Cambridge University Press.

(2005). "The beginnings of a literature in Latin." *JRS*, 95, 226–40.

(2007). *Caesar's Calendar: Ancient Time and the Beginnings of History*, Berkeley: University of California Press.

(2016). *Beyond Greek: The Beginnings of Latin Literature*, Cambridge, MA: Harvard University Press.

Fehling, D. (1989). *Herodotus and his "Sources." Citation, Invention and Narrative Art*. ARCA Classical and Medieval Texts, Papers and Monographs, Vol. 21. Leeds: Francis Cairns Ltd.

Feldherr, A. (1995). "Ships of state: *Aeneid* 5 and Augustan circus spectacle." *CA*, 14(2), 245–65.

(2010). "Hannibalic laughter: Sallust's archaeology and the end of Livy's Third Decade." In W. Polleichtner, ed., *Livy and Intertextuality*. Trier: Wissenschaftlicher Verlag Trier, pp. 203–32.

Ferrari, G. (1999). "The geography of time: the Nile mosaic and the library at Praeneste." *Ostraka*, 8(2), 359–86.

Fink, R. O. (1971). *Roman Military Records on Papyrus*, Cleveland: Press of Case Western Reserve University.

Finley, M. I. (1977). "Aulos Kapreilios Timotheos, slave trader." In M. I. Finley, ed., *Aspects of Antiquity: Discoveries and Controversies*, 2nd edn. New York: Viking, pp. 154–66.

Finnestad, R. B. (1997). "Temples of the Ptolemaic and Roman periods: ancient traditions in new contexts." In B. Shafer, ed., *Temples of Ancient Egypt*. Ithaca: Cornell University Press, pp. 185–237.

Fleury, P., ed. (1990). *Vitruve: De l'architecture, Livre 1*, with trans. and comm., Paris: Les Belles Lettres.

Flohr, M. & Wilson, A. (2011). "The economy of ordure." In G.C.M. Jansen, A. O. Koloski-Ostrow, & E. M. Moormann, eds., *Roman Toilets: Their Archaeology and Cultural History*. Leuven: Peeters, pp. 147–56.

Flower, H. I. (2000). "The tradition of the *spolia opima*: M. Claudius Marcellus and Augustus." *CA*, 19(1), 34–64.

(2006). *The Art of Forgetting: Disgrace & Oblivion in Roman Political Culture*, Chapel Hill: University of North Carolina Press.

(2014). "Memory and memoirs in Republican Rome." In K. Galinsky, ed., *Memoria Romana: Memory in Rome and Rome in Memory*. Ann Arbor: University of Michigan Press, pp. 27–40.

Fögen, T. (2009). *Wissen, Kommunikation und Selbstdarstellung: Zur Struktur und Charakteristik römischer Fachtexte der frühen Kaiserzeit*, Munich: Beck.

Fontaine, M. (2010). *Funny Words in Plautine Comedy*, Oxford University Press.

Fontana, D. (1590). *Della trasportatione dell'obelisco vaticano et delle fabriche di nostro signore papa Sisto V*, Rome: Domenico Basa.

Forsdyke, S. (2012). *Slaves Tell Tales and Other Episodes in the Politics of Popular Culture in Ancient Greece*, Princeton University Press.

Fowden, G. (1987). "Nicagoras of Athens and the Lateran obelisk." *JHS*, 107, 51–7.

Fowler, D. (1991). "Narrate and describe: the problem of ekphrasis." *JRS*, 81, 25–35.

(2000). *Roman Constructions: Readings in Postmodern Latin*, Oxford University Press.

Fraenkel, E. (2007). *Plautine Elements in Plautus.* T. Drevikovsky and F. Muecke, trans., Oxford University Press.

Fraser, P. M. (1970). "Aristophanes of Byzantion and Zoilus Homeromastix in Vitruvius." *Eranos,* 68, 115–22.

Fraser, P. M. & Matthews, E., eds. (1987–). *A Lexicon of Greek Personal Names,* Oxford: Clarendon Press.

Frazel, T. D. (2005). "'*Furtum*' and the description of stolen objects in Cicero *in Verrem* 2.4." *American Journal of Philology,* 126(3), 363–76.

(2009). *The Rhetoric of Cicero's* In Verrem. Hypomnemata 179, Göttingen: Vandenhoeck & Ruprecht.

Frend, W. (1976). "Some Greek and Latin papyri of the period 50 BC–50 AD from Q'asr Ibrim in Nubia." In *Proceedings of the XIV International Congress of Papyrologists, Oxford, 24–31 July 1974.* London: Egypt Exploration Society, pp. 103–11.

Frey-Kupper, S. (2014). "Coins and their use in the Punic Mediterranean: case studies from Carthage to Italy from the fourth to the first century BCE." In J. Crawley Quinn & N. Vella, eds., *The Punic Mediterranean: Identities and Identification from Phoenician Settlement to Roman Rule.* Cambridge University Press, pp. 76–110.

Friedman, Z. (2011). *Ship Iconography in Mosaics: An Aid to Understanding Ancient Ships and Their Construction,* Oxford: Archaeopress.

Frischer, B. & Fillwalk, J. (2014). "New digital simulation studies on the Obelisk, Meridian, and Ara Pacis of Augustus." In L. Haselberger, ed., *The Horologium of Augustus: Debate and Context.* Portsmouth: JRA Supplementary Series No. 99, pp. 77–90.

Gabba, E. (1991). *Dionysius and the History of Archaic Rome,* Berkeley: University of California Press.

Gagliardi, P. (2009). "Per la datazione dei versi di Gallo da Qasr Ibrim." *ZPE,* 171, 45–63.

Galinsky, K. (1996). *Augustan Culture: An Interpretive Introduction,* Princeton University Press.

(2014). *Memoria Romana: Memory in Rome and Rome in Memory,* Memoirs of the American Academy in Rome, Supplementary Vol. 10, Ann Arbor: University of Michigan Press.

Galinsky, K. & Lapatin, K., eds. (2016). *Cultural Memories in the Roman Empire,* Los Angeles: J. Paul Getty Museum.

Gandhi, L. (2006). *Affective Communities: Anticolonial Thought, Fin-de-siècle Radicalism, and the Politics of Friendship,* University of Chicago Press.

García y Bellido, A. (1963). "Hercules Gaditanus." *ArchEspArq,* 36, 70–153.

(1967). *Les religions orientales dans l'Espagne romaine,* Leiden: Brill.

García-Bellido, M. P. (1985–6). "Leyendas e imágenes púnicas en las monedas libio-fenices." In J. Gorrochatequi, J. L. Melena, & J. Santos, eds., *Actas del IV coloquio sobre lenguas y culturas paleohispánicas.* Vitoria-Gasteiz: Universidad del País Vasco, pp. 499–519.

(1990). "Iconografía fenicio-púnica en moneda romano-republicana de la Bética." *Zephyrus,* 43, 371–83.

(1991). "Las religiones orientales en la península Ibérica: documentos numismáticos, I." *AespA*, 64, 37–81.

Gardner, A. (2007). *An Archaeology of Identity: Soldiers and Society in Late Roman Britain*, Walnut Creek, CA: Left Coast Press.

Gardner, A., Herring, E., & Lomas, K., eds. (2013). *Creating Ethnicities and Identities in the Roman World*, London: *Institute of Classical Studies*, School of Advanced Study, University of London.

Garzón Blanco, J. A. (1988). "La propaganda imperial en las monedas de Hércules, 'HERCVLES GADITANVS', Minerva y 'MINERVA GADITANA' emitidas desde Trajano, a Antonino Pio." *Baetica. Estudios de arte, geografía e historia*, 11, 257–65.

Geertz, C. (1983). *Local Knowledge: Further Essays in Interpretive Anthropology*, New York: Basic Books.

Geiger, J. (2009). *The First Hall of Fame: A Study of the Statues in the Forum Augustum*, Leiden: Brill.

Gell, A. (1998). *Art and Agency: An Anthropological Theory*, Oxford: Clarendon Press.

Gibbins, D. (2001). "Shipwrecks and Hellenistic trade." In Z. Archibald *et al.*, eds., *Hellenistic Economies*. New York: Routledge, pp. 273–312.

Gibson, B., trans. and comm. (2006). *Statius Silvae 5*. Oxford: Oxford University Press.

Glare, P.G.W., ed. (1982). *Oxford Latin Dictionary*, Oxford: Clarendon Press.

Gnoli, T. (2011). "La battaglia delle Egadi. A proposito di ritrovamenti recenti." *Rivista storica dell'antichità*, 41, 47–86.

(2012a). "*Classis Praetoria*," *Studi Romagnoli*, 62, 11–21.

(2012b). "Nuova iscrizione su un rostro proveniente dalla battaglia delle Egadi." *Epigraphica*, 74, 59–74.

Goldberg, S. M. (1986). *Understanding Terence*, Princeton University Press.

(2005). *Constructing Literature in the Roman Republic: Poetry and Its Reception*, Cambridge University Press.

Gómez Pallarès, J. (2005). "The 'reading of monuments' in Cornelius Gallus' fragment." *Philologus*, 149, 104–9.

Gómez-Pantoja, J. & García Palomar, F. (2001). "El culto a Hércules y otras novedades epigráficas de San Esteban de Gormaz (Soria)." *Studia philologica valentina*, 5(2), 73–101.

Goodyear, F.R.D., ed. (1981). *The Annals of Tacitus*, Vol. II. Cambridge University Press.

Gordon, A. E. (1983). *Illustrated History to Latin Epigraphy*, Berkeley: University of California Press.

Gorman, R. & Gorman, V. (2014). *Corrupting Luxury in Ancient Greek Literature*, Ann Arbor: University of Michigan Press.

Gowers, E. (1995). "The anatomy of Rome from Capitol to Cloaca." *JRS*, 85, 23–32.

Gowing, A. M. (2005). *Empire and Memory: The Representation of the Roman Republic in Imperial Culture*, Cambridge University Press.

Gozalbes, M. (2012). "Cities, *drachmae, denarii* and the Roman conquest of Hispania." In F. López Sánchez, ed., *The City and the Coin in the Ancient and Early Medieval Worlds*, BAR International Series 2402. Oxford: Archaeopress, pp. 17–35.

Gozalbes Cravioto, E. (1994). "Moneda y proyección económica: la difusión de las monedas de cecas hispano-romanas en el norte de Africa." *Numisma*, 234, 47–59.

Granger, F. (1985). *Vitruvius. On Architecture*. Vol. II, Cambridge, MA: Harvard University Press.

Gransden, K. W. (1976). *Virgil's Aeneid: Book VIII*, Cambridge University Press.

Gratwick, A. S., ed. (1993). *Plautus: Menaechmi*, Cambridge University Press.

Green, J. R. (2012). "Comic vases in South Italy: continuity and innovation in the development of a figurative language." In K. Bosher, ed., *Theater Outside Athens: Drama in Greek Sicily and South Italy*. Cambridge University Press, pp. 289–342.

Greenblatt, S., ed. (2009). *Cultural Mobility: A Manifesto*, Cambridge University Press.

Greenhalgh, M. (2011). "*Spolia*: A Definition in Ruins." In R. Brilliant & D. Kinney, eds., *Reuse Value: Spolia and Appropriation in Art and Architecture, from Constantine to Sherrie Levine*. Surrey: Ashgate, pp. 75–95.

Grenier, J.-Y. (1997). "Économie du surplus, économie du circuit: les prix et les échanges dans l'Antiquité gréco-romaine et dans l'Ancien Régime." In J. Andreau, P. Briant, & R. Descat, eds., *Économie antique: Prix et formation des prix dans les économies antiques*. Saint-Bertrand-de-Comminges, Musée Archéologique Départemental, pp. 385–404.

Gros, P. (1976). *Aurea Templa: Recherches sur l'architecture religieuse de Rome à l'époque d'Auguste*, Rome: École française de Rome.

  (1983). "Statut social et rôle culturel des architectes (période héllenistique et augustéenne)." *Architecture et société. De l'archaïsme grec à la fin de la République. Actes du colloque de Rome (2–3 décembre 1980)*, Collection de l'École française de Rome, 66. Rome: École française de Rome, pp. 425–52.

  (1989). "L'*auctoritas* chez Vitruve: contribution à l'étude de la sémantique des ordres dans le *De architectura*." In H. Geertman & J. J. de Jong, eds., *Munus Non Ingratum: Proceedings of the International Symposium on Vitruvius' De Architectura and the Hellenistic and Republican Architecture*. Bulletin Antieke Beschaving, Supplement 2. Leiden: Peeters, pp. 126–33.

  (1997). "*Vitruvio e il suo tempo.*" In P. Gros, ed., E. Romano and A. Corso, trans. and comm., *Vitruvio, De Architectura*, 2 vols. Turin: Einaudi, pp. ix–lxxvii.

Gruen, E. S. (1990). *Studies in Greek Culture and Roman Policy*, Leiden: Brill.

  (1992). *Culture and National Identity in Republican Rome*, Ithaca: Cornell University Press.

Gurval, R. A. (1995). *Actium and Augustus: The Politics and Emotions of Civil War*, Ann Arbor: University of Michigan Press.

Habachi, L. (2000). *Die unsterblichen Obelisken Ägyptens*, new edn, C. Vogel, ed., Mainz: Philipp von Zabern.

Habermas, J. (1984). *The Theory of Communicative Action, Vol. 1: Reason and the Rationalization of Society*, T. McCarthy, trans., Boston: Beacon Press.

Habinek, T. N. (1998). *The Politics of Latin Literature: Writing, Identity, and Empire in Ancient Rome*, Princeton University Press.

(2005). *The World of Roman Song: From Ritualized Speech to Social Order*, Baltimore: Johns Hopkins University Press.

Haeny, G. (1985). "A short architectural history of Philae." *BIFAO*, 85, 197–233.

Hahn, H. (2012). "Cultural appropriation: power, transformation, tradition." In C. Huck & S. Bauernschmidt, eds., *Travelling Goods, Travelling Moods: Varieties of Cultural Appropriation (1850–1950)*. Frankfurt: Campus Verlag, pp. 15–35.

Hahn, H. & Weiss, H. (2013). *Mobility, Meaning and the Transformations of Things: Shifting Contexts of Material Culture through Time and Space*, Oxford: Oxbow Books.

Haimson Lushkov, A. (2010). "Intertextuality and source criticism in the Scipionic trials." In W. Polleichtner, ed., *Livy and Intertextuality*. Trier: Wissenschaftlicher Verlag Trier, pp. 203–32.

(2013). "Citation and the dynamics of tradition in Livy's *AUC*." *Histos*, 7, 21–47.

Hallett, C. H. (2005). *The Roman Nude: Heroic Portrait Statuary 200 BC–AD 300*, Oxford University Press.

Hallet, J. P. (1977). "*Perusinae Glandes* and the changing image of Augustus." *AJAH*, 2, 151–71.

Hallof, J. (2011). *The Meriotic Inscriptions from Qasr Ibrim I: Meroitic Inscriptions on Ostraka*, Dettelbach: Röll Verlag.

(2014). *The Meriotic Inscriptions from Qasr Ibrim II: Inscriptions on Papyri*, Dettelbach: Röll Verlag.

Hannestad, L. (1993). "Greeks and Celts: the creation of a myth." In P. Bilde, ed., *Centre and Periphery in the Hellenistic World*. Studies in Hellenistic Civilisation 4. Aarhus: Aarhus University Press, pp. 15–38.

Hansen, E. V. (1971). *The Attalids of Pergamon*, Ithaca: Cornell University Press.

Hansen, M. F. (2003). *The Eloquence of Appropriation: Prolegomena to an Understanding of Spolia in Early Christian Rome*, Rome: L'Erma di Bretschneider.

Hardie, A. (2002). "The *Georgics*, the mysteries and the muses at Rome." *PCPS*, 48, 175–208.

Hardie, P. R. (1986). *Virgil's Aeneid: Cosmos and Imperium*, Oxford: Clarendon Press.

(1987). "Ships and ship-names in the *Aeneid*." In M. Whitby, P. R. Hardie & M. Whitby, eds., *Homo viator: Classical Essays for John Bramble*. Bristol Classical Press, pp. 163–73.

(2007). "Poets, patrons, rulers: the Ennian traditions." In W. Fitzgerald & E. Gowers, eds., *Ennius Perennis: The Annals and Beyond*. Cambridge University Press, pp. 129–44.

(2012). *Rumour and Renown: Representations of Fama in Western Literature*, Cambridge University Press.

Harris, W. V. (1979). *War and Imperialism in Republican Rome, 327–70 BC*, Oxford University Press.

(1999). "Demography, geography and the sources of Roman slaves." *JRS*, 89, 62–75.

(2011). *Rome's Imperial Economy: Twelve Essays*, Oxford University Press.

(2015). "Prolegomena to a study of the economics of Roman art." *AJA*, 119(3), 395–417.

Harris-McCoy, D. E. (2012). *Artemidorus' Oneirocritica: Text, Translation, and Commentary*, Oxford University Press.

Harrison, S. J. (1997). "The survival and supremacy of Rome: the unity of the shield of Aeneas." *JRS*, 87, 70–6.

Hartog, F. (2001). *Memories of Odysseus: Frontier Takes from Ancient Greece*, J. Lloyd, trans., University of Chicago Press.

Hasebroek, J. (1933). *Trade and Politics in Ancient Greece*, London: G. Bell and Sons.

Haselberger, L., ed. (2014). *The Horologium of Augustus: Debate and Context*, Portsmouth: JRA Supplement No. 99.

Hauben, H. (1993). "Femmes propriétaires et locataires de navires en Egypte ptolémaïque." *JJurP*, 23, 61–74.

Headlam, W. ed. [1922] (2001). *Herodas: The Mimes and Fragments*. London: Bristol Classical Press. Orig. pub. Cambridge University Press.

Heinze, R. (1925). "*Auctoritas.*" *Hermes*, 60, 348–66.

Hekster, O. (2005). "Propagating power: Hercules as an example for second-century Emperors." In L. Rawlings & H. Bowden, eds., *Herakles and Hercules: Exploring a Graeco–Roman Divinity*. Swansea: The Classical Press of Wales, pp. 205–21.

Hellenkemper Salies, G., von Prittwitz und Gaffron, H.-H., & Bauchhenss, G., eds. (1994). *Das Wrack: der antike Schiffsfund von Mahdia*, Köln: Rheinland Verlag.

Henderson, J. (2010). "Lucan/The word at war." In C. Tesoriero, ed., *Oxford Readings in Classical Studies: Lucan*. Oxford University Press, pp. 433–92. Orig. pub. (1987) *Ramus*, 16, 122–64.

Hendrickson, T. (2015). "An emendation to a fragment of Varro's *De bibliothecis* (fr. 54 *GRF* Funaioli)." *CQ*, 65(1), 395–97.

Herklotz, F. (2007). *Prinzeps und Pharao: Der Kult des Augustus in Ägypten*. Oikumene. Studien zur antiken Weltgeschichte, 4, Frankfurt am Main: Verlag Antike.

Hermary, A. (1992). "Quelques remarques sur les origins proche-orientales de l'iconographie d'Héraclès." In C. Bonnet & C. Jourdain-Annequin, eds., *Héraclès: D'une rive à l'autre de la Méditerranée. Bilan et perspectives*, Brussels: Institut Belge de Rome, pp. 129–43.

Heslin, K. (2011). "Dolia shipwrecks and the wine trade in the Roman Mediterranean." In D. Robinson & A. Wilson, eds., *Maritime Archaeology and Ancient Trade in the Mediterranean*. Oxford: Oxford Centre for Maritime Archaeology, Institute of Archaeology, pp. 157–68.

Heslin, P. (2007). "Augustus, Domitian and the so-called Horologium Augusti." *JRS*, 97, 1–20.

Heyworth, S. J. (1984). "A note on the Gallus fragment." *LCM*, 9, 63–4.

(1995). "Dividing poems." In O. Pecere & M. D. Reeve, eds., *Formative Stages of Classical Traditions: Latin Texts from Antiquity to Renaissance.* Spoleto: Centro Italiano di Studi sull'Alto Medioevo, pp. 117–40.

Hinds, S. (1998). *Allusion and Intertext: Dynamics of Appropriation in Roman Poetry*, Cambridge University Press.

(2001). "Cinna, Statius, and 'immanent literary history' in the cultural economy." In E. A. Schmidt, ed., *L'histoire littéraire immanente dans la poésie latine, Entretiens Hardt 47.* Vandoevres-Geneva: Fondation Hardt, pp. 221–65.

Hingley, R. (2005). *Globalizing Roman Culture: Unity, Diversity and Empire*, London: Routledge.

Hirschfeld, O. (1896). "Zur der lateinisch-griechischen Inschrift." In H. Lyons & L. Borchardt, eds., "Eine trilingue Inschrift von Philae." *Sitzungsberichte der Berliner Akademie der Wissenschaften* 20, pp. 469–82.

Höckmann, O. (1994). "Das Schiff." In G. Hellenkemper Salies, H.-H. von Prittwitz und Gaffron, & G. Bauchhenss, eds., *Das Wrack: der antike Schiffsfund von Mahdia*. Köln: Rheinland Verlag, pp. 53–81.

Hodder, I. (2012). *Entangled: An Archaeology of the Relationships Between Humans and Things*, Malden: Wiley-Blackwell.

Hodge, A.T. (2002). *Roman Aqueducts and Water Supply*, 2nd edn, London: Duckworth.

Hoffmann, F., Minas-Nerpel, M., & Pfeiffer, S. (2009). *Die dreisprachige Stele des C. Cornelius Gallus: Übersetzung und Kommentar*, Berlin: de Gruyter.

Hofter, M. R., ed. (1988). *Kaiser Augustus und die verlorene Republik. Eine Ausstellung im Martin-Gropius-Bau, Berlin, 7. Juni–14. August 1988*, Mainz: Philipp von Zabern.

Hölbl, G. (2000). *Altägypten im Römischen Reich: Der Römische Pharao und Seine Tempel*, Vol. I. Mainz: Philipp von Zabern.

(2004). *Altägypten im Römischen Reich: Der Römische Pharao und Seine Tempel*, Vol. II. Mainz: Philipp von Zabern.

(2006). *Altägypten im Römischen Reich: Der Römische Pharao und Seine Tempel*, Vol. III. Mainz: Philipp von Zabern.

Hölkeskamp, K.-J. (2000). "*Fides–deditio in fidem–dextra data et accepta:* Recht, Religion und Ritual in Rom." In C. Brunn, ed., *The Roman Middle Republic: Politics, Religion, and Historiography, c. 400–133 BC.* Rome: Institutum Romanum Finlandiae, pp. 223–49.

(2006). "History and collective memory in the Middle Republic." In N. Rosenstein & R. Morstein-Marx, eds., *A Companion to the Roman Republic*. Oxford University Press, pp. 479–95.

Holleran, C. (2012). *Shopping in Ancient Rome: The Retail Trade in the Late Republic and the Principate*, Oxford University Press.

Holliday, P. J. (2002). *The Origins of Roman Historical Commemoration in the Visual Arts*, Cambridge University Press.

Hollis, A. (1997). "A fragmentary addiction." In G. Most, ed., *Collecting Fragments–Fragmente sammeln, Aporemata I.* Göttingen: Vandenhoeck & Ruprecht, pp. 111–23.

(2007). *Fragments of Roman Poetry c. 60 BC–AD 20*, Oxford University Press.

Holloway, R. R. (1994). *The Archaeology of Early Rome and Latium*, London and New York: Routledge.

Hölscher, T. (1994). "Hellenistische Kunst und römische Aristokratie." In G. Hellenkemper Salies, H.-H. von Prittwitz und Gaffron, & G. Bauchhenss, eds., *Das Wrack: Der antike Schiffsfund von Mahdia*. Köln: Rheinland Verlag, pp. 875–88.

(2004). *The Language of Images in Roman Art*, A. Snodgrass, trans., Cambridge, UK: Cambridge University Press. Orig. pub. (1987). *Römische Bildsprache als semantisches System*, Heidelberg: C. Winter.

(2006). "Greek styles and Greek art in Augustan Rome: issues of the present versus records of the past." In J. I. Porter, ed., *Classical Pasts*. Princeton University Press, pp. 237–69.

Holz, S. (2009). "*Praeda* und Prestige — Kriegsbeute und Beutekunst im (spät-) republikanischen Rom." In M. Coudry & M. Humm, eds., *Praeda: Butin de guerre et société dans la Rome républicaine/Kriegsbeute und Gesellschaft im republikanischen Rom*. Collegium Beatus Rhenanus 1. Stuttgart: Franz Steiner Verlag, pp. 197–206.

Hoogma, R. P. (1959). *Der Einfluss Vergils auf die Carmina latina epigraphica: eine Studie mit besonderer Berücksichtigung der metrisch-technischen Grundsätze der Entlehnung*, Amsterdam: North–Holland Publishing Company.

Hopkins, K. (1980). "Taxes and trade in the Roman empire (200 BC–AD 400)." *JRS*, 70, 101–25.

Horden, P. & Purcell, N. (2000). *The Corrupting Sea: A Study of Mediterranean History*, Oxford: Blackwell.

Horsfall, N. M. (1984). "Aspects of Virgilian influence in Roman life." In *Atti del Convegno mondiale scientifico di studi su Virgilio, Mantova–Roma–Napoli, 19–24 Settembre, 1981*, Vol. 2. Milan: Mondadori, pp. 47–63.

Houston, G. (1988). "Ports in perspective: some comparative materials on Roman merchant ships and ports." *AJA*, 92(4), 553–64.

Hubbard, M. (1995). "*Pindarici fontis qui non expalluit haustus:* Horace, *Epistles* 1.3." In S. J. Harrison, ed., *Homage to Horace: A Bimillenary Celebration*. Oxford University Press, pp. 219–27.

Huck, C. & Bauernschmidt, S. (2012). "Trans-cultural appropriation." In C. Huck & S. Bauernschmidt, eds., *Travelling Goods, Travelling Moods: Varieties of Cultural Appropriation (1850–1950)*. Frankfurt: Campus Verlag, pp. 229–51.

eds. (2012). *Travelling Goods, Travelling Moods: Varieties of Cultural Appropriation (1850–1950)*, Frankfurt: Campus Verlag.

Huet, V. (1999). "Napoleon I: a new Augustus?" In C. Edwards, ed., *Roman Presences: Receptions of Rome in European Culture, 1789–1945*. Cambridge University Press, pp. 53–69.

Humm, M. (2005). *Appius Claudius Caecus. La République accomplie*, Rome: École française de Rome.

(2007). "Des fragments d'historiens grecs dans l'*Ineditum Vaticanum?* (Fragmente griechischer Historiker im *Ineditum Vaticanum?*)" In M.-L. Freyburger & D. Meyer, eds., *Visions grecques de Rome. Griechische Blicke auf Rome*. Paris: De Boccard, pp. 279–81.

Hunter, R. (1993). "The presentation of Herodas' *Mimiamboi*." *Antichthon*, 27, 31–44.

(1995). "Plautus and Herodas." In L. Benz, E. Stärk, & G. Vogt-Spira, eds., *Plautus und die Tradition des Stegreifspiels*. Tübingen: Gunter Narr, pp. 155–69.

(2006). *The Shadow of Callimachus: Studies in the Reception of Hellenistic Poetry at Rome*, Cambridge University Press.

Hunter, R. & Rutherford, I., eds. (2009). *Wandering Poets in Ancient Greek Culture: Travel, Locality and Pan-Hellenism*, Cambridge University Press.

Hurley, D. W., ed. (2001). *Suetonius: Divus Claudius*, Cambridge University Press.

Hutchinson, G. (1981). "Notes on the new Gallus." *ZPE*, 41, 37–42.

(2013). *Greek to Latin: Frameworks and Contexts for Intertextuality*, Oxford University Press.

Huxley, G. L. (1967). "The Medism of Caryae." *Greek, Roman, and Byzantine Studies*, 8, 29–32.

Idle, E. (1999). *The Road to Mars: A Post-Modern Novel*, New York: Vintage.

Ingold, T. (1993). "The temporality of the landscape." *WorldArch*, 25(2), 152–74.

(2007). "Materials against materiality." *Archaeological Dialogues*, 14(1), 1–16.

(2008). "When ANT meets SPIDER: social theory for arthropods." In C. Knappett & L. Malafouris, eds., *Material Agency*. Berlin: Springer, pp. 209–15.

Inizan, M.-L., *et al.* (1999). *Technology and Terminology of Knapped Stone*, Nanterre: Cercle de Recherches et d'Études Préhistoriques.

Itgenshorst, T. (2004). "Augustus und der republikanische Triumph: Triumphalfasten und summi viri–Galerie als Instrumente der imperialen Machtsicherung." *Hermes*, 132(4), 436–58.

Iversen, E. (1968–80). *Obelisks in Exile*, 2 vols., Copenhagen: Gad.

(1993). *The Myth of Egypt and its Hieroglyphs in European Tradition*, new edn, Princeton University Press.

Jacobson, D. M. and Weitzman, M. P. (1992). "What was Corinthian bronze?" *AJA*, 96(2), 237–47.

Jacobsen, H. (1984). "Aristaeus, Orpheus, and the *laudes Galli*." *AJP*, 105, 271–300.

Jaeger, M. (1997). *Livy's Written Rome*, Ann Arbor: University of Michigan Press.

(2002). "Cicero and Archimedes' tomb." *Journal of Roman Studies*, 92, 49–61.

(2008). *Archimedes and the Roman Imagination*, Ann Arbor: University of Michigan Press.

Jameson, S. (1968). "Chronology of the campaigns of Aelius Gallus and C. Petronius." *JRS*, 58, 71–84.

Jenkyns, G. K. (1978). "Coins of Punic Sicily. Part 4." *Revue Suisse de Numismatique*, 57, 5-68.

Jennison, G. (2005). *Animals for Show and Pleasure in Ancient Rome*, Philadelphia: University of Pennsylvania Press.

Jiménez, A. (2014). "Punic after Punic times? The case of the so-called 'Libyphoenician' coins of Southern Iberia." In J. Crawley Quinn & N. Vella, eds., *The Punic Mediterranean: Identities and Identification from Phoenician Settlement to Roman Rule*. Cambridge University Press, pp. 219–42.

Jones, A.H.M. (1956). "Numismatics and history." In R.A.G. Carson & C.H.V. Sutherland, eds., *Essays in Roman Coinage Presented to Harold Mattingly*. Oxford University Press, pp. 61–91.

Jones, C. P. (1987). "Stigma: tattooing and branding in Graeco-Roman Antiquity." *Journal of Roman Studies*, 77, 139–55.

Jones, P. J. (2005). *Reading Rivers in Roman Literature and Culture*, Lanham: Lexington Books.

Joshel, S. R. (1992). *Work, Identity, and Legal Status at Rome: A Study of the Occupational Inscriptions*, Norman: University of Oklahoma Press.

Kaltsas, N. (2012). "Introduction." In N. Kaltsas, E. Vlachogianni, & P. Bouyia, eds., *The Antikythera Shipwreck: The Ship, the Treasures, the Mechanism; National Archaeological Museum, April 2012–April 2013*. Athens: Kapon Editions, pp. 14–16.

Kaltsas, N., Vlachogianni, E., & Bouyia, P., eds. (2012). *The Antikythera Shipwreck: The Ship, the Treasures, the Mechanism; National Archaeological Museum, April 2012–April 2013*, Athens: Kapon Editions.

Kaster, R. (1995). *C. Suetonius Tranquillus: De Grammaticis et Rhetoribus*, Oxford: Clarendon Press.

Katz, J. T. (2000). "Egnatius' dental fricatives (Catullus 39.20)." *CP*, 95(3), 338–48.

Kay, P. (2014). *Rome's Economic Revolution*, Oxford University Press.

Kayser, F. (1994). *Recueil des inscriptions grecques et latines (non funéraires) d'Alexandrie impériale (1er–IIIe s. apr. J.–C.)*, Cairo: Institut Français d'Archéologie Orientale.

Keay, S. (1998). "The development of towns in Early Roman Baetica." In S. Keay, ed., *The Archaeology of Early Roman Baetica*. Portsmouth: JRA Supplementary Series No. 29, pp. 54–86.

(2001). "Romanization and the Hispaniae." In S. Keay & N. Terrenato, eds., *Italy and the West: Comparative Issues in Romanization*. Oxford: Oxbow Books, pp. 117–44.

Keefe, D. E. (1982). "Gallus and Euphorion." *CQ*, 32, 237–8.

Keenan, J. G. (2009). "The history of the discipline." In Bagnall, R., ed., *The Oxford Handbook of Papyrology*. Oxford University Press, pp. 59–78.

Kees, H. (1958). "Die weiße Kapelle Sesostris' I. in Karnak und das Sedfest." *MDIK*, 16, 194–213.

Keith, A. (2011). "Lycoris Galli/Volumnia Cytheris: a Greek courtesan in Rome." *EuGeStA*, 1, 23–53.

Kellum, B. A. (1990). "The city adorned: programmatic display at the *Aedes Concordiae Augustae*." In K. A. Raaflaub & M. Toher, eds., *Between Republic and Empire: Interpretations of Augustus and his Principate*. Berkeley and Los Angeles: University of California Press, pp. 276–96.

(2010). "Representations and re-presentations of the Battle of Actium." In B. W. Breed, C. Damon, and A. Rossi, eds., *Citizens of Discord: Rome and its Civil Wars*. Oxford University Press, pp. 187–206.

Kelly, G. (2008). *Ammianus Marcellinus: The Allusive Historian*, Cambridge University Press.

Kennedy, D. F. (1982). "Gallus and the *Culex*." *CQ*, 32, 371–89.

Ketterer, R. C. (1986). "Stage properties in Plautine comedy, part III: props in four plays of identity." *Semiotica*, 60, 29–72.

Killgrove, K. & Montgomery, J. (2016). "All roads lead to Rome: exploring human migration to the Eternal City through biochemistry of skeletons from two Imperial-era cemeteries (1st–3rd c. AD)." *PloS ONE*, 11(2): e0147585. doi:10.1371/journal.pone.0147585.

Kinney, D. (1997). "*Spolia, damnatio* and *renovatio memoriae*." *MAAR*, 42, 117–48.

(2001). "Roman architectural spolia." *PAPS*, 145(2), 138–61.

(2006). "The concept of *spolia*." In C. Rudolph ed., *A Companion to Medieval Art: Romanesque and Gothic in Northern Europe*. Malden, Oxford, and Chichester: Wiley-Blackwell, pp. 233–52.

(2011). "Introduction." In R. Brilliant & D. Kinney, eds., *Reuse Value: Spolia and Appropriation in Art and Architecture, from Constantine to Sherrie Levine*. Farnham: Ashgate, pp. 1–11.

(2012). "Instances of appropriation in late Roman and early Christian art." *Essays in Medieval Studies*, 28, 1–22.

Kirk, A. (2014). "The semantics of showcase in Herodotus's *Histories*." *TAPA*, 144(1), 19–40.

Klein, S. (2015). "When actions speak louder than words: mute characters in Roman comedy." *CJ*, 111(1), 53–66.

Knappett, C. (2011a). *An Archaeology of Interaction: Network Perspectives on Material Culture and Society*, Oxford University Press.

(2011b). "Networks of objects, meshworks of things." In T. Ingold, ed., *Redrawing Anthropology: Materials, Movements, Lines*. Farnham: Ashgate, pp. 45–63.

Knox, P. E. (1985). "The old Gallus." *Hermes*, 113, 497.

Koenen, L. (1976). "Egyptian influence in Tibullus." *ICS*, 1, 127–59.

Kondratieff, E. (2004). "The column and coinage of C. Duilius: innovations in iconography in large and small media in the Middle Republic." *SIC*, 23, 1–39.

König, A. (2009). "From architect to *imperator*: Vitruvius and his addressee in the *De Architectura*." In L. Taub & A. Doody, eds., *Authorial Voices in Greco-Roman Technical Writing*. Trier: Wissenschaftlicher Verlag Trier, pp. 31–52.

(2016). "Tracing the ebb and flow of *De Architectura* 8." In S. Cuomo & M. Formisano, eds., *Vitruvius: Text, Architecture, Reception. Arethusa*, 49(2), 161–82.

König, J. & Whitmarsh, T., eds. (2007). *Ordering Knowledge in the Roman Empire*, Cambridge University Press.

Konstan, D. (2013). "Menander's slaves: The banality of violence." In B. Akrigg & R. Tordoff, eds., *Slaves and Slavery in Ancient Greek Comic Drama.* Cambridge University Press, pp. 144–58.

Konstan, D. & Raaflaub, K. A., eds. (2010). *Epic and History*, Malden and Chichester: Wiley-Blackwell.

Kopytoff, I. (1986). "The cultural biography of things: commoditization as a process." In A. Appadurai, ed., *The Social Life of Things: Commodities in Cultural Perspective.* Cambridge University Press, pp. 64–91.

Kostof, S. (1978). "The emperor and the *Duce*: the planning of Piazzale Augusto Imperatore in Rome." In H. A. Millon & L. Nochlin, eds., *Art and Architecture in the Service of Politics.* Cambridge, MA: MIT Press, pp. 270–325.

Kraus, C. S. (1994). "'No second Troy': topoi and refoundation in Livy, Book V.'" *TAPA*, 124, 267–89.

(1998). "Repetition and empire in the *Ab Vrbe Condita*." In C. Foss & P. Knox, eds., *Style and Tradition: Studies in Honor of Wendell Clausen.* Stuttgart: de Gruyter, pp. 264–83.

(2005). "Hair, hegemony, and historiography: Caesar's style and its earliest critics." In J. N. Adams, M. Lapidge, & T. Reinhardt, eds., *Aspects of the Language of Latin Prose.* Oxford University Press, pp. 97–115.

(2011). "The language of Latin historiography." In J. Clackson, ed., *A Companion to the Latin Language.* Malden: Wiley-Blackwell, pp. 408–25.

Krautheimer, R. (1969). "The architecture of Sixtus III: a fifth-century Renascence?" In R. Krautheimer, ed., *Studies in Early Christian, Medieval, and Renaissance Art.* New York University Press, pp. 181–96.

Künzl, E. (1971). *Die Kelten des Epigonos von Pergamon*, Beiträge zur Archäologie, 4, Würzburg: K. Triltsch.

Kuttner, A. (1995a). *Dynasty and Empire in the Age of Augustus: The Case of the Boscoreale Cups*, Berkeley and Los Angeles: University of California Press.

(1995b). "Republican Rome looks at Pergamon." *HSCP*, 97, 157–78.

Kutzko, D. (2012). "In pursuit of Sophron: Doric mime and Attic comedy in Herodas' *Mimiambi*." In K. Bosher, ed., *Theater Outside Athens: Drama in Greek Sicily and South Italy.* Cambridge University Press, pp. 367–90.

Labate, M. & Rosati, G. (2013). *La costruzione del mito augusteo*, Heidelberg: Universitätsverlag Winter.

Lacau, P. & Chevrier, H. (1956). *Une chapelle de Sésostris Ier à Karnak*, Cairo: Imprimerie de l'Institut Français d'Archéologie Orientale.

Lamboglia, N. (1952). "La nave romana di Albenga." *RStLig*, 18, 131–213.

(1961a). "La nave romana di Spargi (La Maddalena). Campagna di scavo 1958." In *Atti del II Congresso internazionale di archeologia sottomarina (Albenga 1958).* Bordighera: Istituto internazionale di studi liguri, pp. 143–66.

(1961b). "Il rilevamento totale della nave romana di Albenga." *RStLig*, 27, 211–9.

(1965). "Albenga." In J. du Plat Taylor, ed., *Marine Archaeology: Developments During Sixty Years in the Mediterranean*. New York: Thomas Y. Crowell Company, pp. 53–66.

(1971). "La seconda campagna di scavo sulla nave romana di Spargi (1959)." *Atti del III Congresso internazionale di archeologia sottomarina, (Barcelona 1961)*. Bordighera: Istituto internazionale di studi liguri, pp. 205–14.

Lane, M. (2015). *Birth of Politics: Eight Greek and Roman Political Ideas and Why They Matter*, Princeton University Press.

Lange, C. H. (2009). *Res Publica Constituta: Actium, Apollo and the Accomplishment of the Triumviral Assignment*, Leiden: Brill.

(2013). "Triumph and civil war in the late Republic." *PBSR*, 81, 67–90.

Laporte, D. (2000). *History of Shit*, N. Benabid and R. el-Khoury, trans., Cambridge, MA: MIT Press.

La Rocca, E. (2014). "Augustus' solar meridian and the Augustan urban program in the northern Campus Martius: an attempt at a holistic view." In L. Haselberger, ed., *The Horologium of Augustus: Debate and Context*. Portsmouth: JRA Supplementary Series No. 99, pp. 121–65.

La Rocca, E., Ruesch, V., & Zanardi, B. (1983). *Ara Pacis Augustae: in occasione del restauro della fronte orientale*, Rome: L'Erma di Bretschneider.

et al. (2013). *Augusto*, Milan: Mondadori Electa.

Laroche, R. (1977). "Valerius Antias and his numerical totals." *Historia*, 26(3), 358–68.

Laroche-Traunecker, F. (1998). "Les restaurations et transformations d'époque gréco-romaine du temple de Khonsou à Karnak." In W. Clarysse, A. Schoors, & H. Willems, eds., *Egyptian Religion: The Last Thousand Years, Part I. Studies Dedicated to the Memory of Jan Quaegebeur*. Leuven: Uitgeverij Peeters en Departement Oosterse Studies, pp. 903–16.

Latour, B. (2005). *Reassembling the Social: An Introduction to Actor-Network-Theory*, Oxford University Press.

Laubenheimer, F. (2013). "Amphoras and shipwrecks: wine from the Tyrrhenian coast at the end of the Republic and its distribution in Gaul." In J. D. Evans, ed., *A Companion to the Archaeology of the Roman Republic*. Chichester: Wiley-Blackwell, pp. 97–109.

Laurence, R. (1999). *Roman Roads of Italy*, New York: Routledge.

Leach, E. W. (1969). "*Meam quom formam noscito*: language and characterization in the *Menaechmi*." *Arethusa*, 2, 30–45.

Lee, G. R. (1957). *Gypsy: A Memoir*, New York: Harper.

Leemreize, M. (2014). "The Egyptian past in the Roman present." In J. Ker & C. Pieper, eds., *Valuing the Past in the Greco-Roman World: Proceedings of the Penn-Leiden Colloquia on Ancient Values*, Vol. VII. Leiden: Brill, pp. 56–82.

Leen, A. (1991). "Cicero and the rhetoric of art." *AJP*, 112(2), 229–45.

Lefèvre, E. (2001). "*Nimium familiariter* - plautinische Sklaven unter sich: *Epidicus* I 1 (mit einem Blick auf das Original)." In U. Auhagen, ed., *Studien zu Plautus' Epidicus*. Tübingen: Gunter Narr, pp. 105–29.

Le Guen, B. (2014). "The diffusion of comedy from the age of Alexander to the beginning of the Roman Empire." Trans. Christopher Welser. In M. Fontaine & A. C. Scafuro, eds., *The Oxford Handbook of Greek and Roman Comedy*. Oxford University Press, pp. 359–77.

Lehmann, K. & Spittle, D. (1964). *Samothrace: Excavations Conducted by the Institute of Fine Arts of New York University*, Vol. IV.2: *The Altar Court*, New York: Pantheon Books.

Leigh, M. (2004). *Comedy and the Rise of Rome*, Oxford University Press.

(2010). "Early Roman epic and the maritime moment." *CP*, 105(3), 265–80.

Lembke, K. (1994). *Das Iseum Campense in Rom: Studie über den Isiskult unter Domitian*, Heidelberg: Verlag Archäologie und Geschichte.

Lennon, J. J. (2014). *Pollution and Religion in Ancient Rome*, New York: Cambridge University Press.

Lepore, J. (2001). "Historians who love too much: reflections on microhistory and biography." *Journal of American History*, 88(1), 129–44.

Leroi-Gourhan, A. (1964). *Le geste et la parole*, Paris: A. Michel.

Levene, D. S. (1994). Review of *The Temples of Mid-Republican Rome and their Historical and Topographical Context*, by A. Ziolkowski, *JRS*, 84, 220–1.

(2010). *Livy and the Hannibalic War*, Oxford University Press.

(2011). "Historical Allusion and the Nature of the Historical Text." *Histos* Working Papers 2011.1. <http://research.ncl.ac.uk/histos/documents/WP2011.01LeveneHistoricalAllusion.pdf >. Last accessed December 2016.

Levick, B. M. (1982). "Propaganda and imperial coinage." *Antichthon*, 16, 104–16.

(1999a). "Messages on the Roman coinage: types and inscriptions." In G. M. Paul & M. Ierardi, eds., *Roman Coins and Public Life Under the Empire: E. Togo Salmon Papers II*. Ann Arbor: University of Michigan Press, pp. 41–60.

(1999b). *Vespasian*, London: Routledge Press.

Lewis, N. (1974). *Papyrus in Classical Antiquity*, Oxford: Clarendon Press.

Liddle, A., ed. (2003). *Arrian: Periplus Ponti Euxini*, new edn, London: Bristol Classical Press.

Lightfoot, J. L. (1999). *Parthenius of Nicaea: Extant Works Edited with Introduction and Commentary*, Oxford University Press.

Lintott, A. (1972). "Imperial expansion and moral decline in the Roman Republic." *Historia*, 21(4), 626–38.

Lipiński, E. (1995). *Dieux et déesses de l'univers phénicien et punique*, Leuven: Peeters.

Liu, J. (2009). *Collegia Centonariorum: The Guilds of Textile Dealers in the Roman West*, Leiden: Brill.

Loar, M. P. (2017). "Hercules, Mummius, and the Roman triumph in *Aeneid* 8." *CP*, 112(1), 45–62.

Locher, J. (1999). *Topographie und Geschichte der Region am ersten Nilkatarakt in griechisch-römischer Zeit*, Stuttgart: Teubner.

Long, P. O. (1991). "Invention, authorship, 'intellectual property,' and the origin of patents: notes toward a conceptual history." *Technology and Culture*, 32(4), 846–84.

(2001). *Openness, Secrecy, Authorship: Technical Arts and the Culture of Knowledge from Antiquity to the Renaissance*, Baltimore: Johns Hopkins University Press.

López Castro, J. L. (1995). *Hispania Poena: Los fenicios en la Hispania romana*, Barcelona: Crítica.

(1998). "Familia, poder y culto a Melqart Gaditano." *ARYS*, 1, 93–108.

(2007). "The Western Phoenicians under the Roman Republic: integration and persistence." In P. van Dommelen & N. Terrenato, eds., *Articulating Local Cultures: Power and Identity under the Expanding Roman Republic*. Portsmouth: JRA Supplementary Series No. 63, pp. 103–25.

Lopéz-Ruiz, C. (2015). Review of *The Punic Mediterranean: Identities and Identification from Phoenician Settlement to Roman Rule*, edited by J. Crawley Quinn and N. Vella, *Bryn Mawr Classical Review* 2015.09.53.

Lowenstam, S. (1993). "The pictures on Juno's temple in the Aeneid." *CJ*, 87, 37–49.

Lucas, H. (1904). *Zur Geschichte der Neptunsbasilica in Rom*, Berlin: A.W. Hayn's Erben.

Luce, T. J. (1977). *Livy: The Composition of His History*, Princeton University Press.

(1990). "Livy, Augustus, and the Forum Augustum." In K. A. Raaflaub & M. Toher, eds., *Between Republic and Empire: Interpretations of Augustus and His Principate*. Berkeley and Los Angeles: University of California Press, pp. 123–38.

Lulof, P. (2000). "Archaic terracottas representing Athena and Heracles: manifestations of power in Central Italy." *JRA*, 13, 207–19.

MacCormack, S. (1981). *Art and Ceremony in Late Antiquity*, Berkeley: University of California Press.

Magi, F. (1963). "Le inscrizioni recentemente scoperte sull'obelisco vaticano." *Studi Romani*, 11, 50–6.

Maischberger, M. (1997). *Marmor in Rom: Anlieferung, Lager- und Werkplätze in der Kaiserzeit*, Wiesbaden: Dr. Ludwig Reichert Verlag.

Malkin, I. (2003). "Networks and the emergence of Greek identity." *MHR* 18, 56–74.

(2005). "Herakles and Melqart: Greeks and Phoenicians in the middle ground." In E. Gruen, ed., *Cultural Borrowings and Ethnic Appropriations in Antiquity*. Oriens et Occidens 8. Stuttgart: Franz Steiner Verlag, pp. 238–57.

(2011). *A Small Greek World: Networks in the Ancient Mediterranean*, Oxford University Press.

Malkin, I., Constantakopoulou, C., & Panagopoulou, K., eds. (2009). *Greek and Roman Networks in the Mediterranean*, London: Routledge.

Mangas Manjarrés, J. (1989). "El Hercules Gaditanus, dios heredero." In M. J. Hidalgo de la Vega, ed., *Homenaje a Marcelo Vigil Pascual: La historia en el contexto de las ciencias humanas y sociales*. Salamanca: Universidad de Salamanca, pp. 55–60.

(1996). "El culto de Hercules en la Bética." In J. M. Blázquez and J. Alvar, *La Romanización en Occidente*. Madrid: Actas Editorial, pp. 279–97.

Mann, M. (1986). *The Sources of Social Power, Vol. 1: A History of Power from the Beginning to AD 1760*, Cambridge University Press.

Manolaraki, E. (2015). "*Hebraei liquores*: the balsam of Judaea in Pliny's *Natural History.*" *AJP*, 136(4), 633–67.

Manzoni, G. E. (1995). *Foroiuliensis poeta: Vita e poesia de Cornelio Gallo*, Milan: Vita e pensiero.

Marincola, J. (1997). *Tradition and Authority in Ancient Historiography*, Cambridge University Press.

Marín Martínez, A. P. (2011). "Iconografia sagrada fenicio-púnica en las monedas de Hispania siglos III al I a. C." *El Futuro del Pasado*, 2, 579–600.

Markovits, C., Pouchepadass, J., & Subrahmanyam, S. (2003). "Introduction: circulation and society under colonial rule." In C. Markovits, J. Pouchepadass, & S. Subrahmanyam, eds., *Society and Circulation: Mobile People and Itinerant Cultures in South Asia, 1750–1950*. Delhi: Permanent Black, pp. 1–22.

   eds. (2003). *Society and Circulation: Mobile People and Itinerant Cultures in South Asia, 1750–1950*, Delhi: Permanent Black.

Marsden, P. (1994). *Ships of the Port of London: First to Eleventh Centuries AD*, London: English Heritage.

Marshall, C. W. (1999). "*Quis hic loquitur?* Plautine Delivery and the 'Double Aside.'" In J. Porter *et al.*, eds., *Crossing the Stages: The Production, Performance, and Reception of Ancient Theater. Syllecta Classica*, 10, pp. 105–29.

   (2006). *The Stagecraft and Performance of Roman Comedy*, Cambridge University Press.

   (2013). "Sex slaves in New Comedy." In B. Akrigg & R. Tordoff, eds., *Slaves and Slavery in Ancient Greek Comic Drama*. Cambridge University Press, pp. 173–96.

Marszal, J. R. (2000). "Ubiquitous barbarians: representations of the Gauls at Pergamon and elsewhere." In N. T. de Grummond & B. S. Ridgway, eds., *From Pergamon to Sperlonga: Sculpture and Context*. Berkeley: University of California Press, pp. 191–234.

Marvin, M. (2008). *The Language of the Muses: The Dialogue between Roman and Greek Sculpture*, Los Angeles: J. Paul Getty Museum.

Marx, G. (1959). *Groucho and Me*, New York: Bernard Geis Associates.

Marx, H., with Barber, R. [1962] (2000). *Harpo Speaks*, New York: Limelight Editions.

Marzano, A. (2013). *Harvesting the Sea: The Exploitation of Maritime Resources in the Roman Mediterranean*, Oxford University Press.

Masterson, M. (2004). "Status, pay and pleasure in the *De Architectura* of Vitruvius." *American Journal of Philology*, 125(3), 387–416.

Mastromarco, G. (1984). *The Public of Herondas*, Amsterdam: Gieben.

Matthews, J. (1989). *The Roman Empire of Ammianus*, London: Duckworth.

Mattingly, D. J. (2003). "Family values: art and power at Ghirza in the Libyan pre- desert." In S. Scott & J. Webster, eds., *Roman Imperialism and Provincial Art*. Cambridge University Press, pp. 153–70.

(2007). *An Imperial Possession: Britain in the Roman Empire, 54 BC–AD 409*, London: Penguin.

Mattingly, H. (1929). "The first age of Roman coinage." *JRS*, 19(1), 19–37.

et al. (1962). *The Roman Imperial Coinage*, London: Spink.

Mattusch, C. (2003). "Corinthian bronze: famous, but elusive." *Corinth*, 20, 219–32.

Mazzarino, S. (1980). "Un nuovo epigramma di Gallus e l'antica 'lettura epigrafica' (Un problema di datazione)." *QC*, 2, 7–50.

(1982). "L'iscrizione latina nella trilingue di Philae e i carmi di Gallus scoperti a Qasr Ibrîm." *RhM*, 125, 312–37.

Mbembe, A. (1992). "Provisional notes on the postcolony." *Africa: Journal of the International African Institute*, 62(1), 3–37.

McCarthy, K. (2000). *Slaves, Masters, and the Art of Authority in Plautine Comedy*, Princeton University Press.

McDermott, W. C. (1941). "Varro Murena." *TAPA*, 72, 255–65.

McDonnell, M. (2006). "Roman aesthetics and the spoils of Syracuse." In S. Dillon & K. E. Welch, eds., *Representations of War in Ancient Rome*. Cambridge University Press, pp. 68–90.

McEwen, I. K. (2003). *Vitruvius: Writing the Body of Architecture*. Cambridge, MA: MIT Press.

McGill, S. (2012). *Plagiarism in Latin Literature*, Cambridge University Press.

McGinn, T.A. (2004). *The Economy of Prostitution in the Roman World: A Study of Social History and the Brothel*, Ann Arbor: University of Michigan Press.

McGrail, S. (1989). "The shipment of traded goods and of ballast in Antiquity." *OJA*, 8, 353–8.

McKenzie, J. (2007). *The Architecture of Alexandria and Egypt: 300 BC to AD 700*, New Haven: Yale University Press.

Meban, D. (2008). "Temple building, *primus* language, and the proem to Virgil's third *Georgic*." *CP*, 103(2), 150–74.

Melliti, K. (2006). "Religion et hellénisme à Carthage: la politique aristocratique à l'épreuve." *Pallas*, 70, 381–94.

Mercati, M. (1589). *De gli obelischi di Roma*, Rome: Domenico Basa.

Meyboom, P. G. P. (1995). *The Nile Mosaic of Palestrina: Early Evidence of Egyptian Religion in Italy*, Leiden: Brill.

Michaelis, A. (1893). "Der Schöpfer der attalischen Kampfgruppen." *JdI*, 8, 119–34.

Mierse, W. E. (1993). "Temple images on the coinage of Southern Iberia." *Revue belge de numismatique et de sigillographie*, 139, 37–57.

(1999). *Temples and Towns in Roman Iberia: The Social and Architectural Dynamics of Sanctuary Designs from the Third Century BC to the Third Century AD*, Berkeley and Los Angeles: University of California Press.

(2004). "The architecture of the lost temple of Hercules Gaditanus and its Levantine associations." *AJA*, 108(4), 545–75.

Mignolo, W. (2003). *The Darker Side of the Renaissance: Literacy, Territoriality and Colonization*, 2nd edn, Ann Arbor: University of Michigan Press.

Milanese, M., Ruggeri, P., & Vismara, C., eds. (2010). *L'Africa romana: i luoghi e le forme dei mestieri e della produzione nelle province africane. Atti del XVIII convegno di studio, Olbia, 11–14 dicembre 2008*, 3 vols., Rome: Carocci.

Miles, G. B. (1995). *Livy: Reconstructing Early Rome*, Ithaca: Cornell University Press.

Miles, M. M. (2008). *Art as Plunder: The Ancient Origins of Debate about Art as Cultural Property*, Cambridge University Press.

Miles, R. (2010). *Carthage Must Be Destroyed: The Rise and Fall of an Ancient Civilization*, London and New York: Allen Lane.

(2011). "Hannibal and propaganda." In D. Hoyos, ed., *A Companion to the Punic Wars*. Malden and Oxford: Wiley-Blackwell, pp. 260–79.

Millar, F. (1993). *The Roman Near East: 31 BC–AD 337*, Cambridge, MA: Harvard University Press.

(1998). "Looking east from the classical world: colonialism, culture, and trade from Alexander the Great to Shapur I." *International History Review*, 20(3), 507–31.

Miller, J. (1969). *The Spice Trade of the Roman Empire, 29 BC to AD 641*, Oxford: Clarendon Press.

Miller, J. F. (1981). "Propertius 2.1 and the new Gallus papyrus." *ZPE*, 44, 173–6.

(2009). *Apollo, Augustus, and the Poets*, Cambridge University Press.

Miller, P. A. (2004). *Subjecting Verses: Latin Love Elegy and the Emergence of the Real*, Princeton University Press.

Milnor, K. L. (2005). *Gender, Domesticity and the Age of Augustus: Inventing Private Life*, Oxford University Press.

Mithen, S. (2012). *Thirst: Water and Power in the Ancient World*, Cambridge, MA: Harvard University Press.

Mocchegiani Carpano, C. (1986). *Archeologia subacquea: note di viaggio nell'Italia sommersa*, Rome: Fratelli Palombi.

Momigliano, A. (1975). *Alien Wisdom: The Limits of Hellenization*, Cambridge University Press.

Moore, T. J. (1998). *The Theater of Plautus: Playing to the Audience*, Austin: University of Texas Press.

(2001). "Music in *Epidicus*." In U. Auhagen, ed., *Studien zu Plautus' Epidicus*. Tübingen: Gunter Narr, pp. 313–34.

(2012). *Music in Roman Comedy*, Cambridge University Press.

Mora Serrano, B. (2006). "Metrología y sistemas monetarios en la península Ibérica (siglos V–I a.C.)." In *Actas del XII congreso nacional de numismática (Madrid–Segovia, 25–27 de octubre de 2004)*. Madrid: Real Casa de la Moneda, 23–61.

Moretti, F. (2000). "Conjectures on world literature." *New Left Review*, 1, 54–68.

(2003). "More conjectures." *New Left Review*, 20, 73–81.

Moretti, G. (1948). *Ara Pacis Augustae*, Rome: Libreria dello Stato.

Morris, I. (2003). "Mediterraneanization." *Mediterranean Historical Review*, 18(2), 30–55.

Murphy, C. (2007). *Are We Rome? The Fall of an Empire and the Fate of America*, Boston: Houghton Mifflin Co.

Murphy, L. (1983). "Shipwrecks as a database for human behavioral studies." In R. Gould, ed., *Shipwreck Anthropology*. Albuquerque: University of New Mexico, pp. 65–89.

Murphy, T. (2004). *Pliny the Elder's Natural History: The Empire in the Encyclopedia*, Oxford University Press.

Myers, M. Y. (2015). *"Gallus: a guide to selected sources."* Durham: https://livingpoets.dur.ac.uk/w/Gallus:_A_Guide_to_Selected_Sources. Last accessed December 2016.

Mynors, R. A. B. (1969). P. Vergili Maronis Opera, Oxford: Clarendon Press.

(1990). *Virgil: Georgics*, Oxford: Clarendon Press.

Nachtergael, G. (1977). *Les Galates en Grèce et les Sôtéria de Delphes: recherches d'histoire et d'épigraphie hellénistiques*. Académie Royale de Belgique: Mémoires de la Classe des Lettres 63.1, Brussels: Palais des Académies.

Nappa, C. (2005). *Reading after Actium: Vergil's Georgics, Octavian, and Rome*, Ann Arbor: University of Michigan Press.

Nauta, R. (2002). *Poetry for Patrons: Literary Communication in the Age of Domitian*, Leiden: Brill.

Nelis, D. P. (2008). "Caesar, the Circus and the charioteer in Vergil's *Georgics*." In J. Nelis-Clément & J.-M. Roddaz, eds., *Le cirque romain et son image*. Mémoires, 20. Bordeaux: Ausonius Éditions, pp. 497–520.

Nelis-Clément, J. & Nelis, D. P. (2011). "Vergil, *Georgics* 1.1–42 and the *pompa circensis*." *Dictynna*, 8, 1–14.

(2014). "Poésie, topographie et épigraphie à l'époque augustéenne." In D. P. Nelis & M. Royo, eds., *Lire la ville. Fragments d'une archéologie littéraire de Rome antique*. Scripta antiqua, 65. Bordeaux: Ausonius Éditions, pp. 125–58.

Nelson, R. S. (1996). "Appropriation." In R. S. Nelson & R. Shiff, eds. *Critical Terms for Art History*. University of Chicago Press, pp. 116–28.

(2003). "Appropriation," in R. S. Nelson & R. Schiff, eds., *Critical Terms for Art History*, 2nd edn. University of Chicago Press, pp. 160–73.

Nenci, G. (1978). "'Graecia capta ferum victorem cepit.' Hor. Ep. II 1, 156." *AnnPisa*, 8, 1007–23.

Neudecker, R. (1998). "The Roman villa as a locus of art collections." In A. Frazer, ed., *The Roman Villa: Villa Urbana*. Philadelphia: University of Pennsylvania Museum, pp. 77–92.

Newlands, C. E., ed. (2011). *Statius Silvae Book 2*, Cambridge University Press.

Newman, J. K. (1980). *"De novo Galli fragmento in Nubia eruto."* *Latinitas*, 28, 83–94.

Nicholls, M. C. (2011). "Galen and libraries in the *Peri Alupias*." *JRS*, 101, 123–42.

Nichols, M. F. (2009). "Social status and the authorial personae of Horace and Vitruvius." In L. Houghton & M. Wyke, eds., *Perceptions of Horace: A Roman Poet and His Readers*. Cambridge University Press, pp. 109–22.

(2017). Vitruvius on Display: Roman Author and Audience in De *architectura*, Cambridge University Press.

Nicholson, C. & Nicholson, O. (1989). "Lactantius, Hermes Trismegistus and Constantinian obelisks." *Journal of Hellenic Studies*, 109, 198–200.

Nicolet, C. (1991). *Space, Geography, and Politics in the Roman Empire*, Ann Arbor: University of Michigan Press.

Nieto Prieto, X. (1997). "Le commerce de cabotage et de distribution." In P. Pomey, ed., *La navigation dans l'antiquité*. Aix-en-Provence: Edisud, pp. 146–59.

Nisbet, R. G. M. & Hubbard, M. (1978). *A Commentary on Horace: Odes Book II*, Oxford University Press.

Nissen, H. (1863). *Kritische Untersuchungen über die Quellen der vierten und fünften Dekade des Livius*, Berlin: Weidmannsche Buchhandlung.

Nitschke, J. (2013). "Interculturality in image and cult in the Hellenistic East: Tyrian Melqart revisited." In E. Stravrianopoulou, ed., *Shifting Social Imaginaries in the Hellenistic Period*. Leiden: Brill, pp. 253–82.

Noreña, C. F. (2011). *Imperial Ideals in the Roman West: Representation, Circulation, Power*, Cambridge University Press.

(2013). "Locating the Ustrinum of Augustus." *MAAR*, 58, 51–64.

Norry, C. (1800). *An Account of the French Expedition to Egypt*, London: Gosnell.

Noy, D. (2000). *Foreigners at Rome: Citizens and Strangers*, London: Duckworth.

Oakley, S. (2005). *A Commentary on Livy, Books VI–X. Vol. 3: Book XI*. Oxford: Clarendon Press.

O'Donnell, D. (1993). "The Pacific Guano islands: the stirring of American Empire in the Pacific Ocean." *Pacific Studies*, 16(1), 43–66.

Ogilvie, R. M. (1965). *A Commentary on Livy Books 1–5*, Oxford: Clarendon Press.

O'Hara, J. (1989). "The New Gallus and the *alternae voces* of Propertius 1.10.10." *CQ*, 39, 561–2.

Oksanish, J. (2016). "Vitruvius and the programmatics of prose." In S. Cuomo & M. Formisano, eds., *Vitruvius: Text, Architecture, Reception. Arethusa*, 49(2), 263–80.

(Forthcoming). *Vitruvian Man: Rome Under Construction*.

Oleson, J., Brandon, C., & Hohlfelder, R. (2011). "Technology, innovation, and trade: research into the engineering characteristics of Roman maritime concrete." In D. Robinson & A. Wilson, eds., *Maritime Archaeology and Ancient Trade in the Mediterranean*. Oxford: Oxford Centre for Maritime Archaeology, Institute of Archaeology, pp. 107–19.

Oliver, A., Jr. & Shelton, J. (1979). "Silver on papyrus. A translation of a Roman silver tableware inventory." *Archaeology*, 32, 21–28.

O'Neill, P. (2012). *The Culture of Curating and the Curating of Culture(s)*, Cambridge, MA: MIT Press.

Oria Segura, M. (1989). "Distribución del culto a Hércules en Hispania según los testimonios epigráficos." *Habis*, 20, 263–73.

(1993). "Los templos de Hércules en la Hispania romana." *AAC*, 4, 221–32.

(1997). "Et cum signo Herculis dedicavit. Imágenes de Hércules y culto oficial en Hispania." *Habis*, 28, 143–51.

Orlin, E. M. (2002). *Temples, Religion, and Politics in the Roman Republic*, Leiden: Brill.

Ormerod, H. A. (1924). *Piracy in the Ancient World: An Essay in Mediterranean History*, Liverpool University Press.

Östenberg, I. (2009). *Staging the World: Spoils, Captives, and Representation in the Roman Triumphal Procession*, Oxford University Press.

Ousterhout, R. (2014). "The life and afterlife of Constantine's column." *JRA*, 27, 305–26.

Palma, B. (1981). "Il piccolo donario pergameno." *Xenia*, 1, 45–84.

Palmer, R. E. A. (1997). *Rome and Carthage at Peace*, Historia Einzelschriften 113, Stuttgart: Franz Steiner Verlag.

Panayotakis, C. (2014). "Hellenistic mime and its reception in Rome." In M. Fontaine & A. C. Scafuro, eds., *The Oxford Handbook of Greek and Roman Comedy*. Oxford University Press, pp. 378–96.

Pansiéri, C. (1997). *Plaute et Rome, ou, les ambiguïtés d'un marginal*, Brussels: Latomus.

Parker, A. J. (1992a). *Ancient Shipwrecks of the Mediterranean and the Roman Provinces*, Oxford: Tempus Reparatum.

(1992b). "Cargoes, containers and stowage: the ancient Mediterranean." *IJNA*, 21(2), 89–100.

Parker, G. (2003). "Narrating monumentality: the Piazza Navona obelisk." *Journal of Mediterranean Archaeology*, 16(2), 193–215.

(2007). "Obelisks still in exile: monuments made to measure?" In L. Bricault, M. J. Versluys, & P.G.P. Meyboom, eds., *Nile into Tiber: Egypt in the Roman World*. Leiden and Boston: Brill, pp. 209–22.

(2014). "Mobile monumentality: the case of obelisks." In J. F. Osborne, ed., *Approaching Monumentality in Archaeology*. Albany: SUNY Press, pp. 273–87.

Parker, H. N. (2009). "Books and reading Latin poetry." In W. A. Johnson & H. N. Parker, eds., *Ancient Literacies: The Culture of Reading in Greece and Rome*. Oxford University Press, pp. 186–232.

Parks, T. (2015). *Where I'm Reading From: The Changing World of Books*, New York: New York Review Books.

Parsons, P. J. (1980). "Cornelius Gallus lives." *The London Review of Books*, 2(2), 9–10.

(1983). "164: Latin Letter." In *Papyrus Erzherzog Rainer (P. Rainer Cent.): Festschrift zum 100-jährigen Bestehen der Papyrussammlung der Österreichischen Nationalbibliothek*. Vienna: Verlag Brüder Hollinek, pp. 483–9.

Pearce, S. (1995). *On Collecting: An Investigation into Collecting in the European Tradition*, London: Routledge.

Pelling, C. (1997). Review of *Actium and Augustus: The Politics and Emotions of Civil War*, by R. A. Gurval, *JRS*, 87, 289–90.

Peña, J. T. (2007). *Roman Pottery in the Archaeological Record*, Cambridge University Press.

Penwill, J. L. (2000). "Quintilian, Statius and the lost epic of Domitian." *Ramus*, 29, 60–83.

Perry, E. (2005). *The Aesthetics of Emulation in the Visual Arts of Ancient Rome*, Cambridge University Press.

Petersen, L. H. (2006). *The Freedman in Roman Art and Art History*, Cambridge University Press.

Pietilä-Castrén, L. (1987). *Magnificentia Publica: The Victory Monuments of the Roman Generals in the Era of the Punic Wars.* Commentationes Humanarum Litterarum, 84, Helsinki: Societas Scientiarum Fennica.

Pitard, W. T. (1988). "The identity of the Bir-Hadad of the Melqart Stela." *BASOR*, 272, 3–21.

Pitassi, M. (2009). *The Navies of Rome*, Woodbridge: The Boydell Press.

Pitcher, L. (2009). *Writing Ancient History. An Introduction to Classical Historiography*, London: I. B. Tauris.

Pitts, M. (2015). "Globalisation, circulation and mass consumption in the Roman world." In M. Pitts & M. J. Versluys, eds., *Globalisation and the Roman World: World History, Connectivity and Material Culture.* New York: Cambridge University Press, pp. 69–98.

Pitts, M. & Versluys, M. J. (2015). "Globalisation and the Roman world: perspectives and opportunities." In M. Pitts & M. J. Versluys, eds., *Globalisation and the Roman World: World History, Connectivity and Material Culture.* Cambridge University Press, pp. 3–31.

Pococke, R. (1803). *The Travels of Richard Pococke, L.L.D., F.R.S., through Egypt, Interspersed with Remarks and Observations by Captain Norden*, Philadelphia: Joseph and James Crukshank.

Pollard, E. A. (2009). "Pliny's *Natural History* and the Flavian *Templum Pacis*: botanical imperialism in first-century C.E. Rome." *Journal of World History*, 20(3), 309–38.

Polleichtner, W., ed. (2010). *Livy and Intertextuality*, Trier: Wissenschaftlicher Verlag Trier.

Pollini, J. (2012). *From Republic to Empire: Rhetoric, Religion, and Power in the Visual Culture of Ancient Rome*, Oklahoma Series in Classical Culture, 48, Norman: University of Oklahoma Press.

Pollitt, J. J. (1986). *Art in the Hellenistic Age*, Cambridge University Press.

Pomey, P. (2011). "Les conséquences de l'évolution des techniques de construction navale sur l'économie maritime antique: quelques exemples." In W. V. Harris & K. Iara, eds., *Maritime Technology in the Ancient Economy: Ship-Design and Navigation.* Portsmouth: JRA Supplementary Series No. 84, pp. 39–55.

Pope, M. (1975). *The Story of Decipherment: From Egyptian Hieroglyphic to Linear B*, London: Thames and Hudson.

Porter, J. I., ed. (2006). *Classical Pasts: The Classical Traditions of Greece and Rome*, Princeton University Press.

Potter, D. (2014). "The Roman army and navy." In H.I. Flower, ed., *The Cambridge Companion to the Roman Republic*, rev. ed. Cambridge University Press, 57-77.

Powell, A. & Welch, K. (2002). *Sextus Pompeius*, London: Duckworth and The Classical Press of Wales.

Prag, J. (2011) "Siculo-Punic coinage and Siculo-Punic interactions." In M. Dalla Riva, ed., *Meeting Between Cultures in the Ancient Mediterranean. Bollettino di Archeologia online* 1, 2010: http://www.bollettinodiarcheologiaonline .beniculturali.it/documenti/generale/2_PRAG.pdf. Last accessed May 2017.

Prag, J. (2014). "Inscribed bronze rostra from the site of the Battle of the Aegates Islands, Sicily, 241 BC." In W. Eck & P. Funke, eds., *Corpus Inscriptionum Latinarum*, Vol. 4. *Öffentlichkeit – Monument –Text. XIV Congressus Internationalis Epigraphiae Graecae et Latinae. Akten.* Berlin: de Gruyter, pp. 727–29.

(2015). "Sicily and the Punic Wars." In D. Burgersdijk *et al.*, eds., *Sicily and the Sea.* Zwolle: W Books, pp. 83–6.

Prusac, M. & Seim, T. K., eds. (2012). *Recycling Rome,* Rome: Scienze e lettere.

Pugh, S. (2010). *Herrick, Fanshawe and the Politics of Intertextuality: Classical Literature and Seventeenth-Century Royalism,* Burlington: Ashgate.

Purcell, N. (1983). "The *apparitores*: a study in social mobility." *PBSR,* 51, 125–73.

(1996). "Rome and the management of water: environment, culture and power." In G. Shipley & J. Salmon, eds., *Human Landscapes in Classical Antiquity: Environment and Culture.* New York and London: Routledge, pp. 180–212.

(2012). "Rivers and the geography of power." *Pallas,* 90, 373–87.

(2013). "On the significance of East and West in today's 'Hellenistic' history: reflections on symmetrical worlds, reflecting through world symmetries." In J.R.W. Prag & J. Crawley Quinn, eds., *The Hellenistic West: Rethinking the Ancient Mediterranean.* Cambridge University Press, pp. 367–90.

Putnam, M.C.J. (1980). "Propertius and the new Gallus fragment." *ZPE,* 39, 49–56.

Putnam, M. (1998). *Virgil's Epic Designs,* New Haven: Yale University Press.

Raaflaub, K. A. & Toher, M., eds. (1990). *Between Republic and Empire: Interpretations of Augustus and His Principate,* Berkeley and Los Angeles: University of California Press.

Rathbone, D. (2003). "The financing of maritime commerce in the Roman Empire, I–II AD." In E. Lo Cascio, ed., *Credito e moneta nel mondo romano: Atti degli Incontri capresi di storia dell'economia antica (Capri 12–14 ottobre 2000).* Bari: Edipuglia, pp. 197–229.

(2007). "Merchant networks in the Greek world: the impact of Rome." *Mediterranean Historical Review,* 22, 309–20.

(2009). "Merchant networks in the Greek world: the impact of Rome." In I. Malkin, C. Constantakopoulou, & K. Panagopoulou, eds., *Greek and Roman Networks in the Mediterranean.* London: Routledge, pp. 299–310.

Rauh, N. (2003). *Merchants, Sailors & Pirates in the Roman World,* Stroud: Tempus.

Rawlings, L. (2005). "Hannibal and Hercules." In L. Rawlings & H. Bowden, eds., *Herakles and Hercules: Exploring a Graeco-Roman Divinity.* Swansea: The Classical Press of Wales, 153–84.

Rawlings, L. & Bowden, H., eds. (2005). *Herakles and Hercules: Exploring a Graeco-Roman Divinity*, Swansea: The Classical Press of Wales.

Rawson, E. (1985). *Intellectual Life in the Late Roman Republic*, London: Duckworth.

Ray, J. D. (2005). *Demotic Papyri and Ostraca from Qasr Ibrim*, London: Egypt Exploration Society.

Rebeggiani, S. (2013). "Reading the republican Forum: Virgil's *Aeneid*, the Dioscuri, and the Battle of Lake Regillus." *CP*, 108(1), 53–69.

   (Forthcoming). *Statius' Thebaid and the Destiny of the Empire*, Oxford University Press.

Rebuffat, R. (1966). "Les Phéniciens à Rome." *Mélanges d'archéologie et d'histoire*, 78, 7–48.

Reed, J. (1998). "The death of Osiris in *Aeneid* 12.258." *AJP*, 119, 399–418.

   (2011). "The *Bellum Civile* as a Roman epic." In P. Asso, ed., *Brill's Companion to Lucan*. Leiden: Brill, pp. 21–31.

Remesal Rodríguez, J. (2004). *Epigrafía anfórica*, Barcelona: Publicacions de la Universitat de Barcelona.

Rhodes, R. (2007). *The Acquisition and Exhibition of Classical Antiquities: Professional, Legal, and Ethical Perspectives*, Notre Dame: University of Notre Dame Press.

Ribbeck, O., ed. (1962). *Comicorum Romanorum praeter Plautum et Terentium fragmenta*, Hildesheim: Georg Olms.

Richardson, B. (2001). "Denarration in fiction: erasing the story in Beckett and others." *Narrative*, 9(2), 168–75.

Richardson, J. S. (1986). *Hispaniae: Spain and the Development of Roman Imperialism, 218–82 BC*, Cambridge University Press.

Richardson, L. (1992). *A New Topographical Dictionary of Ancient Rome*, Baltimore: Johns Hopkins University Press.

Richlin, A. (2014). "Talking to slaves in the Plautine audience." *CA*, 33(1), 174–226

   (2015). "Slave-woman drag." In D. Dutsch, S. L. James, and D. Konstan, eds., *Women in Roman Republican Drama*. Madison: University of Wisconsin Press, pp. 37–67.

   (2016). "The kings of comedy." In S. Frangoulidis, S. J. Harrison, and G. Manuwald, eds., *Roman Drama and Its Contexts*. Trends in Classics - Supplementary Volume 34. Berlin: de Gruyter, pp. 67–95.

Richlin, A. (Forthcoming a). "The ones who paid the butcher's bill: soldiers and war captives in Roman comedy." In J. M. Clark & B. Turner, eds., *Brill's Companion to Loss and Defeat in the Ancient World*. Leiden: Brill.

   (Forthcoming b). *Slave Theater in the Roman Republic: Plautus and Popular Comedy*, Cambridge University Press.

Rickman, G. (2008). "Ports, ships, and power in the Roman world." In R. Hohlfelder, ed., *The Maritime World of Ancient Rome*. Ann Arbor: University of Michigan Press, pp. 5–20.

Ridgway, B. S. (1999). *Prayers in Stone: Greek Architectural Sculpture (600–100 BCE)*, Berkeley and Los Angeles: University of California Press.

Ripollès, P. P. (2007). "Coinage and identity in the Roman provinces: Spain." In C. Howgego, V. Heuchert, & A. Burnett, eds., *Coinage and Identity in the Roman Provinces*. Oxford University Press, 79–93.

Robinson, E. G. D. (2004). "Reception of comic theatre amongst the indigenous South Italians." *Mediterranean Archaeology*, 17, 193–214.

Roby, C. (2016). *Technical Ekphrasis in Greek and Roman Science and Literature: The Written Machine Between Alexandria and Rome*, Cambridge University Press.

Rodríguez Almeida, E. (1989). *Los tituli picti de las ánforas olearias de la Bética*, Madrid: Editorial de la Universidad Complutense.

Rodríguez Cortés, J. (1991). *Sociedad y religion clásica en la Bética romana*, Salamanca: Universidad de Salamanca.

Rogers, R. S. (1959). "The emperor's displeasure — *amicitiam renuntiare.*" *TAPA*, 90, 224–37.

Roller, D. W. (2003). *The World of Juba II and Kleopatra Selene: Royal Scholarship on Rome's African Frontier*, New York and London: Routledge.

Roller, M. (2004). "Exemplarity in Roman culture: the cases of Horatius Cocles and Cloelia." *CP*, 99, 1–56.

  (2009). "The exemplary past in Roman history and culture: the case of Gaius Duilius." In A. Feldherr, ed., *The Cambridge Companion to the Roman Historians*. Cambridge University Press, pp. 214–30.

  (2010). "Demolished houses, monumentality, and memory in Roman culture." *CA*, 29(1), 117–80.

  (2013). "On the intersignification of monuments in Augustan Rome." *AJP*, 134 (1), 119–31.

Romano, E. (1987). *La capanna e il tempio: Vitruvio o dell'architettura*, Palermo: Palumbo.

  (2011). "Vitruvio fra storia e antiquaria." *Cahiers des études anciennes*, 48, 201–17.

Romm, J. S. (1992). *The Edges of the Earth in Ancient Thought: Geography, Exploration, and Fiction*, Princeton University Press.

Roscalla, F. (2006). "Storie di plagi e di plagiari." In F. Roscalla, ed., *L'autore e l'opera: attribuzioni, appropriazioni, apocrifi nella Grecia antica. Atti del convegno internazionale (Pavia, 27–28 maggio 2005)*. Memorie e atti di convegni 34. Pisa: Edizioni ETS, pp. 69–102.

Rose, P. (1996). *Qasr Ibrim: The Hinterland Survey*, London: Egypt Exploration Society.

  (1998). "Excavations at Qasr Ibrim: Qasr Ibrim 1998." *Sudan & Nubia* 2, 61–75.

  (2011). "Qasr Ibrim: the last 3000 Years." *Sudan & Nubia* 15, 1–9.

Rosenberg, H. (1971). *Barnett Newman: Broken Obelisk and Other Sculptures*, Seattle: Henry Art Gallery.

Rosenstein, N. (2004). *Rome at War: Farms, Families, and Death in the Middle Republic*, Chapel Hill: University of North Carolina Press.

  (2012). *Rome and the Mediterranean, 290 to 146 BC: The Imperial Republic*, Edinburgh University Press.

Roth, R. & Keller, J., eds. (2007). *Roman by Integration. Dimensions of Group Identity in Material Culture and Text*. Portsmouth: JRA Supplementary Series No. 66.

Rougé, J. (1975). *La marine dans l'Antiquité*, Paris: Presses universitaires de France.

(1980). "Prêt et société maritimes dans le monde romain (Maritime loans and maritime associations in the Roman world)." *MAAR*, 36, 291–303.

Roullet, A. (1972). *The Egyptian and Egyptianizing Monuments of Imperial Rome*, Leiden: Brill.

Rubin, G. (1975). "The traffic in women." In R. R. Reiter, ed., *Toward an Anthropology of Women*. New York: Monthly Review Press, pp. 157–210.

Rubincam, C. (2003). "Numbers in Greek poetry and historiography: quantifying Fehling." *CQ* 53(2), 448–63.

Russell, B. (2015). "Transport and distribution." In E. Friedland, M. Sobocinski, & E. Gazda, eds., *The Oxford Handbook of Roman Sculpture*. Oxford University Press, pp. 189–207.

Rusten, J. & Cunningham, I. C., eds. and trans. (2002). *Theophrastus: Characters, Herodas: Mimes, Sophron and Other Mime Fragments*, Cambridge, MA: Harvard University Press.

Rutledge, S. H. (2012). *Ancient Rome as a Museum: Power, Identity and the Culture of Collecting*, Oxford University Press.

Said, E. W. (1993). *Culture and Imperialism*, New York: Vintage Books.

Sailor, D. (2006). "Dirty linen, fabrication, and the authorities of Livy and Augustus." *TAPA*, 136(2), 329–88.

Sánchez, R. C. (2004). "Sobre la imagen de Hercules Gaditanus." *Romula*, 3, 37–62.

Santangelo, F. (2007). "Pompey and Religion." *Hermes*, 135(2), 228–33.

Sauron, G. (1994). *Quis Deum? L'expression plastique des idéologies politiques et religieuses à Rome à la fin de la République et au début du principat, BÉFAR 285*, Rome: École française de Rome.

Scafuro, A. C. (2014). "Comedy in the late fourth and early third centuries BCE." In M. Fontaine & A. C. Scafuro, eds., *The Oxford Handbook of Greek and Roman Comedy*. Oxford University Press, pp. 199–217.

Scappaticcio, M. C. (2009). "Virgilio, allievi e maestri a Vindolanda: per un'edizione di nuovi documenti dal forte britannico." *ZPE*, 169, 59–70.

(2010). "Tra ecdotica e performance: Per un *Corpus Papyrorum Vergilianarum*." *APF*, 56, 130–48.

Scheidel, W. (2001). *Death on the Nile: Disease and the Demography of Egypt*, Leiden: Brill.

(2005). "Human mobility in Roman Italy, II: the slave population." *JRS*, 95, 64–79.

(2009). "In search of Roman economic growth." *JRA*, 138, 46–70.

(2011). "The Roman slave supply." In K. Bradley & P. Cartledge, eds., *The Cambridge World History of Slavery*, Vol. 1: *The Ancient Mediterranean World*. Cambridge University Press, pp. 287–310.

Scheidel, W. & Meeks, E. (2014). "*ORBIS: The Stanford Geospatial Network Model of the Roman World.*" Stanford: Stanford University Libraries. http://orbis.stanford.edu.

Schmidt, M. (2011). "*A Gadibus Romam*: myth and reality of an ancient route." *BICS*, 54(2), 71–86.

Schneider, A. (2003). "On 'appropriation'. A critical reappraisal of the concept and its application in global art practices." *Social Anthropology*, 11(2), 215–29.

Schneider, R. M. (2004). "Nicht mehr Ägypten, sondern Rom: der neue Lebensraum der Obelisken." *Städel-Jahrbuch*, 19, 155–79.

(2005). "Römische Bilder ägyptischer Obelisken." In H. Beck *et al.*, eds., *Ägypten, Griechenland, Rom. Abwehr und Berührung.* Frankfurt: Das Städel, pp. 416–25, 721–28.

(2008). "Image and empire: the shaping of Augustan Rome." In F.-H. Mutschler & A. Mittag, eds., *Conceiving the Empire: China and Rome Compared.* Oxford University Press, pp. 269–98.

Schober, A. (1938). "Zur Geschichte pergamenischer Künstler." *ÖJh*, 31, 142–9.

(1951). *Die Kunst von Pergamon*, Vienna: Rohrer.

Schrijvers, P. H. (1989). "Vitruve et la vie intellectuelle de son temps." In H. Geertman & J. J. de Jong, eds., *Munus Non Ingratum: Proceedings of the International Symposium on Vitruvius' De Architectura and the Hellenistic and Republican Architecture.* Bulletin Antieke Beschaving, Supplement 2. Leiden: Peeters, pp. 13–21.

Schuler, S. (1999). *Vitruv im Mittelalter: die Rezeption von "De architectura" von der Antike bis in die frühe Neuzeit*, Köln: Böhlau.

Schütz, M. (1990). "Zur Sonnenuhr des Augustus auf dem Marsfeld." *Gymnasium*, 97, 432–57.

Schwarz, S. J. (2009). "Hercle." *Lexicon Iconographicum Mythologiae Classicae, Supplementum 2009*, Vol. I. Düsseldorf: Patmos Verlag, pp. 244–64.

Sciarrino, E. (2011). *Cato the Censor and the Beginnings of Latin Prose: From Poetic Translation to Elite Transcription*, Columbus: Ohio State University Press.

Sehlmeyer, M. (1999). *Stadtrömische Ehrenstatuen der republikanischen Zeit: Historizität und Kontext von Symbolen nobilitären Standesbewusstseins*, Historia: Einzelschriften 130, Stuttgart: Franz Steiner Verlag.

Severy-Hoven, B. (2007). "Reshaping Rome: space, time, and memory in the Augustan transformation." *Arethusa*, 40(1), 1–111.

Shackleton Bailey, D. R. (1965). *Cicero's Letters to Atticus*, Cambridge University Press.

(1980). *Cicero: Epistulae ad Quintum fratrem et M. Brutum*, Cambridge University Press.

Sharrock, A. (2009). *Reading Roman Comedy: Poetics and Playfulness in Plautus and Terence*, Cambridge University Press.

Shatzman, I. (1972). "The Roman general's authority over booty." *Historia*, 21(2), 177–205.

Shaw, B. D. (1984). "Bandits in the Roman Empire." *PastPres*, 105, 3–52.

Sherratt, S. & Sherratt, A. (1993). "The growth of the Mediterranean economy in the early first millennium BC." *WorldArch*, 24, 361–78.

Sherwin-White, A. N. (1985). *The Letters of Pliny: A Historical and Social Commentary*, Oxford University Press.

Shils, E. (1965). "Charisma, order, and status." *American Sociological Review*, 30 (2), 199–213.

Shipley, F. W. (1933). *Agrippa's Building Activities in Rome*, St. Louis: Washington University Studies.

Shipley, G. (2011). *Pseudo-Skylax's Periplous: The Circumnavigation of the Inhabited World: Text, Translation and Commentary*, Exeter: Bristol Phoenix Press.

Silver, M. (2007). "Those exotic Roman elites: behavior vs. preferences." *Historia*, 56(3), 347–55.

Simon, E. (1967). *Ara Pacis Augustae*, Tübingen: Verlag Ernst Wasmuth.

(1986). *Augustus: Kunst und Leben in Rom um die Zeitenwende*, München: Hirmer.

Simpson, W. K. (1991). "Mentuhotep, vizier of Sesostris I, patron of art and architecture." *MDIK*, 47, 331–40.

Sirks, A. (1991). *Food for Rome: The Legal Structure of the Transportation and Processing of Supplies for the Imperial Distributions in Rome and Constantinople*, Amsterdam: J. C. Gieben.

Skibo, J. & Schiffer, M. (2008). *People and Things: A Behavioral Approach to Material Culture*, New York: Springer.

Skutsch, F. (1901). *Aus Vergils Frühzeit*, Leipzig: Teubner.

Skutsch, O. (1985). *The Annals of Q. Ennius*, Oxford: Clarendon Press.

Slater, N. W. (1985). *Plautus in Performance: The Theatre of the Mind*, Princeton University Press.

Smil, V. (2010). *Why America Is Not a New Rome*, Cambridge, MA: MIT Press.

Smith, C. S. (2006). *The Roman Clan: The Gens from Ancient Ideology to Modern Anthropology*, Cambridge University Press.

Smith, R. R. R. (1988). "*Simulacra gentium*: the *ethne* from the Sebasteion at Aphrodisias." *JRS*, 78, 50–77.

Somerville, T. (2009). "The literary merit of the New Gallus." *CP*, 104, 106–13.

Sommers, M. (2014). "*OIKOYMENH*: *Longue durée* perspectives on ancient Mediterranean 'globality'." In M. Pitts & M. J. Versluys, eds., *Globalisation and the Roman World: Archaeological and Theoretical Perspectives*. Cambridge University Press, pp. 175–97.

Spawforth, A. J. (2012). *Greece and the Augustan Cultural Revolution*, Cambridge University Press.

Speidel, M. P. (1988). "Nubia's Roman garrison." *ANRW*, 2.10(1), 768–98.

Sponsler, C. (2002). "In transit: theorizing cultural appropriation in Medieval Europe." *Journal of Medieval and Early Modern Studies*, 32, 17–39.

Stafford, E. (2012). *Herakles*, London and New York: Routledge.

Starr, R. J. (1987). "The circulation of literary texts in the Roman world." *CQ*, 37, 213–23.

Steffy, J. R. (1994). *Wooden Ship Building and the Interpretation of Shipwrecks*, College Station: Texas A&M University Press.

Stein, C. W., ed. (1984). *American Vaudeville as Seen by Its Contemporaries*, New York: Alfred A. Knopf.

Stephens, S. (2003). *Seeing Double: Intercultural Poetics in Ptolemaic Alexandria*, Berkeley: University of California Press.

(2010). "Ptolemaic Alexandria." In J. J. Clauss & M. Cuypers, eds., *A Companion to Hellenistic Literature*. Oxford: Wiley-Blackwell, pp. 46–61.

Stevenson Smith, W. (1981). *The Art and Architecture of Ancient Egypt*. Revised with additions by William Kelly Simpson. New Haven and London: Yale University Press.

Stewart, A. (2000). "*Pergamo ara marmorea magna*: on the date, reconstruction, and functions of the Great Altar of Pergamon." In N. T. de Grummond & B. S. Ridgway, eds., *From Pergamon to Sperlonga: Sculpture and Context*. Berkeley: University of California Press, pp. 32–57.

(2004). *Attalos, Athens, and the Akropolis. The Pergamene "Little Barbarians" and Their Roman and Renaissance Legacy. With an essay by Manolis Korres*, Cambridge University Press.

Stewart, D. (1999). "Formation processes affecting submerged archaeological sites: an overview." *Geoarchaeology*, 14(6), 565–87.

Stewart, D. T. [Trav S.D.] (2005). *No Applause—Just Throw Money, or, The Book That Made Vaudeville Famous: A High-Class, Refined Entertainment*, New York: Faber and Faber.

Stewart, R. L. (2012). *Plautus and Roman Slavery*, Malden: Wiley-Blackwell.

Stickler, T. (2002). *"Gallus amore peribat"?: Cornelius Gallus und die Anfänge der augusteischen Herrschaft in Ägypten*, Rahden/Westfalen: Verlag Marie Leidorf.

Strack, P. (1931). *Untersuchungen zur römischen Reichsprägung des zweiten Jahrhunderts. I: Die Reichsprägung des Traian*, Stuttgart: W. Kohlhammer.

Strazzulla, M. J. (2009). "War and peace: housing the Ara Pacis in the Eternal City." *AJA*, 113(2), http://www.ajaonline.org/online-review-museum/370. Last accessed December 2016.

Strzelecki, W., ed. (1964). *Cn. Naevii Belli Punici carminis quae supersunt*, Leipzig: Teubner.

Sumi, G. (2009). "Monuments and memory: the *Aedes Castoris* in the formation of Augustan ideology." *CQ*, 59(1), 167–86.

Susan, A. S. (2015). *Callimachus: The Hymns*, Oxford; New York: Oxford University Press.

Swain, J. W. (1940). "The theory of the four monarchies: opposition history under the Roman empire." *CP*, 35(1), 1–21.

Swann, M. (2001). *Curiosities and Texts: The Culture of Collecting in Early Modern England*, Philadelphia: University of Pennsylvania Press.

Swetnam-Burland, M. (2007). "Egyptian objects, Roman contexts: a taste for Aegyptiaca in Italy." In L. Bricault, M. J. Versluys, & P.G.P. Meyboom, eds., *Nile into Tiber: Egypt in the Roman World*. Leiden and Boston: Brill, pp. 113–36.

(2010). "'Aegyptus Redacta': the Egyptian obelisk in the Augustan Campus Martius." *ArtB*, 92(3), 135–53.

(2015). *Egypt in Italy: Visions of Egypt in Roman Imperial Culture*, Cambridge University Press.

Syme, R. (1938). "The origin of Cornelius Gallus." *CQ*, 32, 39–44.

(1939). *The Roman Revolution*, Oxford University Press.

(1959). "Livy and Augustus." *HSCP*, 64, 27–87.

(1964). "Hadrian and Italica." *JRA*, 54(1) and (2), 142–49.

Takács, S. A. (1995). *Isis and Serapis in the Roman World*, Leiden and New York: Brill.

Tartaron, T. (2013). *Maritime Networks in the Mycenaean World*, Cambridge University Press.

Tchernia, A. (2011). *Les Romains et le commerce*, Naples: Centre Jean Bérard.

(2016) The Romans and trade, Oxford University Press.

et al. (1978). *L'épave romaine de la Madrague de Giens, campagnes 1972–1975: Fouilles de l'institut d'archéologie méditerranéenne*, Paris: Éditions du Centre national de la recherche scientifique.

Thiel, W. (2006). "Die Pompeius–Säule in Alexandria und die Viersäulenmonumente Ägyptens. Überlegungen zur tetrarchischen Repräsentationskultur in Nordafrika." In D. Boschung & W. Eck, eds., *Die Tetrarchie: ein neues Regierungssystem und seine mediale Präsentation*. Wiesbaden: Reichert, pp. 249–322.

Thomas, R. (1983). "Virgil's ecphrastic centerpieces." *HSCP*, 87, 175–84.

(1988). *Vergil: Georgics*. Vol. I: Books I–II. Cambridge University Press.

(2004). "'Stuck in the middle with you': Virgilian middles." In S. Kyriakidis & F. De Martino, eds., *Middles in Latin Poetry*. Bari: Levante, pp. 123–50.

Thompson, H. (1952). "The altar of pity in the Athenian agora." *Hesperia*, 21, 79–82.

Tomlinson, R. A. (1989). "Vitruvius and Hermogenes." In H. Geertman & J. J. de Jong, eds., *Munus Non Ingratum: Proceedings of the International Symposium on Vitruvius' De Architectura and the Hellenistic and Republican Architecture*. Bulletin Antieke Beschaving, Supplement 2. Leiden: Peeters, pp. 71–5.

Tordoff, R. (2013). "Introduction: slaves and slavery in ancient Greek comedy." In B. Akrigg & R. Tordoff, eds., *Slaves and Slavery in Ancient Greek Comic Drama*. Cambridge University Press, 1–62.

Török, L. (1997). *The Kingdom of Kush: Handbook of the Napatan–Meriotic Civilization*, Leiden: Brill.

(2009). *Between Two Worlds: The Frontier Region between Ancient Nubia and Egypt. 3700 BC–AD 500*, Leiden: Brill.

Toynbee, J. M. C. (1934). *The Hadrianic School: A Chapter in the History of Greek Art*. Cambridge University Press.

(1953). "The Ara Pacis reconsidered and historical art in Roman Italy." *ProcBritAc*, 39, 67–95.

Tran, N. (2006). *Les membres des associations romaines: le rang social des collegiati en Italie et en Gaules, sous le haut-empire*, Rome: École française de Rome.

Trimble, J. (2011). *Women and Visual Replication in Roman Imperial Art and Culture*, Cambridge University Press.

Tuchelt, K. (1975). "Buleuterion und Ara Augusti: Bemerkungen zur Rathausanlage von Milet." *IstMitt*, 25, 91–140.

Turner, V. (1968). *The Drums of Affliction: A Study of Religious Processes among the Ndembu of Zambia*, Oxford: Clarendon Press.

Tusa, S. & Royal, J. (2012). "The landscape of the naval battle at the Egadi Islands (241 BC)." *JRA*, 25, 7–48.

Tylawsky, E. I. (2002). *Saturio's Inheritance: The Greek Ancestry of the Roman Comic Parasite*, New York: Peter Lang Publishing.

Tzalas, H. (1997). "Bronze Statues from the Depths of the Seas." In P. Valavanes & A. Delevorrias, eds., *Great Moments In Greek Archaeology*. Los Angeles: J. Paul Getty Museum, pp. 342–63.

Ulrich, R. B. (1994). *The Roman Orator and the Sacred Stage: The Roman Templum Rostratum*, Brussels: Latomus Revue d'Études Latines.

Untermann, J. (1995). "La latinización de Hispania a través del documento monetal." In M. P. García-Bellido & R.M.S. Centeno, eds., *La moneda hispánica: ciudad y territorio*. Madrid: CSIC, 305–16.

Van Berchem, D. (1967). "Sanctuaires d'Hercule-Melqart: contribution à l'étude de l'expansion phénicienne en Méditerranée." *Syria*, 44, 73–109.

van der Vliet, J. (2013). "Qasr Ibrim in Lower Nubia: cultural interaction at the southernmost Roman *limes*." In J. van der Vliet & J. L. Hagen, eds., *Qasr Ibrim: Between Egypt and Africa*. Leuven: Peeters, pp. 1–22.

van Minnen, P. (1986). "A woman ναύκληροϲ in *P. Tebt.* II 370." *ZPE*, 66, 91–2.

Van't Dack, E. (1983). "L'armée romaine d'Égypte de 55 à 30 av. J.-C." In G. Grimm, H. Heinen, & E. Winter, eds., *Das Römisch-Byzantinische Ägypten: Akten des Internationalen Symposions 26.–30. September 1978 in Trier*. Mainz: Philipp von Zabern, pp. 19–29.

van Tilburg, C. (2007). *Traffic and Congestion in the Roman Empire*, London: Routledge.

Van Sickle, J. (1981). "Style and imitation in the New Gallus." *QUCC*, 9, 115–23.

Verboven, K. (2002). *The Economy of Friends: Economic Aspects of Amicitia and Patronage in the Late Republic*, Brussels: Editions Latomus.

(2007). "The associative order. Status and ethos among Roman businessmen in Late Republic and Early Empire." *Athenaeum*, 95, 861–94.

Verducci, F. (1984). "On the sequence of Gallus' epigrams: *molles elegi, vasta triumphi pondera*." *QUCC*, 16, 119–36.

Versluys, M. J. (2002). *Aegyptiaca Romana: Nilotic Scenes and the Roman Views of Egypt*, Leiden: Brill.

Vives Y Escudero, A. (1924–6). *La moneda hispánica*, Vols. I–III. Madrid: Real Academia de la Historia.

Vivliodetis, E. (2012). "The *lagynoi*." In N. Kaltsas, E. Vlachogianni, & P. Bouyia, eds., *The Antikythera Shipwreck: The Ship, the Treasures, the Mechanism; National Archaeological Museum, April 2012–April 2013*. Athens: Kapon Editions, pp. 152–63.

Vlachogianni, E. (2012). "The sculpture." In N. Kaltsas, E. Vlachogianni, & P. Bouyia, eds., *The Antikythera Shipwreck: The Ship, the Treasures, the Mechanism; National Archaeological Museum, April 2012–April 2013*. Athens: Kapon Editions, pp. 62–115.

Vogt-Spira, G. (1991). "*Stichus* oder Ein Parasit wird Hauptperson." In E. Lefèvre, E. Stärk, & G. Vogt-Spira, eds., *Plautus Barbarus: Sechs Kapitel zur Originalität des Plautus*. Tübingen: Gunter Narr, pp. 163–74.

(1995). "Traditionen improvisierten Theaters bei Plautus: einige programmatische Überlegungen." In B. Zimmermann, ed., *Griechisch-römische Komödie und Tragödie*. Stuttgart: M&P, pp. 70–93.

(2001). "Traditions of theatrical improvisation in Plautus: some considerations." Trans. L. Holford-Stevens. In E. Segal, ed., *Oxford Readings in Menander, Plautus, and Terence*. Abridged and revised version of Vogt-Spira (1995). Oxford University Press, pp. 95–106.

Volk, K. (2010). "Literary theft and Roman water rights in Manilius' second proem." *Materiali e discussioni per l'analisi dei testi classici*, 65, 187–97.

von Blanckenhagen, P. H. & Alexander, C. (1990). *The Augustan Villa at Boscotrecase*, Mainz: Philipp von Zabern.

von Staden, H. (1992). "Women and dirt." *Helios*, 19, 7–30.

Walbank, F.W. (1957–79). *A Historical Commentary on Polybius*, 3 vols. Oxford University Press.

Wallace-Hadrill, A. (1987). "Time for Augustus: Ovid, Augustus and the *Fasti*." In M. Whitby, P. Hardie, & M. Whitby, eds., *Homo Viator: Classical Essays for John Bramble*. Bristol Classical Press, pp. 221–30.

(2008). *Rome's Cultural Revolution*, Cambridge University Press.

Wallinga, H. (1964). "Nautika (I): The Unit of Capacity for Ancient Ships." *Mnemosyne*, 17, 1–40.

Wallochny, B. (1992). *Streitszenen in der griechischen und römischen Komödie*, Tübingen: Gunter Narr.

Walsh, J. (2014). *Consumerism in the Ancient World: Imports and Identity Construction*, New York: Routledge.

Walter, U. (2004). Memoria und res publica. *Zur Geschichtskultur im republikanischen Rom*, Frankfurt am Main: Verlag Antike.

Weber, W. (1910). "Ein Hermes-Tempel des Kaisers Marcus," *Sitzungsberichte der Heidelberger Akademie der Wissenschaften, Philosophisch-Historische Klasse*, 7, 1–43.

Webster, J. (2001). "Creolizing the Roman provinces." *AJA*, 105(2), 209–25.

Weinstein, M. E. & Turner, E. G. (1976). "Greek and Latin papyri from Qasr Ibrim." *JEA*, 62, 115–30.

Weinstock, S. (1957). "Victor and Invictus." *Harvard Theological Review*, 50(3), 211–47.

Weis, A. (2003). "Gaius Verres and the Roman art market: consumption and connoisseurship in *Verrine* II 4." In A. Haltenhoff, A. Heil, & F.-H. Mutschler, eds., *O tempora, o mores! Römische Werte und römische*

Literatur in den letzten Jahrzehnten der Republik. München: Saur, pp. 355–400.

Welch, K. E. (2006). "*Domi militiaeque*: Roman domestic aesthetics and war booty in the Republic," In S. Dillon & K. E. Welch, eds., *Representations of War in Ancient Rome.* Cambridge University Press, pp. 91–161.

(2012). *Magnus Pius: Sextus Pompeius and the Transformation of the Roman Republic,* Swansea: The Classical Press of Wales.

Welsby, D. A. (1998). "Roman military installations along the Nile south of the first cataract." *Archéologie du Nil Moyen,* 8, 157–82.

Wenning, R. (1978). *Die Galateranatheme Attalos I.: eine Untersuchung zum Bestand und zur Nachwirkung pergamenischer Skulptur,* Pergamenische Forschungen Bd. 4, Berlin: de Gruyter.

Wesenberg, B. (1984). "Augustusforum und Akropolis." *Jahrbuch des Deutschen Archäologischen Instituts,* 99, 161–85.

West, D. (1983). "*Pauca meo Gallo.*" *LCM,* 8(6), 92–3.

(1998). *Horace: Odes II. Vatis Amici. Text, Translation and Commentary,* Oxford: Clarendon Press.

West, D. & Woodman, A. J., eds. (1979). *Creative Imitation and Latin Literature,* Cambridge University Press.

Wheeler, E. L. (2012). "Roman fleets in the Black Sea: mysteries of the '*classis Pontica*'." *Acta Classica,* 55, 119–54.

White, H. (1913). *Appian's Roman History,* 4 vols. Cambridge, MA: Harvard University Press.

Whitewright, J. (2011). "The potential performance of ancient Mediterranean sailing rigs." *IJNA,* 40(1), 2–17.

Whitmarsh, T. (2010). "Thinking local." In T. Whitmarsh, ed., *Local Knowledge and Microidentities in the Imperial Greek World.* Cambridge University Press, pp. 1–16.

Whittaker, C. R. (1997). "Imperialism and culture: the Roman initiative." In D. J. Mattingly, ed., *Dialogues in Roman Imperialism: Power, Discourse, and Discrepant Experience in the Roman Empire.* Portsmouth: JRA Supplementary Series No. 23, pp. 143–61.

Wilkins, A., Barnard, H., & Rose, P. (2006). "Roman artillery balls from Qasr Ibrim, Egypt." *Sudan & Nubia,* 10, 64–78.

Williams, J. H. C. (2001). *Beyond the Rubicon: Romans and Gauls in Republican Italy,* Oxford: Clarendon Press.

Williams, R. D. (1960). "The pictures on Dido's temple." *CQ,* 10, 145–51.

Williams, R. (1983). *Culture and Society: 1780–1950,* New York: Columbia University Press.

Willis, I. (2007). "The Empire never ended." In L. Hardwick & C. Gillespie, eds., *Classics in Post-Colonial Worlds.* Cambridge University Press, pp. 329–48.

Wilson, A. (2009). "Approaches to quantifying Roman trade." In A. Bowman & A. Wilson, eds., *Quantifying the Roman Economy: Methods and Problems.* Oxford University Press, pp. 213–49.

(2011). "Developments in Mediterranean shipping and maritime trade from the Hellenistic period to AD 1000." In D. Robinson & A. Wilson, eds., *Maritime Archaeology and Ancient Trade in the Mediterranean*. Oxford: Oxford Centre for Maritime Archaeology, Institute of Archaeology, pp. 33–59.

Winterling, A. (2009). *Politics and Society in Imperial Rome*, Malden: Wiley-Blackwell.

Wiseman, T. F. (2000). "The Games of Hercules." In E. Bispham & C. Smith, eds., *Religion in Archaic and Republican Rome and Italy: Evidence and Experience*. New York and London: Routledge, 108–13.

Woerther, F., ed. (2015). *Caecilius de Calè-Actè. Fragments et témoignages*, Paris: Les Belles Lettres.

Woodman, A. J. (2004). Tacitus. *The Annals*, Indianapolis and Cambridge: Hackett.

Woolf, G. (1998). *Becoming Roman: The Origins of Provincial Civilization in Gaul*, Cambridge University Press.

(2012). *Rome: An Empire's Story*, Oxford University Press.

(2015). "Pliny/Trajan and the poetics of empire." *CP*, 110(2), 132–51.

Wray, D. (2007). "Wood: Statius' *Silvae* and the poetics of genius." *Arethusa*, 41 (2), 127–43.

Wright, J. (1974). *Dancing in Chains: The Stylistic Unity of the Comoedia Palliata*, PMAAR 25. Rome: American Academy in Rome.

Wyetzner, P. (2002). "Sulla's law on prices and the Roman definition of luxury." In J.-J. Aubert & A. Sirks, eds., *Speculum iuris: Roman Law as a Reflection of Social and Economic Life in Antiquity*. Ann Arbor: University of Michigan Press, pp. 15–33.

Yarrow, L. M. (2006a). *Historiography at the End of the Republic: Provincial Perspectives on Roman Rule*, Oxford University Press.

(2006b). "Lucius Mummius and the spoils of Corinth." *Scripta Classica Israelica*, 25, 57–70.

Yon, M. (1992). "Héraclès à Chypre." In C. Bonnet & C. Jourdain-Annequin, eds., *Héraclès: D'une rive à l'autre de la Méditerranée. Bilan et perspectives*. Brussels: Institut Belge de Rome, pp. 145–63.

Young, E. M. (2015). *Translation as Muse: Poetic Translation in Catullus's Rome*, University of Chicago Press.

Zanda, E. (2011). *Fighting Hydra-Like Luxury: Sumptuary Regulation in the Roman Republic*, London: Bristol Classical Press.

Zanker, P. (1968). *Forum Augustum: das Bildprogramm*, Tübingen: E. Wasmuth.

(1970). "Das Trajansforum in Rom." *Archäologischer Anzeiger*, 85, 499–544.

(1987). *Augustus und die Macht der Bilder*, Munich: Beck.

(1988). *The Power of Images in the Age of Augustus*, A. Shapiro, trans., Ann Arbor: University of Michigan Press.

Zarmakoupi, M. (2014). *Designing for Luxury on the Bay of Naples: Villas and Landscapes (c. 100 BCE–79 CE)*, Oxford University Press.

Zimmer, G. (1994). "Republikanisches Kunstverständnis: Cicero gegen Verres." In G. Hellenkemper Salies, H.-H. von Prittwitz und Gaffron, & G. Bauchhenss, eds., *Das Wrack: Der antike Schiffsfund von Mahdia*. Köln: Rheinland Verlag, pp. 867–74.

Ziolkowski, A. (1988). "Mummius' temple of Hercules Victor and the round temple on the Tiber." *Phoenix*, 42(4), 309–33.

  (1992). *The Temples of Mid-Republican Rome and their Historical and Topographical Context*, Rome: L'Erma di Bretschneider.

Index

Page numbers in italics are figures; with 'n' are notes.